The Metamorphoses of Ovid

Translated into English blank verse by J.J. Howard

Publius Ovidius Naso but better known to us as simply Ovid was born on 20th March 43 BC in Sulmo (modern day Sulmona) in Italy.

He was educated in rhetoric in Rome in preparation for the practice of Law. Accounts of his character say that he was emotional and not able to stay within the argumentative boundaries of rhetoric disclipine. After the early death of his brother, Ovid ceased his law studies and travelled to Athens, Asia Minor, and Sicily. He held a number of minor public posts but, around 29-25 BC began to pursue poetry, a decision that brought with it his father's disapproval.

Ovid's first recitation occurred when he was eighteen (around 25 BC). He was part of the circle centered on the patron Marcus Valerius Messalla Corvinus, and appears to have been a friend of poets in the circle of Maecenas.

He married three times and divorced twice by the time he was thirty years old. He fathered a daughter, who eventually bore him grandchildren. His last wife was connected to the influential gens Fabia (an ancient Roman patrician family) and would help him during his later exile.

The first decades of Ovid's literary career were mostly spent writing poetry with erotic themes. The chronology of these early works cannot, however, be relied upon.

His earliest extant work is thought to be the 'Heroides', letters of mythological heroines to absent lovers, which is believed to have been published in 19 BC.

The first five-book collection of the 'Amores', erotic poems addressed to a lover, Corinna, is believed to have been published in 16–15 BC The surviving three book version appears to have been published c. 8–3 BC.

Between these two editions of the 'Amores' his tragedy 'Medea', which was much admired in antiquity but is no longer extant, was performed.

Ovid buoyed by his glowing reputation now increased the tempo of his writing. 'Medicamina Faciei', was followed by the 'Ars Amatoria, the Art of Love' and immediately followed by 'Remedia Amoris'. This body of elegiac, erotic poetry saw Ovid cited as the equal of the Roman elegists Gallus, Tibullus, and Propertius.

By AD 8, he had completed his most ambitious work, the 'Metamorphoses', a 15-book hexameter epic poem. It catalogued Greek and Roman mythology, from the emergence of the universe to the apotheosis of Julius Caesar.

Concurrent with this, he worked on the 'Fasti', planned as 12-books but only 6 volumes (January to June were completed) in elegiac couplets on the calendar of Roman festivals and astronomy were completed. The remaining six books were interrupted by Ovid's sentence to exile.

In AD 8, Ovid was banished to Tomis, on the Black Sea, by the Emperor Augustus. This event shadowed his life and shaped his remaining poetic output. Ovid wrote that his exile was for carmen et error – "a poem and a mistake", claiming his crime was worse than murder, more harmful than poetry.

Ovid was also a contemporary of the older Virgil and Horace, with whom he is often ranked as one of the three canonical poets of Latin literature. The Imperial scholar Quintilian considered him the last of the Latin love elegists.

His poetry was much imitated during Late Antiquity and the Middle Ages, and greatly influenced Western art and literature. The Metamorphoses remains one of the most important sources of classical mythology.

In exile, Ovid wrote 'Tristia' and 'Epistulae ex Ponto', pointedly focused on his sadness and desolation. He was far from Rome and his beloved third wife.

The five books of the elegiac Tristia, a series of poems expressing the poet's despair in exile and advocating his return to Rome, are dated to AD 9–12.

'The Ibis', an elegiac curse poem attacking an adversary at home is also dated to this period. 'The Epistulae ex Ponto', a series of letters to friends in Rome asking them to effect his return, are thought to be his last compositions.

Ovid died at Tomis in AD 17 or 18. It is thought that the Fasti, which he spent time revising, were published posthumously.

Index of Contents

Dedication
VOLUME I - THE FIRST BOOK OF THE METAMORPHOSES OF OVID
The First Book
The Second Book
The Third Book
The Fourth Book
The Fifth Book
The Sixth Book
The Seventh Book
VOLUME II - THE SECOND BOOK OF THE METAMORPHOSES OF OVID
The Eighth Book
The Ninth Book
The Tenth Book
The Eleventh Book
The Twelfth Book
The Thirteenth Book
The Fourteenth Book
The Fifteenth Book

VOLUME I

THE FIRST BOOK OF THE METAMORPHOSES OF OVID

From bodies various form'd, mutative shapes
My Muse would sing:—Celestial powers give aid!
From you those changes sprung,—inspire my pen;
Connect each period of my venturous song
Unsever'd, from old Chaös' rude misrule,
Till now the world beneath Augustus smiles.

While yet nor earth nor sea their place possest,
Nor that cerulean canopy which hangs
O'ershadowing all, each undistinguish'd lay,
And one dead form all Nature's features bore;
Unshapely, rude, and Chaos justly nam'd.
Together struggling laid, each element
Confusion strange begat:—Sol had not yet
Whirl'd through the blue expanse his burning car:
Nor Luna yet had lighted forth her lamp,
Nor fed her waning light with borrowed rays.
No globous earth pois'd inly by its weight,
Hung pendent in the circumambient sky:
The sky was not:—Nor Amphitrité had
Clasp'd round the land her wide-encircling arms.
Unfirm the earth, with water mix'd and air;
Opaque the air; unfluid were the waves.
Together clash'd the elements confus'd:
Cold strove with heat, and moisture drought oppos'd;
Light, heavy, hard, and soft, in combat join'd.

Uprose the world's great Lord,—the strife dissolv'd,
The firm earth from the blue sky plac'd apart;

Roll'd back the waves from off the land, and fixt
Where pure ethereal joins with foggy air.
Defin'd each element, and from the mass
Chaötic, rang'd select, in concord firm
He bound, and all agreed. On high upsprung
The fiery ether to the utmost heaven:
The atmospheric air, in lightness next,
Upfloated:—dense the solid earth dragg'd down
The heavier mass; and girt on every side
By waves circumfluent, seiz'd her place below.

   This done, the mass this deity unknown
Divides;—each part dispos'd in order lays:
First earth he rounds, in form a sphere immense,
Equal on every side: then bids the seas,
Pent in by banks, spread their rude waves abroad,
By strong winds vext; and clasp within their arms
The tortuous shores: and marshes wide he adds,
Pure springs and lakes:—he bounds with shelving banks
The streams smooth gliding;—slowly creeping, some
The arid earth absorbs; furious some rush,
And in the watery plain their waves disgorge;
Their narrow bounds escap'd, to billows rise,
And lash the sandy shores. He bade the plains
Extend;—the vallies sink;—the groves to bloom;—
And rocky hills to lift their heads aloft.
And as two zones the northern heaven restrain,
The southern two, and one the hotter midst,
With five the Godhead girt th' inclosed earth,
And climates five upon its face imprest.
The midst from heat inhabitable: snows
Eternal cover two: 'twixt these extremes
Two temperate regions lie, where heat and cold
Meet in due mixture; 'bove the whole light air
Was hung:—as water floats above the land,
So fire 'bove air ascends. Here he bade lodge,
Thick clouds and vapors; thunders bellowing loud
Terrific to mankind, and winds; which mixt
Sharp cold beget. But these to range at large
The air throughout, his care forbade. E'en now
Their force is scarce withstood; but oft they threat
Wild ruin to the universe, though each
In separate regions rules his potent blasts.
Such is fraternal strife! Far to the east
Where Persian mountains greet the rising sun
Eurus withdrew. Where sinking Phœbus' rays
Glow on the western shores mild Zephyr fled.
Terrific Boreas frozen Scythia seiz'd,

Beneath the icy bear. On southern climes
From constant clouds the showery Auster rains.
The liquid ether high above he spread,
Light, calm, and undefil'd by dregs terrene.
Scarce were those bounds immutable arrang'd,
When upward sprung the stars so long press'd down
Beneath the heap chaötic, and along
The path of heaven their blazing courses ran.

Next that each separate element might hold
Appropriate habitants,—the vault of heaven,
Bright constellations and the gods receiv'd.
To glittering fish allotted were the waves:
To earth fierce brutes:—to agitated air,
Light-plumag'd birds. A being more divine,
Of soul exalted more, and form'd to rule
The rest was wanting. Then he finish'd MAN!
Or by the world's creator, power supreme,
Form'd from an heavenly seed; or new-shap'd earth
Late from celestial ether torn, and still
Congenial warmth retaining, moisten'd felt,
Prometheus' fire, and moulded took the form
Of him all-potent. Others earth behold
Pronely;—to man a face erect was given.
The heavens he bade him view, and raise his eyes
High to the stars. Thus earth of late so rude,
So shapeless, man, till now unknown, became.

First sprung the age of gold. Unforc'd by laws
Strict rectitude and faith, spontaneous then
Mankind inspir'd. No judge vindictive frown'd;
Unknown alike were punishment and fear:
No strict decrees on brazen plates were seen;
Nor suppliant crowd, with trembling limbs low bent,
Before their judges bow'd. Unknown was law,
Yet safe were all. Unhewn from native hills,
The pine-tree knew the seas not, nor had view'd
Regions unknown, for man not yet had search'd
Shores distant from his own. The towns ungirt
By trenches deep, laid open to the plain;
Nor brazen trump, nor bended horn were seen,
Helmet, nor sword; but conscious and secure,
Unaw'd by arms the nations tranquil slept.
The teeming earth by barrows yet unras'd,
By ploughs unwounded, plenteous pour'd her stores.
Content with food unforc'd, man pluck'd with ease
Young strawberries from the mountains; cornels red;
The thorny bramble's fruit; and acorns shook

From Jove's wide-spreading tree. Spring ever smil'd;
And placid Zephyr foster'd with his breeze
The flowers unsown, which everlasting bloom'd.
Untill'd the land its welcome produce gave,
And unmanur'd its hoary crop renew'd.
Here streams of milk, there streams of nectar flow'd;
And from the ilex, drop by drop distill'd,
The yellow honey fell. But, Saturn down
To dusky Tartarus banish'd, all the world
By Jove was govern'd. Then a silver age
Succeeded; by the golden far excell'd;—
Itself surpassing far the age of brass.
The ancient durance of perpetual spring
He shorten'd, and in seasons four the year
Divided:—Winter, summer, lessen'd spring,
And various temper'd autumn first were known.
Then first the air with parching fervor dry,
Glow'd hot;—then ice congeal'd by piercing winds
Hung pendent;—houses then first shelter'd man;
Houses by caverns form'd, with thick shrubs fenc'd,
And boughs entwin'd with osiers. Then the grain
Of Ceres first in lengthen'd furrows lay;
And oxen groan'd beneath the weighty yoke.
Third after these a brazen race succeeds,
More stern in soul, and more in furious war
Delighting;—still to wicked deeds averse.
The last from stubborn iron took its name;—
And now rush'd in upon the wretched race
All impious villainies: Truth, faith, and shame,
Fled far; while enter'd fraud, and force, and craft,
And plotting, with detested avarice.
To winds scarce known the seaman boldly loos'd
His sails, and ships which long on lofty hills
Had rested, bounded o'er the unsearch'd waves.
The cautious measurer now with spacious line
Mark'd out the land, in common once to all;
Free as the sun-beams, or the lucid air.
Nor would the fruits and aliments suffice,
The rich earth from her surface threw, but deep
Within her womb they digg'd, and thence display'd,
Riches, of crimes the prompter, hid far deep
Close by the Stygian shades. Now murderous steel,
And gold more murderous enter'd into day:
Weapon'd with each, war sallied forth and shook
With bloody grasp his loud-resounding arms.
Now man by rapine lives;—friend fears his host;
And sire-in-law his son;—e'en brethren's love
Is rarely seen: wives plot their husbands' death;

And husbands theirs design: step-mothers fierce
The lurid poisons mix: th' impatient son
Enquires the limits of his father's years:—
Piety lies neglected; and Astræa,
Last of celestial deities on earth,
Ascends, and leaves the sanguine-moisten'd land.

Nor high-rais'd heaven was more than earth secure.
Giants, 'tis said, with mad ambition strove
To seize the heavenly throne, and mountains pile
On mountains till the loftiest stars they touch'd.
But with his darted bolt all-powerful Jove,
Olympus shatter'd, and from Pelion's top
Dash'd Ossa. There with huge unwieldy bulk
Oppress'd, their dreadful corses lay, and soak'd
Their parent earth with blood; their parent earth
The warm blood vivify'd, and caus'd assume
An human form,—a monumental type
Of fierce progenitors. Heaven they despise,
Violent, of slaughter greedy; and their race
From blood deriv'd, betray.

Saturnian Jove
This from his lofty seat beheld, and sigh'd;
The recent bloody fact revolving deep,
The Lycaönian feast, to few yet known.
Incens'd with mighty rage, rage worthy Jove,
He calls the council;—none who hear delay.
A path subl me, in cloudless skies fair seen,
They tread when tow'rd the mighty thunderer's dome,
His regal court, th' immortals bend their way.
On right and left by folding doors enclos'd,
Are halls where gods of rank and power are set;
Plebeians far and wide their place select:
More potent deities, in heaven most bright,
Full in the front possess their shining seats.
This place, (might words so bold a form assume)
I'd term Palætium of the lofty sky.
Here in his marble niche each god was plac'd
And on his eburn sceptre leaning, Jove
O'er all high tower'd; the dread-inspiring locks
Three times he shook; and ocean, earth, and sky,
The motion felt and trembled. Then in rage
The silence thus he broke:—"Not more I fear'd
"Our kingdom's fate in those tempestuous times,
"When monsters serpent-footed furious strove,
"To clasp w thin their hundred arms the heavens,
"Already captive deem'd. Though fierce our foe,

"One race alone warr'd with us, sprung from one.
"Now all must perish; all within the bounds
"By Nereus circled with his roaring waves.
"I swear by Styx, by those infernal streams,
"Through shades slow creeping. All I could I've try'd.
"But lest to parts unsound the taint should spread,
"What baffles cure, the knife must lop away.
"Our demi-gods we have,—we have our nymphs,
"Our rustic deities,—our satyrs,—fawns,
"And mountain sylvans—whose deserts we grant
"Celestial honors claim not,—yet on earth,
"By us assign'd, they safely sure should rest.
"But, oh! ye sacred powers,—but oh! how safe
"Are these, when fierce Lycaön plots for me!
"Me! whom the thunders and yourselves obey?"

Loud murmurs fill the skies—swift vengeance all
With eager voice demand. When impious hands
With Cæsar's blood th' immortal fame of Rome,
Rag'd to extinguish—all the world aghast,
With horror shook, and trembled through its frame.
Nor was thy subjects' loyalty to thee
More sweet, Augustus, than was theirs to Jove.
His hand and voice, to still their noise he rais'd:
Their clamors loud were hush'd, all silence kept;
When thus the thunderer ends his angry tale:
"Dismiss your care, his punishment is o'er;
"But hear his crimes, and hear his well-earn'd fate.
"Of human vice the fame had reach'd mine ear,
"With hop'd exaggeration; gliding down,
"From proud Olympus' brow, I veil'd the god,
"And rov'd the world in human form around.
"'Twere long to tell what turpitude I saw
"On every side, for rumor far fell short,
"Of what I witness'd. Through the dusky woods
"Of Mænalus I pass'd, where savage lurk
"Fierce monsters; o'er the cold Lycean hill,
"With pine-trees waving; and Cyllené's height.
"Thence to th' Arcadian monarch's roof I came,
"As dusky twilight drew on sable night.
"Gave signs a god approach'd. The people crowd
"In adoration: but Lycaön turns
"Their reverence and piety to scorn.
"Then said,—not hard the task to ascertain,
"If god or mortal, by unerring test:
"And plots to slay me when oppress'd with sleep.
"Such proof his soul well suited. Impious more,
"An hostage from Molossus sent he slew;

"His palpitating members part he boil'd,
"And o'er the glowing embers roasted part:
"These on the board he serves. My vengeful flames
"Consume his roof;—for his deserts, o'erwhelm
"His household gods. Lycaön trembling fled
"And gain'd the silent country; loud he howl'd,
"And strove in vain to speak; his ravenous mouth
"Still thirsts for slaughter; on the harmless flocks
"His fury rages, as it wont on man:
"Blood glads him still; his vest is shaggy hair;
"His arms sink down to legs; a wolf he stands.
"Yet former traits his visage still retains;
"Grey stil his hair; and cruel still his look;
"His eyes still glisten; savage all his form.
"Thus one house perish'd, but not one alone
"The fate deserves. Wherever earth extends,
"The fierce Erinnys reigns; men seem conspir'd
"In impious bond to sin; and all shall feel
"The scourge they merit: fixt is my decree."

  Part loud applaud his words, and feed his rage;
The rest assent in silence; yet to all,
Man's loss seems grievous; anxious all enquire
What form shall earth of him depriv'd assume?
Who ther shall incense to their altars bring?
And if those rich and fertile lands he means
A spoil for beasts ferocious? Their despair
He bade them banish, and in him confide
For what the future needed; held them forth
The promise of a race unlike the first;
Originating from a wonderous stock.

  And now his lightenings were already shot,
And earth in flames, but that a fire so vast,
He fear'd might reach Olympus, and consume
The heavenly axis. Also call'd to mind
What fate had doom'd, that all in future times
By fire should perish, earth, and sea, and heaven;
And all th unwieldy fabric of the world
Should waste to nought. The Cyclops' labor'd bolts
Aside he laid. A different vengeance now,
To drench with rains from every part of heaven,
And whelm mankind beneath the rising waves,
Pleas'd more th' immortal. Straightway close he pent
The dry north-east, and every blast to showers
Adverse, in caves Æolian, and unbarr'd
The cell of Notus. Notus rushes forth
On pinions dropping rain; his horrid face

A pitchy cloud conceals; pregnant with showers
His beard; and waters from his grey hairs flow:
Mists on his forehead sit; in dews dissolv'd
His arms and bosom, seem to melt away.
With broad hands seizing on the pendent clouds
He press'd them—with a mighty crash they burst,
And thick and constant floods from heaven pour down.
Iris meantime, in various robe array'd,
Collects the waters and supplies the clouds.
Prostrate the harvest lies, the tiller's hopes
Turn to despair. The labors of an year,
A long, long year, without their fruit are spent.
Nor Jove's own heaven his anger could suffice,
His brother brings him his auxiliar waves.
He calls the rivers,—at their monarch's call
His roof they enter, and in brief he speaks:
"Few words we need, pour each his utmost strength,
"The cause demands it; ope' your fountains wide,
"Sweep every mound before you, and let gush
"Your furious waters with unshorten'd reins."
He bids—the watery gods retire,—break up
Their narrow springs, and furious tow'rd the main
Their waters roll: himself his trident rears
And smites the earth; earth trembles at the stroke,
Yawns wide her bosom, and upon the land
A flood disgorges. Wide outspread the streams
Rush o'er the open fields;—uproot the trees;
Sweep harvests, flocks, and men;—nor houses stood;
Nor household gods, asylums hereto safe.
Where strong-built edifice its walls oppos'd
Unlevell'd in the ruin, high above
Its roof the billows mounted, and its towers
Totter'd, beneath the watery gulf oppress'd.
Nor land nor sea their ancient bounds maintain'd,
For all around was sea, sea without shore.
This seeks a mountain's top, that gains a skiff,
And plies his oars where late he plough'd the plains.
O'er fields of corn one sails, or 'bove the roofs
Of towns immerg'd;—another in the elm
Seizes th' intangled fish. Perchance in meads
The anchor oft is thrown, and oft the keel
Tears the subjacent vine-tree. Where were wont
The nimble goats to crop the tender grass
Unwieldy sea-calves roll. The Nereid nymphs,
With wonder, groves, and palaces, and towns,
Beneath the waves behold. By dolphins now
The woods are tenanted, who furious smite
The boughs, and shake the strong oak by their blows.

Swims with the flock the wolf; and swept along,
Tigers and tawny lions strive in vain.
Now not his thundering strength avails the boar;
Nor, borne away, the fleet stag's slender limbs:
And land, long sought in vain, to rest her feet,
The wandering bird draws in her weary wings,
And drops into the waves, whose uncheck'd roll
The hills have drown'd; and with un'custom'd surge
Foam on the mountain tops. Of man the most
They swallow'd; whom their fierce irruption spar'd,
By hunger perish'd in their bleak retreat.

   Between th' Aönian and Actæian lands
Lies Phocis; fruitful were the Phocian fields
While fields they were, but now o'erwhelm'd, they form
A region on y of the wide-spread main.
Here stands Parnassus with his forked top,
Above the clouds high-towering to the stars.
To this Deucalion with his consort driven
O'er ridgy billows in his bark clung close;
For all was sea beside. There bend they down;
The nymphs, and mountain gods adore, and she
Predicting Themis, then oraculous deem'd.
No man more upright than himself had liv'd;
Than Pyrrha none more pious heaven had seen.

   Now Jove beheld a mighty lake expand
Where late was earth, and from the swarming crowds
But one man sav'd—of woman only one:
Both guiltless,—pious both. He chas'd the clouds
And bade the dry north-east to drive the showers
Far distant, and display the earth to heaven,
And unto earth the skies. The ocean's rage
Remains no more. Mild Neptune lays aside
His three-fork'd weapon, and his surges smoothes;
Then calls blue Triton from the dark profound.
Above the waves the god his shoulders rears,
With inbred purple ting'd: He bids him sound
His shelly trump, and back the billows call;
And rivers to their banks again remand.
The trump he seizes,—broad above it wreath'd
From narrow base;—the trump whose piercing blast
From east to west resounds through every shore.
This to his mouth the watery-bearded god
Applies, and breathes within the stern command.
All hear the sound, or waves of earth or sea,
And all who hear obey. Sea finds a shore;
Floods flow within their channels; rivers sink;

Hills lift their heads; and as the waves decrease,
In numerous islets solid earth appears.
A tedious time elaps'd, and now the woods
Display'd their leafless summits, and their boughs
Heavy with mud. At length the world restor'd
Deucalion saw, but empty all and void;
Deep silence reigning through th' expansive waste:
Tears gush'd while thus his Pyrrha he address'd:
"O sister! wife! O woman sole preserv'd!—
"By nature, kindred, and the marriage-bed,
"To me most closely join'd. Now nearer still
"By mutual perils. We, of all the earth
"Beheld by Sol in his diurnal course,
"We two alone remain. The mighty deep
"Entombs the rest. Nor sure our safety yet;
"Still hang the clouds dark louring. Wretched wife,
"What if preserv'd alone? What hadst thou done
"Of me bereft? How singly borne the shock?
"Where found condolement in thy load of grief?
"For me,—and trust, my dearest wife, my words,—
"Hadst thou amidst the billows been ingulph'd,
"Me also had they swallow'd. Oh! for power
"To form mankind, as once my father did,
"And in the shapen earth true souls infuse!
"In us rests human race, so will the gods,
"A sample only of mankind we live."
He spoke and Pyrrha's tears join'd his. To heaven
They raise their hands in prayer, and straight resolve
To ask through oracles divine its aid.
Nor long delay. Quick to Cephisus' streams
They hasten; muddy still Cephisus flows,
Yet not beyond its wonted boundaries swol'n.
Libations thence they lift, and o'er their heads
And garments cast the sprinklings;—then their steps
To Themis' temple bend. The roof they found
With filthy moss o'ergrown;—the altars cold.
Prone on the steps they fell, and trembling kiss'd
The gelid stones, and thus preferr'd their words:
"If righteous prayers can move the heavenly mind,
"And soften harsh resolves, and soothe the rage
"Of great immortals, say, O Themis, say,
"How to the world mankind shall be restor'd;
"And grant, most merciful, in our distress
"Thy potent aid." The goddess heard their words,
And instant gave reply. "The temple leave,
"Ungird your garments, veil your heads, and throw
"Behind your backs your mighty mother's bones."
Astonish'd long they stood! and Pyrrha first

The silence broke; the oracle's behest
Refusing to obey; and earnest pray'd,
With trembling tongue for pardon for her sin:
Her mother's shade to violate she dreads,
Her bones thus rudely flinging. But meantime
Deep in their minds, in dark mysterious veil
Obscurely hid, the sentence they revolve.
At length Deucalion sooths his wife with words
Of cheering import: "Right, if I divine,
"No impious deed the deity desires:
"Earth is our mighty mother, and her bones
"The stony rocks within her;—these behind
"Our backs to cast, the oracle commands."
With joy th' auspicious augury she hears,
But joy with doubt commingled, both so much
The heavenly words distrust; yet still they hope
The essay cannot harm. The temple left,
Their heads they cover, and their vests unbind;
And o'er their heads as order'd heave the stones.
The stones—(incredible! unless the fact
Tradition sanction'd doubtless) straight began
To lose their rugged firmness,—and anon,
To soften,—and when soft a form assume.
Next as they grew in size, they felt infus'd
A nature mild,—their form resembled man!
But incorrectly: marble so appears,
Rough hewn to form a statue, ere the hand
Completes the shape. What liquid was, and moist,
With earthy atoms mixt, soft flesh became;
Parts solid and unbending chang'd to bone;
In name unalter'd, veins the same remain'd.
Thus by the gods' beneficent decree,
And brief the change, the stones Deucalion threw,
A manly shape assum'd; but females sprung
From those by Pyrrha cast behind; and hence
A patient, hard, laborious race we prove,
And shew the source, by actions, whence we sprung.

   Beings all else the teeming earth produc'd
Spontaneous. Heated by the solar rays,
The stagnant water quicken'd;—marshy fens
Swell'd up their oozy loads to meet the beams:
And nourish'd by earth's vivifying soil,
The fruitful elements of life increas'd,
As in a mother's womb; and in a while
Assum'd a certain shape. So when the floods
Of seven-mouth'd Nile desert the moisten'd fields,
And to their ancient channels bring their streams,

The soft mud fries beneath the scorching sun;
And midst the fresh-turn'd earth unnumber'd forms
The tiller finds: some scarcely half conceiv'd;
Imperfect some, their bodies wanting limbs:
And oft he beings sees with parts alive,
The rest a clod of earth: for where with heat
Due moisture kindly mixes, life will spring:
From these in concord all things are produc'd.
Though fire with water strives; yet vapour warm,
Discordant mixture, gives a birth to all.

Thus when the earth, with filthy ooze bespread
From the late deluge, felt the blazing sun;
His burning heat productive caus'd spring forth
A countless race of beings. Part appear'd
In forms before well-known; the rest a group
Of monsters strange. Then, but unwilling, she
Produc'd terrific Python, serpent huge!
A mighty mountain with his bulk he hid;
A plague unknown, the new-born race to scare.
The quiver-shoulder'd god, unus'd before
His arms to launch, save on the flying deer,
Or roebuck fleet, the horrid monster slew:
A thousand arrows in his sides he fix'd,
His quiver's store exhausting; through the wounds
Gush'd the black poison. To contending games,
Hence instituted for the serpent slain,
The glorious action to preserve through times
Succeeding, he the name of Pythian gave.
And here the youth who bore the palm away
By wrestling, racing, or in chariot swift,
With beechen bough was crown'd. Nor yet was known
The laurel's leaf: Apollo's brows, with hair
Deck'd graceful, no peculiar branches bound.

Penæian Daphne first his bosom charm'd;
No casual flame but plann'd by Love's revenge.
Him, Phœbus flush'd with conquest late obtain'd,
His bow saw bend, and thus exclaim'd in taunt:
"Lascivious boy! How ill with thee assort
"Those warlike arms?—how much my shoulders more
"Beseem the load, whose arm can deadly wounds
"In furious beasts, and every foe infix!
"I who but now huge Python have o'erthrown;
"Swol'n with a thousand darts; his mighty bulk
"Whole acres covering with pestiferous weight?
"Content in vulgar hearts thy torch to flame,
"To me the bow's superior glory leave."

Then Venus' son: "O Phœbus, nought thy dart
"Evades, nor thou canst 'scape the force of mine:
"To thee as others yield,—so much my fame
"Must ever thine transcend." Thus spoke the boy,
And lightly mounting, cleaves the yielding air
With beating wings, and on Parnassus' top
Umbrageous rests. There from his quiver drew
Two darts of different power:—this chases love;
And that desire enkindles; form'd of gold
It glistens, ending in a point acute:
Blunt is the first, tipt with a leaden load;
Which Love in Daphne's tender breast infix'd.
The sharper through Apollo's heart he drove,
And through his nerves and bones;—instant he loves:
She flies of ove the name. In shady woods,
And spoils of captive beasts alone she joys;
To copy Dian' emulous; her hair
In careless tresses form'd, a fillet bound.
By numbers sought,—averse alike to all;
Impatient of their suit, through forests wild,
And groves, in maiden ignorance she roams;
Nor cares for Cupid, nor hymeneal rites,
Nor soft connubial joys. Oft cry'd her sire;
"My Daphne, you should bring to me a son;
"From you, my child, I hope for grandsons too."
But she detesting wedlock as a crime,
(Suffus'd her features with a bashful glow)
Around his aged neck, her beauteous arms,
Winds blandishing, and cries, "O sire, most dear!
"One favor grant,—perpetual to enjoy
"My virgin curity;—the mighty Jove
"The same indulgence has to Dian' given."
Thy sire complies;—but that too beauteous face,
And lovely form, thy anxious wish oppose:
Apollo loves thee;—to thy bed aspires;—
And looks with anxious hopes, his wish to gain:
Futurity, by him for once unseen.
As the light stubble when the ears are shorn,
The flames consume: as hedges blaze on high
From torches by the traveller closely held,
Or heedless flung, when morning gilds the world:
So flaming burnt the god;—so blaz'd his breast,
And with fond hopes his vain desires he fed.
Her tresses careless flowing o'er her neck
He view'd, and, "Oh! how beauteous, deck'd with care,"
Exclaim'd: her eyes which shone like brilliant fire,
Or sparkling stars, he sees; and sees her lips;
Unsated with the sight, he burns to touch:

Admires her fingers, and her hands, her arms,
Half to the shoulder naked:—what he sees
Though beauteous, what is hid he deems more fair.
Fleet as the wind, her fearful flight she wings,
Nor stays his fond recalling words to hear:
"Daughter of Peneus, stay! no foe pursues,—
"Stay, beauteous nymph!—so flies the lamb the wolf;
"The stag the lion;—so on trembling wings
"The dove avoids the eagle:—these are foes,
"But love alone me urges to pursue.
"Ah me! then, shouldst thou fall,—or prickly thorns
"Wound thy fair legs,—and I the cause of pain!—
"Rough is the road thou runnest; slack, I pray,
"Thy speed;—I swear to follow not so fast.
"But hear who loves thee;—no rough mountain swain;
"No shepherd;—none in raiments rugged clad,
"Tending the lowing herds: rash thoughtless nymph,
"Thou fly'st thou know'st not whom, and therefore fly'st!
"O'er Delphos' lands, and Tenedos I sway,
"And Claros, and the Pataræan realms.—
"My sire is Jove. To me are all things known,
"Or present, past, or future. Taught by me
"Melodious sounds poetic numbers grace.—
"Sure is my dart, but one more sure I feel
"Lodg'd in this bosom; strange to love before.—
"Medicine me hails inventor; through the world
"My help is call'd for; unto me is known
"The powers of plants and herbs:—ah! hapless I,
"Nor plants, nor herbs, afford a cure for love;
"Nor arts which all relieve, relieve their lord."
All this, and more:—but Daphne fearful fled,
And left his speech unfinish'd. Lovely then
She running seem'd;—her limbs the breezes bar'd;
Her flying raiment floated on the gale;
Her careless tresses to the light air stream'd;
Her flight increas'd her beauty. Now no more
The god to waste his courteous words endures,
But urg'd by love himself, with swifter pace
Her footsteps treads: the rapid greyhound so,
When in the open field the hare he spies,
Trusts to his legs for prey,—as she for flight;
And now he snaps, and now he thinks to hold,
And brushes with his outstretch'd nose her heels;—
She trembling, half in doubt, or caught or no,
Springs from his jaws, and mocks his touching mouth.
Thus fled the virgin and the god;—he fleet
Through hope, and she through fear,—but wing'd by love
More rapid flew Apollo;—spurning rest,

Approach'd her close behind, and panting breath'd
Upon her floating tresses. Pale with dread,
Her strength exhausted in the lengthen'd flight,
Old Peneus' streams she saw, and loud exclaim'd:—
"O sire, assist me, if within thy streams
"Divinity abides. Let earth this form,
"Too comely for my peace, quick swallow up;
"Or change those beauties to an harmless shape."
Her prayer scarce ended, when her lovely limbs
A numbness felt; a tender rind enwraps
Her beauteous bosom; from her head shoots up
Her hair in leaves; in branches spread her arms;
Her feet but now so swift, cleave to the earth
With roots immoveable; her face at last
The summit forms; her bloom the same remains.
Still loves the god the tree, and on the trunk
His right hand placing, feels her breast yet throb,
Beneath the new-grown bark: around the boughs,
As yet her limbs, his clasping arms he throws;
And burning kisses on the wood imprints.
The wood his lips repels. Then thus the god:—
"O laurel, though to be my bride deny'd,
"Yet shalt thou be my tree; my temples bind;
"My lyre and quiver shalt thou still adorn:
"The brows of Latian conquerors shalt thou grace,
"When the glad people sing triumphant hymns,
"And the long pomp the capitol ascends.
"A faithful guard before Augustus' gates,
"On each side hung;—the sturdy oak between.
"And as perpetual youth adorns my head
"With locks unshorn, thou also still shalt bear
"Thy leafy honors in perpetual green."
Apollo ended, and the laurel bow'd
Her verdant summit as her grateful head.

　Within Æmonia lies a grove, inclos'd
By steep and lofty hills on every side:
'Tis Tempé call'd. From lowest Pindus pour'd
Here Peneus rolls his foaming waves along:
Thick clouds of smoke, and dark and vapoury mists
The violent falls produce, sprinkling the tops
Of proudest forests with the plenteous dew;
And distant parts astounding with the roar.
Here holds the watery deity his throne;—
Here his retreat most sacred;—seated here,
Within the rock-form'd cavern, to the streams
And stream-residing nymphs, his laws he gives.
Here flock the neighbouring river-gods, in doubt

Or to condole, or gratulate the sire.
Here Spercheus came, whose banks with poplars wave;
Rapid Enipeus; Apidanus slow;
Amphrysos gently flowing; Æäs mild;
And other streams which wind their various course,
Till in the sea their weary wanderings end,
By natural bent directed. Absent sole
Was Inachus;—deep in his gloomy cave
Dark hidden, with his tears he swells his floods.
He, wretched sire, his Iö's loss bewails;
Witless if living air she still enjoys,
Or with the shades she dwells; and no where found
He dreads the worst, and thinks her not to be.
The beauteous damsel from her father's banks
Jove saw returning, and, "O, maid!" exclaim'd,
"Worthy of Jove, whose charms will shortly bless
"Some youth desertless; come, and seek the shade,
"Yon lofty groves afford,"—and shew'd the groves,—
"While now Sol scorches from heaven's midmost height.
"Fear not the forests to explore alone,
"But in their deepest shades adventurous go;
"A god shall guard thee:—no plebeian god,
"But he whose mighty hand the sceptre grasps
"Of rule celestial, and the lightening flings.
"O fly me not"—for Iö fled, amaz'd.
Now Lerna's pastures, and Lyrcæa's lands
With trees thick-planted, far behind were left;
When with a sudden mist the god conceal'd
The wide-spread earth, and stopp'd her eager flight;
And in his arms the struggling maid compress'd.
Meantime did Juno cast her eyes below,
The floating clouds surpris'd to see produce
A night-like shade amidst so bright a day.
No common clouds, from streams exhal'd, she knew;
Nor misty vapours from the humid earth.
Suspicions rise; her sharpness oft had caught
Her amorous husband in his thefts of love.
She search'd around the sky, its lord explor'd,—
But not in heaven he sate;—then loud exclaim'd:
"Much must I err, or much my bed is wrong'd."
Down sliding from the topmost heaven, on earth
She lights, and bids the cloudy mists recede.
Prepar'd already, Jove the nymph had chang'd,
And in a lovely heifer's form she stood.
A shape so beauteous fair,—though sore chagrin'd,
Unwilling Juno prais'd; and whence she came,
And who her owner asks; and of what herd?
Her prying art, as witless of the truth,

To baffle, from the earth he feigns her sprung;
And straight Saturnia begs the beauteous gift.
Embarrass'd now he stands,—the nymph to leave
Abandon'd, were too cruel;—to deny
His wife, suspicious: shame compliance urg'd;
Love strong dissuaded: love had vanquish'd shame,
Save that a paltry cow to her refus'd,
Associate of his race and bed, he fear'd
More than a cow the goddess would suspect.
Her rival now she holds; but anxious, still
She Jove distrusts, and fears her prize to lose;
Nor safe she deem'd her, till to Argus' care
Committed. Round the jailor's watchful head
An hundred eyes were set. Two clos'd in turn;
The rest with watchful care, kept cautious guard.
Howe'er he stands, on Iö still he looks;
His face averse, yet still his eyes behold.
By day she pastures, but beneath the earth
When Phœbus sinks, he drags her to the stall,
And binds with cords her undeserving neck.
Arbutus' leaves, and bitter herbs her food:
Her wretched bed is oft the cold damp earth;
A strawy couch deny'd:—the muddy stream
Her constant drink: when suppliant she would raise
Her arms to Argus, arms to raise were none.
To moan she tries; loud bellowings echo wide,—
She starts and trembles at her voice's roar.
Now to the banks she comes where oft she'd play'd,—
The banks of Inachus, and in his streams
Her new-form'd horns beheld;—in wild affright
From them she strove, and from herself to fly.
Her sister Naïads know her not, nor he
Griev'd Inachus, his long-lost daughter knows.
But she her sisters and her sire pursues;
Invites their touch, as wondering they caress.
Old Inachus the gather'd herbs presents;
She licks his hands, and presses with her lips
His dear paternal fingers. Tears flow quick,
And could words follow she would ask his aid;
And speak her name, and lamentable state.
Marks for her words she form'd, which in the dust
Trac'd by her hoof, disclos'd her mournful change.
"Ah wretch " her sire exclaim'd, "unhappy wretch!"
And o'er the weeping heifer's snowy neck,
His arms he threw, and round her horns he hung
With sobs redoubled:—"Art thou then, my child,
"Through earth's extent so sought? Ah! less my grief,
"To find thee not, than thus transform'd to find!

"But dumb thou art, nor with responsive words,
"Me cheerest. From thy deep chest sighs alone
"Thou utterest, and loud lowings to my words:
"Thou canst no more. Unwitting I prepar'd
"Thy marriage torches, anxious to behold
"A son, and next a son of thine to see.
"Now from the herd a husband must thou seek,
"Now with the herd thy sons must wander forth.
"Nor death my woes can finish: curst the gift
"Of immortality. Eternal grief
"Must still corrode me; Lethé's gate is clos'd."
Thus griev'd the god, when starry Argus tore
His charge away, and to a distant mead
Drove her to pasture;—he a lofty hill's
Commanding prospect chose, and seated there
View'd all around alike on every side.

But now heaven's ruler could no more contain,
To see the sorrows Iö felt:—he calls
His son, of brightest Pleiäd mother born,
And bids him quickly compass Argus' death.
Instant around his heels his wings he binds;
His rod somniferous grasps; nor leaves his cap.
Accoutred thus, from native heights he springs,
And lights on earth; removes his cap; his wings
Unlooses; and his wand alone retains:
Through devious paths with this, a shepherd now,
A flock he drives of goats, and tunes his pipe
Of reeds constructed. Argus hears the sound,
Junonian guard, and captivated cries,—
"Come, stranger, sit with me upon this mount:
"Nor for thy flock more fertile pasture grows,
"Than round this spot;—and here the shade thou seest
"To shepherds' ease inviting."—Hermes sate,
And with his converse stay'd declining day.
Long he discours'd, and anxious strove to lull
With music sweet, the all-observant eyes;
But long he strove in vain: soft slumber's bonds
Argus opposes;—of his numerous lights,
Part sleep, but others jealous watch his charge.
And now he questions whence the pipe was form'd,
The pipe but new-discover'd to the world.

Then thus the god:—"A lovely Naiäd nymph,
"With bleak Arcadia's Hamadryads nurs'd,
"And on Nonacriné for beauty fam'd
"Was Syrinx. Oft the satyrs wild she fled;
"Nor these alone, but every god that roves

"In shady forests, or in fertile fields.
"Dian' she follows, and her virgin life.
"Like Dian cinctur'd, she might Dian' seem,
"Save that a golden bow the goddess bears;
"The nymph a bow of horn: yet still to most
"Mistake was easy. From Lycæum's height,
"His head encompass'd with the pointed pine,
"Returning, her the lustful Pan espy'd,
"And cry'd:—Fair virgin grant a god's request,—
"A god who burns to wed thee. Here he stays.
"Through pathless forests flies the nymph, and scorns
"His warm intreaties, till the gravelly stream
"Of Ladon, smoothly winding, she beheld.
"The waves impede her flight. She earnest prays
"Her sister-nymphs her human form to change.
"Now thirks the sylvan god his clasping arms
"Inclose her, whilst he grasps but marshy reeds.—
"He mournful sighs; the light reeds catch his breath,
"And soft reverberate the plaintive sound.
"The dulcet movement charms th' enraptur'd god,
"Who,—thus forever shall we join,—exclaims!
"With wax combin'd th' unequal reeds he forms
"A pipe, which still the virgin's name retains."
While thus the god, he every eye beheld
Weigh'd heavy, sink in sleep, and stopp'd his tale.
His magic rod o'er every lid he draws,
His sleep confirming, and with crooked blade
Severs his nodding head, and down the mount
The bloody ruin hurls,—the craggy rock
With gore besmearing. Low, thou Argus liest!
Extinct thy hundred lights; one night obscure
Eclipsing all. But Juno seiz'd the rays,
And on the plumage of her favor'd bird,
In gaudy pride, the starry gems she plac'd.

With furious ire she flam'd, and instant sent
The dread Erinnys to the Argive maid.
Before her eyes, within her breast she dwelt
A secret torment, and in terror drove
Her exil'd through the world. 'Twas thou, O Nile!
Her tedious wandering ended. On thy banks
Weary'd she kneel'd, and on her back, supine
Her neck she lean'd:—her sad face to the skies,
What could she more?—she lifted. Unto Jove
By groans, and tears, and mournful lows she plain'd,
And begg'd her woes might end. The mighty god
Around his consort's neck embracing hung.
And pray'd her wrath might finish. "Fear no more

"A rival love, in her," he said, "to see;"
And bade the Stygian streams his words record.
Appeas'd the goddess, Iö straight resumes
Her wonted shape, as lovely as before.
The rough hair flies; the crooked horns are shed;
Her visual orbits narrow; and her mouth
In size contracts; her arms and hands return;
Parted in five small nails her hoofs are lost:
Nought of the lovely heifer now remains,
Save the bright splendor. On her feet erect
With two now only furnish'd, stands the maid.
To speak she fears, lest bellowing sounds should break,
And timid tries her long-forgotten words.
Of mighty fame a goddess now, she hears
Of nations linen-clad the pious prayers.

  Then bore she Epaphus, whose birth deriv'd
From mighty Jove, his temples through the land,
An equal worship with his mother's claim.
Him Phaëton, bright Phœbus' youthful son,
In years and spirit equall'd,—whose proud boasts,
To all his sire preferring, Iö's son
Thus check'd: "O simple! thee thy mother's arts
"To ought persuade. A feigned sire thou boast'st."
Deep blush'd the youth, but shame his rage repress'd,
And each reproach to Clymené he bore.
"This too," he says, "O mother, irks me more,
"That I so bold, so fierce, urg'd no defence:
"Which shame is greater? that they dare accuse,
"Or that accus'd, we cannot prove them false?
"Do thou my mother,—if from heaven indeed
"Descent I claim,—prove from what stock I spring.
"My race divine assert." He said,—and flung
Around her neck his arms; and by his life,
The life of Merops, and his sisters' hopes
Of nuptial bliss, adjures her to obtain
Proofs of his birth celestial. Prayers like these
The mother doubtless mov'd;—and rage no less
To hear the defamation. Up to heaven
Her arms she raises, gazing on the sun,
And cries,—"My child! by yon bright rays I swear
"In brilliance glittering, which now hear and view,
"Our every word and action—thou art sprung
"From him, the sun thou see'st;—the sun who rules
"With tempering sway the seasons:—If untrue
"My words, let me his light no more behold!
"Nor long the toil to seek thy father's dome,
"His palace whence he rises borders close

"On our land's confines.—If thou dar'st the task,
"Go forth, and from himself thy birth enquire."
Elate to hear her words, the youth departs
Instant, and all the sky in mind he grasps.
Through Æthiopia's regions swiftly went,
With India plac'd beneath the burning zone:
And quickly reach'd his own paternal east.

THE SECOND BOOK

Palace of the Sun. Phaëton's reception by his father. His request to drive the chariot. The Sun's useless arguments to dissuade him from the attempt. Description of the car. Cautions how to perform the journey. Terror of Phaëton, and his inability to rule the horses. Conflagration of the world. Petition of Earth to Jupiter, and death of Phaëton by thunder. Grief of Clymené, and of his sisters. Change of the latter to poplars, and their tears to amber. Transformation of Cycnus to a swan. Mourning of Phœbus. Jupiter's descent to earth; and amour with Calistho. Birth of Arcas, and transformation of Calistho to a bear; and afterwards with Arcas to a constellation. Story of Coronis. Tale of the daw to the raven. Change of the raven's color. Esculapius. Ocyrrhoë's prophecies, and transformation to a mare. Apollo's herds stolen by Mercury. Battus' double-dealing, and change to a touchstone. Mercury's love for Hersé. Envy. Aglauros changed to a statue. Rape of Europa.

THE SECOND BOOK OF THE METAMORPHOSES OF OVID

   By towering columns bright with burnish'd gold,
And fiery gems, which blaz'd their light around,
Upborne, the palace stood. The lofty roof
With ivory smooth incas'd. The folding doors,
Of silver shone, but much by sculpture grac'd,
For Vulcan there with curious hand had carv'd
The ocean girding in the land; the land;
And heaven o'ershadowing: here cerulean gods
Sport in the waves, grim Triton with his shell;
Proteus shape-changing; and Ægeon huge,—
His mighty arms upon the large broad backs
Of whales hard pressing: Doris and her nymphs:
Some sportive swimming; on a rocky seat
Some their green tresses drying: others borne
By fish swift-gliding: nor the same all seem'd,
Yet sister-like a close resembling look
Each face pervaded. Earth her natives bore,
Mankind;—and woods, and cities, there were seen;
Wild beasts, and streams, and nymphs, and rural gods.
'Bove all the bright display of heaven was hung—
Six signs celestial o'er each portal grav'd.

The daring youth, the steep ascent attain'd,
O'erstepp'd the threshold of his dubious sire,
And hasty rush'd to meet paternal eyes;
But sudden stay'd: so fierce a blaze of light
No nearer he sustain'd. In purple clad,
The god a regal emerald throne upheld;
Encircled round by hours which space the day;
By days themselves; and ages, months, and years.
Crown'd with a flowery garland Spring appear'd:
Chaplets of grain the swarthy brows adorn'd
Of naked Summer: smear'd with trodden grapes
Stood Autumn: icy Winter fill'd the groupe;—
Snow-white his shaggy locks. Sol from the midst
His eyes all-seeing glanc'd upon the youth,
Startled and trembling at the wonderous sight;
And cried:—"What brings my Phaëton, my son,
"Whose sire shall ne'er disclaim him? tell me now,
"What here thou seekest?" Thus the youth replies:—
"O father, Phœbus, universal light!
"If justly, I thy honor'd name may use,
"Nor proudly boasting Clymené conceals
"A crime by falshood; grant paternal signs,
"The world convincing that from thee I spring;
"Reproachful doubts erasing from my mind."
He said;—the sire the glittering rays removes
That blaz'd around his head,—invites him nigh,
And thus embracing:—"Proud I own thee, son,
"For all is true by Clymené disclos'd.
"If still thou doubtest, name the gift thou lik'st,—
"That shalt thou have; for that will I bestow.
"Ye streams unseen, which hear celestial oaths
"My vows attest!" But scarce had Phœbus spoke,
When Phaëton, the fiery car demands,—
Demands his sway the winged-footed steeds
One day should suffer. Soon the solemn oath
Phœbus lamented: three times mournful shook
His glorious tresses and in sorrow cry'd—
"Would I could yet deny thee!—O my son!
"All else with gladness will I hear thee ask;—
"List to persuasion,—perseverance sure
"Will risk thy ruin. Phaëton, my child!
"The task thou seek'st is arduous; far unfit
"For those weak arms, and age so immature.
"Mortal,—thou would'st a seat immortal press.
"Ignorant of grasping more than all the gods
"Attempt to manage. Every power we grant
"Diverse excels; but I of all the gods,

"Have force in that igniferous car to stand.
"Ev'n Jove, the ruler of Olympus vast,
"Whose right hand terrible fierce lightenings hurls,
"This chariot never rul'd: and who than Jove,
"More mighty deem we? Steep the first ascent,
"The fresh steeds clamber up the height with pain:
"High in mid heaven arriv'd, to view beneath
"Ocean and earth, oft strikes even me with fear,
"And with dread palpitation shakes my breast.
"Prerupt the end, and asks a firm restraint;
"Tethys herself who nightly me receives,
"Beneath the waves, fears oft my headlong fall.
"Nor all;—the skies a constant whirling bears
"In rapid motion, and the heavenly orbs
"Sweep with them swift; I strive the adverse my;
"Nor can th' impetuous force which whirls the rest
"Bear with them me; I stem the rapid world
"With force superior. Grant, the car I yield,—
"Could'st thou the swift rotation of the poles
"Stem nervous, nor be borne with them along?
"Perchance imagination fills thy mind,
"With groves, and dwellings of celestial gods,
"And temples richly deck'd with offer'd gold,
"Where thou shall pass. Far else;—thy journey lies,
"Through ambushes, and savage monsters' forms.
"Ev'n shouldst thou lucky not erratic stray,
"Yet must thou pass the Bull's opposing horns;
"The bow Hæmonian, by the Centaur bent;
"The Lion's countenance grim; the Scorpion's claws
"Bent cruel in a circuit large; the Crab
"In lesser compass curving. Hard the task
"To rule the steeds with those fierce fires inflam'd,
"Within their breasts, which through their nostrils glow.
"Scarce bear they my control, when mad with heat
"Their high necks spurn the rein. But, oh! my son,
"Beware lest I a fatal gift bestow.
"Retract, while yet thou may'st, thy rash demand.
"Sure tokens thou requir'st to prove thee sprung
"From me,—the genuine offspring of my blood:
"My anxious trembling is a token true;
"Paternal terrors plainly prove the sire.
"Lo! on my features fix thine eyes; as well,
"I would thou could'st them place within my breast,
"And view the anguish of a father's cares.
"Last throw thy looks around; the riches view,
"Whatever earth contains, and some demand;
"Some of so many and such mighty gifts:
"In heaven, or earth, or sea, 'tis undeny'd.

"This only would I grant not, as its grant
"Is punishment, not favor. Phaëton
"Asks evil for a gift. Why, foolish boy,
"Hang on my neck thus coaxing with thine arms?
"Whate'er thou would'st, thou shalt. The Stygian streams
"Have heard me swear. But make a wiser wish."
His admonition ceas'd, but all advice
Was bootless: still his resolution holds;
To guide the chariot still his bosom burns.
The sire, his every effort vain, at length
Forth to the lofty car, Vulcanian gift,
Brings the rash youth. Of gold the axle shone;
The pole of gold; by gold the rolling wheels
Were circled; every spoke with silver bright;
Upon the seat bright chrysolites display'd,
With various jewels shed a dazzling light,
From Sol reflected. All the high-soul'd youth
Admir'd, and while he curious view'd each part,
Behold Aurora from the purple east
Wide throws the ruddy portals, and displays
The halls with roses strewn: the starry host
Fly, driven by Lucifer,—himself the last
To quit his heavenly station. Sol beheld
The earth and sky grow red, and Luna's horns
Blunt, and prepar'd to vanish. Straight he bade
The flying hours to yoke the steeds: his words
The nimble goddesses obey, and lead
The steeds fire-breathing from their lofty stalls,
Ambrosia fed, and fix the sounding reins.
Then with a sacred ointment Phœbus smear'd
The face of Phaëton,—unscorch'd to bear
The fervid blaze; and on his head a crown
Of rays he fix'd. His smother'd sighs within
His anxious breast, sad presages of woe
Suppressing, thus he spoke:—"If now my words
"Though late, thou heedest, spare, O boy! the lash,
"But tightly grasp the reins: unbid they run,
"They fly; to check their flight thy labor asks.
"Not through the five bright zones thy journey lies:
"Obliquely winds the path, with spacious curve,
"Three girdles only touching; leaving far
"The pole Antarctic, and the northern Bear:
"Be this thy track; there plain thou may'st discern
"The marks my wheels have made. Since heaven and earth
"An equal portion of my influence claim;
"Press not the car too low, nor mount aloft
"Near topmost heaven: there would'st thou fire the roof
"Celestial;—here the earth thou would'st consume.

"For safety keep the midst. Let thy right wheel
"Approach the tortuous Snake not: nor thy left
"Press near the Altar:—hold the midmost course.
"Fortune the rest must rule; may she assist
"Thy undertaking; for thy safety act
"Better than thou. But more delay deny'd,
"Lo! whilst I speak the dewy night has touch'd
"The boundaries plac'd upon th' Hesperian shore.
"I'm call'd.—for, darkness fled, Aurora shines.
"Seize then, the reins, or if thy mind relents,
"My counsel rather than my chariot take.
"Now whilst thou can'st; whilst on a solid base
"Thou standest, ere thou yet unskilful mount'st
"The chariot ev'lly wish'd: give me to dart
"Those rays on earth which thou may'st safely view:"
Agile the youth bounds from his sire, and stands
Proud in the chariot; joyously he holds
Th' entrusted reigns, and from the seat glad thanks
Th' unwilling parent gives. Meantime neigh'd loud
In curling flames, the winged steeds of Sol,
Pyroeis, Æthon, Phlegon, Eous swift;
And with impatient hoofs the barrier beat;
Which Tethys, ignorant of her grandson's fate,
Drove back, and open laid the range of heaven.
Swiftly they hasten,—swiftly fly their heels,
Through the thin air, and through opposing clouds.
Pois'd by their wings the eastern gales they pass,
Which started with them: but their burthen light,
Small felt the pressure on the chariot seat:
Not what the steeds of Sol had felt before.
As ships unpois'd reel tottering through the waves,
Light and unsteady, rambling o'er the main;
So bounds the car, void of its 'custom'd weight,
High-toss'd as though unfill'd. This quick perceiv'd,
Fierce rush the four-yok'd steeds, and quit the path
Beaten before, and tread a road unknown.
Trembling the youth nor knows to pull the reins
Which side, nor knowing would the steeds obey.
Then first the frozen Triönes from Sol
Felt warm, and try'd, but try'd in vain, to dip
Beneath the sea. The frozen polar snake,
Sluggish with cold, and indolently mild,
Warm'd, and dire fierceness gather'd from the flames.
Thou too, Boötes, fled'st away disturb'd,
Though slow thy flight, retarded by thy teams.
And now the luckless Phaëton his eyes
Cast on the earth remote,—far distant spread
Beneath the lofty sky; pale grew his face

With sudden terror; trembled his weak knees;
O'ercome with light his eyes in darkness sunk:
Glad were he now, his father's steeds untouch'd:
Griev'd that his race he knows; griev'd his request
Was undeny'd: glad were he now if call'd
The son of Merops. Ev'n as Boreas sweeps
Furious the vessel, when the pilot leaves
The helm to heaven, and puts his trust in prayers
So was he hurry'd. What remains to do?
Vast space of heaven behind him lies;—much more
He forward views. Each distance in his mind
Compar'd he measures. Now he forward bends
To view the west, forbidden him to reach;
Now to the east he backward turns his eyes.
With terror stunn'd his trembling hands refuse
To hold the reins with vigor; yet he holds.
The coursers' names, affrighted he forgets:
Trembling he views the various monsters spread
Through every part above; and figures huge
Of beasts ferocious. Heaven a spot contains,
Where Scorpio bends in two wide bows his arms,
His tail, and doubly-stretching claws;—the space
Encompassing of two celestial signs.
Soon as the youth the monstrous beast beheld,
Black poison sweating, and with crooked sting
Threatening fierce wounds, he nerveless dropp'd the reins:
Pale dread o'ercame him. Quick the steeds perceiv'd
The loose thongs playing on their backs, and rush'd
Wide from the path, uncheck'd;—through regions strange,
Now here, now there, impetuous;—unrestrain'd,
Amidst the loftiest stars they dash, and drag
The car through pathless places: upward now
They labor;—headlong now they down descend,
Nearing the earth. With wonder Luna sees
Her brother's coursers run beneath her own;
And sees the burnt clouds smoking. Lofty points
Of earth, feel first the flames, and fissures wide,
Departing moisture prove. The forage green,
Whitens; trees crackle with their burning leaves;
And ripe corn adds its fuel to the blaze.
Why mourn we trifles? Mighty cities fall;
Their walls protect them not; their dwellers sink
To ashes with them. Woods on mountains flame;—
Athos, Cilician Taurus, Tmolus, burn;
Oeté, and Ide, her pleasant fountains dry;
With virgin Helicon, and Hæmus high,
Œagrius since. Now with redoubled flames
Fierce Etna blazes;—Eryx, Othrys too;

Cynthus, and fam'd Parnassus' double top,
And Rhodopé, at length of snow depriv'd:
Dindyma, Mimas, and the sacred hill
Cythæron nam'd, and lofty Mycalé:
Nor aid their snows the Scythians: Ossa burns,
Pindus, and Caucasus, and, loftier still,
The huge Olympus; with the towering Alps;
And cloud-capt Apennines. Now the youth,
Beholds earth flaming fierce from every part;—
The heat o'erpowers him; fiery air he breathes
As from a furnace; and the car he rides
Glows with the flame beneath him: sore annoy'd
On every side by cinders, and by smoke
Hot curling round him. Whither now he drives,
Or where he is, he knows not; in a cloud
Of pitchy night involv'd; swept as the steeds
Swift-flying will. The Æthiopians then,
'Tis said, their sable tincture first receiv'd;
Their purple blood the glowing heat call'd forth
To tinge their skins. Then dry'd the scorching fire
From arid Lybia all her fertile streams.
Now with dishevell'd locks the nymphs bewail'd
Their fountains and their lakes. Bœotia mourns
The loss of Dircé: Argos Amymoné:
Corinth laments Pirené. Nor yet safe
Were rivers bounded by far distant shores,
Tanais' midmost waves fume to the sky;
And ancient Peneus smokes: Ismenos swift;
Caïcus, Teuthrantean; and the flood
Of Phocis, Erymanthus: Xanthus too,
Doom'd to be fir'd again: Lycormas brown;
Mæander's sportive oft recircling waves;
Mygdon an Melas; and the Spartan flood,
Eurotas; with Euphrates burn: and burn,
Orontes; and the rapid Thermodoon;
Ganges; and Phasis; and the Ister swift.
Alpheus boils; the banks of Spercheus burn;
And Tagus' golden sands the flames dissolve.
Stream-loving swans, whose song melodious rung
Throughout Mæonian regions, feel the heat,
Caïster's streams amid. In terror Nile
Fled to the farthest earth, and sunk his head,
Yet undiscover'd!—void the seven-fold stream,
His mouth seven dry and dusty vales disclos'd.
Now Hebrus dries, and Strymon, Thracian floods:
And streams Hesperian, Rhine; and Rhone; and Po;
And Tiber, destin'd all the world to rule.
Asunder split the globe, and through the chinks

Darted the light to hell: the novel blaze,
Pluto and Proserpine with terror view'd.
The ocean shrinks;—a dry and scorching plain
Where late was sea appears. Hills lift their heads
Late by the deep waves hid, and countless seem
The scatter'd Cyclades. Deep crouch the fish;—
The crooked dolphins dare not leap aloft,
As, custom'd in the air; with breasts upturn'd
The gasping sea-calves float upon the waves:
Nereus, with Doris and her daughter-nymphs
Deep plung'd to seek their low, but tepid caves.
Thrice Neptune ventur'd to upraise his arms
Grim frowning,—thrice the flames too fierce he found,
And shrunk beneath the waters. Earth at length,
(By streams and founts encircled,—for her womb
Trembling they sought for refuge) rais'd on high
Her face omniferous, dry and parch'd with heat;
Her burning forehead shaded with her hand;
Shook all with tremor huge; then shrank for shade
Beneath, and gasping, thus to heaven she plain'd:

  "Almighty lord! if such thy sovereign will,
"And I deserve it, why thy lightenings hold
"Thus idle? If by fire to perish doom'd,—
"Be it by thine,—an honorable fate!
"Scarce can my lips now utter forth my pains!—
Volumes of smoke oppress'd her—"See, my hair
"Sing'd with the flames! Behold my face,—my eyes,
"Scorch'd with hot embers! Is no better boon
"Due for the fruits I furnish? Such reward,
"Suits it my fertile crops? or cruel wounds
"Of harrow, rake, and plough, which through the year
"Enforc'd I suffer? For the herds I bring
"Green herbs and grass; bland aliments, ripe fruit
"For man; and incense for ye mighty gods:
"Faulty is this? But grant thy wrath deserv'd,
"How do the waves, thy brother's realm offend?
"Why does the main, to him by lot decreed,
"Shrink and retreat from heaven? Thy brother's weal,
"Say it concerns thee not, nor my distress;
"Care for thy own paternal heaven may move.
"Thine eyes cast round,—black smoke from either pole
"Mounts!—soon the greedy flames your halls will seize.
"Lo! Atlas labors;—scarcely he sustains
"The burning load. If earth and ocean flame,
"And heaven too perish, all to chaös turn'd,
"Confounded we shall sink. Snatch from the flames
"What yet, if ought, remains, and nature save."

No more could Earth, for now thick vapors rose,
Her speech obstructing; down she shrunk her head,
And shelter'd 'midst the cool Tartarian shades.

  Now Jove, the gods, all witness to the fact
Conven'd; ev'n Sol, the donor of the car,
That but for him the world in ruins soon
Would lie. The loftiest height of heaven he gains,
Whence clouds he wont upon the wide-spread earth
To shower;—from whence his thunders loud he hurl'd;
And quivering lightenings flung: but now nor clouds,
Nor showers to rain on earth the sovereign had.
He thunders;—from his right-ear pois'd, the bolt
Hurls on the charioteer. Life, and the car,
Phaëton quits at once;—his fatal fires,
By fires more fierce extinguish'd. Startled prance
The steeds confounded; free their fiery necks
From the torn reins: here lie the traces broke;
There the strong axle, sever'd from the seat;
Spokes of the shatter'd wheels are here display'd;
And scatter'd far and wide the car's remains.
Hurl'd headlong falls the youth, his golden locks,
Flame as he tumbles, swept through empty air,
A lengthen'd track he forms: so seems a star
In night serene, but only seems, to shoot.
Far from paternal home, the mighty Po
Receiv'd his burning corps, and quench'd the flames.

  Due rites the nymphs Hesperian gave the limbs
From the fork'd lightening flaming. On his tomb
This epitaph they grav'd: "Here Phaëton
"Intombed rests; the charioteer so bold,
"Of Phœbus' car, which though he fail'd to rule,
"He perish'd greatly daring." Griev'd his sire,
Veil'd his sad face; and, were tradition true,
One day saw not the sun; the embers blaz'd
Sufficient light: thus may misfortune aid.

  When Clymené with all that sorrow could
To ease her woes give utterance, loud had wail'd
In wild lament; all spark of reason fled,
Her bosom tearing, through the world she roam'd.
And now his limbs inanimate she sought;
Then for his whiten'd bones: his bones she found,
On banks far distant from his home inhum'd.
Prone on his tomb her form she flung, and pour'd
Her tears in floods upon the graven lines:
And with her bosom bar'd, the cold stone warm'd.

His sisters' love their fruitless offerings bring,
Their griefs and briny droppings; cruel tear
Their beauteous bosoms; while they loudly call
Phaëton, deaf to all their mournful cries.
Stretch'd on his tomb, by night, by day they call'd.
Till Luna's circle four times fill'd was seen;
Their blows still given as 'custom'd, (use had made
Their forms of grief as nature). Sudden plain'd
Fair Phaëthusa, eldest of the three,
Of stiffen'd feet; as on the tomb she strove
To cast her body prone. Lampetie bright,
Rushing in hope to aid, a shooting root
Abruptly held. With lifted hands the third
Her locks to tear attempted; but green leaves
Tore off instead. Now this laments her legs,
Bound with thin bark; that mourns to see her arms
Shoot in long branches. While they wonder thus,
Th' increasing bark their bodies upward veils,
Their breasts, their arms, and hands, with gradual growth:
Their mouths alone remain; which loudly call
Their mother. What a mother could, she did:
What could she do? save, here and there to fly,
Where blind affection dragg'd her; and while yet,
'Twas given to join, join with them mouth to mouth.
Nor this contents; she strives to tear the rind,
Their limbs enwrapping; and the tender boughs
Pluck from their hands: but from the rended spot
The sanguine drops flow swift. Each suffering nymph
Cries,—"Spare me, mother!—spare your wounded child;
"I suffer in the tree.—farewell!—farewell!"—
For as they spoke the rind their mouths inclos'd.
From these new branches tears were dropp'd, and shap'd
By solar heat, bright amber straight compos'd.
Dropt in the lucid stream, the prize was borne
To Latium, and its gayest nymphs adorn'd.

This wonderous change Sthenelian Cycnus saw;
To thee, O Phaëton, by kindred join'd,
But by affection closer. He his realms,
(For o'er Liguria's large and populous towns
He reign'd) had then relinquish'd. With his plaints,
The Po's wide stream was fill'd; and fill'd the banks
With his lamentings; ev'n the woods, whose shade
The sister poplars thicken'd. Soon he feels
His utterance shrill and weak: his streaming locks
Soft snowy plumes displace: high from his chest,
His lengthen'd neck extends: a filmy web
Unites his ruddy toes: his sides are cloth'd

With quills and feathers: where his mouth was seen
Expanded, now a blunted beak obtains;
And Cycnus stands a bird;—but bird unknown
In days of yore. Mistrustful still of Jove,
His heaven he shuns; as mindful of the flames
From thence unjustly hurl'd. Wide lakes and ponds
He seeks to habit now;—indignant shuns
What favors fire, and joys in purling streams.

 Meantime was Phœbus dull, his blaze obscur'd,
As when eclips'd his orb: his rays he hates;
Himself; and even the day. To grief his soul
He gives, and anger to his grief he joins;
Depriving earth of all its wonted light.
"Troubled my lot has been," he cry'd, "since first
"Was publish'd my existence:—urg'd my toil
"Endless,—still unremitted, still unprais'd.
"Now let who will my furious chariot drive
"Flammiferous! If every god shall shrink
"Inadequate,—let Jove the task attempt:
"Then while my reins he tries, at least those flames,
"Which cause parental grief must peaceful rest.
"Then when the fiery flaming coursers strain
"His nervous arms, no more he'll judge the youth
"Of death deserving, who could less control."
Sol, grieving thus, the deities surround,
And suppliant beg that earth may mourn no more,
By darkness 'whelm'd. Ev'n Jove concession gave,—
And why his fiery bolts were launch'd explain'd;
But threats and prayers majestically mix'd.
The steeds with terror trembling, Phœbus seiz'd,
Wild from their late affright, and rein'd their jaws;
Furious he wields his goad and lash, and fierce
He storms, and their impetuous fury blames
At every blow, as murderers of his son.

 High heaven's huge walls the mighty sire explores,
With eye close searching, lest a weakening flaw,
Might hurl some part to ruin. All he found
Firm in its pristine strength;—then glanc'd his eye
Around the earth, and toils of man below.
'Bove all terrestrial lands, Arcadia felt—
His own Arcadia—his preserving care.
Her fountains he restores; her streams not yet
To murmur daring; to her fields he gives
Seed-corn; and foliage to her spreading boughs;
And her scorch'd forests bids again look green.
Through here as oft he journey'd, and return'd,

A virgin of Nonacriné he spy'd,
And instant inward fire the god consum'd.
No nymph was she whose skill the wool prepar'd;
Nor comb'd with art her tresses seem'd; full plain,
Her vest a button held; a fillet white
Careless her hair confin'd. Now pois'd her hand
A javelin light, and now a bow she bore:
In Dian's train she ran, nor nymph more dear
To her the mountain Mænalus e'er trode.
But brief the reign of favor! Sol had now
Beyond mid-heaven attain'd; Calistho sought
A grove where felling axe had never rung:
Here was her quiver from her shoulder thrown;
Her slender bow unstrung; and on the ground
With soft grass clad she rested: 'neath her neck
Was plac'd the painted quiver. Jove, the maid
Weary'd beheld, and from her wonted troop
Far distant. "Surely now, my wife," he cries,
"This theft can ne'er discover. Should she know,
"What is her rage with such a prize compar'd?"
Then Dian's face and form the god conceal'd;
Loud calling,—"Where, O virgin, hast thou stray'd?
"What hills, my comrade, hast thou crost in chase?"
Light springing from the turf, the nymph reply'd,—
"Hail goddess, greater, if with me the palm,
"Than Jove himself, though Jove himself should hear."
The feign'd Diana smil'd, and joy'd to hear
Him to himself preferr'd; then press'd her lips
With kisses, such as virgins never give
To virgins. Her, prepar'd to tell the woods
Where late she hunted, with a warm embrace
He hinder'd; and his crime the god disclos'd.
Hard strove the nymph,—and what could female more?
(O Juno, hadst thou seen her, less thy ire!)
Long she resists, but what can nymph attain,
Or any mortal, when to Jove oppos'd?
Victor the god ascends th' ethereal court.

The groves and forests, conscious of the deed,
Calistho hates; so swift she flies the spot,
Her quiver, and her darts, and slender bow
Suspended on the tree, through eager haste
Were nigh forgotten. Lo! Diana comes,
By clustering nymphs attended, o'er the hills
Of lofty Mænalus, from slaughter'd beasts,
Proudly triumphant. She Calistho sees,
And calls her;—as the goddess calls she flies,
Fearing another Jove disguis'd to meet.

But when th' attendant virgin-troop appear'd,
Fraud she no more suspected, but the train
Join'd fearless. Hard the countenance to form,
And not betray a perpetrated crime!
Scarce from the ground she dar'd her looks to raise;
Nor with her wonted ardor press'd before,
First of the throng, close to Diana's side.
Silent she moves; her blushes prove a wound
Her modesty had felt. E'en Dian' might,
(But that a virgin,) all the truth have known.
By numerous proofs and strong. Nay, fame reports
Her sister-nymphs had long her shame perceiv'd.
Nine times had Luna now her orb renew'd,
When Dian' from the chase retreating faint
By Phœbus' rays, had gain'd a forest cool,
Where flow'd a limpid stream with murmuring noise,
The shining sand upturning. Much the spot
The goddess tempted, and her feet she dipp'd
Light in the waves, as to the nymphs she cry'd:—
"Hence far each prying eye, we'll dare unrobe
"And lave beneath the stream." Calistho blush'd;—
Quick while the other nymphs their bodies bare,
Protracting she undresses. From her limbs,
Suspicious they the garments rend, and view
Her body naked, and her fault is plain.
To her, confus'd, whose trembling hands essay'd
Her shame to hide, Diana spoke;—"Hence fly,—
"Far hence, nor more these sacred streams pollute."
And drove her instant from her spotless train.

  Long time the mighty thunderer's queen had known
Calistho's state; but curb'd her furious ire
Till ripe occasion suited: longer now
Delay were needless; now the nymph produc'd
Arcas; whom Juno more enrag'd beheld.
With savage mind, and furious look she ey'd
The boy, and spoke;—"Adulteress! this alone
"Was wanting! fruitful, harlot, hast thou prov'd?
"Must by this birth my wrongs in public glare?
"And what dishonor I from Jove receive
"Be palpable to sight. Expect not thou
"Impunity to find. Thy form I'll change,—
"To thee so pleasing, and so dear to Jove."
She said; and on the flowing tresses seiz'd
Which o'er her forehead stream'd, and prostrate dragg'd
The nymph to earth. She rais'd her suppliant hands,—
With black hairs cover'd, rough her arms appear'd;
Bent were her hands, and, with her lengthen'd nails

To claws transform'd, press'd on the ground as feet;
Her mouth so beauteous, late of Jove admir'd,
Yawn'd wide deformity;—and lest soft prayers
And flowing words, might pity move, no power
To speak she left. Now through her hoarse throat sounds
An angry threatening voice that fear instills;
A bear becoming, though her sense the same:
Her sufferings proving by her constant groans.
Lifting to heaven such hands as lift she could,
Jove she ungrateful found, but Jove to call
Ungrateful, strove in vain. Alas! how oft
In woods and solitudes, to sleep afraid,
She roam'd around the house and fertile fields
Of late her own!—Alas, how oft thence driven
By yelping hounds o'er craggy steeps she fled!
Thou dread'st the hunters though an huntress thou!
Oft was her form forgotten, and in fear
From beasts she crouch'd conceal'd: the shaggy bear
Shudder'd to see the bears upon the hills;
And at the wolves she trembled, though with wolves
Her sire Lycaön howl'd. Now Arcas comes;
Arcas, her son, unconscious of his race.
Near fifteen suns the youth had seen revolv'd;
And while the game he chases, while he seeks
Thickets best suited for his sports, and round
The Erymanthean woods his toils he sets,
He meets his mother:—at his sight she stay'd,
The well-known object viewing. Arcas fled
Trembling, unconscious why those eyes were fix'd
On him immoveably. His spear, prepar'd
To pierce his mother's breast, as near she draws
The youth protends. But Jove the deed prevents:
Both bears away, and stays the matricide.
Swept through the void of heaven by rapid whirl
They're borne, and neighbouring constellations made,
Loud Juno rag'd, to see the harlot shine,
Amid the stars; and 'neath the deep descends,
To hoary Tethys, and her ancient spouse;
Where reverence oft the host of heaven had shewn.
And thus to them, who anxious seek the cause,
Why there she journeys. "Wish ye then to know
"Why I the queen of heaven, my regal seat
"Now leave? Another fills my lofty throne!
"Nor false I speak,—for when gray night shall spread
"O'er all,—new constellations shall you see
"Me irking,—on the utmost bounds of heaven,
"Where the last shorten'd zone the axis binds.
"Now surely none, t' insult shall rashly dare

"The thunderer's spouse, but tremble at her frown;
"For she who most offends is honor'd most!
"Much has my power perform'd!—vast is my sway!
"Her human form I chang'd,—and lo! she shines
"A goddess;—thus the guilty feel my ire!
"Thus potent I. Why not her form restore,
"And change that beastly shape, as Iö once
"In Argolis, the same indulgence felt.
"Why drives he not his consort from his bed,
"Calistho placing there;—for sire-in-law
"The wolf Lycaön chusing? If to you
"Your foster-daughter's insults ought import,
"Forbid these stars to touch the blue profound:
"Repel those constellations, plac'd in heaven,
"Meed of adultery; lest the harlot dip
"In your pure waves."—The gods their promise gave
And through the liquid air Saturnia flies,
Borne in her chariot by her peacocks bright;
Their coats gay studded from fall'n Argus' eyes.

  Less beauteous was the change, loquacious crow,
Thy plumage suffer'd,—snowy white to black.
With silvery brightness once his feathers shone;
Unspotted doves outvying; nor to those
Preserving birds the capital whose voice
So watchful sav'd;—nor to the stream-fond swans,
Inferior seem'd his covering: but his tongue,
His babbling tongue his ruin wrought; and chang'd
His hue from splendid white to gloomy black.

  No fairer maid all Thessaly contain'd,
Than young Coronis,—to the Delphic god
Most dear while chaste, or while her fault unknown.
But Corvus, Phœbus' watchman, spy'd the deed
Adulterous,—and inexorably bent
To tell the secret crime, his flight directs
To seek his master. Him the daw pursues,
On plumes quick waving, curious all to learn.
His errand heard, she cries;—"Thy anxious task,
"A journey vain, pursue not: mark my words;—
"Learn what I have been;—see what now I am;
"And hear from whence my change: a fault you'll find
"Too much fidelity, which wrought my woe.

  "Time was, when Pallas, Ericthonius took,
"Offspring created motherless, and close
"In basket twin'd with Attic twigs conceal'd.
"The charge to keep, three sister-maids she chose,

"Daughters of Cecrops double-form'd, but close,
"Conceal'd what lodg'd within; and strict forbade
"All prying, that her secret safe might rest.
"On a thick elm, behind light leaves conceal'd,
"I mark'd their actions. Two their sacred charge
"Hold faithful; Pandrosos, and Hersé they:
"Aglauros calls her sisters cowards weak;
"The twistings with bold hand unloosening, sees
"Within an infant, and a dragon stretch'd.
"The deed I tell to Pallas, and from her
"My service this remuneration finds:
"Driven from her presence, she my place supplies
"Of favorite with the gloomy bird of night.
"All other birds my fate severe may warn,
"To seek not danger by officious tales.
"Pallas, perhaps you think, but lightly lov'd
"One whom she thus so suddenly disgrac'd.
"But ask of Pallas;—she, though much enrag'd
"Will yet my truth confirm. A regal maid
"Was I,—of facts to all well-known I speak:
"Coroneus noble, of the Phocian lands
"As sire I claim. Me wealthy suitors sought—
"Contemn me not,—my beauty was my bane.
"While careless on the sandy shore I roam'd,
"With gentle pace as wont, the ocean's god
"Saw me and lov'd: persuasive words in vain
"Long trying, force prepar'd, and me pursu'd.
"I fled; the firm shore left, and tir'd my limbs
"Vainly, upon the light soft sinking sand.
"There to assist me men and gods I call'd;
"Deaf to the sound was every mortal ear:
"But by a virgin's cries a virgin mov'd,
"Assistance gave. Up to the skies my arms
"I stretch'd; and black my arms began to grow,
"With waving pinions. From my shoulders, back
"My robes I strove to fling,—my robes were plumes;
"Deep in my skin the quills were fix'd: I try'd
"On my bare bosom with my hands to beat;
"Nor hands nor naked bosom now were found:
"I ran; the sand no longer now retain'd
"My feet, but lightly o'er the ground I skimm'd;
"And soon on pinions through the air was borne;
"And Pallas' faultless favorite I became.
"What now avail to me my pure deserts?
"Nyctimené, whose horrid crime deserv'd
"Her transformation, to my place succeeds.
"The deed so wide through spacious Lesbos known,
"Ere this has reach'd thee;—how Nyctimené—

"Her father's bed defil'd,—a bird became.
"Conscious of guilt, she shuns the sight of man;
"Flies from the day, and in nocturnal shades
"Conceals her shame; by every bird assail'd
"And exil'd from the skies." The crow in rage
To her still chattering, cry'd;—"May each delay
"Thy babbling causes, prove to thee a curse.
"I scorn thy foolish presages,"—and flew
His journey urging. When his master found,
He told him where Coronis he had seen
Claspt by a young Thessalian. Down he dropp'd
His laurel garland, when the crime he heard
Of her he lov'd;—his harp away he flung;
His countenance fell, and pale his visage grew.
Now with fierce rage his swelling bosom fires;
His wonted arms he seizes; draws his bow,
Bent to the horns; and through that breast so oft
Embrac'd,—th' inevitable weapon drove.
Deep groan'd the wounded nymph, and tearing out
The arrow from her breast, a purple flood
Gush'd o'er her shining limbs. She sighing cry'd,—
"This fate, O Phœbus, I deserv'dly meet,
"Were but thy infant born;—two now in one
"Thy dart has slain!"—She spoke,—her vital blood
Fast flow'd, and stay'd her voice. A deadly chill
Seiz'd all her members, now of life bereft.
Too late, alas! her sorrowing lover mourns
His cruel vengeance; and himself he hates,
Too credulous listening, and too soon enflam'd:
The bird he hates, who first betray'd the deed
And caus'd him first to grieve: his bow he hates;
His bowstring; arm; and with his arm the dart,
Shot vengeful. Fond he clasps her fallen form;
And strives by skill, by skill too late apply'd
To conquer fate:—his healing arts he tries,—
All unavailing. Fruitless he beholds
His each attempt, and sees the pile prepar'd;
And final flames her limbs about to burn.
Then from his deepest bosom burst his groans;
(For tears on cheeks celestial ne'er are seen,)
Such groans are utter'd when the heifer sees,
The weighty mallet, from the right ear pois'd,
Crush down the forehead of her suckling calf.
And now his useless odors in her breast
He pour'd; embrac'd her; to her last rites gave
Solemnization due. The greedy fires
His offspring were not suffer'd to consume.
Snatch'd from the curling flames, and from the womb

Of his dead mother, he the infant bore
To double-body'd Chiron's secret cave.
But bade the self-applauding crow, fill'd big
With hopes of favor for his faithful tale,
With snowy-plumag'd birds no more to join.

Meantime while Chiron, human half, half beast,
Proud of his deity-descended charge,
Joy'd in the honor with the task bestow'd:—
Behold, her shoulders with her golden locks
Shaded, the daughter of the Centaur comes;
Whom fair Chariclo, on a river's brink
Swift-rolling, bore, and thence Ocyrrhoë nam'd.
She not content her father's arts to know,
The hidden secrets of the fates disclos'd.
Now was her soul with fate-foretelling sounds
Fill'd, and within her fiercely rag'd the god:
The infant viewing;—"Grow," she said, "apace,
"Health-bearer through the world. To thee shall oft
"Expiring mortals owe returning life!
"To thee 'tis given to render souls again
"Back to their bodies! Once thou'lt dare the deed;—
"The angry god's forbidding flames, thy power
"Further preventing:—and a bloodless corps
"Heaven-born, thou ly'st;—but what thy body form'd
"A god becomes,—resuscitated twice.
"Thou too, my dearest and immortal sire!
"To ages never-ending, born to live,
"Shalt wish for death in vain; when writhing sad
"From the dire serpent's venom in thy limbs,
"By wounds instill'd. The pitying gods will change
"Thy destin'd fate, and let immortal die:
"The triple sisters shall thy thread divide.
"More yet untold remains;"—Deep from her chest
The sighs burst forth, and starting tears stream down,
Laving her cheeks, while thus the maid pursues:
"The fates prevent me, and forbid to tell
"What more I would;—all power to speak deny.
"Those arts, alas! heaven's anger which have drawn,—
"What were they? Would I ne'er the future knew!
"Now seems my human shape to leave me. Now
"The verdant grass a pleasing food appears.
"Now am I urg'd along the plain to bound;
"Chang'd to a mare: unto my sire ally'd
"In form,—but why sole chang'd? my father bears
"A two-form'd body;"—Wailing thus, her words
Confus'd and indistinct at length are heard.
Next sounds are utter'd partly human, more

A mare's resembling:—then she neighs aloud;
Treading with alter'd arms the ground: fast join'd
Her fingers now become: a slender hoof
Her toes connecting with continuous horn.
Her head enlarges; and her neck expands;
Her spreading garment floats a beauteous tail:
Her scatter d tresses o'er her shoulders flung,
Form a thick mane to clothe her spacious neck:
Her voice is alter'd with her alter'd shape:
And change of name the wonderous deed attends.

Deep Chiron mourn'd, O Phœbus, and thy aid
In vain invck'd; for bootless was thy power
Jove's mandate to resist; nor if thou could'st
Then wast thou nigh to help. In Elis far,
And fields Messenian then was thy abode.
Then was the time when shepherd-like a robe
Of skins enwrapp'd thee;—when thy left hand bore
A sylvan staff;—thy right a pipe retain'd,
Of seven unequal reeds. While love engag'd
Thy thoughts, and dulcet music sooth'd thy cares,
'Tis said, thy herds without their herdsman stray'd,
Far to the Pylian meadows. These the son
Of Atlantean Maiä espy'd;
And, slily driven away, within the woods
The cattle artful hid. None saw the deed,
Save one old hoary swain, well known around,
And Battus nam'd; whose post it was to guard
The groves, the grassy meads, and high-bred mares
Of wealthy Neleus. Him the robber fear'd;
Drew him aside, and coaxing thus address'd;—
"Whoe'er thou art, good friend, if here perchance,
"Someone should seek an herd,—say that thou here
"No herd hast seen;—thou shall not lack reward:
"Take this bright heifer:"—and the cow he gave.
The bribe receiv'd, the shepherd thus replies;
"Friend, thou art safe,—that stone shall sooner speak
"And tell thy deed than I:"—and shew'd the stone.
The son of Jove departs, or seems to go;
But soon with alter'd form and voice returns.
"Here, countryman," he cries, "hast thou an herd
"This way observ'd to pass?—no secret keep,
"To aid the theft; an heifer with a bull
"Await thy information." Doubly brib'd,
The hoary rogue betray'd his former trust.
"Beneath those hills," he said, "the herd you'll find."
Beneath the hills they were. Loud laugh'd the god
And cry'd,—"Thou treacherous villain, to myself

"Wouldst thou betray me? wouldst thou to myself
"My deeds betray?" And to a flinty stone
His perjur'd breast he chang'd, which still retains
The name of Touchstone;—on the harmless rock
His infamous demerits firmly fix'd.

  Hermes from hence, on waving wings upborne
Darted, and in his flight beneath him saw
The Attic pastures,—the much-favor'd land
Of Pallas; and Lyceum's cultur'd groves.
It chanc'd that day, as wont, the virgins chaste,
Bore on their heads in canisters festoon'd,
Their offerings pure to Pallas' sacred fane.
Returning thence the winged god espy'd
The troop, and straight his onward flight restrain'd;
Wheeling in circles round. As sails the kite,
Swiftest of birds, when entrails seen from far
By holy augurs thick beset,—he fears
A near approach, but circling steers his flight
On beating wings, around his hopes and round.
So 'bove the Athenian towers the light-plum'd god
Swept round in circles on the self-same air.
As Phosphor far outshines the starry host;
As silver Cynthia Phosphor bright outshines;
So much did Hersé all the nymphs excel,
The bright procession's ornament; the pride
Of all th' accompanying nymphs. Her beauteous mien
Stagger'd Jove's son, who hovering in the air
Fierce burns with love. The Balearic sling,
Thus shoots a ball; quick through the air it flies,
Warms in its flight, and feels beneath the clouds
Flames hereto known not. Alter'd now his route
The skies he leaves, and holds a different flight:
Nor veils his figure,—such reliance gave
His beauteous form: and beauteous though that form,
Yet careful did the god his looks adorn;
He smoothes his tresses, and his robe adjusts
To hang in graceful folds, and fair display
The golden fringe; his round and slender wand,
Of sleep-procuring, sleep-repelling power,
His right hand bears; and on his comely feet
His plumed sandals shine. Within the house
Three separate chambers were secluded form'd,
With tortoise and with ivory rich adorn'd.
Thou, Pandrosos, within the right repos'd;
And on the left hand thou Aglauros, slept;
Fair Hersé in the midst. Aglauros first
The god's approach descry'd, and daring ask'd

Who he?—and what he sought?—To whom the god;
"Him you behold, who through the air conveys
"His sire's commands: Almighty Jove that sire.
"Nor will I feign my errand. So may'st thou
"True to thy sister prove, and soon be call'd
"My offspring's aunt. 'Tis Hersé draws me here.
"Help then a lover in his warm pursuit."
Aglauros bends on Mercury those eyes,
Which yellow-hair'd Minerva's secret saw;
And ponderous sums for her assistance claims;
Driving the god meantime without the gates.
With angry glare the warlike goddess view'd
The mercenary nymph, and angry sighs,
Which shook her bosom heav'd; the Ægis shook,
On that strong bosom fix'd. Now calls to mind
Minerva how with hands prophane, the maid
Her strict behests despising, daring pry'd
To know her secrets; and the seed beheld
Of Vulcan, child without a mother form'd:
Now to her sister and the god unkind;
Rich with the gold her avarice had claim'd.
To Envy's gloomy cell, where clots of gore
The floor defl'd, enrag'd Minerva flew:
A darkened vale, deep sunk, the cavern held,
where vivid sun ne'er shone, nor freshening breeze
Health wafted: torpid melancholy rul'd,
And sluggish cold; and cheering light unknown,
Damp darkness ever gloom'd. The goddess here
In conflict dreaded came, but at the doors
Her footsteps staid, for entrance Fate forbade.
The gates she strikes—struck by her spear, the gates
Wide open fly, and dark within disclose,
On vipers gorging, (her accustom'd feast,)
The envious fiend: back from the hideous sight
Recoils the goddess, and averts her eyes.
Slow rising from the ground, her half chew'd food
She quits, advancing indolently forth:
The maid, in warlike brightness clad, she saw,
In form divine, and heavy sighs burst forth
Deep from her bosom's black recess: pale gloom.
Dwells on her forehead; lean her fleshless form;
Askaunce her eyes; encrusted black her teeth;
Green'd deep with gall her breasts; her hideous tongue
With poisons lurid; laughter knows her not,
Save woes and pangs unmerited she sees;
Sleep flies her couch, by cares unceasing wrung;
At men's success she sickens, pining sad;
But stung herself, while others feel her sting

Her torture closely grasps her.—Much the maid
The sight abhors; and thus in brief she speaks:—
"Deep in the breast of Cecrops' daughter fix
"Thy venom'd sting—Aglauros is the nymph.—
"More needs not."—Speaking so Minerva fled,
Upbounding, earth she with her spear repell'd.
Glancing asquint the fury saw her rise,
And inly groan'd,—that she success should gain.
Her staff with prickly thorns enwreath'd she takes,
And forth she sallies, wrapp'd in gloomy clouds.
Where'er she flies she blasts the flowery fields;
Consumes the herbage; and the harvest blights.
Her breath pestiferous felt the cities round,
Houses and 'habitants where'er she flew.
At length the towers of Athens she beheld
With arts and riches flourishing, and blest
With holy peace. Scarce could she tears withhold,
No tearful eye throughout the place to see.
Straight to the room of Cecrops' daughter now
Her route she urges, and her task performs:
Her rusty hand upon the maiden's breast
She plants, and with sharp thorns that bosom fills;
Breathes noxious poison through her frame; imbues
With venom black her heart, and all her limbs.
Lest from her eyes escap'd, the maddening scene
Should cease to vex her, full in view she plac'd
Her sister, and her sister's nuptial rites;
And Hermes beauteous in the bridal pomp:
In beauty all, and splendor all increas'd.
Mad with the imag'd sight, the maid is gnawn
With secret pangs;—deep groans the lengthen'd night,
And deep the morning hears; she wastes away
Silently wretched, lingeringly slow.
As Sol's faint rays the summer ice dissolves:
So burns she to behold the envy'd lot
Of Hersé; not with furious flames,—as weeds
Blaze not when damp, but with slow heat consume.
Oft would she wish to die: and oft the deed
To hinder, thinks to tell her rigid sire
Her sister's fault. At length her seat she takes
Across the threshold, and th' approaching god
Repuls'd; and to his blandishments, and words
Beseeching fair, and soft-alluring prayers,
She cry'd,—"Desist,—from hence I ne'er will move
"Till thou art driven away." Swift Hermes said.—
"Keep firmly that resolve." And with his wand
The sculptur'd portals touching, wide they flew.
But when her limbs to raise, the virgin strove,

A weighty numbness o'er the members crept
Which bend in sitting, and their movement staid.
Strenuous she strives to raise her form erect,
But stiffen'd feels her knees; chill coldness spreads
Through all her toes; and, fled the purple stream,
Her veins turn pallid: cruel cancer thus,
Disease incurable, spreads far and wide,
Sound members adding to the parts diseas'd.
So gradual o'er her breast the chilling frost
Crept deadly, and the gates of life shut close.
Complaint she try'd not; had she try'd, her voice
Had found no passage, for the stone had seiz'd
Her throat,—her mouth; to marble all was chang'd.
She sat a pallid statue;—all the stone
Her envy tainted with a livid hue.

His vengeance, when Jove's son complete had seen,
Due to her avarice, and her envious soul;
He left Minerva's land, and up the sky
On wafting pinions mounted. There his sire,
Him from th' assembly drew; nor yet disclos'd,
The object of his love:—"Son, quickly haste,—
"Thou faithful messenger of my commands,
"Urge rapid thy descending flight, and seek
"The realm whose northern bounds thy mother star
"O'erlooks,—the land by natives Sidon call'd.
"There wilt thou pasturing find the royal herd,
"'Neath hills not distant from the sea: turn down
"This herd to meadows bordering on the beach."
He said;—the cattle tow'rd the sea shore move,
Where sported with her Tyrian maids as wont,
The monarch's daughter. Ill majestic state
And love agree; nor long combin'd remain.
The sire and ruler of the gods resigns
His weighty sceptre: he whose right hand bears
The three-fork'd fires; whose nod creation shakes,
Assumes a bull's appearance:—with the herd
Mingles; and strolling lets the tender shrubs
Brush his fair sides. Of snowy white his skin;
Such snow as rugged feet has never soil'd,
Nor southern showers dissolv'd: his brawny neck,
Strong from his shoulders stands: beneath extends
The dewlap pendulous: small are his horns;
But smooth as polish'd by the workman's hand;—
Pellucid as the brightest gems they shine:
No threatenings wear his brow; no fire his eyes
Flame fierce; but all his countenance peace proclaims.
Him much Agenor's royal maid admir'd;—

His form so beauteous, and his look so mild.
Yet peaceful as he seem'd, she fear'd at first
A close approach;—but nearer soon she drew,
And to his shining mouth the flowery food
Presented. Joy'd th' impatient lover stands,
Her fingers kissing; and with sore restraint
Defers his look'd for pleasures. Sportive now
He wantons, frisking in the grass; now rolls
His snowy sides upon the yellow sand.
Her apprehensions chas'd, by slow degrees,
The virgin's fingers playful stroke his breast;
Then bind with wreaths his horns: more daring now
Upon his back the royal maid ascends;—
Witless a god she presses. From the fields,
His steps deceitful gradual turn'd, he bends,
And seeks the shore; then playful in the waves
Just dips his feet;—thence plunging deep, he swims
Through midmost ocean with his ravish'd prize.
Trembling the nymph beholds the lessening shore;—
Firm grasps one hand his horn; upon his back,
Secure the other resting: to the wind,
Her fluttering garments floating as she sails.

THE THIRD BOOK

Unsuccessful search of Cadmus for his sister. Death of his companions by the dragon. Overthrow of the dragon, and production of armed men from his teeth. Thebes. Actæon devoured by his hounds. Semelé destroyed by lightening, and the birth of Bacchus. The prophet Tiresias. Echo: and the transformation of Narcissus. Impiety of Pentheus. Change of the Tyrrhenian sailors to dolphins. Massacre of Pentheus.

THE THIRD BOOK OF THE METAMORPHOSES OF OVID

  And now the god, his bestial form resign'd,
Shone in his form celestial as he gain'd
The Cretan shore. Meantime, the theft unknown,
Mourn'd her sad sire, and Cadmus sent to seek
The ravish'd maid; stern threatening as he went,
Perpetual exile if his searching fail'd:—
Parental love and cruelty combin'd!
All earth explor'd in vain, (for who shall find
The amorous thefts of Jove?) the exile shuns
His father's anger, and paternal soil.
A suppliant bends before Apollo's shrine,

To ask his aid;—what region he should chuse
To fix his habitation. Phœbus thus;—
"A cow, whose neck the yoke has never prest,
"Strange to the crooked plough, shall meet thy steps,
"Lone in the desert fields: the way she leads
"Chuse thou,—rand where upon the grass she rests,
"Erect thy walls;—Bœotia call the place."
Scarce had the cave Castalian Cadmus left,
When he a heifer, gently pacing, spy'd
Untended; one whose neck no mark betray'd
Of galling service. Closely treads the youth,
Slow moving in her footsteps, and adores
In silence Phœbus, leader of his way.
Now had he pass'd the Cephisidian stream,
And meads of Panopé, when stay'd the beast;
Her broad front lifted to the sky; reverse
Her lofty horns reclining, shook the air
With lowings loud; back then her face she bent,
And saw the comrades following close behind:
Down low she couch'd, and press'd the yielding grass,
Glad thanks to Phœbus, Cadmus gave, and kiss'd
The foreign soil;—the unknown hills, and land
Saluted. Then a sacrifice to Jove
Preparing, sent his followers to explore
Streams flowing from the living fountain clear.

An ancient forest hallow'd from the axe,
Not far there stood; in whose dark bosom gloom'd
A cavern:—twigs and branches thick inwove
With rocky crags, a low arch'd entrance form'd;
Where pure and copious, gush'd transparent waves.
Deep hid within a monstrous serpent lay,
Sacred to Mars. Bright shone his crested head;
His eyeballs glow'd with fire; his body swell'd
Bloated with poison; o'er a threefold row
Of murderous teeth, three quivering tongues he shook.
This grove the Tyrians with ill-fated feet
Now enter'd; and now in the waters threw,
With noisy dash, their urns. Uprears his head,
The azure serpent from the cavern deep;
And breathes forth hisses dire: their urns they drop;
The blood forsakes their bodies; sudden fear
Chills their astonish'd limbs. He writhing quick,
Forms scaly circles; spiral twisting round,
Bends in an arch immense to leap, and rears
In the thin air erect, 'bove half his height;
All the wide grove o'erlooking. Such his size,
Could all be seen, than that vast snake no less,

Whose huge bulk lies the Arctic bears between.
The Tyrians quick he seizes; some their arms
Vain grasping,—flying some,—and some through fear
To fight or fly unable:—these his jaws
Crash murderous; those his writhing tail surrounds;
Others his breath, with poison loaded, kills.

  Now loftiest Phœbus shorten'd shadows gave,
When Cadmus, wondering much why still his friends
Tarried so long, their parting footsteps trac'd.
His robe an hide torn from a lion's back;
A dart and spear of shining steel his arms;
With courage, arms surpassing. Now the grove
He enters, and their breathless limbs beholds;—
Their victor foe's huge bulk upon them stretch'd;
Licking with gory tongue their mournful wounds.
"My faithful friends," he cry'd, "I will avenge
"Your fate,—or perish with you." Straight a rock
His right hand rais'd, and with impetuous force,
Hurl'd it right on. A city's lofty walls
With all its towers, to feel the blow had shook!
Yet lay the beast unwounded; safely sheath'd
With scaly armour, and his harden'd hide:—
His skin alone the furious blow repell'd.
Not so that hardness mocks the javelin,—fixt
Firm in the bending of the pliant spine
His weapon stood,—and all the iron head
Deep in his entrails sunk. Mad with the pain,
Reverse he writhes his head;—beholds the wound;
Champs the fixt dart;—by many forceful tugs
Loosen'd at length, he tears the shaft away;
But deep the steel within his bones remains.
Now to his wonted fury fiercer flames
This torture adding, big with poison swells
His throat; and flowing, round his venom'd jaws,
White foam appears; deep harrow'd with his scales
Loud sounds the earth; and vapours black, breath'd out
His mouth infernal, taint with death the air.
Now roll'd in spires, he forms an orb immense:
Now stretch'd at length he seems a monstrous beam:
Now rushing forward with impetuous force,
As sweeps a torrent swell'd by rain, his breast
Bears down th' opposing forest. Cadmus back
A step recedes, and on his lion's hide
The shock sustains;—then with protended spear
Checks his approaching jaws. Furious he strives
To wound the harden'd steel;—on the sharp point
He grinds his teeth: now from his poisonous mouth,

Began the blood to flow, and sprinkling ting'd
The virid grass; but trivial still the hurt;
For shrinking from the blow, and twisting back
His wounded neck, the stroke he still prevents
Deeper to pierce, by yielding to its force.
But pushing arduous on, Agenor's son,
Fix'd in his throat the steel;—and the sharp point
Forc'd through his neck: an oak oppos'd behind;—
The tree and neck the spear at once transfix'd.
Dragg'd by the monster's weight low bends the tree,
And groans and cracks, as lashing blows, his tail
Immense, deals round. Now whilst the victor stands
And wondering views the conquer'd serpent's size,
Sudden a voice is heard, (from whence unknown,—
But plain the words he hears) "Why view'st thou thus,
"Agenor's son, the foe by thee destroy'd?
"Thou one day like this serpent shalt be seen."
Aghast he stood,—the warm blood fled his cheeks;
His courage chang'd to terror; freezing fear
Rais'd his stiff locks erect. Lo! Pallas comes,
Pallas, the known protectress of the brave.
Smooth sliding from the higher clouds she comes;
Bids him remove the soil, and place beneath,
The serpent's fangs, a future offspring's pledge.
The prince obeys; and as with crooked share,
The ground he opens, in the furrows throws
The teeth directed. Thence, (beyond belief!)
The clods of earth at once began to move;
Then in the furrows glitter'd, first, the points
Of spears: anon fair painted crests arose,
Above bright helmets nodding: shoulders next;
And breasts; and arms, with javelins loaded came:
Thickening the harvest grew of shielded men.
Thus shews the glad theatric curtain; rais'd
The painted figures' faces first appear,
Gradual display'd; and more by slow degrees;
At length the whole stand forth, their feet all fix'd
Firm on the lower margin. Wondering, he
His new-made foe beheld; and grasp'd his arms.
But one whom earth had just produc'd, exclaim'd;—
"Arm not, nor meddle in our civil broils."
He said,—an earth-born brother, hand to hand
With sword keen-edg'd attacking; but from far,
A javelin hurl'd, dispatch'd him. Short the boast
Of him who sent it;—his death wound infix'd,—
He breathes the air out he so late receiv'd.
So rage the rest, and in the furious war
The new-made brethren fall by mutual wounds:

And on their blood-stain'd mother, dash, the youths
To short existence born, their damp cold breasts.
Five only stand unhurt,—Echion one,—
Who threw, by Pallas prompted, down his arms
And peace propos'd: his brethren took his pledge.
These join the Tyrian prince, and social aid
His efforts, when th' appointed walls he builds;
Obedient to the Delphic god's commands.

  The Theban walls now rais'd, thou, Cadmus seem'd
Blest in thy exile. Mars and Venus gave
Their daughter to thy wife. This spouse so fam'd,
Thee daughters brought, and sons,—a numerous tribe;
And grandsons, pledges dear of nuptial joys,
Already risen to manhood. But too true
That man should still his final day expect;
Nor blest be deem'd till flames his funeral pyre.
Thy grandson's fate, O, Cadmus! first with grief
Thy bosom wrung, amid thy prosperous state:
The alien horns which nodded o'er his brow;
And ye, voracious hounds, with blood full-gorg'd,
Your master's life-stream. Yet by close research,
We find unlucky chance, not vice, his crime.
What sin in error lies?

       The hills were drench'd
With blood of numerous slaughter'd savage beasts;
And objects shorten'd shadows gave: the sun
Exalted view'd each equi-distant goal;
When the young Theban hunter thus address'd,
His fellow sportsmen with a friendly call;
As wide they rov'd the savage lairs among.
"Our weapons, comrades, and our nets are moist
"With blood of spoil; sufficient sport this day
"Has given. But when Aurora next appears,
"High on her saffron car, and light restores,
"Then be our pleasing exercise resum'd.
"Now Phœbus, distant far from west and east,
"Cracks the parch'd ground with heat;—desist from toil,
"And fold your knotted snares." His words obey,
His men, and from their sportive labor cease.

  Near stood a vale, where pointed cypress form'd
With gloomy pines a grateful shade, and nam'd
Gargaphié;—sacred to the girded maid:
Its deep recess a shrubby cavern held,
By nature modell'd,—but by nature, art
Seem'd equall'd, or excell'd. A native arch

Of pumice light, and tophus dry, was form'd;
And from the right a stream transparent flow'd,
Of trivial size, which spread a pool below;
With grassy margin circled. Dian' here,
The woodland goddess, weary'd with the chace,
Had oft rejoic'd to bathe her virgin limbs.
As wont she comes;—her quiver, and her dart,
And unstrung bow, her armour-bearing nymph
In charge receives. Disrob'd, another's arms
Sustain her vest. Two from her feet unloose
Her sandals. Crocalé, Ismenian nymph,
Than others more expert, her tresses binds,
Loose o'er her shoulders floating, in a knot;
Her own wild flowing still. Five more the streams
In huge urns lifting; Hyalé, and Niphé,
Phialé, Rhanis, Psecas, lave her limbs.
Here while the goddess in the limpid wave
Washes as 'custom'd,—lo! Actæon comes;—
His sportive toil till morning dawn deferr'd:
And roving through the vale with random steps,
By hapless fate conducted, he arrives
Close to the sacred grove. Within the grot
Stream-pouring, when he stept, the naked nymphs,—
Then first by man beheld,—their bosoms beat;
Fill'd the deep grove with outcries loud; and round
Diana crowded, screening as they could
Her limbs with theirs. Yet high above them tower'd
The goddess, and her neck their heads o'erlook'd.
As blush the clouds by Phœbus' adverse rays
Deep ting'd;—or as Aurora in the morn;
So blush'd the virgin-goddess, seen unrob'd.
Sideway she stood, though closely hemm'd around
By clustering nymphs, and backward bent her face:
Then anxious praying she could reach her darts,
In vain,—she seiz'd the waters which she could,
And dash'd them o'er his features:—as his locks,
The vengeful drops besprinkled, thus in rage,
She cry'd,—"Now tell thou hast Diana seen
"Disrob'd;—go tell it, if thou canst,"—no more,
With threatenings storm'd, but on his sprinkled head,
The antlers of the long-liv'd stag are plac'd.
His neck is lengthen'd; with a sharpen'd point,
His upright ears are form'd; to feet his hands,—
To long and slender legs his arms are chang'd;
And round his body clings a dappled coat.
Fear in his bosom she instils: the youth,
The bold Actæon flies, and wondering feels
His bounding feet so rapid in the race.

But soon the waters shew'd his branching horns;
And,—"ah unhappy me!" he strove to cry:
His voice he found not; sighs and sobs were all;
And tears fast streaming down his alter'd face.
Still human sense remains. Where shall he turn?
His royal palace seek,—or in the woods
Secluded hide?—To tarry fear forbids,
And shame prevents returning. While he doubts
His hounds espy him. Quick-nos'd Tracer first,
And Blackfoot give the signal by their yell:
Tracer of Crete, and Blackfoot Spartan bred.
Swifter than air the noisy pack rush on;
Arcadian Quicksight; Glutton; Ranger, stout;
Strong Killbuck; Whirlwind, furious; Hunter, fierce;
Flyer, swift-footed; and quick-scented Snap:
Ringwood, late wounded by a furious bear;
And Forester, by savage wolf begot:
Flock-tending Shepherdess; with Ravener fierce,
And her two whelps; and Sicyonian Catch:
The thin flank'd greyhound, Racer; Yelper; Patch;
Tiger; Robust; Milkwhite, with snowy coat;
And coalblack Soot. First in the race, fleet Storm;
Courageous Spartan Swift; and rapid Wolf;
Join'd with his Cyprian brother, Snatch, well mark'd
With sable forehead on a coat of white:
Blackcoat: and thickhair'd Shag: Worrier; and Wild,—
Twins from a dam Laconian sprung, their sire
Dictæan: Babbler with his noisy throat:—
But all to name were endless. Urg'd by hope
Of prey they crowd; down precipices rush;
O'er rocks, and crags; through rugged paths, and ways
Unpass'd before. His hounds he flies, where oft
His hounds he had pursu'd. Poor wretch! he flies
His own domestics, striving hard to call,
"Actæon am I!—villains, know your lord."
Words aid him not: loud rings the air with yells,
Howlings, and barkings:—Blackhair first, his teeth
Fix'd in his back; staunch Tamer fasten'd next;
And Rover seiz'd his shoulder: tardy these,
The rest far left behind, but o'er the hills
Athwart, the chase they shorten'd. Now the pack,
Join'd them their lord retaining; join'd their teeth
Their victim seizing:—now his body bleeds,
A wound continuous: deep he utters groans,
Not human, yet unlike a dying deer;
And fills the well-known mountains with his plaint.
Prone on his knees in suppliant form he bends;
And low beseeching waves his silent head,

As he would wave his hands. His witless friends,
The savage pack with joyous outcries urge;
Actæon anxious seeking: echoing loud
Eager his name as absent. At the name,
His head he turns. His absence irks them sore,
As lazy loitering, not the noble prey
Obtain'd, beholding. Joyful could he be,
At distance now,—but hapless is too near:
Glad would he see the furious dogs their fangs,
On other prey than his torn limbs infix.
On every side they crowd; their dying lord,
A well-seem'd deer, they rend; their ravenous teeth
Deep tear his members. With a thousand wounds,
(Dian's insatiate anger less despis'd)
The hapless hunter yielded forth his breath.

  Report flies dubious; some the goddess blame
For disproportion'd vengeance; others warm
Applaud the deed as worthy one so pure;
And reasons weighty either party urge:
Jove's consort only silent: she nor blames
The action, nor approves; but inward joys,
Agenor's house should such misfortune feel.
The hatred nourish'd for the Tyrian maid,
Her brother's offspring visits. Now fresh cause
Of wrath succeeds; enrag'd the goddess learns
That Semelé, embrac'd by mighty Jove,
Is pregnant. Straight broke loose her angry tongue,
And loud she storm'd:—"Advantage much I gain
"By endless railing at unfaithful Jove!
"This harlot will I find,—and, if with truth
"They potent Juno stile me, she shall die.
"Destruction shall o'erwhelm her, if beseems
"My hand the sparkling sceptre of the sky:
"If queen   am I to Jove;—if sister;—wife:—
"His sister doubtless am I, if no more.
"Content perchance is Semelé to joy
"In pleasures briefly tasted; and my wrongs
"Though deep, not lasting. No!—she must conceive
"Foul aggravation of her shameless deed!
"Her swelling womb unblushing proves her crime:
"By Jove she longs to be a mother hail'd;
"Which scarcely I can boast. Such faith her pride,
"In conscious beauty places. Trust me not,
"Or she mistaken proves. As I am child
"Of hoary Saturn, she shall sink o'erwhelm'd
"By her own Jove; and dip in Stygian waves."

She said, and starting from her regal throne,
Wrapt in a dusky cloud descended; o'er
The threshold stepp'd of Semelé, nor chas'd
Her darkening veil, till like an ancient dame
She stood display'd. White hairs her temples strew'd;
Deep furrows plough'd her skin; her bending limbs
Quiver'd beneath her weight; her tremulous voice
Exhausted age betray'd: she stood to view
Old Beroë, from Epidaurus come,
The nurse of Semelé. With tedious tales
She garrulous amus'd:—when in her turn
Listening, the name of Jupiter she heard
She sigh'd, and said,—"May he be truly Jove!
"But age is still suspicious. Chastest beds
"Have been by these pretended gods defil'd:
"For if the deity supreme he be,
"Why comes he thus disguis'd? If true his love,
"Why prove it not? Urge thou an anxious wish
"To clasp him in his might, in such a sort,
"As lofty Juno he embraces;—round
"Begirt with all the ensigns of his power."
Thus Juno artful, Semelé's desires
Apt moulded to her mind. From Jove she prays
A nameless boon: the ready god consents;—
"Chuse what thou wilt, nor least denial dread:
"To prove my faith, I call the Stygian streams
"To witness, terror of the god of gods."
Joy'd at her fatal prayer's too large success;
And by her lover's prompt compliance, doom'd
To sure destruction;—"This," said she, "I wish;—
"When with me next you love's delights enjoy,
"Appear as when Saturnia fills your arms."
Fain would the god have stopp'd her mouth:—too soon
The hasty words found entrance to his ears.
Deep mourn'd he. Equal now the fates forbid,
The wish retracted, or the oath absolv'd.
Sorrowing he seeks the lofty heaven: his nod
Dark rolling clouds collects: here form black showers;
And hurricanes; and flashing lightenings mixt;
Thunders; and his inevitable bolt:
Anxious he strives with all his power to damp,
The fierceness of his flames: nor arm'd him now,
With those dread fires that to the earth dash'd down
The hundred-handed foe:—too powerful they.
He chose a milder thunder;—less of rage,
Of fire, and fury, had the Cyclops given
The mass when forg'd; a second-rated bolt.
Clad in mild glory thus, the dome he seeks

Of Semelé;—her mortal frame too weak,
To bear th' ethereal shock, fierce scorcht she sunk,
Beneath the nuptial grant. Th' imperfect babe,
Snatcht from his mother's smoking womb, was sew'd
(If faith the tale deserves) within his thigh;
There to complete the period of his growth.
Ino, his aunt maternal, then receiv'd
The boy; in private rear'd him, till the nymphs
Of Nysa's mountains, in their secret caves
Shelter'd, and fed with milk, th' entrusted charge.

  While the rash promise caus'd on earth those deeds,
And twice-born Bacchus' cradle safe was hid;
'Tis said that Jove with heavenly nectar flush'd,
All serious cares dismiss'd. With sportive jests,
At ease conversing, he and Juno sate:
When he:—"The thrilling ecstasies of love,
"Are surely strongest on the female side."
She differs,—and the question both agree
Tiresias, who each sex had prov'd, shall judge.
Two mighty snakes he spy'd upon the grass,
Twisted in Venus' wreaths; and with his staff
Hard smote them;—instant alter'd was his sex.
Wonderous! he woman of a man became,
Seven winters so he liv'd:—the eight, again
He spy'd the same; and cry'd,—"If such your power,
"That whoso strikes you must their gender change,
"Once more I'll try the spell." Straight as the blow
The snakes receiv'd, his pristine form return'd:
Hence was he chosen, in the strife jocose,
As umpire; and the words of Jove confirm'd.

  Much, say they, Juno rag'd; more than beseem'd
The trivial cause, or sentence justly given;
And veil'd the judge's eyes in endless night.
But Jove omnipotent, him gave to know,
(For fate forbids to cancel others' deeds)
What future times conceal; a light divine;
An honor'd gift to mitigate his pain.

  Fam'd far and wide through all Bœotia's towns,
Unerring answers still the prophet gave,
To all who sought him. Blue Liriopé,
First prov'd his faith, and ne'er-deceiving words.
Her once Cephisus, in his winding stream
Entwin'd, and forceful in his waves enjoy'd.
The beauteous nymph's full womb, in time produc'd
A babe, whose features ev'n from birth inspir'd

Th' attendant nymphs with love; Narcissus nam'd.
For him enquiring, whether doom'd to see,
The peaceful period of maturest age,
The fate-foretelling prophet thus reply'd:—
"Yes,—if himself he never knows." The words
Were long absurd esteem'd: but well th' event
Their justice prov'd; his strange unheard of death;
And love of object never lov'd before.

Now sixteen summers had Narcissus seen,
A boy in beauty, but in growth a man;
And crowds of youths his friendship sought, and crowds
Of damsels sought his love: but fiercely pride
Swell'd in his snowy bosom; and he spurn'd
His friends' advances, and the love-sick maids.
A chattering nymph, resounding Echo, saw
The youth, when in his toils the trembling deer
He drove;—a nymph who ne'er her words retain'd,
Nor dialogue commenc'd. But then she bore
A body palpable; and not, as now,
Merely a voice:—yet garrulous, she then
That voice, nor other us'd; 'twas all she could,
The closing words of speakers to repeat.
Juno had this ordain'd: for oft the dame
The frailer nymphs upon the hills had caught,
In trespass with her Jove; but Echo sly
With lengthen'd speech the goddess kept amus'd,
Till all by flight were sav'd. Soon Juno saw
The trick:—"The power of that delusive tongue,"—
She cry'd, "I'll lessen, and make brief thy words;"
Nor stay'd, but straight her threaten'd vengeance took.
Now she redoubles (all she can) the words
Which end another's speech; reporting back,
But only what she hears.

Through pathless woods
As roves Narcissus, Echo sees, and burns;
Steals in his footsteps, following close, but flames
More fierce, more near approaching. Sudden thus,
The sulphurous daubing o'er the torches spread,
Snatches th' approaching flame. How oft she wish'd
With bland and soothing words to hail the youth;
But nature harsh forbids, nor grants to make
The first commencement; what she grants she takes,
And anxious waits to catch the wish'd-for sounds;
And speak responsive. Chance the youth had led
Far from his social troop, and loud he cry'd,—
"Who's he that hither comes?" Attentive she,—

Reply'd, "O hither come!" Amaz'd he stood,
Round searching whence the voice; and louder still,
"Here come!" exclaim'd,—and Echo answer'd,—"Come!"
To every part his eyes in vain are bent;
And, "why," laments he, "dost thou me avoid?"
Again he hears her,—"dost thou me avoid?"
Still he persists; th' alternate voice deceives,—
And,—"come, approach, together let us join,"
Impatient now he utters: ardent she
Exclaims, in joyful accents,—"let us join!"
Her wish in person urging, from the grove
She springs, and wide extends her arms to clasp
His neck:—Narcissus flies, and flying calls,—
"Desist!—hold off thy hands;—may sooner death
"Me seize, than thou enjoy me." Nought the maid
Re-echoes, but,—"enjoy me." Close conceal'd,
By him disdain'd, amid the groves she hides
Her blushing forehead, where the leaves bud thick;
And dwells in lonely caverns. Still her flame
Clings close around her heart; and sharper pangs
Repulse occasions: cares unceasing waste
Her wretched form: gaunt famine shrivels up
Her skin; and all the moistening juice which fed
Her body, flies in air: her voice and bones
Alone are left: her voice, unchang'd;—her bones
To craggy stones are harden'd. Still in groves
She hides secluded; nor on hills appears:
Heard frequent; only heard, and nought but sound.

  Thus slighted he the nymph; nor her alone,
But numbers else who o'er the mountains rov'd;
Or sported in the waves. Nor less his pride,
When more mature: keen smarting from his scorn,
To heaven one rais'd her hands, and ardent pray'd;—
"Ordain that he may love, but love like me
"One ne'er to be enjoy'd!" Rhamnusia grants
To prayers so just, th' assenting nod. There stood,
A mudless pool, whose waters silvery bright,
The shepherds touch'd not,—nor the mountain goats,
Nor lowing herds: which birds, and fierce wild beasts,
Dabbling disturb'd not:—nor a wither'd branch,
Dropt from a tree o'erhanging. Round the brink,
Fed by the moisture, virid grass arose;
And trees impervious to the solar beam,
Screen'd the cool surface. Weary'd with the chase,
And faint with heat, here laid Narcissus down;
Charm'd with the place, and tempted by the pool.
Here as he seeks to quench his burning thirst,

He burns with other fires: and while he drinks,
Caught by the image of his beauteous face,
He loves th' unbody'd form: a substance thinks
The shadow:—loves enraptur'd,—loves himself!
Fixes with eager gaze upon the sight
As on a face in Parian marble wrought.
Stretcht on the ground, his own bright eyes he views,
Twin stars;—his fingers, such as Bacchus grace;
His tresses like Apollo's;—downy cheeks,
Unbearded yet; his neck as ivory white;
The roseate blooming fading into snow:
Each trait admiring which the hapless nymphs,
In him admir'd. Unwitting youth, himself
He wants;—at once beloving, and belov'd:
Himself desiring, by himself desir'd:
Burning with love, while by himself he burns.
Oft, stooping, were his fruitless kisses given:
Oft were his arms outstretch'd to clasp the neck
So plainly seen beneath the waters. No!—
Himself he could not clasp. Whom he beholds,
He knows not; but for whom he sees he burns.
The error that his eye deceives, provokes
His rage. O, foolish youth! why vainly grasp
A fleeting shadow? What thou seek'st is not:—
And what thou lov'st thou now destroy'st:—thou see'st
A semblance only;—a reflected shade—
Nought of itself: with thee it came;—with thee
It stays;—and with thee, if thou could'st, would go.
Not hunger's power has force to drag him thence;
Nor cares of sleep oppress him. Thrown along
The shaded grass, he bends insatiate eyes
Tow'rds the fallacious beauty;—by those eyes
He perishes. Now half-uprais'd, his arms
Outspread, to all the groves around he cry'd:—
"Ye woods, whose darken'd shades so oft have given
"Convenient privacies to lovers, say,
"Saw you e'er one so cruelly who lov'd?
"In ages heap'd on ages you have stood,
"Remember ye a youth who pin'd as I?
"Pleas'd with the object, I its form behold;
"But what I see, and what so pleases flies.
"I find it not: in such bewilder'd maze
"The lover stands. And what my grief augments,
"No mighty seas divide us; lengthen'd roads;
"Nor lofty hills; nor high embattled walls,
"With portals clos'd: asunder are we held
"By trivial drops of water. It no less
"Than I, would give th' embrace; for when I bend

"My lips to kiss it in the limpid stream;
"With rising lips to meet, it anxious strives:
"Then might you think we touch, so faint a line
"Sunders us lovers. Come! whate'er thou art,
"Come hither! why thus mock me, dearest form?
"Why fly my wooing thus? My beauty sure,
"Nor youth are such as should provoke thy flight:
"For numerous nymphs for me have burn'd. Some hope
"Thy kindly sympathizing face affords;
"And when my anxious arms I stretch,—thy arms
"Advance to clasp me:—when I smile, thou smil'st:
"And often have I noted, when the tears
"Stream'd down my cheeks, a rivulet on thine:
"I nod,—thou, answering, noddest: and those lips,
"Those beauteous lips, whose movements plain I see,
"Words utter sure to mine,—though I forbid,
"The sounds to hear. In thee am I!—no more
"My shadow me deceives: I see the whole;
"Love for myself consumes me:—flames self-rais'd,
"Myself torment. What hope? be woo'd,—or woo?
"Wooing, or being woo'd, where is my gain?
"Myself I wish, and plenty makes me poor.
"Would that my body from itself could part!
"Strange wish for lovers, what most dear they love,
"Absent to pray. Grief undermines my strength;
"Nor long my life can linger;—immature,
"In youth I perish: but in me no fears,
"Can death infuse, of all my woes the end;
"Might I but leave this lovely object, still
"Existing: now two images, alas!
"Sink with one soul in death." Narcissus wails;
And raving turns to view the face again.
His tears the waters trouble; and the face
So beauteous, scarce is seen. Griev'd, he exclaims,
When disappearing,—"Whither fly'st thou? stay—
"Stay, I beseech thee; cruel, fly me not,—
"Thy lover: grant me still to view the form,
"To touch forbidden:—food, at least, afford
"To this unhappy flame." Lamenting thus,
He from his shoulders tore his robe, and beat
With snow-white hands his bosom; at the blow
His bosom redden'd: so the cherry seems,
Here ruddy blushing, there as fair as snow:
Or grapes unripe, part purpling to the sun,
In vary'd clusters. This he soon espy'd,
Reflected in the placid pool; no more
He bore it, but as gentle fire dissolves
The yellow wax: as Phœbus' morning beams

Melt the light hoar;—so wasted he,—by love
Gradual consum'd, as by a secret fire.
No more the ruddy teints appear, with white
Soft blended. All his active strength decays;
And all that pleas'd so lately. Ev'n his form
So much by Echo lov'd, no more remains.

All Echo saw; and though of former slights
Still mindful, griev'd; and when the hapless youth
"Alas!" exclaim'd; responsive sigh'd, "Alas!"
When on his breast the blows resounded; blows
Loud answering his were heard. His final words,
Gazing still earnest on the wonted wave,
Were,—"dearest form, belov'd in vain!"—the words
Resounded from the grove: "farewel," he cry'd,
And Echo cry'd, "farewel." Weary'd he threw,
On the green turf his head. Night clos'd his eyes;
Their owner fond admiring. Now retir'd
To regions far beneath, the Stygian lake
Reflects his form. The Naiäd sisters wail,
Shorn of their tresses, which to him they throw:
The Dryads also mourn; their bosoms beat;
And Echo answers every tearful groan.
A pile they build; the high-tost torches bring;
And funeral bier; but, lo! the corpse is gone:
A saffron-teinted flower alone is found,
Rising encircled with its snowy leaves.

Th' adventure spread through all the Achaian towns,
And much repute th' unerring augur gain'd.
Great now his prophesying fame. Alone,
Pentheus despis'd him;—(he the gods despis'd)
And only he;—he mock'd each holy word
Sagely prophetic:—with his rayless eyes
Reproach'd him. Angrily, his temples hoar
With reverend locks, the prophet shook, and said;—
"Happy for thee, if thus of light bereft,
"The Bacchanalian orgies ne'er to see!
"The day approaches, nor far distant now;
"My sight prophetic tells,—when here will come
"Bacchus new-born, of Semelé the son,
"Whose rites, if thou with honor due, not tend'st
"In temples worthy,—scatter'd far and wide,
"Thy limbs dismember'd shall the ground bestrew:
"Thy blood the forests shall distain;—thy gore
"Thy aunts,—nay e'en thy mother, shall pollute:
"For thou such honors, as immortals claim,
"Shalt to the god deny; then wilt thou find

"Beneath this darkness I but see too well."
Thus speaking, Echion's son the prophet push'd
Harshly away; but his too faithful words
Time prov'd;—the threaten'd deeds accomplish'd all.

  Lo! Bacchus comes, and all the country rings
With joyous outcries; crowds on crowds thick swarm;—
Matrons, and wives new-wedded, mixt with men;
Nobles, and commons; all the impulse bears,
To join the stranger's rites. But Pentheus thus;—
"Offspring of Mars! O nation, serpent born!
"What madness fills your minds? Can piercing sounds
"Of brass from brass rebounding; winding horns,
"And magic cheatings, then possess such power?
"You whom the warlike sword, the trumpet's clang,
"And battle's edge, dread bristling close with arms,
"Appal not; yield ye thus to female howls;
"Wine's maddening fumes; a filthy shameless crowd;
"And empty cymbals? In amaze, I see,
"You venerable men who plough'd the seas,
"And here, a refuge for your exil'd gods,
"This second Tyre have built,—without a blow,
"Yield it a spoil! Ye too, robuster youths,
"Of hardier age, and years more near my own;—
"Whom warlike arms, than Thyrsi more become;
"And brows with helmets than with leaves comprest:
"Think whence you sprang, and let the thought inspire
"Your souls with all the dragon's fierceness: he
Singly slew hosts: he for his fountain fell;
You for your honor vanquish. He destroy'd
The valiant; you th' effeminate expel;
And all the glory of your sire regain.
"If fate to Thebes a speedy fall decrees,
"May heroes, O, ye gods! with battering force
"O'erturn her walls;—may the sword rage, and flames
"Crackling, devour her. Wretched though our lot;
"Not criminal: our fate, though much bemoan'd,
"Would need concealment not: tears then might flow,
"But not from shame. Now unresisting Thebes,
"Yields to a boy unarm'd; who never joys
"In armies, steeds, nor swords;—but more in locks
"With myrrh moist-dropping, garlands soft, and robes
"Of various teints, with gold and purple gay.
"Rest ye but tranquil, and without delay,
"Him will I force to own his boasted sire
"Untrue; and forg'd those new invented rites.
"Had not Acrisius bravery to despise
"The counterfeited deity, and close

"The gates of Argos on him? And must now
"This wanderer come, and Pentheus terrify,
"With all the power of Thebes! Haste, quickly haste,"—
He bade his servants,—"hither drag, firm chain'd,
"This leader. Quick, nor brook my words delay!"
His grandsire, Athamas, and all the crowd
Reprove;—while thus he rails, with fruitless toil
Labor to stop him. Obstinate he stands,
More raging at remonstrance; and his ire
Restrain'd, increases; goading more and more;
Restraint itself enkindling more his rage.
So may be seen a river rolling smooth,
With murmuring nearly silent, while unchecked;
But when by rocks, or bulky trees oppos'd,
Foaming and boiling furious, on it sweeps
Impetuous raging; fiercer, more withstood.

 With blood besmear'd, his men return;—their lord
For Bacchus anxious asks;—but Bacchus they,
To find, arriv'd too late;—"but here," they cry,—
"Here have we seiz'd his comrade;—one who joins
"His train, and joins his rites." (The Tuscans once
The Bacchanalian orgies follow'd.) Bound
Behind, his hands, their prisoner they present.
Pentheus survey'd the stranger, while his eyes
Sparkled with rage terrific: with constraint
His torture so deferring, thus he spoke;—
"Wretch! ere thou sufferest,—ere thy death shall give
"A public warning,—tell thy name;—confess
"Thy sire; declare thy country; and the cause
"Those rites thou celebratest in a mode
"Diverse from others." Fearless, he reply'd;—
"Acœtes is my name: my natal land,
"Tyrrhenia: from an humble stock I spring.
"Lands by strong oxen plough'd, or wool-clad flocks,
"Or lowing herds my father left me none:
"For poor was he;—his daily toil to catch
"With nets and lines the fish, and as they leap'd,
"Draw with his bending rod the prey to land:
"His skill his sole estate. When unto me
"This art he taught,—receive, said he, my wealth;
"Such wealth as I possess; heir to my toil,
"And to my toil successor: dying, he
"To me bequeath'd the waters;—nothing more:
"These only as paternal wealth I claim.
"But soon, disliking on the self-same rock
"To dwell, I learn'd the art to rule the track
"Plough'd by the keel, with skilful guiding hand;

"And learn'd th' Olenian sign, the showery goat;
"Taygeté; and the Hyädes; the Bear;
"The dwellings of the winds; and every port
"Where ships could shelter. Once for Delos bound,
"By chance, the shore of Chios' isle we near'd;
"And when our starboard oars the beach had touch'd,
"Lightly I leap'd, and rested on the land.
"Now, night expir'd, Aurora warmly glow'd,
"And rousing up from sleep, my men I bade
"Supplies of living waters bring; and shew'd
"What path the fountain led to. I meanwhile,
"A lofty hill ascending, careful mark'd
"The wish'd-for wind approaching;—loud I call'd
"My fellows, and with haste the vessel gain'd.
"Lo! cry'd Opheltes, chief of all my crew,—
"Lo! here we come;—and from the desart fields,
"(A prize obtain'd, he thought),—he dragg'd along
"A boy of virgin beauty tow'rd the sands:
"Staggering, the youth, with wine and sleep opprest,
"With difficulty follow'd. Closely I
"His dress, his countenance, and his gait remark;
"And all I see, displays no mortal man.
"Conscious, I speak my comrades thus:—Unknown
"To me, what deity before us stands,
"But sure I am, that form conceals a god.
"O thou! whoe'er thou art, assist us;—aid
"Our undertakings;—who have seiz'd thee, spare,
"Unknowing what they did. Bold Dictys cries,—
"Than whom none swifter gain'd the topmost yards,
"Nor on the cordage slid more agile down;—
"Prayers offer not for us. Him Lybis joins;
"And brown Melanthus, ruler of the helm;
"Alcimedon unites; Epopeus too,
"Who rul'd the rowers, and their restings mark'd;
"(Arduous they urg'd their sinews by his voice)—
"Nay all Opheltes join,—the lust of gain,
"So blinded all their judgments. Still I cry;—
"Ne'er will I yield my vessel to behold
"Burthen'd with such a sacrilegious load:
"Pre-eminent is here my right. I stand
"To those who strive to hoist him in, oppos'd.
"Bold and outrageous, far beyond the rest,
"Was Lycabas; from Tuscan shore exil'd
"For deeds of murderous violence: he grasp'd
"My throat with force athletic, as I stood,
"And in the waves had flung me; but sore stunn'd,
"A cable caught, and sav'd me. Loud the crew
"The impious deed applauded. Bacchus rose,

"(The boy was Bacchus!) with the tumult loud
"Rous'd from his sleep;—the fumes of wine dispell'd,
"His senses seem'd restor'd. What is't you do?
"What noise is this? he cry'd;—What brought me here?
"O, mariners! inform me;—tell me where
"You carry me! Fear not,—the pilot said,—
"Say but the port, where most thou'dst chuse to land;—
"Thither we straight will steer. The god reply'd;—
"To Naxos then your course direct; that isle
"My native soil I call:—to you that isle
"A friendly shore shall prove. False men, they swear,
"By ocean, and by all the sacred gods,
"This to perform; and order me to loose,
"The painted vessel's sails. Full on the right
"Stood Naxos. Loudly one to me exclaims;
"As tow'rd the right I trim the sails to steer;—
"What now, Acœtes? madman! fool! what now?
"Art thou distracted? to the left we sail.—
"Most nod significant their wishes: some
"Soft whisper in my ear. Astounded, I
"Let others guide!—exclaim,—and quit the helm;
"Guiltless of aiding in their treacherous guile.
"Loud murmurings sound from all; and loudly one,
"Ethalion, cries;—in thee alone is plac'd
"Our safety, doubtless!—forward steps himself;—
"My station seizes; and a different course
"Directs the vessel, Naxos left behind.
"The feigning god, as though but then, the fraud
"To him perceptible, the waves beholds
"From the curv'd poop, and tears pretending, cries;—
"Not this, O, seamen! is the promis'd shore:
"Not this the wish'd-for land! What deed of mine
"This cruel treatment merits? Where the fame
"Of men, a child deceiving; numbers leagu'd
"Misleading one? Fast flow'd my tears with his;
"Our tears the impious mob deride, and press
"The ocean with their strong-propelling oars.
"Now by the god himself, I swear, (and none
"To vows more ready listens) that the tale,
"Though in appearance credence far beyond,
"Is strictly true. Firm fixt amid the waves
"The vessel stands, as in a harbour laid
"Dry from the ocean! Wondering, they their oars,
"With strokes redoubled ply; loose to the wind
"More sails; and with this double aid essay
"Onward to urge. Their oars with ivy twin'd,
"Are clogg'd; the curving tendrils crooked spread;
"The sails with clustering berries loaded hang.

"His temples girded with a branchy crown,
"Whence grapes hang dangling, stands the god, and shakes
"A spear entwisted with the curling vine.
"Round seem to prowl the tiger, and the lynx,
"And savage forms of panthers, various mark'd.
"Up leap'd the men, by sudden madness mov'd;
"Or terror only: Medon first appear'd
"Blackening to grow, with shooting fins; his form
"Flatten'd; and in a curve was bent his spine.
"Him Lycabas address'd;—what wonderous shape
"Art thou receiving?—speaking, wide his jaws
"Expanded; flatten'd down, his nose appear'd;
"A scaly covering cloth'd his harden'd skin.
"Lybis to turn the firm fixt oars attempts,
"But while he tries, perceives his fingers shrink;
"And hands, now hands no longer, fins he sees.
"Another round the cordage strives his arms
"To clasp,—but arms he has not,—down he leaps
"Broad on his crooked back, and seeks the waves.
"Forkt is their new-made tail; like Luna's form
"Bent in the skies, ere half her orb is fill'd.
"Bounding all round they leap;—now down they dash,
"Besprinkling wide the foamy drops; now 'merge;
"And now re-diving, plunge in playful sport:
"As chorus regular they act, and move
"Their forms in shapes lascivious; spouting high,
"The briny waters through their nostrils wide.
"Of twenty now, (our ship so many bore)
"I only stand unchang'd; with trembling limbs,
"And petrify'c with fear. The god himself,
"Scarce courage in my mind inspires; when thus,—
"Pale terror from thy bosom drive, and seek
"The isle of Naxos.—Thither come, I tend
"On smoking altars, Bacchus' sacred rites."

  Him Pentheus angry stopp'd. "Thy tedious tale,
"Form'd to divert my rage, in vain is told.
"Here, men, swift drag him hence!—dispatch his soul,
"Driven from his body, down to Stygian night;
"By pangs excruciating." Straight close pent,
In solid dungeon is Acœtes thrown,
While they the instruments of death prepare;
The cruel steel; the flames;—spontaneous fly
Wide ope the dungeon doors; spontaneous fall
The fetters from his arms, and freed he goes.
Stubborn, the son of Echion still persists;
But sends no messenger: himself proceeds,
To where Cythæron, for the sacred rites

Selected, rings with Bacchanalian songs,
And outcries shrill. As foams an high-bred steed,
When through the speaking brass the warlike trump,
Sounds the glad signal; and with ardor burns
For battle: so the air, with howlings loud
Re-echoing, Pentheus moves, and doubly flames
His rage, to hear the clangor. Clear'd from trees,
A plain extends, from every part fair seen,
And near the mountain's centre: round its skirt,
Thick groves grow shady. Here his mother saw
His eye unhallow'd view the sacred rites;
And first,—by frantic madness urg'd,—she first
Furious the Thyrsus at her Pentheus flung:
Exclaiming loud;—"Ho, sisters! hither haste!
"Here stands the furious boar that wastes our grounds:
"My hand has smote him." Raging rush the crowd,
In one united body. All close join,
And all pursue the now pale trembling wretch.
No longer fierce he storms; but grieving blames
His rashness, and his obstinacy owns.
Wounded,—"dear aunt, Autonoë!"—he cries,
"Help me!—O, let your own Actæon's ghost
"Move you to pity!" She, Actæon's name
Nought heeding, tears his outstretcht arm away;
The other, Ino from his body drags!
And when his arms, unhappy wretch, he tries
To lift unto his mother, arms to lift
Were none;—but stretching forth his mangled trunk
Of limbs bereft;—"look, mother!"—he exclaims.
Loud howl'd Agavé at the sight; his neck
Fierce grasping,—toss'd on high his streaming locks,
Her bloody fingers twisted in his hair.
Then clamor'd loudly;—"joy, my comrades, joy!
"The victory is mine!" Not swifter sweep
The winds those leaves which early frosts have nipp'd,
And lightly to the boughs attach'd remain,
Than scatter'd flew his limbs by furious hands.

THE FOURTH BOOK

Feast of Bacchus. Impiety and infidelity of Alcithoë and her sisters. Story of Pyramus and Thisbe. Amour of Mars and Venus. The lovers caught by Vulcan in a net. Sol's love for Leucothoë, and her change to a tree of frankincense. Clytié transformed to a sunflower. Tale of Salmacis and Hermaphroditus. Transformation of Alcithoë and her sisters to bats. Juno's fury. Madness of Athamas; and deification of Ino and Melicertes. Change of the Theban women to rocks and birds. Cadmus and

Hermione changed to serpents. Perseus. Transformation of Atlas to a mountain. Andromeda saved from the sea monster. Story of Medusa.

Warn'd by the dreadful admonition, all
Of Thebes the new solemnities approve;
Bring incense, and to Bacchus' altars bend.
Alcithoë only, Minyäs' daughter views
His orgies still with unbelieving eyes.
Boldly, herself and sisters, partners all
In impious guilt, refuse the god to own,
The progeny of Jove. The prophet bids
Each mistress with her maids, to join the feast:
(Sacred the day from toil). Their breasts to clothe
In skins; the fillets from their heads to loose;
With ivy wreathe their brows; and in their hands
The leafy Thyrsus grasp. Threatening, he spoke,
In words prophetic, how th' affronted god
Would wreak his ire. Matrons and virgins haste;
Throw by their baskets; quit the loom, and leave
Th' unfinish'd threads: sweet incense they supply
Invoking Bacchus by his various names.
Bromius! Lyæus! power in flames produc'd!—
Produc'd a second time! god doubly born!
Born of two mothers! Nyseus! they exclaim;
Long-hair'd Thyoneus!—and the planter fam'd
Of genial grapes! Lenæus! too, they sing;
Nyctelius! Elelcus! and aloud
Iäcchus! Evan! with the numerous names,
O Liber! in the Grecian land thou hold'st.
Unwaning youth is thine, eternal boy!
Most beauteous form in heaven! a virgin's face
Thou seem'st to bear, when seen without thy horns.
Stoops to thy arms the East, where Ganges bounds
The dusky India:—Deity rever'd!
Thou impious Pentheus sacrific'd; and thou,
The mad Lycurgus punish'd with his axe:
By thee the Tyrrhene traitors, in the main
Were flung: Adorn'd with painted reins, thou curb'st
The lynxes in thy chariot yok'd abreast:
Thy steps the Satyrs and Bacchantes tread;
And old Silenus; who with wine o'ercharg'd,
With a long staff his tottering steps sustains:
Or on a crooked ass, unsteady sits:
Where'er thou enterest shout the joyous youth,

Females and males immingled: loud the drums
Struck by their hands resound;—and loudly clash
The brazen cymbals: soft the boxen flutes
Deep and melodious sound!

Now prays all Thebes
The god's approach in mildness; and perform
His sacred rites as bidden. Sole remain
At home secluded, Minyäs' daughters,—they
With ill-tim'd industry the feast prophane.
Busy, they form the wool, and twirl the thread;
Or to the loom stick close, and all their maids
Urge to strict labor. One with dexterous thumb
The slender thread extending, cries;—"while all,
"Idly, those rites imaginary tend,
"Let us, whom Pallas, deity more great,
"Detains, our useful labors lighter make
"By vary'd converse. Each in turn relate
"Her tale, while others listen; thus the time
"Less tedious shall appear." All pleas'd applaud
The proposition; and her sisters beg
That she the tales commence. Long she demurs,
What story first, of those she knew, to tell;
For numerous was her store. In doubt, thy tale,
Dercetis Babylonian, to relate,
Whose form, the Syrians think, with scales is cloth'd;
The stagnant pools frequenting: or describe
Thy daughter's change, on waving pinions borne;
Who lengthen'd age obtain'd, on lofty towers
Safe dwelling: or of Naïs, who the youths
With magic works, and potent witching words
To silent fishes turn'd; till she the same
Vile transformation suffer'd: or the tree,
Which once in clusters white its berries bore,
Now blood besprinkled, growing black. This tale
Most novel, pleas'd the most: and as she spun
Her slender thread, the nymph the tale began.

   "Thisbe, the brightest of the eastern maids;
"And Pyramus, the pride of all the youths,
"Contiguous dwellings held, in that fam'd town,
"Where lofty walls of stone, we learn were rais'd,
"By bold Semiramis. Their neighbouring scite,
"Acquaintance first encourag'd,—primal step
"To further intimacy: love, in time,
"Grew from this chance connection; and they long'd
"To join by lawful rites: but harsh forbade,
"Their rigid sires the union fate had doom'd.

"With equal ardor both their minds inflam'd,
"Burnt fierce; and absent every watchful spy
"By nods and signs they spoke; for close their love
"Conceal'd they kept;—conceal'd it burn'd more fierce.
"The severing wall a narrow chink contain'd,
"Form'd when first rear'd;—what will not love espy?
"This chink, by all for ages past unseen,
"The lovers first espy'd.—This opening gave
"A passage for their voices; safely through,
"Their tender words were breath'd in whisperings soft.
"Oft punctual at their posts,—on this side she,
"And Pyramus on that;—each breathing sighs,—
"By turns inhaling, have they mutual cry'd;—
"Invidious wall! why lovers thus divide?
"Much were it, did thy parts more wide recede,
"And suffer us to join? were that too much
"A little opening more, and we might meet
"With lips at least. Yet grateful still we own
"Thy kind indulgence, which a passage gives,
"And amorous words conveys to loving ears.
"Thus they loquacious, though on sides diverse,
"Till night their converse stay'd;—then cry'd, adieu!
"And each imprinted kisses, which the stones
"Forbade to taste. Soon as Aurora's fires
"Remov'd the shades of night, and Phœbus' rays
"From the moist earth the dew exhal'd, they meet
"As 'custom'd at the wall: lamenting deep,
"As wont in murmuring whispers: bold they plan,
"Their guards evading in the silent night,
"To pass the outer gates. Then, when escap'd
"From home, to leave the city's dangerous shade;
"But lest, in wandering o'er the spacious plains
"They miss to meet, at Ninus' sacred tomb
"They fix their assignation,—hid conceal'd
"Beneath th' umbrageous leaves. There grew a tree,
"Close bordering on a cooling fountain's brink;
"A stately mulberry;—snow-white fruit hung thick
"On every branch. The plot pleas'd well the pair.

   "And now slow seems the car of Sol to sink;
"Slow from the ocean seems the night to rise;
"Till Thisbe, cautious, by the darkness veil'd,
"Soft turns the hinges, and her guards beguiles.
"Her features veil'd, the tomb she reaches,—sits
"Beneath th' appointed tree: love makes her bold.
"Lo! comes a lioness,—her jaws besmear'd
"With gory foam, fresh from the slaughter'd herd,
"Deep in th' adjoining fount her thirst to slake.

"Far off the Babylonian maid beheld
"By Luna's rays the horrid foe,—quick fled
"With trembling feet, and gain'd a darksome cave:
"Flying, she dropp'd, and left her robe behind.

"Now had the savage beast her drought allay'd,
"And backward to the forest roaming, found
"The veiling robe;—its tender texture rent,
"And smear'd the spoil with bloody jaws. The youth
"(With later fortune his strict watch escap'd)
"Spy'd the plain footsteps of a monster huge
"Deep in the sand indented!—O'er his face
"Pale terror spread: but when the robe he saw,
"With blood besmear'd, and mangled; loud he cry'd,—
"One night shall close two lovers' eyes in death!
"She most deserving of a longer date.
"Mine is the fault alone. Dear luckless maid!
"I have destroy'd thee;—I, who bade thee keep
"Nocturnal meetings in this dangerous place,
"And came not first to shield thy steps from harm.
"Ye lions, wheresoe'er within those caves
"Ye lurk! haste hither,—tear me limb from limb!
"Fierce ravaging devour, and make my tomb
"Your horrid entrails. But for death to wish
"A coward's turn may serve. The robe he takes,
"Once Thisbe's, and beneath th' appointed tree
"Bearing it, bath'd in tears; with ardent lips
"Oft fondly kissing, thus he desperate cries;—
"Now with my blood be also bath'd!—drink deep!
"And in his body plung'd the sword, that round
"His loins hung ready girt: then as he dy'd,
"Hasty withdrew, hot reeking from the wound,
"The steel; and backwards falling, press'd the earth.
"High spouts the sanguine flood! thus forth a pipe,
"(The lead decay'd, or damag'd) sends a stream
"Contracted from the breach; upspringing high,
"And loudly hissing, as the air it breaks
"With jets repeated. Sprinkled with the blood,
"The tree's white fruit a purple tinge receiv'd;
"Deep soak'd with blood the roots convey the stain
"Inly, and tinge each bough with Tyrian dye.

"Now Thisbe comes, with terror trembling still,
"Fearful, she Pyramus expecting waits:
"Him seek her beating bosom, and her eyes;
"Anxious the peril she escap'd to tell.
"Well mark'd her eyes the place,—and well the tree;
"The berries chang'd in color, long she doubts

"The same or no. While hesitating thus,
"The panting members quivering she beholds,
"Upon the sanguin'd turf; and back recoils!
"Paler than box her features grow; her limbs
"More tremble than when ocean fretful sounds,
"Its surface briskly by the breezes swept.
"Nor long the pause, her lover soon is known;
"And now her harmless breast with furious blows
"She punishes; her tresses wild she rends;
"Clasps the lov'd body; and the gaping wound
"Fills with her tears,—their droppings with the blood
"Immingling. On his clay-cold face she press'd
"Her kisses, crying;—Pyramus! what chance
"Has torn thee from me thus? My Pyramus!
"Answer me,—'tis thy dearest Thisbe speaks!
"She calls thee,—hear me,—raise that dying face!
"At Thisbe's name, his lids, with death hard weigh'd,
"He rais'd—beheld her,—and forever clos'd.

"Him dying thus,—her lacerated veil;
"The ivory scabbard empty'd of its sword;
"She saw,—at once the truth upon her mind
"Flash'd quick. Alas! thy hand, by love impell'd,
"Has wrought thy ruin: but to me the hand,
"In this, at least, shall equal force display,
"For equal was my love; and love will grant
"Sufficient strength the deadly wound to give.
"In death I'll follow thee; with justice call'd
"Thy ruin's wretched cause,—but comrade too.
"Thou whom, but death seem'd capable to part
"From me, shalt find ev'n death too weak will prove.
"Ye wretched mourning parents, his and mine!
"The dying prayers respect of him,—of me:
"Grant that, entomb'd together, both may rest;
"A pair by faithful love conjoined,—by death
"United close. And thou fair tree which shad'st
"Of one the miserable corse; and two
"Soon with thy boughs wilt cover,—bear the mark
"Of the sad deed eternal;—ting'd thy fruit
"With mournful coloring: monumental type
"Of double slaughter. Speaking thus, she plac'd
"The steely point, while yet with blood it smok'd,
"Beneath her swelling breast; and forward fell.
"Her final prayer reach'd heaven; her parents reach'd:
"Purple the berries blush, when ripen'd full;
"And in one urn the lovers' ashes rest."

She ceas'd: a silent interval, but short,

Ensu'd; and next Leuconoë thus address'd
Her listening sisters:—"Ev'n the sun himself,
"Whose heavenly light so universal shines,
"To love is subject: his amours I tell.
"This deity's keen sight the first espy'd—
"(For all things penetrating first he sees)
"The crime of Mars and Venus; sore chagrin'd,
"To Vulcan he th' adulterous theft display'd,
"And told him where they lay. Appall'd he heard,—
"And dropp'd the tools his dexterous hand contain'd;
"But soon recover'd. Slender chains of brass,
"And nets, and traps he form'd; so wonderous fine,
"They mock'd the power of sight: for far less fine,
"The smallest thread the distaff forms; or line,
"Spun by the spider, pendent from the roof.
"Curious he form'd it; at the lightest touch
"It yielded; each momentum, slight howe'er,
"Caus'd its recession: this he artful hung,
"The couch enfolding. When the faithless wife,
"And paramour upon the bed embrac'd,
"Both in the lewd conjunction were ensnar'd;
"Caught by the husband's skill, whose art the chains
"In novel form had fram'd. The Lemnian god
"Instant wide threw the ivory doors, and gave
"Admittance free to every curious eye:
"In shameful guise together bound they laid.
"But some light gods, not blaming much the sight,
"Would wish thus sham'd to lie: loud laugh'd the whole,
"And long in heaven the tale jocose was told.

  "The well-remember'd deed, the Cyprian queen
"Retorting, made the god remember too:
"And him who her conceal'd amours disclos'd,
"In turn betray'd. What now, Hyperion's son,
"Avails thy beauty!—or thy radiant flames?
"For thou, whose fires warm all the wide-spread world,
"Burn'st with a new-felt heat! Thou, whose wide view,
"Should every object grasp, with partial ken
"Leucothoë only see'st! that nymph alone,
"Attracts those eyes, whose lustre all the world
"Expect to view. Oft in the eastern skies,
"More early rising, art thou seen; and oft
"More tardy 'neath the waves thou sinkest: long
"The wintry days thou stretchest, with delay
"Thy object lov'd to see. Meantime pale gloom
"O'ercasts thy orb; the dullness of thy mind
"Obstructs thy brightness; and thy rays obscure,
"Terror in mortal breasts inspire. Not pale

"Thou fadest, as, when nearer whirl'd to earth,
"Faint Luna's shadow o'er thy surface glooms:
"But love, and only love the paleness gives.
"Her only, now thy amorous soul pursues;
"Rhodos, nor Clymené, nor Persé fair,
"Of Colchian Circé mother, tempt thee now;
"Nor Clytié, whom thy cold neglect still spurns;
"Yet still she burns to clasp thee: deep she mourns,
"Stung more acutely by this fresh amour.
"Now in Leucothoë, every former love
"Is lost. Leucothoë, whom the beauteous nymph,
"Eurynomé, in odoriferous climes
"Of Araby brought forth. Full-grown, matur'd,
"Leucothoë's beauteous form no less surpass'd
"Her mother's, than her mother's all beside.
"Her sire, the royal Orchamus (who claim'd
"A seventh descent from ancient Belus) rul'd
"The Achæmenian towns. The rapid steeds
"Of Phœbus pasture 'neath the western sky;
"Not grass, ambrosia, eating; heavenly food,
"Which nerves their limbs, faint with diurnal toil,
"Restoring all their ardor. Whilst the steeds,
"This their celestial nourishment enjoy;
"And night, as 'custom'd, governs in her turn;
"The god the close apartments of his nymph
"Beloved, enters;—form'd to outward view,
"Eurynomé her mother. Her he saw
"The slender threads from spindle twirling fine,
"Illumin'd by the lamp; and circled round
"By twice six female helpers. Warm he gave
"As a lov'd daughter, his maternal kiss,
"And said;—our converse secrecy demands.—
"Th' attendant maids depart,—nor hinderance give,
"Loitering, a mother's secret words to hear.
"When he, the chamber free from spy or guard,
"Exclaims,—no female I! behold the god,
"The lengthen'd year who spaces! who beholds
"Each object earth contains! the world's great eye
"By which it all surveys. My tender words
"Believe, I dearly love thee. Pale she look'd,
"While thus he spoke;—started, and trembling dropp'd
"Her distaff, and her spindle from her hand
"Nerveless. But ev'n her terror seem'd to add
"Fresh beauty to her features. Longer he
"Delay'd not, but his wonted form assum'd;
"In heavenly splendor shining. Mild the maid,
"Won by his beauteous brightness, (though at first,
"His sudden shape surpriz'd her) sunk beneath

"The force he urg'd, with unresisting power.

  "The jealous Clytié (who with amorous flame
"Burn'd for Apollo) urg'd by harlot's rage,
"Straight to the sire, Leucothoë's crime betray'd;
"Painting the nymph's misdeed with heighten'd glow.
"Fierce rag'd the father,—merciless inhum'd
"Her living body deep in earth! Outstretcht
"High to the sun her arms, and praying warm
"For mercy;—he by force, she cry'd, prevail'd!
"O'er her untimely grave a lofty mound
"Of sand, her sire uprear'd. Hyperion's son
"Through this an opening with his beams quick form'd,
"Full wide for her, her head intomb'd to lift,
"Once to the light again. Thy bury'd corse
"No more thou now couldst raise; the ponderous load
"Of earth prevents thee; and a bloodless mass,
"Exanimate, thou ly'st! Not deeper grief
"'Tis said, the ruler of the swift-wing'd steeds,
"Display'd, when o'er the earth the hapless flames
"By Phaëton were thrown. Arduous he strives,
"Her gelid limbs, with all his powerful rays
"To vivid heat recal: stern fate withstands
"His utmost urg'd endeavours: bathing then
"Her pallid corse, and all the earth around
"With odorous nectar, sorrowing sad he cries;—
"Yet, shalt thou reach the heavens! And soon began
"Her limbs, soft melting in celestial dew,
"With moistening drops of strong perfume to flow:
"Slowly a frankincense's rooted twigs
"Spread in the earth,—its top the hillock burst.

  "Angry the god (though violent love the pain
"Of jealousy might well excuse,—the pain
"Of jealousy the tale) from Clytié now
"Abstains; no more in amorous mood they meet.
"Rash now the deed her burning love had caus'd,
"Too late she found;—she flies her sister-nymphs;
"And pining, on the cold bare turf she sits;
"By day,—by night,—sole shelter'd by the sky;
"Her dripping tresses matted round her brows:
"Food,—drink, abhorring. Nine long days she bore
"Sharp famine, bath'd with dew, bath'd with her tears;
"Still on the ground prone lying. Yet the god
"In circling motion still she ardent view'd;
"Turning her face to his. Tradition tells,
"Her limbs to earth grew fasten'd: ghastly pale
"Her color; chang'd to bloodless leaves she stood,

"Streak'd ruddy here and there;—a violet flower
"Her face o'erspreading. Still that face she turns,
"To meet the sun;—though binding roots retain
"Her feet, her love unalter'd still remains."

  She ended; all their listening ears, well pleas'd,
The wonderous story heard. Some hard of faith
Its truth, its probability deny.
To true divinities such power some grant;
And power to compass more;—to Bacchus none
Such potence own. The sisters, silent now,
Alcithoë beg to speak: she shooting swift
Her shuttle through th' extended threads, exclaims;—
"Of Daphnis' love, so known, on Ida's hill,
"His flocks who tended, whom his angry nymph,
"To stone transform'd (such fury fires the breast
"Of those who desperate love!) I shall not tell:
"Nor yet of Scython, of ambiguous form,
"Now male, now female; nature's wonted laws
"Inconstant proving: thee, O Celmis! too
"I pass; once faithful nurse to infant Jove,
"Now chang'd to adamant: Curetes! sprung
"From showery floods: Crocus, and Smilax, both
"To blooming flowers transform'd: unnotic'd these,
"My tale from novelty itself shall please:
"How Salmacis so infamous became,
"Then list; whose potent waves, the luckless limbs
"Enerve, of those they bathe. Conceal'd the cause;
"Yet far and wide the fountain's power is known.

  "Deep in the sheltering caves of Ida's hill,
"The Naiäc nymphs a beauteous infant nurs'd;
"Whom Cyprus' goddess unto Hermes bore.
"His father's beauty, and his mother's, shone
"In every feature; in his name conjoin'd
"He bore their appellations. When matur'd
"By fifteen summers, from paternal hills
"Straying, he wander'd from his nursing Idé:
"In lands unknown he joy'd, and joy'd to see
"Strange rivers,—pleasure lessening every toil.
"Through Lycia's towns he stray'd; and further still,
"To bordering Caria, where a pool he spy'd,
"Whose lowest depth a gleam transparent shew'd:
"No marshy canes,—no filthy barren weeds,
"Nor pointed bulrush near the margin grew:
"Full on the eye the water shone, yet round
"Its brink a border smil'd of verdant turf,
"And plants forever green. Here dwelt a nymph,

"But one who never join'd the active chace;
"The bow who never bent; who never strove
"To conquer in the race: of all the nymphs,
"Alone no comrade of Diana fleet.
"Oft, as 'tis said, her sister-nymphs exclaim'd;—
"Come, Salmacis, thy painted quiver take;
"Or take thy javelin;—with soft pleasures mix
"Laborious sporting: but nor javelin she,
"Nor painted quiver took;—with sportive toil,
"Soft pleasures mingling: sole intent to bathe,
"Her beauteous limbs amidst her own clear waves;
"And through her flowing tresses oft to draw
"The boxen comb, while o'er the fountain bent,
"She studies all her graces: now, her form
"Clad in a robe transparent, stretcht she lies,
"Or on the yielding leaves, or bending grass;
"Now flowers she culls;—and so it chanc'd to fall,
"Flowers she was gathering, when she first beheld
"The charming youth; no sooner seen than lov'd.
"Not forth she rush'd at first, though strongly urg'd,
"Forward to spring, but all adjusted fair:
"Closely survey'd her robe; her features form'd;
"And every part in beauteous shape compos'd.
"Then thus address'd him;—O, most godlike youth!
"And if a god, the lovely Cupid sure!
"But if of mortal mould, blest is thy sire!
"Blest is thy brother! and thy sister blest!—
"If sister hast thou;—and the fostering breast
"Which fed thy infant growth: but far 'bove all
"In rapturous bliss, is she who calls thee spouse;
"Should nymph exist thou deem'st that bliss deserves!
"If wedded, grant a stol'n embrace to me;
"If not, let me thy nuptial couch ascend.
"The Naiäd ceas'd: a bashful glow suffus'd
"His face, for nought of love to him was known:
"Yet blushing seem'd he lovely: thus warm glows
"The apple, to the ripening sun expos'd;
"Or teinted ivory; or the redden'd moon,
"Whom brazen cymbals clash to help in vain.
"To her, warm praying for at least a kiss,
"A chaste, a sister's kiss,—her arms firm claspt
"Around his ivory neck;—desist! he cries,
"Desist! or sole to thee the place I'll leave.
"His flight she dreaded, and reply'd,—I go,
"Dear youth, and freely yield the spot to thee.
"And seems indeed, her steps from him to turn;
"But still in sight she kept him; lurking close
"Shelter'd by shadowy shrubs, on bended knees.

"Of spy unconscious, he in boyish play
"Frisks sportive here and there; dips first his feet,
"Then ancles deeper in the wantoning waves;
"Pleas'd with the temper of the lucid pool:
"Till hasty stript from off his tender limbs
"His garments soft he flings. More deeply struck
"Stood Salmacis; more fiercely flam'd her love,
"His naked beauty seen. Her gloating eyes
"Sparkled no less than seem bright Phœbus' rays,
"When shining splendid, midst a cloudless sky,
"A mirror's face reflecting gives them back.
"Delay ill brooking, hardly she contains
"Her swelling joy; frantic for his embrace,
"She pants, and hard from rushing forth refrains.
"His sides he claps, and agile in the steam
"Quick plunges, moving with alternate arms.
"Bright through the waves he shines; thus white appears
"The sculptur'd ivory, or the lily fair,
"Seen through a crystal veil. The Naiäd cries;—
"Lo! here I come;—he's mine,—the youth's my own!
"And instant far was every garment flung.
"Midst of the waves she leaps;—the struggling youth
"Clasps close: and on his cold reluctant lips,
"Forces her kisses; down she girds his arms;
"And close to hers hugs his unwilling breast:
"Final, around the youth who arduous strives
"In opposition, and escape essays,
"Her limbs she twines: so twines a serpent huge,
"Seiz'd by the bird of Jove, and borne on high,
"Twisting his head, the feet close-bracing holds;
"The wide-spread wings entangled with his tail:
"So twines the ivy round the lengthen'd bough:
"So numerous Polypus his foe confines,
"Seiz'd in the deep, with claws on every side
"Firm graspt. But Hermes' son persisting still,
"The Naiäd's wish denies; she presses close,
"And as she cleaves, their every limb close join'd
"Exclaims;—ungallant boy! but strive thy most,
"Thou shalt not fly me. Grant me, O ye gods!
"No time may ever sunder him from me,
"Or me from him.—Her prayer was granted straight;—
"For now, commingling, both their bodies join'd;
"And both their faces melted into one.
"So, when in growth we boughs ingrafted see,
"The bark inclosing both at once, they sprout.
"Thus were their limbs, in strong embrace comprest,
"Wrapp'd close; no longer two in form, yet two
"In feature; nor a nymph-like face remain'd,

"Nor yet a boy's: it both and neither seem'd.

   "When Hermes' son beheld the liquid stream,
"Where masculine he plung'd, the power possess
"To enervate his body, and his limbs
"Effeminately soften; high he rais'd
"His arms, and pray'd (but not with manly voice)
"O, sire! O, mother dear! indulge your son,
"Your double appellation bearing, this
"Sole-urg'd petition. Whoso in these waves
"In strong virility, like me, shall plunge,
"Hence let him go, like me enervate made;
"Spoilt by the stream his strength. Each parent god
"Nodding, confirm'd their alter'd son's request;
"And ting'd the fountain with the changing power."

   She ceas'd: the nymphs Minyeian still persist
Their toil to urge, despising still the god;
His festival prophaning. Sudden heard,
The rattling sounds of unseen timbrels burst
Full on their ears! the pipe; the crooked horn;
And brazen cymbals loudly clash; perfumes
Of myrrh and saffron blended smell:—but more,
And what belief surpasses, straight their looms
Virid to sprout begin; the pendent threads
Branch into shoots like ivy: part becomes
The vine: what now were threads, curl'd tendrils seem:
Shot from the folded web, the branches climb;
And the bright red in purpling grapes appears.

   Now was the sun declining, and approach'd
The twilight season, when nor day it seems,
Nor night confirm'd; but a gray mixture forms;
Of each an indetermin'd compound. Deep
The roof appear'd to shade; the oily lamps,
Ardent to glow; the torches bright to burn,
With reddening flames; while round them seem'd to howl,
Figures of beast ferocious. Fill'd with smoke
The room,—th' affrighted maidens seek to hide;
And each in different corners tries to shun
The fires and flaming light. But while they seek
A lurking shelter, o'er their shorten'd limbs
A webby membrane spreading, binds their arms
In waving wings. The gloom conceal'd the mode,
Of transformation from their former shape.
Light plumage bears them not aloft,—yet rais'd
On wings transparent, through the air they skim,
To speak they strive, but utter forth a sound

Feeble and weak; then, screeching shrill, they plain:
Men's dwellings they frequent,—nor try the woods;
And, cheerful day avoiding, skim by night;
Their name from that untimely hour deriv'd.

  Now were the deeds of heaven-born Bacchus fam'd
Through every part of Thebes; and all around,
His aunt proud boasts the new-made god's great power:
She, of the sisters all, from sorrow spar'd,
Save what to view her sisters' sorrowing gave.
Juno beheld her lofty thus, her breast
Elate to view her sons; her nuptial fruits
With Athamas; and her great foster child,
The mighty Bacchus. More the furious queen
Bore not, but thus exclaim'd;—"Has the whore's son
"Power to transform the Tyrrhene crew, and plunge
"Them headlong in the deep? Can he impel
"The mother's hands to seize her bleeding son
"And tear his entrails? Dares he then to clothe
"The Minyëid sisters with un'custom'd wings?
"And is Saturnia's utmost power confin'd
"Wrongs unreveng'd to weep? Suffices such
"For me? Is this a goddess' utmost might?
"But he instructs me;—wisdom may be taught
"Ev'n by a foe. The wretched Pentheus' fate,
"Shews all-sufficient, what may madness do.
"Why should not Ino, stung with frantic rage,
"The well-known track her sisters trode pursue?"

  A path declivitous, with baleful yew
Dark shaded, leads, a dreary silent road,
Down to th' infernal regions: sluggish Styx
Dank mists exhales: here travel new-made ghosts,
With rites funereal blest: pale winter's gloom
Wide rules the squalid place: the stranger shades
Wander, unknowing which the path to tread,
Straight to the infernal city, where is held
Black Pluto's savage court. A thousand gates,
Wide ope, surround the town on every side.
As boundless ocean every stream receives,
From earth pour'd numerous,—so each wandering soul
Flocks to this city; whose capacious bounds
Full space for all affords; nor ever feels
Th' increasing crowd: of flesh depriv'd, and bones,
The bloodless shadows wander. Some frequent
The forum; some th' infernal monarch's court;
Some various arts employ, resembling much
Their former daily actions; numbers groan

In punishments severe. Here Juno came,
Braving the region's horrors, from her throne
Celestial,—so did ire and hatred goad
Her bosom with their stings! Sacred she press'd
The groaning threshold,—instant as she stepp'd,
Fierce Cerberus his triple head uprais'd,
And howl'd with triple throat. The goddess calls
The night-born sisters, fierce, implacable:
Before the close-barr'd adamantine gates
They sit; their tresses twisting round with snakes.
The queen through clouds of midnight gloom they see,
And instant rise. Here dwell the suffering damn'd.
Here Tityus, stretcht o'er nine wide acres, yields
His entrails to be torn. Thou, Tantalus,
Art seen, the stream forbid to taste;—the fruit
Thy lips o'erhanging, flies! Thou, Sisyphus,
Thy stone pursuing downwards; or its weight
Straining aloft, with oft exerted power!
Ixion whirling, too; with swift pursuit,
Thou follow'st, and art follow'd! Belides!
Your husband-cousins who in death dar'd steep,
And ceaseless draw the unavailing streams!
All Juno view'd with unrelenting brow;
But, view'd Ixion sterner far than all:
And when on Sisyphus again she cast
Her eyes, behind Ixion, angry cry'd;—
"What justice this?—of all the brethren he
"Sharp torture suffers! Shall proud Athamas
"A regal dwelling boast,—whose scornful taunts,
"And scornful spouse have still my power contemn'd?"
Then straight her hatred's cause disclos'd. They see
Her journey's object, and revenge's aim.
This her desire, that Cadmus' regal house
Perish'd should sink; and Athamas, fierce urg'd
By madness should some dreadful vengeance claim.
Commands, solicitations, prayers,—at once
The goddesses besiege: and as she speaks,
Angrily mov'd, Tisiphoné replies,—
(Shaking her hoary locks,—the twining snakes
Back from her mouth repelling) hasty thus;—
"A tedious tale we need not; what thou wilt
"Believe accomplish'd. Fly this hateful gloom;—
"Up to the wholesome breeze of heaven repair."
Glad, Juno left the spot;—when near approach'd
Heaven's entrance, there Thaumantian Iris met,
And with her sprinklings purify'd the queen.

Quick now Tisiphoné, the savage fiend,

Seizes her torch, with gory droppings wet;
Flings round her limbs a garment, deeply dy'd
With streaming blood; a twisting snake supplies
A girdle:—thus array'd she sallies forth,
Follow'd by loud lament, by terror, fear,
And quivering-featur'd madness. When she press'd
The threshold, fame declares the pillars shook;
The maple doors, with terror mov'd, grew pale:
Back shrunk the sun! Ino, with trembling dread
Beheld these wonders;—Athamas beheld;
And both prepar'd the haunted place to fly.
Escape the fury hinders: fierce she stands,
Blocking the entrance: wide her arms she spreads,
With viperous twistings bound; and threatening shakes
Her tresses: loud the serpents noise, disturb'd;
Sprawl o'er her shoulders some; some, lower fall'n,
Twine hissing round her breasts, with brandish'd tongue,
Black poison vomiting. With furious gripe,
Two from her locks she tore;—her deadly hand
Hurl'd them straight on; the breasts of Athamas,
And Ino, hungry, with their fangs they seiz'd;
Fierce pains infixing, but external wounds
Their limbs betray'd not: mental was the blow,
So direly struck. Venoms most mortal, too,
From Tartarus she bore:—the foam high-churn'd
From jaws of Cerberus; the poisonous juice
Of Hydra; urgent wish for roaming wide;
Oblivion mental-blinded; wicked deeds;
Weeping; and furious fierceness, slaughter fond.
On these commingled, fresh-drawn gore she pour'd,
And warm'd them bubbling in a brazen vase;
Stirr'd by a sprouting hemlock. Trembling, they
Shudder, while in their breasts the poison fierce
She pours: both bosoms feel it deep instill'd;—
Their inmost vitals feel it. Then her torch,
Whirl'd flaming round and round, in triumph glares,
Fires from the circling gathering. Powerful thus;
Victorious in her aims, and deeds desir'd,
To mighty Pluto's shadowy realm she speeds;
And from her loins untwists the girding snakes.

  Mad bounded Athamas amid the hall,
"Ho! friends," exclaiming;—"here spread wide your toils,
"Here, in this thicket, where ev'n now I saw
"With young twin cubs, a lioness!"—and mad,
Pursu'd his consort for a savage beast;
Snatching Learchus, who with playful smile,
Outstretch'd his infant hands to meet him. Torne

Rough from his mother's bosom, round in air
And round, sling-like he whirl'd; then savage dash'd
Upon a rugged rock the tender bones.

  Loud howls the frantic mother; frantic made
By grief, or by the scatter'd poison's power:
And, raving, with dishevell'd tresses spread
Wide o'er her shoulders, flies. Her naked arms
Young Melicertes bear; madly she shrieks;—
"Evoë, Bacchus!"—Loud at Bacchus' name
Revengeful Juno laugh'd, and said;—"Such boon
"Thy foster-son upon his nurse confers!"
A lofty rock the foaming waves o'erhangs,
Whose dashing force deep in its base have scoop'd
A cavern, safely sheltering from the showers:
The adamantine summit high extends,
And o'er the wide main stretches. Swift this height,
Active and strong with madness, Ino gain'd
And fearless, with the infant in her arms,
Sprung from the cliff, and sunk beneath the waves.
White foam'd the surge around her!

               Venus, griev'd,
Such sufferings, undeserv'd, her race should bear,
Thus with bland coaxings Ocean's god address'd:
"Lord of the azure deep, whose high command
"Sways next to heaven's,—a vast demand I ask;—
"But pity my poor offspring, whom thou see'st
"Plung'd in th' Ionian billows;—with their forms
"Thy deities increase. Some influence sure,
"In ocean I should hold, from thence produc'd;
"Sprung from the froth that on the deep main swims:
"Whence Grecian poets name me." Neptune nods,
Assenting to her prayer; and from their limbs
Abstracts the mortal portion; on their forms
Breathes majesty; and with their alter'd mien,
Their names he changes too; Palæmon he,
Now stil'd, his mother as Leucothoë known.

  The princess' anxious comrades trac'd her steps
With care; the last with arduous search they found,
Just on the giddy brink, nor dubious deem'd
Her fate a moment. Cadmus' house they wail;
With beating hands their tresses tear, and robes;
And highly Juno blame, as one unjust:
Too ireful for the hapless sister's fault.
Juno, fierce flaming, these reproaches stung;—
"Ye too," she cry'd, "shall monuments become

"Of the fierce ire ye blame!" Deeds words pursu'd.
The nymph who most her hapless queen held dear,
Exclaim'd;— "deep in the roaring main I'll plunge,
"To join her fate,"—and sprung to take the leap;
But motionless she stood,—fixt to the rock!
Her wounding blows, upon her bosom one
Strives to renew, as wont; her striving arms
Stiffen'd to stone she sees. This tow'rd the waves
Her hands extends; a rocky mass she stands,
In the same waves far stretching. Lifted high,
The locks to rend, the fingers might be seen
Stiffen'd, and rigid with the hair become.
In posture whatsoever caught, each nymph,
In that same posture stands. Thus part are chang'd:
The rest, to birds transform'd, by wings upborne,
Skim o'er the surface of the neighbouring sea.

  Cadmus, the wond'rous change which rais'd his child,
And his young grandson to the rank of gods,
Yet knew not. By his load of grief o'erwhelm'd;
A chain of woes; and supernatural scenes,
So numerous which he sees; the founder quits
His town, suspicious that the city's fate,
And not his own, misfortune on him showers.
Borne o'er the main, his lengthen'd wanderings end,
When with his exil'd consort, safe he gains
Illyria's shores. Opprest with grief and age,
The primal fortunes of their house, with care
They scan, and in their converse all their woes
Again recounting, Cadmus thus exclaims;—
"Was then that serpent, by my javelin pierc'd,
"When driven from Tyre; whose numerous teeth I sow'd,
"Sacred to some divinity?—If he
"Thus, vengeful for the deed, his anger pours,
"May I a serpent stretcht at length become."
He said,—and serpent-like extended lies!
Scales he perceives, upon his harden'd skin;
And sees green spots on his black body form;
Prone on his breast he falls; together twin'd,
His legs commingling stretch, and gradual end
Lessen'd in rounded point; his arms remain
Still, and those arms remaining he extends;
While down his face yet human tears flow fast.
"O, hapless wife! approach," he cries, "approach,
"And touch me now, while ought of me remains;
"Receive my hand, while yet a hand I bear;
"Ere to a serpent wholly turns my form."—
More he prepar'd to utter, but his tongue,

Cleft sudden, to his wishes words refus'd:
And often when his sorrows sad he try'd
To wail anew, he hiss'd!—that sound alone,
Nature permitted. While her naked breast
With blows resounded, loud his wife exclaim'd;—
"Stay,—O, my Cadmus! hapless man, shake off
"This monstrous figure! Cadmus what is this?
"Where are thy feet,—and where thy arms and hands?
"Where are thy features,—thy complexion? Where,
"Whilst I bewail, art thou? Celestial powers!
"Why not this transformation work on me?"
She ended; he advancing, lick'd her face,
And creep'd, as custom'd, to her bosom dear,
And round her wonted neck embracing twin'd.
Now draw their servants nigh, and as they come
With terror start. The crested serpents play,
Smooth on their necks,—now two; and cordial slide,
In spires conjoin'd; then in the darksome shades
Th' adjoining woods afford them, close they hide.
Mankind they fly not, nor deep wounds inflict;
Harmless, their pristine form is ne'er forgot.

  Still, though in alter'd shapes, the pair rejoic'd
Their grandson's fame to hear; whom vanquish'd Ind'
Low bending worshipp'd; Greece adoring prais'd,
In lofty temples. Sole Acrisius stands,
Like Bacchus sprung from Jove's celestial seed,
Opposing; and from Argos' gates propels
The god;—his birth deny'd, against him arms.
Nor Perseus would he own from heaven deriv'd;
Conceiv'd by Danaë, from a golden shower:
Yet soon,—so mighty is the force of truth,—
Acrisius grieves he e'er so rashly brav'd
The god; his grandson driving from his court,
Disown'd. Now one in heaven is glorious plac'd;
The other, laden with the well-known spoil
Of the fierce snaky monster, cleaves the air,
On sounding pinions. High the victor sails
O'er Lybia's desarts, and the gory drops
Fall from the gorgon's head; the Ground receives
The blood, and warms it into writhing snakes.
Hence does the country with the pest still swarm.

  Thence borne by adverse winds, he sweeps along,
Through boundless ether driven; now here, now there,
As watery clouds are swept. From lofty skies,
The earth far distant viewing, round the globe
He skimm'd: three times he saw the Arctic pole

And thrice the warmer Crab. Oft to the west,
Th' adventurous youth was borne; back to the east,
As often. Now the day in darkness sank,
When he, nocturnal flight mistrusting, lights
In Atlas' kingdom 'neath th' Hesperian sky;
A short repose requests, till Phosphor' bright,
Should call Aurora forth;—she ushering in
The chariot of the day. Japetus' son
All men in huge corporeal bulk surpass'd.
He to th' extremest confines of the land,
And o'er the ocean sway'd, whose waves receive
Apollo's panting steeds, and weary'd car.
A thousand bleating flocks; a thousand herds,
Stray'd through the royal pastures. Neighbouring lords
Not near him plough'd their lands. Trees grew, whose leaves
With splendor glittering, threw a golden shade
O'er golden branches, and o'er fruit of gold.
Thus Perseus;—"Friendly host, if glorious birth
"Thee pleases, here one born of Jove behold.
"If deeds of merit more attraction move,
"Mine thy app ause may claim. At present grant
"An hospitable shelter here, and rest."
But Atlas, fearing these oraculous words,—
(Long since by Themis on Parnassus given)
"The time, O king! will come, thy golden tree
"Shall lose its fruit. The glory of the spoil
"A son of Jove shall boast:" and dreading sore;
Around his orchards massy walls he rears;
A dragon huge and fierce the guard maintains.
"Whatever strangers to his realm approach,
Far thence he drives; and thus to Perseus too;—
"Haste, quickly haste from hence, lest soon I prove
"Thy glorious deeds but feign'd,—feign'd as thy birth."
Then force to threats he added,—strove to thrust
The hero forth; who struggling, efforts urg'd
Resisting, while he begg'd with softening words.
Proving in strength inferior (who in strength
Could vie with Atlas?) "Since my fame," he cries,
"Such small desert obtains, a gift accept."
And, back his face averting, holds display'd,
On his left side Medusa's ghastly head.
A mountain now the mighty Atlas stands!
His hair and beard as lofty forests wave;
His arms and hands high hilly summits rear;
O'er-topp'd above, by what was once his head:
His bones are rocks; then, so the gods decree,
Enlarg'd to size immense in every part,
The weight of heaven, and all the stars he bears.

His blustering vassals Æolus had pent,
In ever-during prisons. Phosphor' bright,
Most splendid 'midst the starry host of heaven;
Admonitor of labor, now was risen;
When Perseus bound again on either foot,
His winnowing wings; girt on his crooked sword;
And cleft the air, on waving pinions borne.
O'er numerous nations, far beneath him spread,
He sail'd, till Ethiopia's realms he saw;
Where Cepheus rul'd. There Ammon, power unjust,
Andromeda had sentenc'd,—guiltless maid,
To what her mother's boastful tongue deserv'd.
Her soon as Perseus spy'd, fast by the arms
Chain'd to the rugged rock;—where but her locks
Wav'd lightly to the breeze; and but her eyes
Trickled a tepid stream; she might be deem'd
A sculptur'd marble: him the unknown sight
Astonish'd, dazzled, and enflam'd with love.
His senses in the beauteous view sole wrapt,
Scarce he remembers on his wings to wave:—
Alights, exclaiming;—"O, whom chains like these
"Should never bind, nor other chains than such,
"As lovers intertwist! declare thy name;
"Thy country tell; and why thou bear'st those bonds."
Silent awhile the virgin stood; abash'd,
Converse with man to hold: her blushing face,
Her hands, if free, had long before conceal'd.
Quick starting tears, 'twas all she could, her eyes
Veil'd swimming: then her name and country told;
And all the conscious pride her mother's charms
Inspir'd, in full acknowledg'd; lest for crimes
Her own, just suffering, Perseus might conceive.
All yet untold, when loud the billows roar'd;
Upheav'd the monster's bulk: far 'bove the waves
He stood uprear'd, and then right onward plung'd;
His ample bosom covering half the main.

   Loud shrieks the virgin! Sad her father comes;
And sad her raving mother, wretched both,
The mother most deserv'dly. Help in vain
From them she seeks; with tears, and bosoms torn,
Her fetter'd limbs they clasp, they can no more.
Then Perseus thus;—"for tears and loud laments,
"Long may the time be: but effective aid
"To give, the time is short. Suppose the nymph
"I ask;—I, Perseus! sprung from mighty Jove,
"By her whose prison in a golden shower

"Fecundative, he enter'd. Perseus, who
"The Gorgon snaky-hair'd o'ercame; who bold
"On waving pinions winnows through the air.
"Him for a son in preference should ye chuse,
"Arduous he'll strive to these high claims to add,
"If heaven permits, some merits more his own.
"Agree she s mine, if by my arm preserv'd."
The parents promise;—(who in such a case
Would waver) beg his help; and promise, more,
That all their kingdom shall her dower become.
Lo! as a vessel's sharpen'd prow quick cleaves
The waves, by strenuous sweating arms impell'd,
The monster comes! his mighty bosom wide
The waters sideway breasting; distant now,
Not more than what the Balearic sling
Could with the bullet gain, when high in air,
The sod repelling, upward springs the youth.
Soon as the main reflected Perseus' form,
The ocean-savage rag'd: as Jove's swift bird
When in the open fields a snake he spies
Basking, his ivid back to Phœbus' rays
Expos'd, behind attacks him; plunges deep,
His hungry talons in his scaly neck,
To curb the twisting of his sanguine teeth.
With rapid flight, thus Perseus shooting cleaves
The empty air; lights on the monster's back;
Burying his weapon to the crooked hilt,
Full in the shoulder of the raging beast.
Mad with the deepen'd wound, now rears aloft
The savage high in air; now plunges low,
Beneath the waters; now he furious turns,
As turns the boar ferocious, when the crowd
Of barking dogs beset him fiercely round.
With rapid waft the venturous hero shuns
His greedy jaws: now on his back, thick-arm'd
With shells, he strikes where opening space he sees;
Now on his sides; now where his tapering tail
In fish-like form is finish'd, bites the steel.
High spouts the wounded monster from his mouth;
The waves with gore deep purpling: drench'd, the wings
Droop nagging; and no longer Perseus dares
To trust their dripping aid. A rock he spies
Whose summit o'er the peaceful waters rose,
But deep was hid when tempests mov'd the main.
Supported here, his left hand firmly grasps
The craggy edge; while through his sides, and through,
The dying savage feels the weapon drove.

Loud shouts and plaudits fill the shore, the noise
Resounding echoes to the heavenly thrones.
Cassiopé and Cepheus joyful greet
Their son, and grateful own him chief support,
And saviour. From her rugged fetters freed,
The virgin walks; the cause, the great reward
Of all his toil. His victor hands he laves
In the pure stream: then with soft leaves defends
A spot, to rest the serpent-bearing head,
Lest the bare sand should harm it. Twigs marine
He likewise strews, and rests Medusa there.
The fresh green twigs as though with life endow'd,
Felt the dire Gorgon's power; their spongy pith
Hard to the touch became, the stiffness spread
Through every twig and leaf. The Nereïd nymphs
More branches bring, and try the wonderous change
On all, and joy to see the change succeed:
Spreading the transformation from the seeds,
With them throughout the waves. This nature still
Retains the coral: hardness still assumes
From contact with the air; beneath the waves
A bending twig; an harden'd stone above.

Three turfy altars to three heavenly gods
He builds: to Hermes sacred stands the left;
The right to warlike Pallas; in the midst
The mighty Jove's is rear'd: (To Pallas bleeds
An heifer: to the plume-heel'd god a calf:
Almighty Jove accepts a lordly bull)
Then claims Andromeda, the rich reward,
without a dower, of all his valorous toil.

Now Love and Hymen wave their torches high,
Precursive of their joys: each hearth is heap'd
With odorous incense: every roof is hung
With flowery garlands: pipes, and harps, and lyres,
And songs which indicate their festive souls,
Resound aloud. Each portal open thrown,
Display'd appears the golden palace wide.
By every lord of Cepheus' court, array'd
In splendid pomp, the nuptial feast is grac'd.
The banquet ended, while the generous gift
Of Bacchus circles; and each soul dilates,
Perseus, the modes and customs of the land
Curious enquires. Lyncides full relates
The habits, laws, and manners of the clime.
His information ended;—"now,"—he cry'd,—
"Relate, O Perseus! boldest of mankind,—

"By what fierce courage, and what skilful arts,"
"The snaky locks in thy possession came."
Then Perseus tells, how lies a lonely vale
Beneath cold Atlas; every side strong fenc'd
By lofty hills, whose only pass is held,
By Phorcus' twin-born daughters. Mutual they
One eye possess'd, in turns by either us'd.
His hand deceiving seiz'd it, as it pass'd
'Twixt them alternate; dexterous was the wile.
Through devious paths, and deep-sunk ways he went;
And craggy woods, dark-frowning, till he reach'd
The Gorgon's dwelling: passing then the fields,
And beaten roads, there forms of men he saw,
And shapes of savage beasts; but all to stone
By dire Medusa's petrifying face
Transform'd. He then the horrid countenance mark'd,
Bright from the brazen targe his left arm bore,
Reflected. While deep slumber safe weigh'd down,
The Gorgon and her serpents, he divorc'd
Her shoulders from her head. He adds how sprung,
Chrysaör, and wing'd Pegasus the swift,
From the prolific Gorgon's streaming gore.
Relates the perils of his lengthen'd flight;
What seas, what kingdoms from the lofty sky,
Beneath him he had view'd; what sparkling stars
His waving wings had brush'd;—thus ceas'd his tale:
All more desiring. Then uprose a peer,—
And why Medusa, of the sisters sole
The serpent-twisted tresses wore, enquir'd.
The youth:—"The story that you ask, full well
"Attention claims;—I what you seek recite.
"For match ess beauty fam'd, with envying hope
"Her, crowds of suitors follow'd: nought surpass'd
"'Mongst all her beauties, her bright lovely hair:
"Those who had seen her thus, have this averr'd.
"But in Minerva's temple Ocean's god
"The maid defil'd. The virgin goddess shock'd,
"Her eyes averted, and her forehead chaste
"Veil'd with the Ægis. Then with vengeful power
"Chang'd the Gorgonian locks to writhing snakes.
"The snakes, thus form'd, fixt on her shield she bears;
"The horrid sight her trembling foes appals."

Attack of Phineus and his friends on Perseus. Defeat of the former, and their change to statues. Atchievements of Perseus in Argos, and Seriphus. Minerva's visit to the Muses. Fate of Pyreneus. Song of the Pierides. Song of the Muses. Rape of Proserpine. Change of Cyané, to a fountain. Search of Ceres. Transformation of a boy to an eft. Of Ascalaphus to an owl. Change of the companions of Proserpine to Sirens. Story of Arethusa. Journey of Triptolemus. Transformation of Lyncus to a lynx. The Pierides transformed to magpies.

THE FIFTH BOOK OF THE METAMORPHOSES OF OVID

These wonders, while the son of Danaë tells,
Circled around by Cepheus' noble troop;
Sudden th' imperial hall with tumults loud
Resounds. Not clamor such as oft we hear,
The bridal feasts, in songs of joy attend:
But what stern war announces. Much the change,
(The peaceful feast to instant riot turn'd)
Seem'd like the placid main, when the fierce rage
Of sudden tempests lash its surges high.

First Phineus stepp'd, the leader of the crowd;
Soul of the riot; and his ashen spear,
Arm'd with a brazen point, he brandish'd high;—
"Lo, here!" he shouts, "lo, here I vengeful come
"On him who claims my spouse! Not thy swift wings;
"Nor cheating Jove, chang'd to a golden shower,
"Shall save thee from my arm,"—and pois'd to fling,
The dart was held, but Cepheus loud exclaim'd,—
"Brother! what dost thou? what dire madness sways
"To wicked acts thy soul? Is this the meed
"His gallant deeds deserve? Is this the dower,
"We for the valued life he sav'd bestow?
"List but to truth,—not Perseus of thy wife
"Bereft thee, but the angry Nereïd nymphs,—
"The horned Ammon,—and the monster huge!
"Prepar'd to glut his hunger with my child.
"Then was thy spouse snatch'd from thee, when remain'd
"Of help no hope; to all she lost appear'd.
"Thy savage heart perhaps had ev'n rejoic'd
"To see her perish, that our greater grief
"Might lighten part of thine. Couldst thou her see
"Fast chain'd before thee? uncle! spouse betroth'd!
"And yet no aid afford! And storm'st thou thus?
"She to another now her safety owes;
"And would'st thou snatch the prize? So high if seems
"To thee her precious value, thy bold arm
"Should on the rock where chain'd she lay, have sought

"And have ceserv'd her. Now permit that he
"Who soug⌐t her there; through whom my failing age
"Is not now childless, grant that he enjoy
"Peaceful, what through his merits he no less,
"Than our firm compact claims: not him to thee,
"But him to certain loss I preference gave."

  Nought Phineus answer'd, but his furious eyes
Now Perseus, now the king alternate view;
Doubtful or this to pierce, or that: his pause
Was short; his powerful arm, by fury nerv'd,
At Perseus hurl'd the quivering spear,—in vain!
Fixt in the couch it stood. Quick bounded up
Th' indignant youth, and deep in Phineus' breast,
Had plung'd the point returning, but he shrunk
Behind an altar; which, O shame! preserv'd
The impious villain. Yet not harmless sped
The weapon;—full in Rhætus' front it stuck;
Who lifeless dropp'd; broke in the bone the steel;
He spurn'd, and sprinkled all the feast with gore.
Then rag'd with ire ungovern'd all the crowd,
And hurl'd in showers their weapons; some fierce cry'd,
Cepheus, no less than Perseus, death deserv'd.
But Cepheus left the hall, adjuring loud,
The hospitable gods; justice; and faith;
That he was guiltless of the sanguine fray.

  Minerva comes; her sheltering Ægis shields
Her brother's body; in his breast she breathes
Redoubled valor. Atys, Indian bred,
Whom fair Limnaté, Ganges' daughter, bore,
'Tis told, amid the waters' crystal caves,
Scarce sixteen years had seen. His beauteous form,
In gorgeous dress more beauteous still appear'd.
A purple garment fring'd around with gold,
Enwrapp'd him; round his neck were golden beads;
And pins and combs of gold his lovely locks,
With myrrh sweet-smelling, held. Well skill'd the youth
To hurl the javelin to its distant mark;
But more to bend the bow. Him Perseus smote,
The flexile bow just bending, with a brand
Snatch'd flaming from the altar; crush'd, his face
A horrid mass of fractur'd bones appears.
His beauteous features Lycabas beheld
In blood convuls'd: his dearest comrade he,
And one who proud his ardent love display'd.
Griev'd to behold the last expiring breath,
Of Atys parting from the furious wound,

He seiz'd the bow the youth had bent, and cry'd;—
"The battle try with me!—not long thy boast
"Of conquest o'er a boy; a conquest more
"By hate than fame attended." Railing thus,
The piercing weapon darted from the string.

Now Phineus, fearful hand to hand to meet
The foe, his javelin hurl'd, the point ill-aim'd
On Idas glanc'd, who vainly kept aloof
With neutral weapon. Phineus, stern he view'd,
"With threatening frown, exclaiming;—"though no share
"In this mad broil I took, now, Phineus, feel
"The power of him whom thou hast forc'd a foe;
"And take reciprocally wound for wound."
Then from his side the weapon tore to hurl;
But fast the life-stream gush'd, he instant fell.
Here, by the sword of Clymenus was slain,
Odites, noblest lord in Cepheus' court;
Protenor fell by Hypseus; Hypseus sunk
Beneath Lyncides' arm. Amid the throng
Was old Emathion too, friend to the just,
And fearer of the gods; though ancient years
Forbade his wielding arms, what aid his words
Could give, he spar'd not: curs'd the impious war,
In loud upbraidings. As with trembling arms,
He grasp'd the altar, Chromis' gory sword
His neck divided; on the altar dropp'd
The head; and there the trembling, dying tongue,
Faint imprecations utter'd; 'midst the flames
He breath'd his spirit forth. By Phineus' hand,
Broteas and Ammon fell: the brother-twins
Unconquer'd in the fight, the cæstus shower'd;
Could but the cæstus make the falchion yield:
But Perseus felt it not,—its point hung fixt
Amidst his garments' folds. On him he turn'd,
The falchion, glutted with Medusa's gore,
And plung'd it in his breast. Dying, he looks
Around, with eyes rolling in endless night,
For Atys, and upon him drops: then pleas'd,
Thus join'd in death, he seeks the shades below.
Methion's son, Syenian Phorbas, now
And fierce Amphimedon, in Lybia born,
Rush in the fight to mingle; both fall prone,
The slippery earth wide spread with smoking blood.
The sword attacks them rising; in his throat
Phorbas receives it, and the other's side.
But Erythis, of Actor born, whd rear'd
An axe tremendous, not the waving sword

Of Perseus meets: a cup of massive bulk,
With both his hands high-heaving, fierce he hurls
Full on his foe: he vomits gory floods;
Falls back, and strikes with dying head the earth.
Then Polydæmon falls, sprung from the blood
Of queen Semiramis; Lycetes brave,
The son of Spercheus; Abaris, who dwelt
On frozen Caucasus; and Helicen
With unshorn tresses; Phlegias; Clitus too;
Those with the rest beneath his weapon fall;
And on the rising heaps of dead he stands.
And fell Ampycus; Ceres' sacred priest,
His temples with a snow-white fillet bound.
Thou, O Japetides! whose string to sound
Such discord knew not; but whose harp still tun'd,
The works of peace, in concord with thy voice;
Wast bidden here to celebrate the feast:
And cheer the nuptial banquet with thy song!
Him, when at distance Pettalus beheld,
Handling his peaceful instrument, he cry'd
In mocking laughter;—"go, and end thy song,
"Amid the Stygian ghosts,"—and instant plung'd
Through his left temple, his too deadly sword.
Sinking, his dying fingers caught the strings,
And, chance-directed, gave a mournful sound.
Not long the fierce Lycormas saw his fall
Without revenge: a massy bar of oak
From the right gate he tore, and on the bones
Behind the neck, the furious blow was aim'd:
Prone on the earth, like a crush'd ox he fell.
Pelates of Cinypheus, strove to rend
A like strong fastening from th' opposing door;
The dart of Corythus his tugging hand
Transfix'd, and nail'd him to the wood confin'd:
Here Abas, with his spear, deep pierc'd his side:
Nor dying fell he;—by the hand retain'd,
Firm to the post he hung. Melaneus fell.
The arms of Perseus aiding; Dorilas,
The wealthiest lord in Nasamonia's land,
Fell too beside him: rich was he in fields;
In wide extent no lands with his could vie;
Nor equal his in hoarded heaps of grain.
Obliquely in his groin, the missive spear
Stuck deep,—a mortal spot: his Bactrian foe
His rolling eyes beheld, and dying breath
In sobs convulsive flitting, and exclaim'd;—
"This spot thou pressest, now of all thy lands,
"Possess,"—and turning left the lifeless corse.

Avenging Perseus hurls at him the spear,
Torn from the smoking wound; the point, receiv'd
Full in the nostrils, pierces through the neck:
Before, behind, expos'd the weapon stands.

  Now fortune aids his blows, the brother pair,
Clanis, and Clytius fall, by different wounds.
Hurl'd by his nervous arm, the ashen spear
Transfix'd the thighs of Clytius: Clanis dy'd
Biting the steel that pierc'd his mouth. Now fell
Mendesian Celadon; and Astreus borne
By Hebrew mother, to a doubtful sire.
Now dy'd Ethion, once deep skill'd to see
The future fates; now by his skill deceiv'd.
Thoactes, who the monarch's armor bore;
And base Agyrtes, murderer of his sire.
Crowds though he conquers, thickening crowds remain;
For all united wage on him the war.
In every quarter fight the press, conspir'd
To aid a cause to worth and faith oppos'd.
The sire, with useless piety,—the queen,
And new-made bride, the hero's party take;
And fill the hall with screams. The clang of arms,
And groans of dying men their screamings drown.
The houshold deities, polluted once,
The fierce Bellona bathes with gore again;
With double fury lighting up the war.

  Now Phineus, followed by a furious throng
Surrounds him single; thicker fly their darts
Than wintry hail, on every side; his sight
They cloud, and deafening, whiz his ears around.
By crowds opprest, retreating, Perseus leans
His shoulders 'gainst a massive pillar's height;
And, safe behind, dares all the furious fight.
Chaonian Molpeus rushes on his left;
Ethemon, Nabathæan, on his right:
Thus a fierce tiger, urg'd by famine, hears
Combin'd the lowings of two different herds,
Far distant in the vale; in doubt he stands,
On this, or that to rush; and furious burns
On both at once to thunder. Perseus so,
To left and right inclin'd at once to bear,
Plerc'd first the thigh of Molpeus,—straight he fled
Unfollow'd; for Ethemon fiercely press'd.
He, furious aiming at the hero's neck,
With ill-directed strength, his weapon broke
Against a column;—back the shiver'd point

Sprung, and his throat transfix'd: slight was the wound;
To doom to death unable. Perseus plung'd
His mortal Falchion, as the trembling wretch
His helpless arms extended, in his breast.
But now his valor Perseus found oppress'd
By crowds unequal, and aloud exclaim'd;—
"Since thus you force me, from my very foe
"More aid I'll ask;—my friends avert your eyes!"
Then shew'd the Gorgon's head. "Go, elsewhere seek,"
Said Thescelus,—"for those such sights may move:"—
The deadly javelin poising in his hand,
In act to throw, a marble form he stands,
In the same posture. Near him Ampyx rear'd,
Against the brave Lyncides' breast his sword;
His uprais'd hand was harden'd; here, or there,
To wave unable. Nileus now display'd
Seven argent streams upon a shield of gold;
False boasting offspring from the seven-mouth'd Nile;
And cry'd;—"Lo! Perseus, whence my race deriv'd;
"Down to the silent shades this solace bear
"By such a hand to die." The final words
Were lost; his sounding voice abrupt was stay'd;
His open'd mouth still seem'd the words to form,
Incapable to utter. Eryx storm'd
At these, exclaiming;—"not the Gorgon's hairs
"Freeze ye, but your own trembling, dastard souls:
"Rush forth with me, and on the earth lay low,
"The youth who battles thus with magic arms."
Fierce had he rush'd, but firmly fixt his feet
Held him to earth, a rigid, fasten'd stone;
A statue arm'd. These well their fate deserv'd,
But one, Aconteus, while in aid he fought
Of Perseus, sudden stood to stone congeal'd;
As star'd the Gorgon luckless in his face.
Him saw Astyages, but thought he liv'd;
And fierce attack'd him with a mighty sword.
Shrill tinkling sounds the blow: astonish'd stands
Astyages;—astonish'd seems the stone;
For while he stares, he too to marble turns.
Long were the tale, of each plebeïan death
To tell; two hundred still unhurt remain;
By Gorgon's head two hundred stiffen'd stand:
When Phineus seems the strife unjust to mourn.
But what to act remains? Around him crowd,
The forms of numerous friends: his friends he knows,
Their aid intreats, and calls on each by name:
Still doubting, seizes those his grasp can reach
And finds them stone! Averse he turns his eyes;

Raises his conscious arms and hands oblique,
And suppliant begs;—"go Perseus,—conqueror, go!
"Remove that dreadful monster,—bear away
"That stone-creating visage, Gorgon's head!
"Whate'er it be, I pray thee bear it hence.
"Nor hate, nor lust of empire, rais'd our arms
"Against thee;—for my wife alone we warr'd.
"Thy cause, by merit best; mine, but by time.
"Bravest of men, me much it grieves I e'er,
"Thy claim oppos'd: existence only give,
"All else be thine." To him, as thus he begg'd,
Fearing his eyes, to whom he suppliant spoke
To turn;—"thou dastard, Phineus!" Perseus cry'd,—
"What I can grant, I will; and what I grant
"To souls like thine a mighty boon must seem.
"Dispel thy terror; rest from steel secure.
"Yet must a during monument remain,
"Still in the dwelling of my spouse's sire,
"Conspicuous. So my bride may daily see
"Her imag'd husband." Speaking thus, he held
The Gorgon's head, where pallid, Phineus turn'd;
So turning stiffen'd stood the neck; so turn'd
Appear'd th' inverted eyes; the humid balls
To stone concreted. Still the timid look,
And suppliant face, and tame-petitioning arms,
And guilty awe-struck look, in stone remain'd.

  Now victor, Abantiades re-seeks
His soil paternal, with his well-earn'd bride:
And in his undeserving grandsire's aid,
Avenging war on Prœtus he declares.
Prœtus then all Acrisius' cities held;
From each possession forc'd, his brother fled.
But arms, and battled towns, like ill-possess'd,
The head snake-curl'd, oblig'd at once to stoop.
Yet not the youth's bold valor, amply prov'd,
By all his brave atchievements; nor his toils
Thee, Polydectes, mov'd; who rul'd the isle,
The paltry isle, Seriphus; stubborn still,
Inexorable hatred thou maintain'st:
Endless against him burns thy rage unjust.
Nay, from his true deserts, thou would'st detract;
And swear'st Medusa's death a fiction form'd.
Then Perseus;—"thus if true I speak, or no,
"Experience. Close, my friends, your eyes!"—as forth,
He held the Gorgon;—bloodless stood the face
Of Polydectes, turn'd a marble form.

Thus far, Minerva aided side by side,
Her brother golden-born; then swiftly flew,
Wrapt in a cloud opaque; and distant left
Seriphus. On she flies, to right she leaves
Cythnos, and Gyaros; and cross the main
The shortest route she hastens; speeds to Thebes,
And seeks the Heliconian nymphs, whose mount
Alighting feels her first: the learned nine,
Thus she bespeaks;—"fame tells, a new-made spring,
"Burst from a blow the swift-wing'd horse's hoof
"Inflicted; lo! the cause I hither come.
"That steed I saw spring from his mother's blood:
"Fain would I this new prodigy behold."
Urania gave reply. "O, maid divine!
"What cause soe'er has with thy presence grac'd.
"Our dwelling, proves to us a grateful boon.
"Fame speaks not false. Our fountain surely sprung
"Sole from Pegasus." Speaking thus, she leads
The virgin goddess to the sacred streams:
Who long the spring admir'd;—the spring produc'd
From the hoof's blow:—around surveying views
The groves of ancient trees, the grots, the plants
Of ever-vary'd tint; and happy calls
The learned nymphs, who such a spot possess'd.
Then thus a sister;—"O, divinest maid!
"Our choir to join most worthy, did not aims
"Of loftier import tempt thy warlike soul,
"Right hast thou spoke; our habitation well,
"And well our arts thy highest praises claim.
"Blest were our lot, if still from danger free:
"But nought a villain's daring power restrains,
"And terror soon our virgin minds appals.
"Ev'n now the dread Pyreneus to my eyes
"Stands present: to its wonted calm not yet
"Restor'd my mind. With furious Thracian bands
"Daulis he conquer'd, and the Phocian fields;
"And held the sway unjust. Parnassus' fane
"We sought, th' usurper there beheld us pass,
"And feigning reverence for our power divine
"Worshipp'd, and then address'd us, whom he knew.
"Here, O! ye Muses, rest, nor dubious stand
"But straight beneath my sheltering roof avoid
"The cloudy heaven, and rain (for fast it shower'd)
"Oft mighty deities have enter'd roofs
"Less pompous.—By his invitation urg'd,
"And by the tempest, we accede and step
"Within the hall. The pelting showers now ceas'd,
"Auster by Boreas vanquish'd; fled the clouds

"Black lowering, and the face of heaven left clear:
"Anxious we wish to go: Pyreneus fast
"His dwelling closes, and rough force prepares:
"Wings we assume, and from his force escape.
"He, standing on the loftiest turret's top,
"Like us his flight about to wing, exclaims—
"A path you lead, that path will I pursue.
"Then madly from the tower's most lofty wall,
"Dash'd on his face he fell, and dying strew'd
"His shatter'd bones upon the blood-stain'd ground."

  As spoke the muse thus, loud and strong was heard,
Of fluttering pinions in the air the sound;
And hailing voices from high branches came.
Jove's daughter then around enquiring look'd
(The sounds she hears, so like the human voice,
From human voice she deems them) birds the sound
Emitted: magpies were they;—magpies nine:
Their doom lamenting, on the boughs they sate,
Aping in voice their neighbours all around.
Then to the wondering goddess, thus the muse
Explain'd: "These vanquish'd in the arduous strife
"Of song, to us submitting, swell the crowd
"Of feather'd fliers. In Pellenian lands
"Most rich was Pierus their sire; to him
"Evippé of Pæonia bore the nymphs;
"Nine times invoking great Lucina's aid.
"Vain of their number, proud the sister-crew,
"In folly journey'd through Thessalia's towns,
"And through the towns of Greece; when here arriv'd
"Thus to the test of power their words provoke:—
"At length desist to cheat the senseless crowd
"With harmony pretended, Thespian maids!
"With us contend, if faith your talents give
"For such a trial. Ye in voice and skill
"Surpass us not,—our numbers are the same.
"If vanquish'd, yield the Medusæan fount,
"And Hyantean Aganippé,—we
"If conquer'd, all Emanthæa's regions cede,
"Far as Pæonia's snows. The nymphs around
"The contest shall decide. Deep shame we felt
"Thus to contend, but deeper shame appear'd
"To yield without contention to their boast.
"The nymphs elected to adjudge the prize
"Swear by the floods; and on the living rock
"Seated, await to hear the rival songs.

  "Then one, impatient who should first commence,

"Or we, or they, arises;—sings the war
"Of gods and giants; to the rebels gives
"False pra ses; and the high celestials' power
"Much uncer-rating, tells how Typhon, rais'd.
"From earth's most deep recesses, struck with fear
"All heaven: each god betook him straight to flight
"Far distant, till th' Egyptian land receiv'd
"Each weary'd foot, where Nile's dissever'd stream
"Pours in seven mouths. How earth-born Typhon here,
"They tell, pursu'd them; and each god, conceal'd
"In feign'd resemblance, cheated there his power.
"Jove, (so she sung) a leading ram became;
"(Whence still the Lybians form their Ammon horn'd)
"The crow Apollo hid: a goat the son
"Of Semelé became: Diana skulk'd
"In shape a cat: a snow-white cow conceal'd
"The form of Juno: Venus seem'd a fish:
"And 'neath an Ibis Hermes safely crouch'd.

  "Thus far she mov'd her vocal lips; thus far
"Her lyre her voice attended: then they call
"For our Aönian song. But that to hear,
"Perchance your leisure suits not; pressing deeds
"Unlike our songs must more your time demand."
Pallas replies;—"be hesitation far,
"And all your song from first commence relate."
So saying, in the forest's pleasing shade
She rested; while the Muse proceeding, spoke.

  "To one the sole contending task we give,
"Calliopé;—she rises, neatly bound,
"Her flowirg tresses with an ivy wreath.
"With dexterous thumb the trembling strings she tries,
"Then to their quivering sounds this song subjoins.
"Ceres at first with crooked plough upturn'd
"The glebe; she first mild fruits and milder corn
"Gave to the earth; and rules to tend them gave:
"All gifts from her proceed. To her the song
"I raise. Would that my best exerted power,
"A song to suit thy least deserts could form,
"O, goddess! worthy of our loftiest praise.

  "The vast Sicilian isle, with pressure huge
"Thrown o'er them, deep the limbs gigantic weighs
"Of huge Typhœus, who the heavenly throne
"Had dar'd to hope for: struggling oft he tries,
"His efforts, daily bent to lift his load:
"But hard Pelorus on his right hand lies,

"Ausonia facing; while Pachyné rests
"Heavy to left: wide o'er his giant thighs
"Spreads Lilybœum: Etna presses down
"His head; beneath whose crater, laid supine,
"From his hot mouth he ashes sends, and flames.
"Thus with his body labouring to remove
"The ponderous load of earth;—whole towns o'erwhelm;
"And lofty hills o'erturn; trembles the ground;
"And Hell's dread monarch fears a chasm should gape:
"And through the opening wide his realm display:
"The trembling ghosts with light un'custom'd scar'd.
"The shock to meet expecting, starts the king
"Quick from his cloudy throne; and in his car
"Borne by his sable steeds, with care surveys
"Sicilia's deep foundations; wide around
"Exploring all; then with his toils content,
"No ruin'd part detected, flings aside
"Each apprehension. Strolling now at ease,
"Him Venus from the Erycinian hill
"Espy'd; and to her feather'd son, who lay
"Clasp'd in her arms, exclaim'd;—O, Cupid! son!
"My sole assistant! sole defence and aid!
"Seize now that weapon which o'er all has sway,
"That piercing dart,—and deep within the breast
"Of the dark god whose lot was given to rule
"The nether regions of the triple realm,
"Bury it. All the gods thy might confess;
"Ev'n Jove himself. The ocean powers allow
"Thy rule, and he whom Ocean's powers obey.
"Why then should Tartarus alone evade
"Thy thrall? Why not my empire and thine own
"With that complete? Of all the world's extent
"A third is stak'd. Nay more, our utmost power,
"Heaven our own seat contemns;—thy potent sway,
"And mine alike impair'd. Behold'st thou not
"Minerva, with the quiver-bearing maid
"Deserting me? Thus will the blooming child
"Of Ceres, if we grant it, still remain
"Inviolate a virgin;—thither tend
"Her anxious hopes. But thou, if dear thou hold'st
"Our mutual realm, the virgin goddess link
"In union with her uncle.—Venus spoke:
"His quiver he unlooses; from the heap
"Of darts, by her directed, one selects,
"Than which none bore a keener point; than which,
"None flew more certain,—trusty to the string.
"Bends to his knee the yielding horn, then sends
"Through Pluto's heart the bearded arrow sure.

"Not far from Enna's walls, a lake expands
"Profound in watery stores, Pergusa nam'd:
"Not ev'n Caïsters' murmuring stream e'er heard
"The songster-swans more frequent. Woods o'ertop
"The waters, rising round on every side;
"And veil from Phœbus' rays the surface cool.
"A shade the branches form; the moist earth round,
"Produces purple flowers: perpetual spring
"Here reigns. While straying sportive in this grove
"Here Proserpine the violet cropp'd, and here
"The lily fair; with childish ardor warm'd
"Her bosom filling, and her basket high:
"Proud to surpass her comrades all around
"In skilful culling, she herself was seen;
"Was chosen, and by Dis was snatch'd away.
"Love urg'd him to the deed. Th' affrighted maid,
"Loud on her mother, and her comrades call'd;
"But chief her mother, with lamenting shrieks.
"Then as her robe she rent, the well-cull'd flowers
"Slipp'd through the loosen'd folds: e'en this (so great
"Her girlish innocence) her tears increas'd.
"Swiftly the robber speeds his car along
"Urging his steeds' exertions each by name;
"'Bove their high manes and necks the rusty reins
"Rattling, as o'er the wide Palician lake,
"Where the cleft earth with sulphur boils, he whirls:
"And where the Bacchiads, from the double sea
"Of Corinth wandering, rais'd their lofty walls;
"'Twixt two unequal havens. Midst, the stream,
"Pisæan Arethusa, and the lake
"Of Cyané are seen, close round embrac'd
"By narrowing horns. This Cyané was once,
"Of all Sicilia's nymphs, the fairest deem'd;
"Who gave the lake her name. She to the waist
"Uprais'd, amidst the waters stood, and knew
"The god, and,—here thy speed must stay,—exclaim'd;
"Nor e'er of Ceres hope the son-in-law
"'Gainst her consent to be: beseechings bland,
"Not rugged rape, thy purpos'd hope might gain.
"If lofty things with low I durst compare,
"Anapis lov'd me; but the nuptial couch,
"I press'd, entreated,—not as thus in dread.
"She said;—her arms extended wide, and stopp'd
"His course. The angry son of Saturn flames
"Swelling with rage; exhorts his furious steeds;
"Throws with a forceful arm, and buries deep
"His regal sceptre in the lowest gulph:
"Wide gapes the stricken earth; an opening gives

"To hell, and headlong down, the car descends.

 Now equal Cyané the goddess mourns,
"So forc'd; and her own sacred stream despis'd;
"A cureless wound her silent breast contains;
"And all in tears she wastes: lost in those waves,
"Where lately sovereign goddess she had rul'd.
"Soft grow her limbs, and flexile seem her bones;
"Her nails their hardness lose. The tenderest parts.
"Melt into water long before the rest:
"Her tresses green; her fingers, legs, and feet.
"Quickly this change the smaller limbs perceive,
"To cooling rills transform'd. Next after these,
"Her back, her shoulders, breasts, and sides dissolve,
"And vanish all in streams. A limpid flood
"Now fills the veins that once in purple flow'd;
"Nought of the nymph to fill the grasp remains.

 "Meantime the trembling mother through the earth,
"And o'er the main, the goddess vainly sought.
"Aurora rising, with her locks of gold;
"Nor Hesper sinking, saw her labors cease.
"With either hand at Etna's flaming mouth,
"A torch she lighted, restless these she bore
"In dewy darkness. Then renew'd again
"Her labor, till fair day made blunt the stars;
"From Sol's first rising till his evening fall.
"Weary'd at length, and parch'd with thirst,—no stream
"Her lips to moisten nigh, by chance she spy'd
"A straw-thatch'd cot, and knock'd the humble door.
"An ancient dame thence stepp'd,—the goddess saw,
"And brought her, (who for water simply crav'd)
"A pleasing draught where roasted grain had boil'd.
"Swallowing the gift presented, rudely came
"A brazen-fronted boy, and facing stood:
"Then laughing mock'd to see her greedy drink.
"Angry grew Ceres, all the offer'd draught,
"Yet unconsum'd, she drench'd him as he jeer'd,
"With barley mixt with liquid: straight his face
"The spots imbib'd; and what but now as arms
"He bore, as legs he carries; to his limbs
"Thus chang'd, a tail is added; shrunk in size,
"Small is his power to harm; shorter he seems
"Than the small lizard. Swift away he fled
"(As, wondering, weeping, try'd the dame to clasp
"His changing form) and gain'd a sheltering hole.
"Well suits his star-like skin the name he bears.

"Long were the tale to tell, what tracts of land
"What tracts of sea, the wandering goddess pass'd.
"Earth now no spot unsearch'd affording, back
"To Sicily she turns; with close research
"Each part exploring, till at length she comes
"To Cyané; who all the tale had told
"If still unchang'd: much as she wish'd to speak
"Nor lips, nor tongue can aid her; nought remains
"Speech to afford. Yet plain a sign she gives,
"The zone of Proserpine upon her waves
"Light floating; in the sacred stream it fell;—
"Dropt as she pass'd the place. Well Ceres knew
"The sight, and then—as then her loss first known,
"Tore her dishevell'd tresses, beat her breast
"With blows on blows redoubled. Still unknown
"The spot that holds her, every part of earth
"Blaming, ungrateful, worthless of her fruits.
"But chief Trinacria, in whose isle was found
"The vestige of her loss. For this she breaks
"With furious hand the glebe up-turning plough:
"And angry, to an equal death she dooms,
"The tiller and his ox: forbids the fields
"Back to return th' entrusted grain; the seeds
"All rotting Now that fertile land, renown'd
"Through the wide earth, lies useless; all the grain
"Dies in the earliest shoots: now scorching rays;
"Now floods of rain destroy it: noxious stars
"Now harm; now blighting winds: and hungry birds
"The scatter'd seed devour: the darnel springs,
"The thistle, and the knot-grass thick, which choke
"The sprouting wheat, and make the harvest void.

  "Now Arethusa from th' Eleian waves
"Exalts her head; her dropping tresses flung
"Back from her forehead, parting shade her ears:
"And thus;—O goddess! mother of the maid,
"So sought through earth, mother of all earth's fruits!
"Cease now thy toilsome labor; cease thine ire,
"Against the land that prov'd to thee so true:
"Thine ire unmerited; unwilling she,
"Op'd for the spoil a passage. Hither I
"No suppliant for my native isle approach;
"An alien here sojourning. Pisa's land
"My country; there near Elis first I sprung:
"A stranger now in Sicily I dwell.
"This soil, more grateful far than is my own;
"This soil, where I my houshold gods have plac'd;
"I, Arethusa, and have fix'd my seat,

"Preserve, mild goddess! Why I chang'd my land,
"Why to Ortygia, through the wide waves borne,
"I came, a more appropriate hour will ask;
"When you, from care reliev'd, can grant your ear
"With brow unclouded. Through the opening earth
"I flow; and borne through subterraneous depths,
"Here lift again my head, again behold
"The long-lost stars. Hence was my lot to see,
"As pass'd my stream close by the Stygian gulph,
"Your Proserpine;—sad still her face appear'd,
"Nor fear had wholly left it. Yet she reigns
"A queen; the mightiest in the realm of shade,
"The powerful consort of th' infernal king.

  "Like marble at the words the mother stands,
"Stupid with grief; and long astounded seems:
"Sorrow by heavier sorrow now surpass'd.
"Then in her chariot mounts th' ethereal sky,
"And stands indignant at th' imperial throne;
"Her locks wild flowing, and her face in clouds.
"Lo! here a suppliant, Jove,—she cry'd,—I come,
"To beg for her, my daughter and thine own;
"For if no favor may the mother find,
"The daughter's claim may move. Let not thy child
"Deserve thy care the less, as born of me.
"Lo! my lost maid, so long, so vainly sought
"At length is found; if finding we may call
"A surer loss; if finding we may call
"The knowledge where she is. Her ravish'd charms
"I'll pardon; let him but my child restore.
"What though a robber might my daughter wed,
"Thine sure is worthy of a different mate!
"Then Jove;—our daughter, our dear mutual pledge,
"As yours, so mine, demands our mutual care.
"But rightly still affairs if we design,
"What you lament will no injustice prove;
"Love only. Sure, a son-in-law like him,
"Can ne'er degrade, will you consent but yield.
"Grant nought beyond,—'tis no such trivial boast,
"Jove's brother to be call'd! How then, if more
"I claim pre-eminence from chance alone!
"Still, if so obstinate your wish remains
"For separation, go,—let Proserpine
"To heaven return, on this condition strict,
"Her lips no food have touch'd. So will the fates.
"He ceas'd.—Glad Ceres, certain to regain
"Her daughter, knew not what the fates forbade.
"Her fast was broken; thoughtless as she stray'd

"Around the garden, from a bending tree
"She pluck'd a fair pomegranate, and seven seeds
"From the pale rind she pick'd, and ate. None saw
"Save one, Ascalaphus, the luckless deed;
"Whom Orphné, fam'd Avernus' nymphs among,
"To Acheron, long since, 'tis said, produc'd
"Beneath a dusky cave. He, cruel, told;
"And his discovery stay'd the hop'd return.

  "Much wept the queen of Pluto, but she chang'd
"The vile informer to an hideous shape:
"Sprinkled with streams of Phlegethon, his head
"Feather'd appears, with beak, and monstrous eyes;
"Spoil'd of his shape, with yellow feathers cloth'd:
"Large grows his head; bent are his lengthen'd nails;
"Scarcely he moves the pinions which are shot
"Light from his lazy arms. A filthy bird
"Becoming;—constant presager of woe;
"An owl inactive; omen dire to man.

  "Well he by his informing tongue deserv'd,
"His doom, but Acheloïdes, from whence
"Your wings, and bird-like feet, whilst still you bear
"Your virgin features? Was it that you mix'd,
"When Proserpine the vernal flowers would cull,
"Amidst her numerous train? The nymph you sought
"Through earth's extent in vain; that ocean too
"Your anxious search might scape not, straight you pray'd
"For waving wings to winnow o'er the deep;
"And favouring gods you found. Of golden hue
"Quick-shooting wings your arms you saw bespread;
"But lest your inbred song, which every ear
"Had charm'd; and lest your highly-gifted voice,
"Your tongue should fail to use;—a virgin face,
"And speech yet human are indulg'd you still.

  "Now Jove as umpire 'twixt the angry pair
"His mourning sister, and his brother, bids
"The year revolving either side oblige:
"Now will the goddess, mutual in each realm,
"Six months with Ceres dwell in heaven; and six
"Reign with her spouse in hell. Straight were perceiv'd
"The goddess' countenance, and demeanour chang'd.
"For now her forehead, which had still retain'd,
"(To Pluto even) a sad and sorrowing gloom,
"Gladden'd: so Phœbus long in cloudy shade
"Envelop'd, shines, their umbrous veil dispers'd.
"Now Ceres calm, her daughter safe regain'd,

"Enquires:—O Arethusa! say the cause,
"Which hither brought thee; why a sacred fount?
"Hush'd were the waves; and from the lowest depths
"The goddess rais'd her head; and as she told,
"The old amours the flood of Elis knew,
"Press'd out the water from her tresses green.

  "Once with the nymphs, that on Achaïa's hills
"Rove, was I seen; none closer beat than I
"The thickets; none than I more skilful spread
"Th' ensnaring net. Yet though no fame I sought
"For beauty; though robust, I bore the name
"Of beauteous. Whilst the constant theme of praise,
"My features fair, to me no pleasure gave;
"What other nymphs inspire with joyful pride,
"Corporeal charms, did but my blushes raise.
"To please I thought a crime. Once tir'd with sport,
"The Stymphalidian forest I had left:
"Warm was the day; I with redoubled heat,
"Glow'd from my toil. A gliding stream I found
"By ripplings undisturb'd; silent and smooth
"It flow'd; so clear, that every stone was seen
"On the deep bottom; gently crept the waves;
"To creep scarce seeming; o'er the shelving banks
"The stream-fed poplar, and the willow hoar,
"A grateful shadow cast. The brink I reach'd
"Dipp'd first my feet, then waded to my knee;
"Not yet content, I loos'd my zone, and hung
"Upon a bending osier my soft robe:
"Then naked plung'd amid the stream; the waves
"Beating, and sporting in a thousand shapes;
"My arms around in every posture flung;
"A strange unusual murmur seem'd to sound,
"Deep from the bottom; terror-struck I gain'd
"The nearest brink;—when,—whither dost thou fly?
"O, Arethusa? whither dost thou fly?
"Alphæus, from his waters, hoarse exclaim'd!
"Vestless I fled, for on th' opposing bank
"My garment hung. Fiercer the god pursu'd;
"Fiercer he burn'd, all naked as I ran:
"Prepar'd more ready for his force I seem'd.
"Such was my flight, and such was his pursuit;
"As when on trembling wings, before the hawk
"Fly the mild doves: as when the hawk fierce drives
"The trembling doves before him. Long the chase
"I bore; Orchomenus, and Psophis soon
"I pass'd, and pass'd Cyllené, and the caves
"Of Mænalus, and Erymanthus' frosts,

"To Elis, ere his speed could cope with mine.
"In strength unequal, I sustain'd no more
"The toilsome race; he stouter flagg'd less soon.
"But still o'er plains I ran; o'er mountains thick
"With forests clad; o'er stones, and rugged rocks;
"And pathless spots. Behind me Phœbus shone.
"I saw, if fear deceiv'd me not, far spread
"His shade before me. What could less deceive,
"I heard his footsteps; and his breath full strong
"Blew on my banded tresses. Weary'd, faint
"With the long flight, I cry'd;—Dictynna, chaste!
"Lost am I,—help a quiver-bearing nymph,
"One who thy bow has oft entrusted borne;
"And oft thy quiver, loaded full with darts.
"Mov'd was the goddess; from the darkest clouds
"She one selected, and around me threw.
"The river-god, about the misty veil
"Pry'd anxious; and unwitting deeply grop'd
"Within the hollow cloud! Unconscious, twice
"The spot he compass'd, where Diana thought
"My safety surest; twice he then aloud
"Ho! Arethusa,—Arethusa! call'd:—
"What terror seiz'd my soul! not less the dread
"Of lambs, when round the sheltering fold they hear
"The wolves loud howling: or the trembling hare
"Close in a bramble hid, who sees approach
"The wide-mouth'd, hostile hounds, and fears to move.
"Further he pass'd not, for beyond the place
"No footsteps he discern'd, but guarding watch'd
"Around the mist. So closely thus besieg'd,
"My limbs a cold sweat seiz'd; cerulean drops
"Fell from my body; when my feet I mov'd,
"A pool remain'd; fast dropp'd my hair in dew;
"And speedier than the wonderous tale I tell,
"Chang'd to a stream I flow'd. But soon the god,
"Knew his lov'd waters; laid the man aside,
"And straight assum'd his proper watery form;
"With mine to mingle. Dian' cleft the ground;
"Sinking, through caverns dark I held my way;
"And reach'd Ortygia, from the goddess nam'd;
"There first ascending view'd the upper skies.

  "Here Arethusa ceas'd. Then Ceres yokes
"The coupled dragons to her car, their mouths
"Curb'd by the reins; and through the air is borne,
"Midway 'twixt heaven and earth. At Pallas' town
"Arriv'd, Triptolemus the car ascends,
"By her commission'd;—bade to spread the seed

"Entrusted: part on ground untill'd before;
"And part on land which long had fallow laid.
"O'er Europe now, and Asia's lands, the youth
"Sublimely sails, and reaches Scythia's clime,
"Where Lyncus rul'd. Beneath the monarch's roof,
"Here enter'd; and to him, who curious sought
"How there he journey'd; what his journey's cause;
"His name, and country; thus the youth reply'd.—
"Athens the fam'd, my country; and my name
"Triptolemus: but neither o'er the main,
"Borne in a ship, nor travelling slow by land,
"I hither came; my path was through the air.
"I bring the gift of Ceres; scatter'd wide
"Through all your spacious fields, quickly restor'd
"In fruitful crops the wholesome food will spring.
"The barbarous monarch, envious he should bear
"So great a blessing, takes him for his guest,
"And when with sleep weigh'd down attacks him. Rais'd
"To pierce his bosom, was the sword;—just then
"The wretch, by Ceres, to a lynx was turn'd.
"Then mounts again the youth, and through the air
"Bids him once more the sacred dragons steer.

"Our chosen champion ended here her lays,
"And all the nymphs unanimous, exclaim'd;—
"The Heliconian goddesses have gain'd.
"Vanquish'd, the others rail'd. When she resum'd:—
"Is not your punishment enough deserv'd?
"Foil'd in the contest, must you swell your crime,
"With base revilings? Patient now no more,
"To punish we begin; what anger bids,
"We now perform.—Loud laugh'd the scornful maids,
"Our threatening words despis'd, and strove to speak,
"And clapp'd with outcries menacing, their hands.
"When from their fingers shooting plumes they spy;
"And feathers shade their arms; her sister's face,
"Each sees to harden in an horny beak;
"To beat their bosoms trying with rais'd arms,
"In air suspended, on those arms they move;
"The new-shap'd birds the sylvan tribes increase:
"Magpies, the scandal of the grove. Thus chang'd,
"Their former eloquence they still maintain,
"In hoarse garrulity, and empty noise."

Trial of skill betwixt Pallas and Arachné. Transformation of Arachné to a spider. Pride of Niobé. Her children slain by Apollo and Diana. Her change to marble. The Lycian peasants changed to frogs. Fate of Marsyas. Pelops. Story of Tereus, Procné, and Philomela. Their change to birds. Boreas and Orithyïa. Birth of Zethes and Calaïs.

  Minerva pleas'd attention to the muse,
While thus she spoke afforded; prais'd the song,
And prais'd the just resentment of the maids.
Then to herself;—"the vengeance others take,
"Merely to praise were mean. I too should claim
"Like praise, for like revenge; nor longer bear
"My power contemn'd, by who unpunish'd live."
And on Arachné, fair Mæönian maid,
She turns her vengeful mind; whose skill she heard
Rivall'd her own in labors of the loom.
No fame her natal town, no fame her sire
On her bestow'd; her skill conferr'd renown.
Idmon of Colophon, her humble sire
Soak'd in the Phocian dye the spongy wool.
Her mother, late deceas'd, from lowest stock,
Had sprung; and wedded with an equal mate.
Yet had she gain'd through all the Lydian towns
For skill a mighty fame. Though born so low,
Though small Hypæpe was her sole abode,
Oft would the nymphs the vine-clad Tmolus leave
To view her wonderous work. Oft would the nymphs
In admiration quit Pactolus' waves.
Nor pleasure only gave the finish'd robe,
When view'd; but while she work'd she gave delight;
Such comely grace in every turn appear'd.
Whether she rounded into balls the wool;
Or with her fingers mollify'd the fleece;
And comb'd it floating light in cloudy waves;
Or her smooth spindle twirl'd with agile thumb;
Or with her needle painted: plain was seen
Her skill from Pallas learnt. This to concede
Unwilling, she ev'n such a tutor scorn'd
Exclaiming:—"come let her the contest try;
"If vanquish'd, let her fix my well-earn'd fate."

  Pallas, an ancient matron's form conceals;
Grey hairs thin strew her temples, and a staff
Supports her tottering limbs; while thus she speaks:—

"Old age though little priz'd, much good attends;
"Experience always grows with lengthen'd years:
"Spurn not my admonition. Great thy fame,
"Midst mortals, for the wonders of the loom.
"Great may it be, but to immortals yield:
"Bold nymph retract, and pardon for thy words,
"With suppliant voice require; Pallas will grant."
Sternly the damsel views her; quits the threads
Unfinish'd; scarce her hand from force restrains:
And rage in all her features flushing fierce,
Thus to the goddess, well-disguis'd, she speaks:—
"Weak dotard, spent with too great gift of years,
"Curst with too long existence, hence, begone!
"Such admonition to thy daughters give,
"If daughters hast thou; or thy sons have wives:
"Enough for me my inbred wisdom serves.
"Hope not, that ought thy vain advice has sway'd
"My purpose; still my challenge holds the same.
"Why comes your goddess not? why shuns she still
"The trying contest?" Then the goddess,—"Lo!
"She comes,"—and flung her aged form aside,
Minerva's form displaying. Every nymph,
And every dame Mygdonian, lowly bent
In veneration. While Arachné sole
Stood stedfast, unalarm'd; but yet she blush'd.
A sudden flush her angry face deep ting'd,
But sudden faded pale. A ruddy glow
Thus teints the early sky, when first the morn
Arises; quickly from the solar ray
Paling to brightness. On her purpos'd boast
Still stubborn bent, she obstinately courts
Her sure destruction, for the empty hope
Of conquest in the strife so madly urg'd.
No more Jove's maid refuses, gives no more
Her empty admonitions, nor delays
The contest: each her station straight assumes,
Tighten each web; each slender thread prepare.
Firm to the beam the cloth is fix'd; the reed
The warp divides, with pointed shuttle, swift
Gliding between; which quick their fingers throw,
Quick extricate, and with the toothy comb
Firm press'd between the warp, the threads unite.
Both hasten now; their garments round them girt,
Their skilful hands they ply: their toil forgot
In anxious wish for conquest. There appear'd,
The wool of Tyrian dye, and softening teints
Lost imperceptible. So seems the arch
Coloring a spacious portion of the sky;

Struck by the rays of Phœbus, when the showers
Recede, a thousand varying tinges shine;
The soft transition mocks the straining eye,
So like the shades which join, though far distinct
Their distant teints. In slender threads they twist
The pliant gold, and in the web display,
Each as she works, an ancient story fair.
Minerva paints the rock of Mars so fam'd
In Cecrops' city, and the well-known strife
To name the town. Twice six celestials sate
On their high thrones, great Jupiter around
In gravity majestic; every god
Bore his celestial features. Jove appear'd
In royal dignity. The Ocean power
Standing she pictur'd, with his trident huge
Smiting the rugged rock; from the cleft stone
Leap'd forth a steed; and thence the town to name
The privilege he claim'd. Herself she paints
Shielded, and arm'd with keenly-pointed spear.
Helm'd was her head; her breast the Ægis bore.
Struck by her spear, the earth a hoary tree
She shews producing, loaded thick with fruit.
The wondering gods the gift admire; the prize
To her awarded, ends the glorious work.

  More, that the daring rival of her art,
Should learn experimental, what reward
Her mad attempt might hope, four parts she adds;
And every part a test of power presents:
Bright the small figures in her colors shine.
This angle Thracian Rhodopé contains,
With Hæmus; both their mortal bodies now,
To frozen mountains chang'd; whose lofty pride
Assum'd the titles of celestial powers.
Another corner held the wretched fate
Felt by Pygmæa's matron; Juno bade
Her vanquish'd rival soar aloft a crane;
And on her people wage continual war.
Antigoné, she paints;—audacious she
With Jove's imperial consort durst contend;
By Jove's imperial queen she flits a bird:
Nor aids her Ilium ought; nor aids her sire,
Laömedon;—upborne on snowy wings,
A stork she rises; loud with chattering bill
She noises. In the sole remaining part,
Was childess Cynaras, in close embrace,
Grasping the temple's steps, his daughters once;
And as he lies extended on the stone,

In marble seems to weep. Around the piece
She spreads the peaceful olive: all complete
Her work is ended with her favorite tree.

  Arachné paints Europa, by a bull
Deceiv'd; the god a real bull appears;
And real seem the waves. She, backward turn'd,
Views the receding shore, and seems to shriek
Loud to her lost companions; seems to dread
The dashing waves, and timid shrinks her feet.
She draws Asteria, by the god o'er-power'd,
Cloth'd in an eagle. Leda, fair she lays
Beneath his wings, when he a swan appears.
She adds how Jove beneath a Satyr's shape
Conceal'd, the beauteous child of Nycteus fill'd,
With a twin-offspring. In Amphytrion's form
Alcmena, thou wert press'd. A golden shower
Danaë deceiv'd. A flame Ægina caught.
A shepherd's shape Mnemosyné beguil'd.
And fair Deöis trusts a speckled snake.
Thee, Neptune, too she painted, for the maid
Æolian, to a threatening bull transform'd.
Thou, as Enipeus, didst the Aloïd twins
Beget. Beneath the semblance of a ram,
Theophané was cheated. Ceres mild,
Of grain inventress, with her yellow locks,
In shape a courser felt thy ardent love.
Medusa, mother of the flying steed,
Nymph of the snaky tresses, in a bird
Conceal'd, you forc'd. Melantho in a fish.
To these the damsel, all well-suiting forms
Dispens'd, and all well-suiting scenes attend.
And there Apollo in a herdsman's guise
Wanders. And now he soars a plumy hawk:
Now stalks a lordly lion. As a swain
Macarean Isse, felt his amorous guile,
Erigoné to Bacchus' flame was dup'd
Beneath a well-seem'd grape. Saturn produc'd
The Centaur doubly-shap'd, in form a steed.
Her web's extremes a slender border girt,
Where flowery wreathes, and twining ivy blend.

  Not Pallas,—not even envy's rankling soul
Could blame the work. The bright immortal griev'd
To view her rival's merit, angry tore
The picture glowing with celestial crimes.
A boxen shuttle, grasping in her hand,
Thrice on the forehead of th' Idmonian maid

She struck. No more Arachné, hapless bore,
But twisted round her neck with desperate pride
A cord. The deed Minerva pitying saw
And check'd her rash suspension.—"Impious wretch!
"Still live," she cry'd, "but still suspended hang;
"Curs'd to futurity, for all thy race,
"Thy sons and grandsons, to the latest day
"Alike shall feel the sentence." Speaking thus,
The juice of Hecat's baleful plant she throws:
Instant besprinkled by the noxious drops,
Her tresses fall; her nose and ears are lost;
Her body shrinks; her head is lessen'd more;
Her slender fingers root within her sides,
Serving as legs; her belly forms the rest;
From whence her thread she still derives and spins:
Her art pursuing in the spider's shape.

    All Lydia rung; the wonderous rumor spread
Through every Phrygian town; the tale employ'd
The tongues of all mankind. The nymph was known,
Ere yet Amphion's nuptial bed she press'd,
To Niobé. She, when a virgin dwelt
In Lydian Sipylus. She still unmov'd,
Arachné's neighboring fate not heeded, still
Proudly refus'd before the gods to bend;
And spoke in haughty boasting. Much her pride
By favoring gifts was swol'n. Not the fine skill
Amphion practis'd; not the lofty birth
Each claim'd; not all their mighty kingdom's power,
So rais'd her soul (of all though justly proud)
As her bright offspring. Justly were she call'd
Most blest of mothers; but her bliss too great
Seem'd to herself, and caus'd a dread reverse.

    Now Manto, sprung from old Tiresias, skill'd
In future fate, impell'd by power divine,
In every street with wild prophetic tongue
Exclaim'd;—"Ye Theban matrons, haste in crowds,
"Your incense offer, and your pious prayers,
"To great Latona, and the heavenly twins,
"Latona's offspring; all your temples bound
"With laurel garlands. This the goddess bids;
"Through me commands it." All of Thebes obey,
And gird their foreheads with the order'd leaves;
The incense burn, and with the sacred flames
Their pious prayers ascend. Lo! 'midst a crowd
Of nymphs attendant, far conspicuous seen;
Comes Niobé, in gorgeous Phrygian robe,

Inwrought with gold, attir'd. Beauteous her form,
Beauteous, as rage permitted. Angry shook
Her graceful head; and angry shook the locks
That o'er each shoulder wav'd. Proudly she tower'd.
Her haughty eyes, round from her lofty stand
Wide darting, cry'd;—"What madness this to place
"Reported gods above the gods you see!
"Why to Latona's altars bend ye low,
"Nor incense burn before my power divine?
"My sire, was Tantalus: of mortals sole,
"Celestial feasts he shar'd. A Pleiäd nymph
"Me bore. My grandsire is the mighty king,
"Whose shoulders all the load of heaven sustain.
"Jove is my father's parent: him I boast
"As sire-in-law too. All the Phrygian towns
"Bend to my sway. The hall of Cadmus owns
"Me sovereign mistress. Thebes' high towering walls,
"Rais'd by my consort's lute; and all the crowd
"Who dwell inclos'd, his rule and mine obey.
"Where'er within my palace turn mine eyes,
"Treasures immense I view. Brightness divine
"I boast: to all seven blooming daughters add,
"And seven fair sons; through whom I soon expect,
"If Hymen favors, seven more sons to see,
"And seven more daughters. Need ye further seek
"Whence I have cause for boasting. Dare ye still
"Latona, from Titanian Cæus sprung,—
"The unknown Cæus,—she to whom all earth
"In bearing pangs the smallest space deny'd:—
"This wretch to my divinity prefer?
"Not heaven your goddess would receive; not earth;
"Not ocean: exil'd from the world, she weep'd,
"Till Delos sorrowing,—wanderer like herself,
"Exclaim'd;—thou dreary wanderest o'er the earth,
"I, o'er the main;—and sympathizing thus,
"A resting spot afforded. There become
"Of two the mother, only—can she vie
"With one whose womb, has sevenfold hers surpass'd?
"Blest am I. Who can slightly e'er arraign
"To happiness my claim? Blest will I still
"Continue. Who my bliss can ever doubt?
"Abundance guards its surety. Far beyond
"The power of fortune is my lot uprais'd:
"Snatch them in numbers from me, crowds more great
"Must still remain. My happy state contemns
"Even now, the threats of danger. Grant the power
"Of fate this nation of my womb to thin,—
"Of part depriv'd, impossible I shrink

"To poor Latona's two. How scant remov'd
"From mothers childless! Quit your rites;—quick haste
"And tear those garlands from your flowing hair."

 Aside the garlands thrown, and incomplete,
The rites relinquish'd, what the Thebans could
They gave: their whispering prayers the matron dame
Address'd. With ire the angry goddess flam'd,
And thus on Cynthus' lofty top bespoke
Her double offspring:—"O, my children! see,
"Your parent, proud your parent to be call'd,—
"To no celestial yielding, save the queen
"Of Jove supreme. Lo! doubted is my claim
"To rites divine; and from the altars, burnt
"To me from endless ages, driven, I go;
"Save by my children succour'd. Nor this grief
"Alone me irks, for Niobé me mocks!—
"Her daring crime increasing, proud she sets
"Her offspring far 'bove you. Me too she spurns,—
"To her in number yielding; childless calls
"My bed, and proves the impious stock which gave
"Her tongue first utterance." More Latona felt
Prepar'd to utter; more beseechings bland
For her young offspring, when Apollo, cry'd:
"Enough, desist to plain;—delay is long
"Till vengeance." Dian' join'd him in his ire.
Swift gliding down the sky, and veil'd in clouds,
On Cadmus' roof they lighted. Wide was spread,
A level plain, by constant hoofs well beat,
The city's walls adjoining; crowding wheels,
And coursers' feet the rolling dust upturn'd.
Here of Amphion's offspring daily some
Mount their fleet steeds; their trappings gaily press
Of Tyrian dye: heavy with gold, the rens
They guide. 'Mid these Ismenos, primal born
Of Niobé, as round the circling course,
His well-train'd steed he sped, and strenuous curb'd
His foaming mouth,—loudly "Ah, me!" exclaim'd,
As through his bosom deep the dart was driv'n:
Dropp'd from his dying hands the slacken'd reins;
Slowly, and sidelong from his courser's back
He tumbled. Sipylus, gave uncheck'd scope
To his, when through the empty air he heard,
The rattling quiver sound: thus speeding clouds
Beheld, the guider of the ruling helm,
A threatening tempest fearing, looses wide
His every sail to catch the lightest breeze.
Loose flow'd his reins. Th' inevitable dart

The flowing reins quick follow'd. Quivering shook,
Fixt in his upper neck, the naked steel,
Far through his throat protruding. Prone he fell
O'er his high courser's head; his smoking gore,
The ground defiling. Hapless Phœdimas,
And Tantalus, his grandsire's name who bore,
Their 'custom'd sport laborious ended, strove
With youthful vigor in the wrestling toil.
Now breast to breast they strain'd with nervous grasp,
When the swift arrow from the bended horn,
Both bodies pierc'd, as close both bodies join'd;
At once they groan'd; at once their limbs they threw,
With agonies convuls'd, prone on the earth;
At once their rolling eyes the light forsook;
At once their souls were yielded forth to air.
Alphenor saw, and smote his grieving breast;
Flew to their pallid limbs, and as he rais'd,
Their bodies, in the pious office fell:
For Phœbus drove his fate-wing'd arrow deep
Through what his heart inclos'd. Sudden withdrawn,
On the barb'd head the mangled lungs were stuck;
And high in air his soul gush'd forth in blood.
But beardless Damasichthon, by a wound
Not single fell, as those; struck where the leg
To form begins, and where the nervous ham
A yielding joint supplies. The deadly dart
To draw essaying, in his throat, full driven,
Up to the feather'd head, another came:
The sanguine flood expell'd it, gushing high,
Cutting the distant air. With outstretcht arms
Ilioneus, the last, besought in vain;
Exclaiming,—"spare me, spare me, all ye gods!"
Witless that all not join'd to cause his woe.
The god was touch'd with pity, touch'd too late,—
Already shot th' irrevocable dart:
Yet light the blow was given, and mild the wound
That pierc'd his heart, and sent his soul aloft.

  The rumor'd ill; the mourning people's groans;
The servant's tears, soon made the mother know,
The sudden ruin: wondering first she stands,
To see so great heaven's power, then angry flames
Indignant, that such power they dare to use.
The sire Amphion, in his bosom plung'd
His sword, and ended life at once, and woe.
Heavens! how remov'd this Niobé, from her
Who drove so lately from Latona's fane,
The pious crowds; who march'd in lofty state,

Through every street of Thebes, an envy'd sight!
Now to be wept by even her bitterest foes.
Prostrate upon their gelid limbs she lies;
Now this, now that, her trembling kisses press;
Her livid arms high-stretching unto heaven,
Exclaims,—"Enjoy Latona, cruel dame,
"My sorrows; feed on all my wretched woes;
"Glut with my load of grief thy savage soul;
"Feast thy fell heart with seven funereal scenes;
"Triumph, victorious foe! conqueror, exult!
"Victorious! said I?—How? To wretched me,
"Still more are left, than joyful thou canst boast:
"Superior I 'midst all this loss remain."

  She spoke;—the twanging bowstring sounded loud!
Terrific noise,—save Niobé, to all:
She stood audacious, callous in her crime.
In mourning vesture clad, with tresses loose,
Around the funeral couches of the slain,
The weeping sisters stood. One strives to pluck
The deep-stuck arrow from her bowels,—falls,
And fainting dies; her brother's clay-cold corse,
Prest with her lips. Another's soothing words
Her hapless parent strive to cheer,—struck dumb,
She bends beneath an unseen wound; her words
Reach not her parent, till her life is fled.
This, vainly flying, falls: that drops in death
Upon her sister's body. One to hide
Attempts: another pale and trembling dies.
Six now lie breathless, each by vary'd wounds;
One sole remaining, whom the mother shields,
Wrapt in her vest; her body o'er her flung,
Exclaiming,—"leave me this, my youngest,—last,
"Least of my mighty numbers,—one alone!"
But while she prays, the damsel pray'd for dies.

  Of all depriv'd, the solitary dame,
Amid the lifeless bodies of her sons,
Her daughters, and her spouse, by sorrows steel'd,
Sits harden'd: no light gale her tresses moves;
No blood her redden'd cheeks contain; her eyes
Motionless glare upon her mournful face;
Life quits the statue: even her tongue congeals,
Within her stony palate; vital floods
Cease in her veins to flow; her neck to bow
Resists; her arms to move in graceful guise;
Her feet to step; and even to stone are turn'd
Her inmost bowels. Still to weep she seems.

Wrapt in a furious whirlwind, distant far
Her natal soil receives her. There fixt high
On a hill's utmost summit, still she melts;
Still does the rigid marble flow in tears.

  Now every Theban, male and female, all,
Dread the fierce anger of the powers of heaven;
And with redoubled fervor lowly bend,
And own the twin-producing goddess' power.
Then, as oft seen, they ancient tales recount,
Reminded by events of recent date.
Thus one relates.—"Long since some clowns, who till'd
"The fertile fields of Lycia, felt the ire
"Of this high goddess, whom they durst despise.
"Obscure the fact itself, for low the race
"Who suffer'd; yet most wonderous was the deed.
"Myself have seen the marsh; the lake have seen
"Fam'd for the prodigy. My aged sire,
"To toil unable on the lengthen'd road,
"Me thither sent; an herd of choicest beeves
"Thence to conduct; to my unpractis'd steps
"A guiding native of the land he gave.
"While we the pastures travers'd, lo! we found
"An ancient altar, 'midst a spacious lake
"Erected; black with sacrificing dust;
"With waving reeds surrounded. Here my guide
"Halted, and softly whisper'd,—bless me, power!
"And I, like softly whispering,—bless me!—cry'd.
"Then ask'd, if nymph, or fawn, or native god
"The altar own'd?—when thus my guide reply'd.
"No mountain god, O youth! this altar claims,
"But her whom once imperial Juno's rage,
"Stern interdicted from firm earth's extent:
"Whom scarce the wandering Delos would receive,
"Ardent beseeching, when the buoyant isle
"Light floated. There at length, Latona, laid
"Betwixt a palm, and bright Minerva's tree,
"Spite of their fierce opposing step-dame's power,
"Her twins produc'd. Even hence, in child-bed driven,
"She fled from Juno; in her bosom bore,
"'Tis said, the twin-celestials. Now the sun
"With fervid rays, had scorch'd the arid meads,
"When faint with lengthen'd toil, the goddess gain'd
"The edge of Lycia's monster-breeding clime;
"Parch'd and exhausted, from the solar heat,
"And infants milking her exhausted breast.
"By chance a lake, far distant she espy'd,
"Deep in a vale's recess, of waters pure.

"There clowns the bulrush gather'd; there they pluck'd
"The shrubby osier, and the marsh-fond grass.
"Approach'd the goddess; on her knees low bent,
"The earth she press'd, and forward lean'd to drink
"The cooling liquid. This the rustic mob
"Forbade. When she to those who thus oppos'd,—
"Water withhold? Water whose use is free?
"Nature to all unsparing gives to take,
"Of light, of air, and of the flowing stream.
"I claim but public gifts: yet suppliant beg
"Those public gifts to share. Not here I come,
"My weary'd arms and limbs within the waves
"To lave: my thirst alone I wish to slake.
"Even now my speaking lips their moisture want;
"Scarce my parch'd throat, a passage to my words
"Can yield. As nectar were the limpid draught.
"Life with the water give me; for to me,
"Water is life; with water life I seek.
"Let these too move you, who their tender hands
"Stretch to your bosoms,—for by chance the babes
"Their little hands held forth. The goddess' words,
"Thus bland-beseeching, who could e'er withstand?
"Yet these persisted;—obstinate refus'd
"To grant her wish, and with opprobrious speech
"And threats revil'd her, should she there remain.
"Nor rested thus,—the lake with hands and feet
"Muddy they trouble; with malicious leaps
"They agitate the pool, and upward stir
"From the deep bottom clouds of slimy ooze.
"Anger her thirst diverted. Rage deny'd
"More supplication from th' indignant dame.
"Their threatening words, no more the goddess brook'd;
"But raising nigh to heaven her hands, she cry'd,—
"Be this your home for ever!—Gracious heard,
"Her prayer was granted. Now they joy to plunge,
"Beneath the waters; now they deep immerge
"Their bodies in the hollow fen; now raise
"Their heads, and skim the surface of the pool,
"Often they rest upon the margin's brink,
"And oft light-springing, in the cool lake plunge.
"Now still their rude contentious tongues they use,
"Still squabbling, lost to shame beneath the waves:
"Beneath the waves they still abusings strive
"To utter. Hoarsely still their voice is heard,
"Through their wide-bloated throats. Their railing words,
"Their jaws more wide dilate. Depriv'd of neck,
"Their head and back in junction seem to meet;
"Green shine their backs; their bellies, hugely swol'n

"Are white; and frogs they plunge within the pool."

Thus as the man, the fate destructive told
Of Lycia's clowns, to mind another call'd
The satyr's fate, who vanquish'd in the strife
Of skill, on Pallas' pipe, Latona's son
Severely punish'd.—"Wherefore thus,"—he cries,
"Rent from myself? O, penitent I bow.
"The pipe," he shrieks, "should not such rage provoke."
Exclaiming thus, o'er his extremest limbs
Stript was his skin; he one continuous wound!
Blood flow'd from every part; the naked nerves
Bare started; and the trembling veins full throbb'd,
By skin uncover'd. Every beating part
Inward, the breast's translucent fibres plain
Display'd to sight. Him every forest fawn;
Each brother satyr; and each sylvan god;
And every nymph, with fam'd Olympus wept:
And every swain, the woolly flock who fed;
Or on the mountain watch'd the horned herd.
Wash'd by their falling tears, the fertile earth
Is soak'd,—absorbs them in her inmost veins;
Then form'd to water, spouts them high in air.
Rapid 'twixt banks declivitous, they seek
The ocean. Marsya, is the river call'd;
The clearest stream through Phrygia's land which flows.

Thus far the crowd;—and then lamenting turn
To present griefs:—Amphion's race extinct,
Unanimous they wail; but hated still
Remains the mother's pride. For her alone
Weep'd Pelops;—rent his garments, bare expos'd
His breast and shoulders lay, and fair display'd
The ivory joint. This shoulder at his birth
In fleshy substance, and carnation tinge,
Equall'd the right. When by his sire his limbs
Disjointed lay, the gods, 'tis said, quick join'd
The sever'd members: every fragment found,
Save what combin'd the neck and upper arm;
The part destroy'd, with ivory they replace;
And Pelops perfect from the gift became.

The neighbouring lords assemble;—every town
Their kings intreat condolence to bestow,
And all to Thebes repair. First Argos sends;
Sparta; Mycené; Calydon, not yet
By stern Diana hated; Corinth, fam'd
For beauteous brass; Orchomenus the fierce;

Messené fertile; Patræ; Pylos, rul'd
By Neleus; Trœzen, yet unus'd to own
The sway of Pittheus; Cleona the low;
And all those towns the two-sea'd isthmus holds;
And all those towns the isthmus views without.
Athens, incredible! was absent sole.
War all her energy demanded. Borne
O'er ocean, fierce barbarian troops, the walls
Mopsopian threaten'd. Thracian Tereus, these
With arms auxiliar routed; bright his name
Shone from the conquest. Him in riches great,
Mighty in power, and from the god-like Mars,
His lineage tracing, Procné's nuptial hand
Close to Pandion bound. Their marriage bed
Nor Grace, nor Hymen, nor the nuptial queen
Attended. Furies held the torches, snatch'd
From biers funereal. Furies spread the couch:
And all night long an owl, ill-omen'd bird,
Perch'd on the roof that crown'd the marriage dome.
Join'd with such omens, with such omens bore
Procné a son to Tereus. Wide through Thrace
Congratulations sound: glad thanks to heaven
The parents give, and hail the happy day
Which gave Pandion's daughter to the king;
And gave the pair a son. So ignorant still
Mankind of real happiness remain!

  Now through five autumns had the cheerful sun
The whirling year renew'd. When Procné, bland
Her spouse besought.—"If grace within thy sight
"Claim my deserts,—or suffer me to see
"In her own clime my sister, or to ours
"My sister bring: a quick return thou well
"Our sire may'st promise. This high boon obtain'd,
"My sister's presence,—to my sight thou'lt seem,
"A deity in goodness."—On the main
He bids them launch the vessel; in the port
Cecropian enters, urg'd by oar and sail;
And treads Piræus' shore. Soon as he gain'd
His audience; soon as hand with hand was clasp'd,
His ill-presaging speech he open'd. First
The journey's cause narrating; fond desire
Of Procné; and the promis'd quick return
Of Philomela, should the sire comply.
Lo! Philomela enters, splendid robes
Attire her; still more splendid shine her charms:
Such they describe within the forests rove
Dryad, and Naiäd nymphs; such would they seem

Their shape like hers adorn'd, like hers attir'd.
Instant was Tereus at the sight inflam'd;
So instant would the hoary harvest burn,
The torch apply'd: so burn the wither'd leaves;
Or hoarded hay. Well might her charms inspire
Such love in any;—him his inbred lust
More goaded, more his country's warmth which burns
Intense; he flames from nature, and from clime.
First to corrupt th' attendants he designs,
And faithful nurse; and Philomel' to tempt
With gifts immense,—his kingdom's mighty price.
Or forceful snatch her, and the rape defend,
With all the powers of war. Nought but he dares.
Impell'd by love's unbridled power; his breast
The raging fire contains not. Irksome seems
Delay:—and eager to the anxious wish
Of Procné, turns his converse; her desires
His wishes aiding. Eloquent he spoke;
For love inspir'd him. Often as he press'd
More close than prudent, all his earnest speech,
Procné, he said, dictated. Heavens! how dark
The gloom that blinds the view of human souls.
Tereus for tenderest piety esteem'd,
More as for vice he labors: praise he gains,
for every crime. Now Philomela begs,
His prayer assisting; flings her winning arms
Around Pandion's neck, and suppliant sues
A sight of Procné; for her woe she begs,
But deems she begs delight. Her Tereus views;—
Anticipates his joys; her every kiss,
Her arms around her parent's neck entwin'd,
But goad his passion: fuel fresh they add;
Food for his flame. And when her sire she clasps,
He longs that sire to be. Parent, not more
His impious purpose would the wretch delay!
The king by both their warm beseechings won,
Consents;—she joyful to her father gives
Glad thanks;—and hapless, deems completely blest,
Herself and sister, both most deeply curst;

  Now Phœbus' toil nigh spent, his coursers' feet
Sweep'd down the slope of heaven. The royal feast,
And golden goblets, fill'd with Bacchus' gift,
The board bespread. From hence in slumbers soft,
Each sought repose. All but the Thracian king,
Though far remov'd, still burning; all her face,
Her hands and gesture he recals, and paints
At pleasure all her beauties yet unseen:

Feeding his flame, and sleep repelling far.

  Twas morn;—Pandion, pressing warm the hand
Of Tereus, as they parted, while the tears
Gush'd sudden, thus bespeaks his friendly care.
"Dear son, to thee I give her, pious claims
"Compel me: suppliant let me thee adjure
"By faith, by kindred, and by all the gods,
"Thy care paternal, shall protect the maid;
"And the soft solace of my anxious years,
"Speedy restore, for each delay is long.
"Quick, Philomela, quick my child, rejoin
"Thy sire, if filial duty sways thee. Much
"Thy sister's absence pains me."—Speaking thus
He press'd with kisses soft, the maiden's lips,
And dripping tears with each behest let fall.
Their hands he asks as pledge of faith, and joins
Their hands in his presented; tender begs
His salutations to his daughter dear;
And his young grandson. Scarce the last adieu,
Chok'd with deep sighs, he breathes: his boding mind
Foreseeing future woes.

          Now Philomel'
Safely on board the painted vessel plac'd,
The land far left, as with their laboring oars
The surges move;—exulting Tereus, cry'd,
"Victorious,—lo! my utmost wishes borne
Safe with me."—Scarce his burning soul defers
His hop'd-for joys. His eyes are never turn'd
From the lov'd face. Thus Jove's protected bird
Rapacious bears, with his sharp talons pierc'd,
An hare defenceless to his lofty nest:
No flight remains, the spoiler calmly views
His prey. Now ended is their voyage, now
Weary'd they quit their ship, and joyful touch
Their native beach; and now the Thracian king
Pandion's daughter to a lofty stall
Conducts: by ancient trees the spot well screen'd.
There he inclos'd the pale, the trembling maid,
Of all things fearful, as with tears she press'd
Her sister's face to see: his purpose dire
Disclosing,—force the helpless maid o'ercame,
Loudly exclaiming to her sire; and loud
Her sister's help invoking, equal vain:
But chief she begs celestial powers to aid.
Trembling she lies; so seems a shuddering lamb
Wounded, and from the hoary wolf's fierce jaws

Just 'scap'd, not sure his safety yet he deems:
So seems a dove, her plumes in blood deep-drench'd,
With fear still shivering; still the hungry claws
Dreading, that lately pierc'd her. Soon restor'd
Her mental powers, while scatter'd hung the locks
Rent in her anguish, high her arms she rais'd,
Livid with blows, as those that mourn the dead;
Exclaiming,—"O, barbarian! wretch supreme!
"In cruelty and vice; whom not the charge
"Parental, seal'd with pious tears could move;
"A sister's charge entrusted: not her state,
"Virgin defenceless; not the sacred vows,
"Conjugal plighted. In confusion all
"Commixt, by thee, adulteress here I lie,
"Against my sister. Thou a double spouse,
"To both. This scourge is sure to me not due.
"Why, villain, not my hated life destroy?
"Perfect in deeds atrocious; would my breath
"Before the horrid act supprest had been:
"Then had I guiltless sought the shades. But still
"If powers celestial view this act; if sway
"On earth they hold; if all not sinks with me,
"Thy fate hence-forward from me dread; myself
"Shall unabash'd, thy acts proclaim. If power
"Is granted, when in public walks I roam:
"If here in woods imprison'd, all the woods
"Shall with my plaints resound; the conscious rocks
"I'll move. May heaven me hear! and if in heaven
"A god abides, me hear!"—Rous'd by her words,
The fierce king's anger burns; no less his fear
Than anger moves him: strongly spurr'd by each,
His weapon from the pendent sheath he drew:
Dragg'd by the hair, her limbs he forc'd to yield
To fetters; twisting rough her arms behind.
Glad Philomel' to him her throat presents,
Death from the glittering sword expecting. Grasp'd
In pincers, fierce her tongue he tore away;
Griev'd, and indignant, as her father's name
She strove to utter: trembling still appear'd
The bloody root; trembling the tongue itself
Murmur'd as on the gore-stain'd earth it lay:
As leaps the serpent's sever'd tail, the tongue,
Quivering in death, still to her feet advanc'd.
This deed of horror done, 'tis said that oft
(Incredible the fact) repeated force
Upon her mangled form the wretch employ'd.

Now dares he, all those acts atrocious done,

Return to Procné. Eager as he comes,
For Philomel' she asks. False tears and groans
He gives: the hapless nymph he feigns deceas'd:
His tears convince. Now from her shoulders torn,
Her robes with gold bright-glittering, sable vests
Her limbs enfolded. High an empty tomb
She rais'd, and pious obsequies perform'd
To manes pretended: for her sister's fate
She mourn'd, whose fate such mourning ill deserv'd.

  Through twice six signs had Phœbus journey'd on,
The year completing. What, alas! remains
For Philomela? Guards prevent her flight.
Of stone erected, high the massive walls
Circle her round. Her lips so mute, refuse
The deed to blazon. Keen the sense of grief
Sharpens the soul:—in misery the mind
Ingenious sparkles. Skillful she extends
The Thracian web, and on the snow-white threads,
In purple letters, weaves the dreadful tale.
Complete, a servant with expressive signs,
The present to the queen she bids to bear.
To Procné was it borne, witless the slave
Of what he carry'd. Savage Tereus' spouse
The web unfolded; read the mournful tale
Her hapless sister told, and wonderous! sate
In silence, grief her rising words repress'd:
Indignant, chok'd, her throat refus'd to breathe,
The angry accents to her plaining tongue.
To weep she waits not, in turmoil confus'd,
Justice and flagrance undistinguished lie;
Her mind sole bent for vengeance on her spouse.

  Now was the time Sithonia's matrons wont,
The rites triennial of the jovial god
To tend. Those rites to conscious shade alone
Confided. Rhodopé, the brazen sound
Shrill tinkling, hears by night;—by night the queen
The palace quits, attir'd as Bacchus' rites
Demand; and weapon'd with the Bacchant arms.
A vine her forehead girds; the nimble deer
Clothes with his skin her sides; her shoulder bears
A slender spear. Thus maddening, Procné seeks
The woods in ire terrific, crowded round
By all her followers: rack'd by inward pangs,
The furious rant of Bacchus veils her woes.
The lonely stable seen at length, she howls
Aloud,—"Evoë, ho!"—and bursts the door;

Drags thence her sister;—her thence dragg'd, invests
In Bacchanalian robes; her face inshrouds
In ivy foliage; and astonish'd leads
The trembling damsel o'er the palace steps.
The horrid dome when Philomela saw,
Perforce she enter'd; through her frame she shook;
The blood her face deserted. Procné sought
A spot retir'd, and from her features flung
The sacred trappings, and her sister's face,
Sorrowing and blushing, to the light unveil'd;
Then ran to clasp her. She the sight not bore;
Her eyes she rais'd not; her dejected brows
Bent to the ground; thus by her sister seen,
Encroacher on her bed. Her hands still spoke,
When oaths she wish'd to utter, and to call
Th' attesting gods, her foul disgrace by force
To prove accomplish'd. Furious, Procné burns,
Nor curbs her ire; her sister's streaming tears
Reproving checks, and cries;—"no period now
"For tears, we ask the sword! But if than sword
"Vengeance more keen thou hop'st for, sister dear,
"Behold me for most horrid deeds prepar'd.
"Shall I with flaming torches blaze on high
"His hall imperial, and the villain king
"Heave in the conflagration? Shall I rend
"As thine his tongue? or from his sockets tear,
"His eye-balls? or what other member maim?
"Or this, or instant send his guilty soul
"Thro' thousand wounds to judgment? What thou speak'st
"Be mighty. I for mightiest acts prepare.
"To fix I hesitate." As Procné speaks,
Lo! infant Itys to his mother runs;
His sight her mind determines; cruel turn
Her eyes, exclaiming;—"See, how like his sire's
"Appear his features!"—More she spoke not, fixt
Was straight her dread resolve: now fiercer burn'd
Within her smother'd rage;—yet when the boy
Approach'd, and round her neck his infant arms
Threw, and his kisses printed on her lips,
With bland caresses mingled, even the soul
Of Procné melted. Mollify'd her rage,
Tears hard constrain'd flow'd from unwilling eyes.
Soon as the mother's feelings softening seem
To melt in extreme fondness; Procné quits
The sight, and to her sister's face reverts
Again her visage; then on each in turn
Full bent her view, she cries;—"Must one me melt
"With blandish'd soothings? Must the other mute,

"With tongue dismember'd stand? Must he exclaim
"O, mother!—she, O, sister! never more?
"To what a spouse, Pandion's daughter, see
"Art thou, degenerate wife, conjoin'd! Thy sin
"A spouse like Tereus to have us'd too well."
More she delays not, infant Itys drags,
Swift as the Indian tiger sweeps the fawn
Through shady forests. Then the lofty dome,
For rooms remote well search'd, in one arrives,
Where she the infant pierces; 'twixt the breast
And side the weapon enters, while his hands,
Suppliant, his fate foreseeing, he extends,
And,—"mother! O, my mother!"—loudly cries.
Nor mov'd her countenance fell;—the single wound
Was deadly. Philomela, with her steel
The throat divided, and the quivering limbs
Dissever'd, whilst of animation still
Some glimmering sparks remain'd. Of these, they part
In brazen cauldrons boil: part on the spit
Crackling they turn: with gore the secret rooms
Offensive float. Her unsuspecting spouse
Procné to feast invites; delusive feigns
Her country's customs,—where 'twas given, but one
The husband should be nigh; all menial slaves
Far distant. On his ancestorial seat
High-lifted, Tereus sate, and feasted there:
And in his bowels deep he there entomb'd
Bowels his own. So blind are human souls,—
"Call Itys to the feast,"—he cries. No more
Could Procné veil her savage joy;—full bent
The slaughter to announce, she loud proclaim'd
"Thou seek'st who with thee rests!"—Around he looks.
Wondering where rests he. Philomela rush'd,
Her tresses sprinkled with the ireful blood,
As griev'd he, Itys calling loud, and flung,
With savage fury Itys' gory head
Full in his father's face; nor ever mourn'd
Lost speech so much; her well-earn'd joy to show,
More griev'd lost power. With outcry loud the king
O'er-turn'd the table; from the Stygian vale,
Invok'd the viper'd sisters: hard he strove
To tear his bosom, and from thence disgorge
The dire repast, the half-digested mass
Of Itys' limbs. Now weeping, wild he mourns,
Himself his offspring's tomb. Now fierce pursues
Pandion's daughters with his unsheath'd sword.
From him escaping, on light wings upborne
Th' Athenians seem'd; light wings their limbs upbore!

One sheltering in the woods: protecting roofs
The other seeking; still the murderous deed,
Mark'd on her breast remains; still on her plumes
The teint of blood is seen. Rapid in rage
And hope of vengeance, Tereus too is chang'd,
And flits a bird; a plumy crest he bears,
High on his head: the lengthen'd sword he bore,
A beak enormous grows. A lapwing now
With fierce-arm'd face he flies.

　　　　　　Untimely sought
Pandion, when the mournful tale he heard,
The Stygian shades, ere yet the lengthen'd date
Of years commanded. Next th' Athenian realm
Erechtheus rul'd, the sceptre dubious held
By right or forceful arms. Proud could he boast
Four sons;—and daughters four to him were given.
Beauteous the maids; in beauty equal two:
Of these Æölian Cephalus was bless'd
With thee as spouse, O, Procris!—Tereus long,
Boreas withstanding, with the power of Thrace,
Long Orithyïa, by the god belov'd,
Was lov'd in vain; while soft beseechings more
And prayers, the power to strenuous force preferr'd.
But now those soothings bland so vainly try'd,
Fierce swol'n with rage, his most accustom'd feel
(Too much that passion knows this wind) he cries;—
"Well I deserve it, all my proper arms
"Relinquish'd: savage fierceness, strength, stern rage,
"And threatening force. With humble softening prayers
"Fool have I su'd; in each attempt have fail'd.
"More apt to me is force! by force I drive
"The lowering clouds before me: Ocean's waves
"Forceful I turn; forceful the knotted oak
"Root from its deep foundation; hard the frost
"I bind; and beat the sounding earth with hail:
"I when in open sky, for there our field
"Lies in display, my blustering brethren meet,
"Oppose such might, that midmost sky resounds
"Echoing our forceful conflict; flashing flames
"From the cleft bodies of the hollow clouds,
"Elicited: I too, earth's secret womb
"Fierce entering, in her deepest caverns strain
"My strength, 'till trembling wide through all her frame,
"The ghosts below are troubled. These the aid
"My nuptial wish should seek; no longer pray
"Erechtheus for my sire;—my sire by force,
"The monarch shall be made."—So spoke the god,

Or thus, or more in fury, as he shook
His plumes, whose motion sweep'd through earth's extent,
And made the wide main tremble. Lofty hills
His dusty mantle covers; as the plains
Rapid he brushes; shrouded deep in mist,
In his dark wings the furious lover clasps
His Orithyïa, trembling, pale with fear:
Flying his flames were fann'd, and fiercer blaz'd.
Nor check'd the ravisher his lofty flight,
Till seen the town of Cicones, whose walls
Receiv'd him. There th' Athenian nymph became
The freezing monarch's bride: a mother there,
A double birth she brought, whose shoulders bear
The father's pinions; all their semblance else
Their mother's. Not at first, 'tis said, appear'd
The feathers: Calaïs and Zethes, boys
Were yet unplum'd; when yet with ruddy hair,
Their beards appear'd not. From each shoulder shot
The feathers bird-like, at the self-same time,
Their manly cheeks were thick with yellow down.
Now when their youth matur'd to man appear'd,
Through seas unplough'd before, they sought the fleece
Splendid with glittering wool; with all the train
Of Minyæ, in the first-built vessel borne.

THE SEVENTH BOOK

Expedition of the Argonauts. Jason obtains the golden fleece, by the assistance of Medea. Æson restored to youth by her magic powers. Murder of Pelias by his daughters. Medea's flight to Corinth. Murder of her rival and infants. Marriage with Ægeus. Adventures of Theseus. War with Minos. Plague in Ægina. Change of ants into Myrmidons. Cephalus and Procris.

THE SEVENTH BOOK OF THE METAMORPHOSES OF OVID

Now in the Pagasæan vessel borne,
Plough'd the wide sea the Argonauts, and saw
The fate of Phineus; whose old age the curse
Of hunger felt, and felt perpetual night.
The youths from Boreas sprung, quick sped to flight
The virgin-featur'd birds, his hapless face,
Far distant. 'Neath great Jason's rule much toil
They bore ere on the oozy banks they stay'd
Of rapid Phasis. Here the king they seek;
And here demand the golden fleece; and here

An answer big with fearful labors learn
The Grecian crew. Meantime the royal maid
Burns with fierce fires: with reason struggling long,
Still her hot flame to quench unable, cries
Aloud Medea;—"vainly I oppose!
"Some unknown god controls. Perhaps 'tis love!
"If love 'tis not, no sentiment more near
"To love can come. Why else my sire's commands
"So harsh appear? But harsh in truth they are.
"But why his failing dread? Why dread his death,
"But barely seen? What cause such fear can give?
"O, hapless maid! would from my virgin breast
"Those flames to fling were given. If mine the power
"More wisdom would I use. But me this force,
"Before unknown, unwilling drags; this love
"Persuades, oppos'd to reason: plain I see
"The better track,—approve it most, yet swerv'd,
"I tread the worse. Why, royal virgin, burn
"Thus for a stranger guest? Why long'st thou thus,
"A foreign partner in the marriage bed
"To clasp? Thy country well can thee supply
"What e'er thou lovest. In the gods' decree
"His death or safety rests. Yet may he live!
"Pray may'st thou for him sure,—love unconcern'd.
"But what has Jason done? Savage, indeed!
"Were those his youth, his birth, and brilliant deeds
"Not touch'd: how savage too the soul must be
"His beauty touch'd not, were there nought beside;
"My bosom sure it moves. But were my aid
"Deny'd, the furious bulls with flaming breath
"His fate would compass; or the foes that spring
"From earth, his harvest, slay him in the fight;
"Or last, he'd fall the ravenous dragon's prey.
"If this I suffer, from the tiger sprung
"Believe me; steel and marble in my breast,
"Deem me to wear. Why not his death behold?
"Why not mine eyes with the dread sight pollute!
"Why not the bulls, the earth-born foes incite,
"And sleepless dragon, with redoubled ire?
"Heaven wills it better. But let deeds, not prayers
"My time employ. How! shall I then betray
"My parent's realm? an unknown stranger aid
"With all my power? who by my power preserv'd,
"Loos'd to the wind his sails, another's spouse
"Becomes,—me left for punishment behind?
"If this to do,—another nymph to me
"Born to prefer, let him, ingrate! be slain.
"But no! his face denies it; his great soul,

"And graceful form forbid the fear of fraud;
"Or benefits forgot. Yet shall he plight
"His solemn faith first, call th' attesting gods
"To witness what he vows. What fear I more?
"All's safe. Medea, hasten, spurn delay,—
"Jason, remaining life to thee shall owe;
"Join'd to his state, the annual torch shall flame
"To thee, preserver! through the Grecian towns
"By crowds of mothers hail'd. Shall I for this
"My sister leave, my brother, and my sire;
"My gods, and natal land? Yes,—fierce my sire;
"My country barbarous; and my brother young:
"With all my wishes, warm my sister joins;
"And dwells within my breast the mightiest god.
"Much I relinquish not, but much I seek.
"The glorious title of the Grecian youth
"Deliverer! gain'd; the sight of lands and towns
"Whose fame even here has journey'd; manners mild,
"And cultur'd arts; and Jason for my spouse,
"For whom all earth's possessions were too small
"To change. His spouse become, supremely blest,
"Dear to the gods, the loftiest stars I'll reach.
"What are those rocks, they tell, which 'mid the waves
"Meet in encounter? Fell Charybdis what,—
"Hostile to ships, now sucking in the tide,
"Now fierce discharging? What the savage bounds,
"Which compass greedy Scylla 'mid the main
"Sicilian? O'er the wide-spread ocean borne,
"Him whom I love embracing; sheltering close
"In Jason's bosom; clasp'd by him, no fear
"My soul could harbor. Or if fear I felt,
"For him alone I'd tremble; for my spouse.
"Spouse, dost thou say, Medea? hid'st thou thus,
"With specious names thy crime? Behold the load
"Of guilt thou goest to bear! While power remains
"The sin avoid."—She said, and duty, shame,
And rectitude, before her eyes appear'd;
And vanquish'd love address'd his wings to flight.
Now to an ancient altar Hecat' own'd,
By shady trees dark veil'd from day, she came:
Her flames abated, and her eager pulse
Subsided. Here Æsonides she saw,
And bright her love reblaz'd. Warm flush'd her cheeks,
Deep all her visage glow'd. The smallest spark
Thus low in embers hid, its vigor shews;
Help'd by the feeding blast, increasing burns,
And stirr'd in all its wonted fury glows.
Just so the languid passion which but now

All but extinct appear'd, the hero seen
Fresh at his beauteous presence flam'd. By chance
More beauteous Jason on that morn appear'd;
Well might a lover all her love excuse.
She looks, his countenance with her eyes devours
As then first seen; and madly fond, she deems
His features more than mortal: bashful turn'd
Her forehead not from his. But when her guest
Address'd her: when he gently took her hands;
And crav'd assistance in an humble tone,
The nuptial promise giving. Plenteous flow'd
Her tears, exclaiming;—"What I should perform
"Plainly I see: not ignorance me misleads
"But love. My gifts shall aid you, you but keep
"The promise pledg'd."—Sacred the hero swears
By her, the tri-form'd goddess, whom that grove
Acknowledges divine; and by the god,
Whence sprung the sire-in-law he hopes to claim;
The god who all beholds; by all his deeds
Atchiev'd; and by his perils all he swears.
His words believ'd, immediate he receives
The magic plants, their use well taught, and seeks
The roof rejoicing. Now the morn had driven
The glimmering stars far distant, crowding press'd
The people in the sacred field of Mars,
The king himself amidst them, seated high,
In purple clad, with ivory sceptre grac'd.
Lo! come the brazen-footed bulls, who breathe
Through nostrils fenc'd with adamant hot flames:
Parch'd by their breath, the herbage blacken'd burns.
Loud as the blazing forge's chimney roars;
Or loud as lime in earthy furnace laid,
Bursts into heat by watery sprinklings touch'd:
So loud, within their flaming chests contain'd,
The struggling fires loud bellow'd. Scorch'd their throats
The sound transmitted. Boldly Æson's son
March'd onward; fiercely as the youth approach'd,
His foes dark lower'd, and bent their steel-tipt horns,
Paw'd with their clefted hoofs the dusty ground,
And fill'd with smoky bellowings all the air.
Pale grew each Grecian face; advancing on
The fiery blasts he feels not, such the power
The mighty charms possess, but boldly strokes
Their dewlaps pendulous, and to the yoke
Subjected, makes them drag the ponderous plough;
And with the iron cut th' uncustom'd soil.
The Colchians wondering gaze; the Grecians loud
Applaud, and with fresh courage fill his soul.

Then from his brazen helmet pluck'd, he sows
The serpent's teeth, deep in the furrow'd ground:
The ground, the teeth with powerful venom ting'd,
Soften'd and swell'd them, and a novel shape
Imparted. Thus within the parent's womb,
An human shape the infant mass receives,
Completed perfect in the dark recess;
Nor till mature, to air external given.
So when the manly forms were perfect made
Within earth's pregnant bowels, up they sprung
Thick in the fruitful field; more wonderous still
Their arms they clash'd when born. Then when the Greeks
Their keenly-pointed spears preparing saw
To hurl at Jason's head, low sunk their souls,
And pallid grew their cheeks; Medea ev'n,
Whose art insur'd his safety, trembling fear'd,
When single she the youth beheld assail'd
By foes in hosts; bloodless her face became,
And tremor seiz'd her limbs: then lest the herbs
Presented first, should fail in power, she sings
An helping magic song, and all her arts
Latent, calls forth. Amidst the hostile crowd
A mighty rock he flings; their martial rage
From him diverted, on each other turns.
By mutual wounds the earth-born brothers fall;
In civil discord perish. Joy'd again
The Grecians clasp the conqueror in their arms.
Thou too, Mecea, wish'd thine arms to fill
With him victorious. (Shame at first repress'd
Thy open fondness, though thou wast embrac'd)
Now reputation awes thee, now prevents
That bliss. What honor gives,—silent to joy,
And pour glad thanks to all thy magic arts,
And gods their authors, those thou dar'st indulge.
Now sole remains by powerful herbs to lull
The wakeful dragon, whose high-crested head
A triple tongue contains, whose crooked fangs
Dreadful the golden fleece protecting guards.
Him when be sprinkled with the juices prest
From plants Lethean; and repeated thrice,
The words which placid sleep inspire; which still
The ruffled ocean; and arrest the course
Of rapid torrents; sleep before unknown
Stole o'er his eyelids, and th' Æsonian youth
Seiz'd on the golden prize. Proud with the spoil,
(A second spoil possessing) she who gave
The power to conquer, as his wife he bears,
And lands triumphant on Thessalia's shores.

Mothers of Thessaly, and aged sires
For sons restor'd, glad offerings bring: bright flames
The high-heap'd incense; votive victims deck'd
With gilded horns are slain: but Æson, far
The grateful crowd avoids, now near his fate,
Bent by a weight of years. Hence Jason spoke;—
"O, spouse! to thee my life and safety ow'd;
"To me, thou all hast given; the high swol'n sum
"Of all thy favors might belief surpass:
"This more attempt, if this thou can'st,—and what
"Thy magic power defies? My years curtail,
"And to my sire's existence add the term."
Fast flow'd his tears while speaking;—while he spoke,
His pious duty mov'd Medea; quick
Her sire Æëta, so deserted, sprung
To thought, and shew'd the two contrasting souls.
But, veil'd her secret thoughts, she thus replies;—
"What impious accents hear I from thy tongue,
"O, spouse religious? Can I then transfer
"Of thy existence part? Not Hecat's power
"Fateful, would sanction this; nor stands thy wish
"In equity. Yet, Jason, will I try
"More than thou seek'st to give. With all my skill
"Thy sire's existence to prolong, thy years
"Unshorten'd; should the tri-form'd goddess aid
"Propitious my designs."—Three nights were now
Deficient, ere the full-form'd horns could meet
The lunar orb to fill. Complete her round;
A solid sphere of light from earth beheld,
Medea wanders forth; loose all her robes;
Naked her feet; bare-headed; while her hair
Wild o'er her shoulders floats; and thus array'd,
Untended, while deep midnight silence reigns
She bends her devious way. Men, beasts, and birds,
In bonds of sleep were chain'd; the hedges still,
No murmur breath'd; nor wav'd the silent trees;
Hush'd was the humid sky; the stars alone
Twinkled: to them her arms extending, thrice
She turn'd around; thrice from the flowing stream
Her tresses sprinkled; thrice with yelling noise
The silence broke; then with her bended knee
The hard earth pressing, cry'd;—"O, night! thou friend
"Of secret deeds; ye glittering stars! whose rays
"With Luna's, Sol's diurnal light succeed;
"And thou, O, Hecat'! tripleform'd, who know'st
"My undertaking, and approaching aid'st
"With incantations, and with magic powers:

"And thou, O, earth! whose bosom witching plants
"Affords: ye winds; ye skies; ye mountains; lakes;
"And flowing streams: O, all ye gods! who dwell
"In shady woods; and all ye gods of night,
"Hither approach! by whose high power, at will,
"Rivers I cause between their wondering banks,
"Back to their springs to flow; the stormy deep
"Hush by my song, or lash it into rage;
"Clouds form, or clouds dispel; raise furious blasts,
"Or furious blasts allay; smite with my song
"The dragon's furious jaws: the living rocks
"I shake;—uproot the oak; the earth upturn;
"Move forests; bid the trembling mountains leap;
"Loud roar the ground; and from the tombs the ghosts
"Affrighted walk. Thee, Luna, too I draw
"From heaven, by all the threatening clash of brass
"Deterr'd not: pale the brighter car becomes,
"My spells once utterr'd: by my poisons charm'd,
"Pallid Aurora seems. You, plants! for me,
"Blunted the ardor of the flaming bulls;
"Press'd with the yoke, their necks impatient bent,
"And dragg'd the crooked plough. You bade the race
"Snake-born, upon themselves their warring rage
"To turn. In sleep the roaring dragon's eyes
"You steep'd; the guard eluded, sent the prize
"To glad the towns of Greece. Now have I need
"Of renovating herbs, to make old age
"Glow once again in all its youthful bloom.
"This will you grant, for sure those stars in vain
"Not sparkle; nor in vain the chariot comes
"Drawn by the dragons wing'd." The chariot comes
Swift sweeping through the air. Active she mounts,
Strokes the rein'd dragons' manes, and shakes the thongs.
On high they soar:—Thessalian Tempé far
Beneath she views; then tow'rd the chalky land
Her snakes directs. On Ossa's top explores
For plants, and seeks what lofty Pelion bears;
Othrys, and Pindus, and Olympus huge.
What please her, part she with their root updrags;
Part with her crooked brazen sickle mows;
Apidanus; Amphrysos, on their banks
Many afforded: nor Enipeus scap'd.
Peneus, and Spercheus, and the rushy shores
Of Bæbé some contributed. She pluck'd
In Anthedon the living grass whose power,
Then Glaucus' form unchang'd, was yet unknown.

Now had nine days, now had nine nights elaps'd,

Borne on her dragon wings, and in her car
Wandering the fields among, ere back she turn'd:
Unfed her dragons, save by odorous smells;
Yet had they shed their scales, with youth renew'd.
Arriv'd, without the palace gate she stays,
And there sole shelter'd by the sky, all touch
Of man denying; altars two she rears
Of turf; sacred to Hecate stood the right,
To Youth the left: when these with vervain bound.
And forest boughs, here sacrifice she makes.
Hard by, two trenches scoops from out the ground;
Smites with her weapon in the sable throat,
A sheep presented; in the open ditch
Empties the blood; then bowls of wine she pours,
And bowls of smoking milk; with mystic words
Invokes the powers terrestrial; begs the king
Of shades, and begs his ravish'd spouse to aid,
Nor of his soul the aged king defraud.
These when with lengthen'd prayers, and murmurings long,
Appeas'd; she bids them tow'rd the altars bring
The feeble Æson; his exhausted limbs
Bound in deep slumber, by her magic power,
Corse-like, she lays extended on the grass.
Then Jason bids, and his attendant crew,
Far thence depart, nor with their view prophane
Her acts mysterious. As she bids they go.
Medea then the flaming altars round,
In Bacchanalian guise her flowing locks,
Circles; and in the ditch's blackening gore
Her splinter'd torches dips; with blood imbu'd,
Burns them upon her altars; thrice with fire,
With sulphur thrice, and thrice with flowing streams,
The sire she lustrates. Heated now in brass,
Her powerful medicines bubble, high and white
The swelling froth appears. There boils she all
The roots in vales Æmonian dug; and seeds,
And flowers, and juices dark: gems unto these,
Sought in the distant East, she adds; and adds
What on the sand the refluent ocean leaves:
More still, the night-long moon collected dew
She brings; the dismal screech-owl's flesh and wings;
The entrails of the wolf ambiguous, wont
His savage face in human guise to wear:
Nor wanted there, the scaly skin which clothes
Th' amphibious snake Cyniphian, long and small:
The beak and head a crow nine ages bore,
She adds. Now was the foreign dame prepar'd,
By help of these, and nameless thousands more,

The promis'd boon to give, the whole she stirs
Deep from the bottom, with a bough long rent,
From the mild olive. Lo! the wither'd branch,
The boiling caldron stirring, sudden shoots
In virid freshness! shortly leaves bud forth;
And soon it bends beneath a load of fruit!
Where'er the fire above the hollow brass,
The bubbling foam high-rais'd, and boiling drops
Sprinkled the ground,—the ground with verdure smil'd;
Flowers and soft herbage sprung. Medea sees,
And with her weapon ope's the senior's throat;
His aged blood exhausted sees, and pours
Her juices copious: part his mouth receives;
And part the wound. When Æson these had drank,
Their hoary whiteness lost, his beard and hair,
An ebon tinge receiv'd; his leanness fled;
His pallid ghastly face no more was seen;
His hollow veins with added blood were fill'd;
And all his limbs in lusty plumpness swell'd.
The wondering Æson, such himself beheld,
As the last forty years he ne'er had past.

  Bacchus, from heaven survey'd the mighty change
Wonderous, and hence that power was given he found;
His nurses to restore to youthful years:
The boon from Tethys asking, he obtain'd.

  Nor cease the frauds yet of the Phasian dame:
Fierce hatred 'gainst her by her spouse she feigns,
And flies to Pelias' court; a suppliant there,
His daughters hail her guest:—the sire bent down
With age. The crafty Colchian these beguiles
Soon, with her well-dissembled friendship's form.
Amid her mighty benefits, she tells
Æson's old age remov'd; relating all,
On this she chiefly dwells. Hope sudden springs
Within their virgin breasts: Pelias their sire,
Such art they trust may yet revivify.
That art they sue for,—highest claim'd reward
To her they promise: mute at first she stands,
And feigning doubt, in hesitation holds,
And anxious poise their eager minds. At last,
She says, when promising,—"That in the deed,
"More faith ye may confide, a leading ram,
"The oldest in your fleecy flocks, a lamb
"My medicine shall transform!"—Instant was dragg'd
The woolly beast, whose wreathing horns around
His hollow temples curl'd; whose wither'd throat

The steel Thessalian stabb'd; the scanty blood
The steel scarce spotting: then th' enchantress steeps
His mangled body in the caldron deep,
With juices powerful: smaller grow his limbs;
Shed are his horns; and vanish'd are his years;
And from the caldron tender bleatings sound:
Instant leaps forth to all the wondering crowd
The bleating lamb, which, frisking, flies and seeks
The swelling teats. With admiration struck,
Now Pelias' daughters faith unshaken give;
More urgent press their wish. Thrice had the sun,
'Merg'd in th' Iberian sea, unyok'd his steeds;
And the fourth night the glittering stars had shone;
When o'er the fire, pure water from the stream,
And powerless plants, the false Medea plac'd.

Now all in sleep relax'd, a death-like sleep,
The monarch's limbs were stretch'd; and with their king,
His guards lay dormant; so her magic words,
And magic tongue had doom'd. Medea leads
Across the steps the daughters; bidd'n by her,
His couch they compass.—"Why, O, feeble souls!
"Thus hesitate?"—she said,—"your swords unsheathe!
"Pour out his far-spent gore, that I may fill
"With youthful, vigorous blood his empty'd veins.
"Your father's life, and years, are in your hands:
"If sways you piety; if empty hopes
"Wavering deceive you not; then well deserve,
"By duty to your sire: quickly expel
"With weapons his old age: let issue forth
"His now congealing blood with brandish'd steel."
Exhorted thus, most pious she who feels,
First impious acts;—a wicked deed performs,
Lest wicked she were call'd: yet on the blow
Not one would bend her sight; with eyes averse
Their savage hands the unseen wounds inflict.
Flowing with gore, he from the bed uprais'd
His limbs; and from his posture strove half-torn
To rise; and stretching forth his pallid arms
'Mid all their threatening swords;—"Daughters!"—he cries,
"What do ye? Why against your parent's life
"Thus arm ye?"—Sink their spirits! drop their hands!
His throat Medea severing, stay'd the words
He more had utter'd,—and the mangled corse,
Deep in the boiling brazen caldron flung.

She now,—but through the air on dragon wings
High borne,—their furious vengeance had not scap'd.

O'er shady Pelion high she flew, and o'er
The cave of Chiron; Othrys; and the spot
For old Cerambus' strange adventure known:
Upborne on wings by kindly-aiding nymphs,
Here, when the solid earth th' incroaching main
Wide delug'd, flying, safe Deucalion's flood
He 'scap'd. Æölian Pitané to left
She quits; and sees the dragon huge, to stone
An image turn'd. And Ida's grove where chang'd
By Bacchus' power, the steer a stag became,
To screen the theft. And where beneath the sand,
A little sand, Corythus' father lies;
And fields which Mæra's new-heard howlings fill.
Euripylus' fam'd town, where Coän dames,
What time the troops of Hercules them left,
With horns were crown'd: and Phœbus' favor'd Rhodes;
Jalysian Telchines, whose hateful eyes
All vitiating, Jove detesting 'whelm'd
Beneath his brother's waves. She passes next
Carthæïa' walls in ancient Cææ's isle,
Where wondering saw Alcidamas the sire,
A placid dove his daughter's body bear.
And Hyrié's lake she sees, and Tempé's pool
Cycneiän, which the swan so sudden form'd
Frequented: Phyllius there, a willing slave,
Birds and fierce beasts, to his capricious boy
Oft brought—e'en lions tam'd; a furious bull
He bade him bring, a furious bull he brought;
But now in croler at his craving soul,
The bull refus'd, though as the last gift claim'd:
Indignant, cry'd he,—"soon you'll wish him given!"—
And from the high rock plung'd: all thought he fell:
But form'd a swan, lightly he pois'd in air
On snowy wings. Hyrié, her son thus sav'd,
Knew not, by constant weeping soon dissolv'd;
The lake becoming that still bears her name.
Near this is Pleuron:—Ophian Combé, here
Wafted on wings, her murderous sons escap'd.
Thence she beholds Latona's favorite isle;
Calaurea, where to birds the royal pair
Were chang'd: Cyllené, on the right is plac'd
Where like the savage herd, Menephron sought
His mother's bed. Far hence she spies in tears
Cephisus, for his nephew's fate who mourn'd,
Chang'd by Apollo to a sea-calf huge;
And saw Eumelus' dome, who wept his child,
A bird become. At length on dragon wings,
Pirenian Corinth she regain'd; where tell

The ancient tales, in primal ages, men
From shower-fed mushrooms sprung. Here first was flam'd
In Colchian venoms fierce, the new-made bride;
Then either sea in blazing spires beheld
The royal dome; and with her children's gore
Her impious sword was stain'd. Thus on herself
Reveng'd; from royal Jason's wrath she fled.

Borne hence, her snakes Titanian reach the walls
Of Pallas' city, where most just of men
O, Phineus! thou, and Periphas the old,
With Polyphemon's niece, as birds are seen,
Soaring aloft in air on new-form'd wings.
Here Ægeus' roof receiv'd her, for this deed
Alone to blame: not satisfy'd as host,
In marriage bonds he makes her more his own.
Now Theseus comes, son to his sire unknown,
Whose brave atchievements, all the two-sea'd land
In peace had settled. For his death she mix'd
The baneful aconite, long since from shores
Of Scythia brought; which thus old tales relate,
From Cerberus' venom'd jaws was first produc'd,
Through a dark den, with gloomy opening, lies
A path steep shelving, where Alcides dragg'd
Fierce Cerberus to light, resisting strong,
Glancing askaunce his eyes from day, whose rays
Sparkled too bright, in adamantine chains.
With rabid anger swol'n, a triple yell
Fill'd all the air; he o'er the virid plain
Sprinkled white foam; increasing fast this shoots;
The fruitful soil fresh virulence imparts,
And ranker grows its power: from hardest rocks
It lively springs, and Aconite hence nam'd.
This did old Ægeus, by his crafty spouse
Deceiv'd, to Theseus, as a foe, present.
Unwitting Theseus, in his hand receiv'd
The cup presented; when the sire espy'd
Upon his ivory-hilted sword a mark,
Which prov'd his offspring; from his lips he dash'd
The poison. Wrapp'd in clouds by magic rais'd,
The sorceress from their furious vengeance fled.

The sire, though joy'd, his son in safety found,
Trembles astonish'd at the narrow 'scape;
And horrid crime premeditated: burns
On every altar fires;—to every god
Piles costly gifts: full on the brawny neck
Of oxen falls, their horns with garlands bound,

The sacrificing axe. Ne'er till that day
Had Athens' town, such joyous feasting seen;
Nobles and commons crowd around the board,
And thus, by wine inspir'd, sublime they sing.

"Thee, mighty Theseus! Marathon admires,
"Stain'd by the vanquish'd Cretan bull's black gore.
"Thy aid the swains of Cromyon own; thou gav'st
"That now secure they till their fields. The land
"Of Epidaurus saw the club-arm'd son
"Of Vulcan slain by thee. By thee, beheld
"Cephisus' shores, the fierce Procrustes die,
"Ceres' Eleusis hail'd Cercyon's fall.
"Sinis thou slew'st, gifted with strength ill-us'd;
"His strength high trees could bend, and oft he dragg'd
"Close down to earth the loftiest tops of pines,
"Thus rent the bodies of his victims wide.
"Safe now extends the road to Lelex' walls,
"Scyron low laid: earth to the robber's limbs,
"Wide scatter'd, rest refuses; to his bones
"Ocean a tomb denies; long widely tost,
"Age hardens into rock his last remains;
"His name the rock still bears. Should we thy age
"And actions count, thy famous deeds by far
"Thy years outnumber. O, most brave of men!
"For thee the public vows ascend; to thee,
"In Bacchus bowl we drink. The royal hall
"Resounds with all the grateful people's praise;
"Nor through the city glooms one sorrowing spot."

And yet (so seldom pleasure comes unmix'd,
But still some cares with joy will intervene)
While Ægeus, gladden'd that his son secure
Arriv'd; Minos, for furious war prepares.
Strong though his troops, and though his navy strong
His utmost strength was in paternal rage;
And with just arms Androgeus' death t' avenge
He wars: yet first auxiliar strength he gains;
And powerful sweeps the seas with flying ships.
First Anaphe joins him, and Astypalæa; urg'd
By promise this, and that by threats constrain'd,
Low Myconé; Cymolus' chalky fields;
Bright Cythnos; Scyros; flat Seriphus' isle;
The marble Paros; and the fort betray'd
For gold, demanded by the impious nymph
Sithonian: still for gold she anxious seeks
Though chang'd a bird; on sable pinions borne,
With sable feet, she flutters as a daw.

But Oliaros, and Didymæ, unite;
And Gyaros, Andros, Tenos, all refuse,
With Peparethos, in bright olives rich,
To aid the Gnossian fleet. Thence to the left
Steering, Œnopia's regions Minos sought;
Œnopia call'd of old, Ægina now,
By Æäcus, his mother's honor'd name.
In crowds the people rush, and pant to view
So highly fam'd a prince: to meet him go
First Telamon, then Peleus next in age,
And Phocas third and last, Ev'n Æäcus
With years opprest, steps tardy forth, and asks
The visit's cause. The hundred-city'd king
Deep sighs, his grief paternal all renew'd,
And thus replies;—"My arms, O, king! assist
"Assum'd, just vengeance for a son to claim.
"Partake this pious war. Peace to his manes
"I seek."—But Asopiades replies;—
"In vain you ask;—my city cannot aid:
"No lands by neighbouring scite more closely bound,
"Than ours and Athens'; hence our league."—The king
Angry departs, exclaiming.—"Much your league
"May cost you!"—But to threaten war more safe
He deems, than wage it there, and waste his force.
Still from Œnopia's walls the fleet was seen,
Not distant far; when sped by swelling sail,
An Attic ship arriv'd; the friendly port
Enter'd. On board was Cephalus who bore
His country's message. Well the royal youths
The hero knew, though long time past beheld;
And gave the friendly hand, and welcome led
To their paternal dome. The graceful chief
Enters, retaining still evincing marks
Of pristine beauty; in his hand he bears
A branch of native olive: in the midst
Senior he stands; and younger on each side,
Clytus, and Butes, Pallas' sons. Complete
Their friendly salutations; next the words
Th' Athenians bade him, Cephalus reports:
Their aid demands; their ancient league recounts;
The oaths their fathers swore; and adds, all Greece
Might perish in their ruin. When their cause
With eloquence the messenger thus urg'd;
On his bright sceptre as his left hand lean'd,
"Take, O Athenians,"—Æäcus exclaim'd,—
"Not ask, our aid! Unhesitating draw
"What force this isle possesses, and with yours

"Employ it: with you shall my strongest power
"March forth: strength want we not; our numerous troops
"Abundant, for ourselves and friends suffice:
"Prais'd be the gods! such is our happy state
"Your wish defies evasion."—"Still may grow,"
Said Cephalus,—"your prosperous city's state,
"And yours!—What transport seiz'd me as I walk'd,
"To see each youth so fair, so equal ag'd,
"Of all who met me. Yet in vain I look'd
"For many features, known when last your walls
"Receiv'd me."—Æacus, with deep-drawn sighs,
And sorrowing voice, thus answers.—"Better fate
"Completed, what a mournful sight began.
"Would I in full could all the facts relate!
"Now unconnected must I speak, or tire
"Your ear with words superfluous. Whom you seek,
"Whom you remember, bones and ashes rest.
"But small their numbers:—Heavens! how small to those,
"My people, who have sunk in death beside.

  "A dreadful plague, the angry Juno shed
"Unjust, upon the natives of the land,
"Detested, that her rival's name it bore.
"While human seem'd the scourge, the noxious cause
"Of slaughter yet conceal'd, with physic's skill
"We strove; in vain! death mock'd the power of art.
"At first thick darkness heavy press'd the earth;
"Pregnant with heat roll'd on the lazy clouds.
"Four times the full-orb'd moon had join'd her horns,
"Four times diminish'd, had she disappear'd;
"Still the hot south-wind blew his deadly blasts.
"Our lakes and fountains, from th' infected air
"Contagion suck'd; millions of vipers swarm'd
"In our uncultur'd fields, our running streams
"Tainting with poison. First the sudden plague
"Its power display'd, on sheep, on dogs, on fowls,
"Cattle, and forest beasts with deadly power.
"The hapless ploughman, wondering, at his work
"Sees his strong oxen in the furrow sink.
"The woolly flocks with sickly bleatings waste
"In body, while their wool spontaneous falls.
"The steed so fiery, on the dusty plain
"So fam'd, the palm contemns; and all despis'd
"His ancient honors, at his manger groans,
"Prey to disease inglorious. His fierce rage
"The boar forgets. The stag neglects his speed.
"Not rush the bears upon the stronger herds.
"A general languor reigns. In woods, in fields,

"In ways, the filthy carcases are seen;
"The stench pollutes the air: and, wonderous! dogs,
"Nor birds rapacious, nor the grizzly wolves,
"Touch the dead spoil. Rotting they melt away,
"Poisoning the gale; and spreading wide the pest.
"Now the disease, a heavier scourge, attacks
"The hapless swains, and in the lofty walls
"Of cities rules. First the scorch'd vitals burn;
"The hidden fire the blushing skin betrays,
"And breath laborious drawn; the furr'd tongue swells;
"The parch'd mouth widely gapes, th' infectious air
"Inhaling copious. On the couch none lie;
"None bear their covering robes; their bodies swol'n,
"On the bare earth they fling; nor coolness find
"Their bodies from the ground;—the ground from them
"Burns hot. Nor aids them now physicians' skill;
"E'en them the dire pest seizes, and their art
"Fails to assist themselves. Who boldly comes,
"With kindly hand his dying friend to aid,
"Sinks straight in death beside him. Fled all hope
"Of health, and in the grave alone an end
"Beheld of their disease,—some wild indulge
"Their fondest passions, void of every care;
"For every care is vain. Of modest shame
"Regardless, in promiscuous throngs they crowd
"To rivers, fountains, and capacious wells,
"Their hot thirst unextinguish'd, but with life.
"To rise unable, many in the stream
"Sink, and there perish: still their followers drink.
"So irksome to the wretched sufferers seem
"Their couches, thence they spring;—and some too weak
"To lift their limbs, roll desperate to the ground.
"Each quits his home,—to each his home appears,
"The fatal spot; and while obscure the cause,
"Each deems the house contagious. Oft were seen
"Beings half-dead, slow crawling o'er the ways,
"Till power to crawl was lost. Others with moans
"Stretch'd on the ground, rolling their half-clos'd eyes,
"In final motion: raising high their arms
"To heaven's o'erhanging stars, breathe out their last,
"Caught here by death, and there. Ah! me, what then
"My mind employ'd? What but to loathe my life,
"And pray with my dear countrymen to die?
"Whatever side mine eyes were bent, I saw
"My people strewn;—thick as the mellow fruit,
"Shook from the branches, or the acorns lie.
"Observe that temple, lofty where it towers;
"To Jove 'tis sacred. Who to that high fane

"Their useless incense brought not? There how oft
"Wife for her husband, parent for her child,
"Before th' inexorable altar, breath'd
"Their dying gasp, 'mid deprecating prayers;
"And half their incense unconsum'd remain'd.
"How oft the oxen to the temple dragg'd,
"While now the priest his voice address'd, and pour'd
"The goblet o'er their foreheads, have they dropp'd
"By stroke unlook'd for. When myself, to Jove
"Wish'd sacrifice to offer up; for me,
"My country, and my sons,—the victim loud
"Dire lowings utter'd, and without a blow
"Fell sudden,—scarce with blood the wounding knife
"Was stain'd. The morbid inwards mock'd our wish,
"To learn the truth, and pleasure of the gods:
"The deep-fixt plague had to the bowels pierc'd.
"Before the sacred portals have I seen,
"The corses spread; before the altars too,
"As death would come in his most hideous form.
"Some with the cord life's passage choke, and seek
"Death, lest they death should meet. Madly they rush
"And voluntary meet approaching fate.
"The bodies plung'd in death, funereal rites
"Custom'd, receiv'd not; nor the numerous dead
"Could all the gates receive: or un-inhum'd
"Above the earth they lie, or on the pyre
"Unhonor'd by due rites, the bodies flame.
"All sense of reverence lost, for piles they fight;
"And burn their dead in fires which others own.
"To mourn are none; unwept the shadows roam,
"Of young and old alike, of sons and sires.
"The ground for graves too small, for fires the woods.
"Aghast this whirlwind of distress to view,
"O, Jove!—I cry'd—if false they not report,
"That once you in Ægina's arms were clasp'd;—
"If not, O, mighty sire! asham'd to own
"Yourself my parent, give my people back,
"Or give me death with them. A rattling sign
"He gave, and prosperous thunders roll'd. I spoke;—
"These omens I accept; and pray these signs
"May indicate your happy will:—as pledge
"I take them.—Nigh by chance an oak there stood,
"Thick-set with spreading boughs, Jove's sacred tree,
"Sprung from Dodona's stock: here I beheld
"Grain-gathering ants, each burthen'd with his load,
"In his small mouth, as o'er the rugged bark
"In lengthen'd file they march'd. The numerous crowds
"Admiring;—Best of fathers, I exclaim'd,

"So many subjects grant me, to refill
"My desert walls.—Trembled the lofty oak,
"Of wind no breath, yet mov'd the sounding boughs;
"With terror shook my limbs, and upright rear'd
"My hair; then kisses to the ground I gave,
"And kiss'd the oak; scarce hope I dar'd to feel:
"Yet still I nourish'd hope within my soul.
"Night comes; my body worn with cares, to sleep
"Obedience yielded. Still before mine eyes
"The oak appear'd; branches the same it bore,
"And on its branches seem'd the swarms the same;
"So mov'd the boughs, and on the grass below,
"Shook the corn-carrying crowd. Sudden they grew;
"Large, and more large they seem'd, as from the ground
"Themselves they rais'd, and stood in form erect.
"Their slender make, their numerous feet, their hue
"Of sable, disappear'd, and all their limbs
"An human shape confess'd. Sleep fled mine eyes;
"And fled my vision:—As by heaven not mark'd,
"Complaining;—far without the hall I heard
"A murmuring loud, and human seem'd the sounds,—
"Though stranger to mine ears: musing if still
"I slept not,—Lo! quick, Telamon approach'd,
"Wide threw the doors; and cry'd,—O, sire! behold;
"What hope, what faith surpasses!—Forth I come;
"Such men as in my dream my fancy saw,
"I see;—I know them, man by man, again:
"They come, and king salute me: unto Jove
"My votive thanks I pay; my city share
"Amongst my subjects new; and all my lands,
"(Of those who till'd them, empty.) Myrmidons,
"From whence they sprung, I call them. You have seen
"Their bodies,—still their habits are the same:
"A frugal race as wont, patient of toil;
"On gain still bent; tenacious of that gain.
"These equal all, in courage and in years,
"Shall follow you to battle; when the east
"Which blew you here so prosperous, (for the east
"Had brought him) to the southern gales shall yield."
With these and such like speeches, all the day
They sit conversing; evening they devote
To banquets; and the night to soft repose.
Sol rais'd his golden head, but Eurus still
Prevail'd, and bound their sails. Now Pallas' sons
To Cephalus, their chief in years, repair,
And to the king with Pallas' sons he goes;
But still deep-wrapt in sleep the king was laid.
Phocus receiv'd them at the gates; employ'd

Were Telamon and Peleus, troops to chuse
For the new war. Th' Athenian chief he leads
Within the palace, to the fairest rooms.
When all were seated, Phocus mark'd the dart
The hero bore, shap'd from a wood unknown,
Pointed with gold; and said, with prefac'd words:
"To range the forests, and fierce beasts to slay
"Is all my joy; yet long in doubt I've stood
"What tree this dart has form'd; for ash too pale,
"Too smooth for cornel; though from whence it comes
"So ignorant, ne'er before mine eyes beheld
"A fairer weapon."—Pallas' son address'd
The youth:—"The javelin's use you'll more admire
"Than beauty;—thrown where'er, its mark it gains,
"Unrul'd by erring chance, and bloody, back
"Instant returns."—Then Phocus curious asks
More full its story, how, and whence it came,
And who the author of so priz'd a gift.
Him Cephalus informs, but shame denies
To tell the whole, and what the present's price.
Full to his mind his consort's loss recall'd,
Tears sudden gush'd:—"O, goddess-born!—he cries,
"This dart (improbable howe'er) my tears
"Has often caus'd,—and long will make them flow;—
"If fate long life should grant. My dear-lov'd spouse
"This dart destroy'd:—O, that this fatal gift
"Had still been unpossess'd! Procris, ally'd
"To stol'n Orithyiä (if Orithyiä's fame
"Your ears has reach'd) was as her sister fair:
"Nay, match'd in form and manners, she might more
"The robber tempt. Her sire Erechthens join'd
"To me the maid; us love more firmly bound:
"Blest was I call'd, and blest I was indeed,
"And still were blest, but heaven else will'd my fate.
"Now had the second month connubial joys
"Beheld; when chasing dusky darkness far,
"Aurora ruddy, saw me on the heights
"Hymettus flowery rears, as there my toils
"For antler'd stags I spread: and there by force
"She clasp'd me. Truth I wish to guide my tongue
"Nor yet displease the goddess, when I swear
"Though bright her roseate cheeks; though wide she sways
"Of night and day the confines; though she quaffs
"Nectarean liquid, still I Procris lov'd:
"Still in my bosom Procris reign'd, and still
"Procris, my tongue repeated. Oft I urg'd
"The sacred couch, the new-felt joys, the rites
"So recent, and the plighted faith just given,

"To her deserted: when the goddess flam'd,
"Exclaiming;—Ingrate! cease thy doleful plaints,
"Enjoy thy Procris,—if I right foresee
"Thou'lt rue that wish'd enjoyment:—Angry thus
"She fled me. Slow returning, much I mus'd,
"The goddess' words recalling: fear me thrill'd,
"Lest Procris had her nuptial oaths profaned.
"Her age, her beauty, much suspicion mov'd;
"Her virtue bade me chase my fears as vain.
"Yet was I absent, and from whence I came,
"Prov'd how adulterous females might indulge,
"Suspicious love fears all. Studious I seek,
"What found would rack with torture; and I burn
"To bribe with gifts, and try her modest faith.
"Aurora aids my fears, my shape transforms:
"(Conscious I felt it.) To Minerva's town,
"To all unknown, I hastened, and my house
"Enter'd: the house in faultless guise I found;
"Chaste all appear'd, and anxious all were seen
"For their lost master. By a thousand arts
"Erechtheus' daughter I at length beheld,
"And seen was stagger'd: near my purpos'd proof
"Relinquish'd of fidelity; most hard
"The cheat to tell not; to refrain most hard
"From conjugal salutes. Sad she appear'd.
"But nought more lovely could in sadness seem:
"Burning in wishes for her absent spouse.
"Image, O, Phocus! what her beauteous face
"Could boast; a face that woe itself became.
"Why should I tell how oft her virtuous soul,
"Repuls'd my tempting offers? Why repeat
"How oft she cry'd;—For one myself I keep,
"For one, where'er he stays, my joys preserve.
"Whose mad suspicion would not this allay?
"This proof of faith? But I, not so content,
"Strive for my own confusion. Lavish gifts
"I proffer for the joys of one short night:
"More and more rich I heap them, till her breast
"Wavers, then loud exclaim,—Lo! here behold,
"Adulteress! one unluckily disguis'd,
"Unluckily betroth'd, thy lawful spouse!
"Perfidious! by those eyes convinc'd I stand.
"Nought she:—with silent shame o'ercome, she fled
"The house deceitful, and her hated spouse.
"With me offended, all the race of men
"Detesting, on the mountain tops she rov'd;
"Diana's sports close following. Fiercer love
"Flam'd in my bosom, thus deserted left.

"I su'd for pardon, and my fault I own'd;
"Swore that myself so tempted, so had err'd,
"By such high offers brib'd. Confessing thus,
"Her wounded modest pride grew more compos'd;
"And shortly I regain'd her. Long in peace
"We liv'd, and cordial spent the smiling years.
"Herself a gift she priz'd not: more she gave,
"An hour d, she from Diana's hand receiv'd,
"Who said,—accept the fleetest of his race—
"And gave this javelin which you see me bear.
"If of the first the fate you seek to know,
"Attend, th' adventure will your wonder move.

  "The son of Laïus had the words explain'd,
"Before h s time to every mind obscure;
"And the dark prophetess, down headlong flung,
"Laid lifeless, all her riddling tales forgot.
"Her, fostering Themis saw, and unreveng'd
"To lie not suffer'd. Straight another plague
"On Thebes was loos'd; and all the country swains
"Fear'd by the savage beast their flocks to lose,
"And fear d their own destruction. With the youths
"Adjacent, I assembled; round the fields
"Our toils we fix; the toils the rapid beast
"O'erleaps high-bounding; 'bove the loftiest ropes,
"Stretch'c o'er the nets, with active spring he flies.
"The hounds uncoupled, in the chace he mocks,
"And like an agile bird before them plays;
"With outcries loud, for Lælaps' aid they call.
"(My Procris' gift, so nam'd.) Long had he tugg'd,
"To extricate him from the chain; to free
"His captive neck: scarce was he loos'd, so swift
"He shot. in vain our eyes his progress mark'd:
"In the light dust his feet were printed, he,
"Rapt from the view, was vanish'd. Swifter flies
"The darted spear not: nor the leaden ball
"Hurl'd from the whirling sling;—nor reedy dart
"Shot from the Cretan bow. A central hill
"High-towering, all the subject plains o'erlooks;
"Thither I climb, and there behold the chase;
"A novel scene. Now seems the beast safe caught;
"Now from the grasp light-springing. Flight right on
"Crafty he shuns, and doubles round the field,
"Cheating his chaser's mouth; and circling turns
"His foe's quick speed eluding. Swift he flies,—
"With equal swiftness follow'd. Now to grasp
"His prey seems Lælaps,—in his grasp deceiv'd,
"His empty jaws seize air. Now to my aid

"I call my javelin,—poize it for the blow,
"And bend mine eyes the thongs to fix secure:
"Again I lift them to behold the chase,
"And see astonish'd in the spacious plain
"Two marble statues! this to fly appears,—
"That barking seems to follow. So decreed
"Doubtless the gods, that in the arduous course
"Unconquer'd, each his glory might retain."

  Thus far he spoke, then silent sate.—"What crime,"
Said Phocus—"has the javelin then perform'd?"—
And thus the javelin's fault the hero tells,
"Since joys supreme my sorrows first forewent,
"Let me, O, Phocus! first those joys recount.
"O, youth! how it delights me to retrace
"Those happy moments, when supremely blest
"In her, the primal years were joyous spent.
"She, equal happy in her darling spouse;
"Each mind of mutual care a portion bore;
"And love's connubial joys each equal shar'd.
"Jove's proffer'd couch, with my embrace compar'd,
"Procris had spurn'd; nor could the loveliest nymph
"Me tempt, though Venus' self had deign'd to sue:
"In either breast an equal ardor flam'd.
"In youthful guise I wont the woods to scour,
"For sport betimes, ere yet the sun had ting'd
"With early beams the lofty mountains' tops:
"Nor took I servants, nor the courser fleet,
"Nor hounds sharp-scented, nor the knotted snares;
"This dart my sole dependence: when my arm
"With slaughtered spoil was satiate, tir'd I sought
"The cooling shade, and sought where Aura breath'd
"In frigid vales her breezes. 'Midst the heat
"Refreshing air I sought, and Aura call'd,
"My labour's recreation; thus I sung,
"I well the words remember;—Aura, come!
"Come, my delight,—within my bosom creep,
"Most grateful friend; come, and as wont remove
"My inward flames.—By chance more tender words
"(So sway'd my destiny) to these I join'd:
"And thus I spoke—O, thou! my greatest joy
"Refreshing, cherishing my strength and power!
"For thee, these woods and lonely spots I love:
"Here does my wishing mouth thy breath inhale.—
"These words ambiguous, busy ears receiv'd,
"And Aura! Aura! oft invok'd, they deem
"A favor'd nymph,—a nymph by me belov'd.
"The rash informer with the imag'd wrong,

"My Procris seeks his whispering tongue relates,
"The words o'erheard. Love credulous believes.
"C'erpress'd with grief, she sudden sunk, when heard
"The tale,—and long she unrecover'd laid.
"Then—hapless wife!—O, wayward fate! she cries:—
"My broken faith bewails, and with my crime
"Imagin'd, troubled, fears what not exists,—
"A name without a being: much she grieves,
"As real were her rival: yet full oft
"Stagger'd, she doubts, and hopes herself deceiv'd:
"Trusts not th' informer; and her husband's fault,
"Unless beheld, refuses to believe.
"When next Aurora bade the darkness fly
"I sally'd forth, and sought th' accustomed wood:
"Then tir'd with conquest, on the grass I stretch'd,
"And,—come, dear Aura, ease my pain,—I cry'd
"Sudden a mournful sigh betwixt my words
"I heard, but still proceeded,—dearest, come!—
"Again the falling leaves a rustling sound
"Causing, a savage beast I thought lay hid,
"And hurl'd my faithful dart. Procris was there!
"And as her tender breast the blow receiv'd
"Alas! she cry'd.—My faithful spouse's voice
"I knew, and with distracted speed I ran;
"Half-dead found her, all her robes distain'd
"With flowing blood,—and dragging from the wound,
"Ah, me!—her fatal gift. My guilty arms,
"Her body, dearer far than mine, support;
"My vest I rend, the cruel gash to bind,
"And check the gushing blood; I fearful pray,
"She will not leave me guilty of her fate.
"She now, her strength fast wasting, dying fast,
"These words to utter try'd:—Suppliant I beg,
"By all the oaths that form'd our nuptial ties;
"By all the gods and goddesses above;
"By all my actions which have given you joy;
"By that strong love which thus my fate has caus'd,
"Which now in death my bosom still retains,
"Let not this Aura to my bed succeed.—
"She said,—too late I learn'd, too late I told
"The error of the name; for what avail'd!
"She sinks, her small remaining strength is fled,
"Her last blood flows. While ought she seems to view,
"On me she bends her eyes; her hapless soul
"My lips inhale, yet pleas'd her brow appears
"In death, more calm from what I just explain'd."
Thus grieving, Cephalus concludes, and all
His audience with him weep. When, lo! appear

King Æacus, his sons, and troops new-rais'd;
Whom Cephalus, in warlike strength, receives.

THE EIGHTH BOOK

Nisus betrayed to Minos by his daughter Scylla; changed to a falcon, and Scylla to a lark. Return of Minos to Crete. The Minotaur and labyrinth. Flight of Dædalus and Icarus. Change of Perdix to a partridge. Chase and death of the Calydonian boar, by Meleager and Atalanta. Murder of Meleager's uncles. Vengeance of his mother. Death of Meleager, and transformation of his sisters to birds. Acheloüs. Nymphs transformed into the isles Echinades. Perimelè into an island. Story of Baucis and Philemon. Changes of Proteus. Story of Erisichthon, and transformations of his daughter.

THE EIGHTH BOOK OF THE METAMORPHOSES OF OVID

Now leading Phosphor' shining day disclos'd,
The darkness flying; and the eastern gales
Lull'd into calm, the vapoury clouds arose:
The placid south befriending, rapid borne,
The hero Cephalus, and aiding troops,
Ride unexpected in their wish'd-for port.

Minos, meanwhile, the Lelegeian coast
Lays waste, and on Alcathoë's town his power
Essays. Here Nisus rul'd, whose reverend locks
Of silvery brightness, in the midst contain'd
One with rich purple splendid, sacred pledge
Of fortune to his kingdom. Six times seen
Were Luna's horns arising fresh renew'd;
Still hover'd conquest doubtful o'er the war,
On wavering pinions, 'twixt opposing hosts.
A regal tower its vocal walls high-rear'd,
Where once Latona's son his golden lyre
Rested; the music still the stones retain'd.
Oft here the beauteous daughter of the king
Ascended, and the latent music drew
Forth to the ear, by smallest pebbles struck.
Thus she in peaceful times, and here she oft
When war was raging, ventur'd: hence she saw
The rough encounters of the furious field.
So long the tedious warfare, well she knew

The leaders' names, their arms, their prancing steeds:
And knew their garments, and their Cretan bows.
Far beyond all Europa's son she knew,
More than became her state: this Minos well
Could prove; whose head in crested helmet hid,
Most beauteous helm'd appear'd: whose arm, adorn'd
With brazen shield refulgent, well became
The brazen shield: whose hand the tough lance whirl'd,
And back withdrawn, the virgin wondering prais'd
Such strength and skill combin'd: to fit the dart
When to the spreading bow his strength he bent,
She vow'd that Phœbus in such posture stood
His arrows fitting: when, his brazen casque
Relinquish'd, all his features shone display'd,
As purple-rob'd his snow-white steed he press'd,
In painted housings gay, and curb'd his jaws
White foaming,—then the lost Nisean maid,
Scarcely herself, in frantic rapture spoke:—
Blest call'd the javelin, that his hands it touch'd;
Blest call'd the reins he curb'd. Arduous she burns,
(Could she) through hostile ranks her virgin steps
To bend: arduous she burns, from loftiest towers
To fling her body in the Cretan camp.
The brazen portals of the city's walls
Wide to the foe she'd ope: what could she not?
That Minos will'd? As resting here she view'd,
The white pavilion of the Gnossian king
Dubious, she cry'd;—"Or should I grieve or joy,
"This mournful war to witness? Grieve I must
"That Minos so belov'd should be my foe.
"But had the war not been, his lovely face
"Had ne'er to me been known. Now war may cease
"Should I become the hostage:—I retain'd,
"As Minos' comrade, and the pledge of peace.
"Fairest of forms! if she who brought thee forth
"Resembled thee, well might an amorous god
"Burn for her beauty. O! thrice blest were I,
"If borne through air on lightly-waving wings,
"The Cretan monarch's camp I might explore,
"And there, my rank and love disclos'd, demand
"What dowry he would ask to be my spouse.
"My country's towers alone, he should not seek.
"Perish the joys of his expected bed,
"Ere I through treason gain them! Yet full oft
"A moderate victor's clemency affords
"Great blessings to the vanquish'd. Doubtless, he
"Just warfare wages for his murder'd son.
"Strong in his cause, and in his armies strong,

"Which aid that cause, he must the conquest gain.
"Why, if this fate my country waits, should war,
"And not my love unbar to him the gates?
"So may he conquer; slaughter, toil, and blood,—
"His own dear blood, avoided. How I dread,
"Lest some rash hand might that lov'd bosom wound!
"None but the ignorant sure, the savage spear
"At him would hurl. The scheme delights my soul:
"Fixt my resolve; my country as my dower
"Will I deliver, finish so the war!
"But what are resolutions? Watchful guards
"The passes keep; of every gate, the keys
"My father careful holds. Hapless! I dread
"My father only; he alone withstands
"My wishes; would that so the gods had doom'd,
"I had no parent! But to each himself
"A god may surely be; and fortune spurns
"Lazy beseechers. With such love inflam'd,
"Another maid had long ere now destroy'd
"All barriers to her bliss; and why than I,
"Should any dare more boldly? Fearless, I
"Thro' swords and flames would pass, but swords and flames
"Oppose me not in this: my sole desire
"Compris'd in one small lock of Nisus' hair:
"Than gold that prize more dear. That purple lock
"Most blest would make me, and my sole desires
"Encompass."—Speaking thus, the gloomy night,
Imperial nurse of cares, approach'd; more bold
Her daring project with the darkness grew.

  Now primal slumbers rul'd o'er weary breasts,
Tir'd with their toil diurnal. Silent, she
Her father's chamber enters, and (O, dire!)
The daughter from her parent's head divides
The fateful lock! Her wicked prize possess'd,
Forth from the gate she issues; and the spoil,
So cursed, with her bears; as through the hosts,
(Such boldness gave the deed,) she seeks the king,
Whom thus, astonish'd and aghast, she hails:—
"To wicked deeds love sways; behold me here,
"Scylla, from royal Nisus sprung; to thee
"My household gods and country I betray:
"Thee, sole reward I seek. Pledge of my faith,
"This purple lock receive, and with this lock
"Receive my parent's head."—Then in her hand
The impious gift presented. Minos spurn'd
The parricidal present; deeply shock'd
A deed so base to witness, and exclaim'd;—

"May all the gods, from every part of earth
"Thee banish, scandal of our age! may land
"And sea alike reject thee; such a soul
"So monstrous! ne'er with me shall touch the shores
"Of Crete, my land, and cradle of high Jove."
He said, and on his captive foes impos'd
Most just his equal laws; his men bade loose
Their cables from the beach, and with their oars
His vessels bright with brass, urge on the deep.

   Launch'd on the main, when Scylla sees the fleet,
Nor from its leader gain'd the hop'd reward,
Her wicked deed had sought, tir'd of her prayers,
In desperate rage she storms; wild throws her hair;
Stretches her hands, exclaiming;—"Where! O, where!
"Fly'st thou. the author of thy fortune left?
"O, priz'd above my country! 'bove my sire!
"O cruel, whither fly'st thou, whose success
"At once my merit, and my fault displays?
"Will not the gifted conquest move thy soul?
"Will not my love thee move? Will not the thought
"That all my hopes centre in thee alone?
"By thee deserted, whither shall I fly?
"Back to my natal town? Ruin'd it lies;
"Or if still standing, fast the gates are barr'd
"Against my treason. To my father's arms,
"Whom I betray'd? Each citizen me hates
"Deserv'dly: neighbours my example dread.
"Banish'd, an exile from each spot of earth,—
"Crete only open lies. Thence dost thou drive
"Me also? Ingrate! dost thou fly me so?
"Europa never bore thee, but some Syrt'
"Inhospitable; or some tigress fell
"Bred in Armenia; or Charybdis vext
"With tempests: Jove was ne'er thy sire, nor feign'd
"A bull's resemblance to delude her, false
"That fable of thy origin. A bull,
"Real and savage thee begot, whose love
"No heifer mov'd. O father Nisus! now
"Exact thy vengeance. Joy, O town! betray'd
"By my transgression; for the woes I feel
"Most merited I grant; guilty I die:
"Yet should the deadly blow be given by one
"My impious fault has injur'd; not by thee,
"Victor through crimes thou with avenging hate
"Now persecutest. This flagitious deed
"Against my country, and against my sire,
"Was all for thee. Th' adultress who beguil'd

"In wooden cavity the furious bull;
"Whose womb an ill-assorted birth produc'd;
"Well for a spouse befits thee. Do my words
"Reach to thine ears, or no? Do the brisk winds,
"Thou ingrate! waft my bootless plainings on,
"And waft thy vessels? Wondrous now no more,
"Pasiphaë, to thy embrace a bull
"Preferr'd; for more unpitying is thy soul.
"Joyful, ah! hapless me,—away thou fly'st;
"Thy cleaving oars dash on the sounding waves:
"Me, and my country far from thee recede.
"O wretch! forgetful of my favoring aid,
"Thou striv'st in vain to fly me. 'Gainst thy wish
"Thee will I follow; on thy crooked ship
"Hanging, embracing, dragg'd through drenching seas.'
Scarce ending, in the waves she furious leaped,
Vigorous by love, and gain'd the flying fleet;
And clasp'd, unwelcome guest, the Gnossian poop.
Here soon her father spy'd her (in the air
He wing'd his way, now cloth'd with yellow plumes
A falcon) and down darted; with his beak
So curv'd, to wound her as she clung. In dread
Her grasp she loos'd, and as she seem'd to fall,
The light air bore her from the waves below:
Plum'd she became, and form'd a feather'd bird,
Ciris they call'd her from the ravish'd lock.

  To Jove now Minos all his vows performs,
An hecatomb of bulls; as from the fleet
He lands on Gnossus' shores: his royal hall
With all his spoils, on high uphung, adorn'd.

  Meantime th' opprobrium of his bed increas'd:
The two-formed monster in a novel birth,
At length the mother's beastly crime proclaim'd.
Minos, the shameful witness from his couch,
Far to remove determines; in a dome
Intricate winding, he resolves to lodge,
From every eye conceal'd, the birth. Intrusts
The work to Dædalus, in cunning arts
Most fam'd, to build. He all the various marks,
Confuses, puzzles; bent on either side,
The various paths confound the searching eye.
So in the fields the soft Mæander plays,
Here refluent, flowing there with dubious course;
Meeting himself, his wandering stream he sees:
And urges now to whence he first arose;
Now to the open outlet of the main.

Thus Dædalus the numerous paths perplex'd
With puzzlings intricate, so much entwin'd,
Himself could scarce the outer threshold gain.
Here was the double monster, man and bull
Inclos'd; till by the third allotted tribe,
The ninth year, vanquish'd; with Athenian blood
Twice gorg'd before. Then was the secret gate,
So often sought in vain, found by the aid
A virgin lent to trace the winding clue.
Instant for Dias, Theseus loos'd his sails,
With Minos' ravish'd daughter: on that shore
Cruel! he left her. The deserted nymph
Wildly lamenting, Bacchus soon embrac'd,
And gave her needful aid; her fame to fix
Immortal in the skies, her sparkling crown,
Mov'd from her forehead, 'mid the stars he plac'd:
Through the thin air it flies, and as it mounts
To blazing stars, the glittering jewels change.
Still as a crown it shines, its station 'midst
Where stout Alcides Ophiuchus grasps.

  Meantime long exile, and the land of Crete
Detesting, burning with a patriot's wish
His native soil to visit, Dædalus,
By sea escape prevented, thus exclaim'd;—
"Let earth and ocean both my flight obstruct,
"Still oper lies the air; through air we'll go.
"Minos controlling all, controls not air."—
He speaks, and bends to unknown arts his skill,
Improving Nature's gift. Quills fixt in rows
He places; small at first in length and size,
Gradual enlarg'd, as if a hill's steep side
Growing, produc'd them: So time past the pipe,
Of rustic origin, by small degrees
Increasing reeds compos'd. Firm fixt with thread
Their middle part he binds, and close with wax
Cements their bottom. All complete he bends
The composition in a gentle curve,
Resembling real wings. Young Icarus
Alone was present; ignorant that the work
Would his destruction cause; with playful tricks
He fingers now the feathers, now his hands
Soften the yellow wax. His sportive wiles
His father's wond'rous essay oft delay.

  Now was the last completing stroke impos'd
Upon his undertaking: First the sire
On artificial wings his body pois'd,

And in the beaten air suspended hung:
Then his young offspring, Icarus, he taught.—
"This I my son advise, a middle course,
"To keep be cautious; low if thou should'st skim,
"Heavy with ocean's spray thy wings would droop:
"If high, the sun would scorch them. Steer thy course
"'Twixt each extreme. Nor would I wish thine eyes
"To view Boötes, or the northern bear;
"Nor yet Orion's naked sword. My track
"Cautious pursue."—With anxious care he gives
Rules thus for flight; and to his shoulders fits
The new-form'd pinions. Tears his ancient cheeks
Bedew'd, as thus his admonitions flow'd:
And his paternal hands as thus employ'd,
Beneath the office trembled. Warm salutes
He gave the boy, nor knew he gave the last;
Then on his feathers borne, explores the way,
Timid for him who follows. So the bird,
Tempts from her lofty nest her new-fledg'd brood,
In the thin air. He bids him close pursue,
Tries in each shape to teach the fatal skill;
Shakes his own pinions, bending back to view
His son's. The angler as with quivering reed,
He drew his prey to land; the shepherd-swain,
As o'er his staff he lean'd; the ploughman-clown,
Their flight astonish'd saw, and deem'd them gods,
That so at will could cleave the liquid sky.

  Now Samos, Juno's favor'd isle they pass'd,
Delos, and Paros, all to left;—to right
Labyrithos lay, and rich in honey'd sweets
Calymné: when the heedless boy o'erjoy'd
In his bold flight, the precepts of his guide
Contemning, soar'd to heaven a loftier range.
The neighbouring sun's fierce heat the fragrant wax
Which bound, his pinions, soften'd. Soon the wax
Dissolves; and now his naked arms he waves;
But destitute of power his course to steer,
No air his arms can gather; loud he calls
His father's name, as in the azure deep
He drops,—the deep which still his name retains.

  The hapless parent, not a parent now,
Loud calls on Icarus;—"Where art thou, son?
"Where shall I seek thee, Icarus?"—He said,
And spy'd his feathers floating on the waves:
Then curs'd his hapless art, as in the earth,
He deep intomb'd him; all the land around

Bears from the youth intomb'd its present name.

  The whirring partridge, from a branchy holm
Beheld him, as beneath the turf he plac'd
His son's lamented body, and with joy
Flutter'd his feathers; while his chirping song
Proclaim'd his gladness: then the only bird
Known of his kind, in elder days unseen;
But lately cloth'd with feathers, through the crime
Flagitious, Dædalus, of thee! To thee,
Thy sister, witless how his fate was doom'd,
Her son committed for instructing art,
When twice six annual suns the youth had seen;
His docile mind best fitted then to learn.
He well th' indented bones remark'd, which form
The fish's spiny back, and in like mode,
Sharp steel indenting, first the saw produc'd
For public service. Two steel arms he join'd
Fixt to one orb above; each widely stretch'd,
One steady rests, the other circling turns.
Him Dæcalus with envy viewing, forc'd
Headlong, from sacred Pallas' lofty tower,
His death feign'd accidental: but the maid
Divine, to all ingenious minds a friend,
Receiv'd him in his fall; chang'd to a bird,
On pinions bore him through the middle air.
His vigorous powers in force remain the same,
But change their seat; rapid he flies, and quick
He races on the ground; his name remains
Unalter'd: still the cautious bird declines
To trust his weight aloft, nor forms his nest
On lofty boughs, or summits of high trees:
Nigh to the earth he skims; beneath the hedge
His shelly brood deposits; of his fall
Still mindful, towering heights he always shuns.

  Now Dædalus, with lengthen'd flight fatigu'd,
Sicilia's realm receiv'd; whose king humane,
Great Cocalus, mov'd with his suppliant pray'r,
Arm'd to assist him. Now by Theseus freed,
Athens no more the mournful tribute paid.
With garlands every temple gay they hang,
Invoke the warlike maid, the mighty Jove,
And every deity: their altars all
With promis'd blood they honor; with rich gifts,
And fragrant incense. Now had wandering fame
Through all the Grecian towns, spread the renown
Of Theseus: and the rich Achaïa's tribes

His aid implor'd, when mighty perils press'd.
Ev'n Calydon, though Meleager brave
Possessing, sought his help with suppliant words.
The cause, a furious boar by Dian' sent,
Avenging instrument of slighted power.

Œneus, from plenteous harvests' full success
Rejoicing, primal fruits to Ceres gave;
To Bacchus pour'd libations of his wine;
To yellow-hair'd Minerva offer'd oil:
The rites invidious, from the rural gods
Commencing, all the bright celestials shar'd.
Latona's daughter only, in her fane,
Nor flames nor offerings on her altar saw.
Rage fires ev'n heavenly breasts.—"Not unreveng'd,"—
She cry'd,—shall this be suffer'd; honor'd not!
"Not unappeas'd by vengeance will I rest."—
Then through th' Œneian fields the maid, despis'd,
Sends the fierce boar to ravage. Such his size,
The bulls that in Epirus' pastures graze
More huge appear not: in Sicilia's meads
Far less are seen. Red are his sparkling eyes,
Fire mixt with blood; high rears his fearful neck,
Thick clustering spears the threatening bristles seem:
Hoarse as he grunts, down his wide shoulders spreads
The boiling foam: his tusks the tusks outvie
Of India's hugest beast: the lightening's blast,
Driven from his mouth, burns all the verdant leaves.
Now o'er the corn, but yet in budding ears,
He tramples, immature he reaps the crop;
The loud-lamenting tiller's hopes destroy'd:
The harvest intercepting in the shoot.
In vain the barns, the granaries in vain,
Their promis'd loads expect. Prostrate alike
Are thrown the fruitful clusters of the vine,
With shooting tendrils; and the olive's fruit
With branches ever-blooming. On the flocks
He rages: these not shepherds, not their dogs
Could save; nor could the furious bull his herd.
Wide fled the people; safety none durst hope
Save in their cities' walls; till thirst of fame
Fir'd Meleager, with his chosen band
Of valiant youths. And first were seen the twins
Of Tyndarus, for wond'rous skill renown'd,
This at the cæstus, that to curb the steed:
Jason, whose art the primal ship design'd:
Theseus, in happy concord with his friend
Pirithous, join'd: Thestius' two valiant sons:

Lynceus, Aphareus' offspring: Idas swift:
Leucippus fierce: Acastus unexcell'd
To dart the javelin: Cæneus, now no more
Cloth'd in a female figure: Phœnix, sprung
From old Amyntor: Actor's equal sons:
Hippothoös: Dryas: and from Elis' town
Dispatch'd, came Phileus. Nor was absent there,
Brave Telamon, nor great Achilles' sire:
Nor stout Eurytion; with Pheretus' son:
Nor Hyantean Iölaüs brave:
Echion in speed unconquer'd: Nestor then
In primal youth: Lelex, Narycian born:
Panopeus: Hyleus: Hippasus the fierce:
Nor those whom Hippocoön sent in aid,
From old Amyclæ: nor Ulysses' sire:
Ancæus of Parrhasia: Mopsus sage:
Amphiareus then by his false spouse's guile
Betray'd not. With them Atalanta came,
The grace and glory of Arcadia's woods.
A shining buckle from the ground confin'd
Her garment's border: simply bound, her hair
One knot confin'd: her ivory quiver, slung
O'er her left shoulder, sounded as she stepp'd:
Her hand sustain'd a bow: and thus array'd
Appear'd her form. Her lineaments disclos'd,
What scarce might feminine in boys appear;
Or hardly boyish in a virgin's face.
The chief of Calydon the maid beheld,—
Beheld, and lov'd: while heaven his love oppos'd.
The secret flames inhaling deep, he cry'd,—
"O, blessed youth! if youth to gain thy hand
"Worthy were deem'd!"—Nor bashful shame, nor time
Would more allow; a mightier deed now claim'd
Their utmost efforts for the furious war.

  Darken'd with trees thick-growing, rose a wood;
From earliest ages there the biting axe
Had never sounded; in the plain it rear'd
Facing the sloping fields. The youths arriv'd;
Some spread the knotted toils; some loose the hounds;
Some strive the foot-prints of the boar to trace,
Their danger anxious seeking. Low beneath
A hollow vale extended, where the floods
Fresh showery torrents gather'd, lazy laid.
The flexile willow, and the waving reed;
The fenny bulrush, osier, and the cane
Diminutive, the stagnant depth conceal'd.
Arous'd from hence, the boar impetuous rush'd

Amidst his host of foes; so lightenings dart
When clouds concussive clash. His rapid force
Levels the grove, the crackling trees resound
Where'er he pushes: loud the joyful youth
Exclaim, each grasping with a nervous hand
His weapon brandish'd, while its broad head shakes.
Forward he darts, the dogs he scatters wide,
And each opposing power; his strokes oblique
Their baying drives to distance. Echion's arm
Hurl'd the first dart, but hurl'd the dart in vain;
Lightly a maple's trunk the weapon graz'd.
The next, but over-urg'd the force that sent,
Had pierc'd the rough back of the wish'd-for prey;
Jason's the steel,—it whizz'd beyond him far.
Then Mopsus pray'd,—"O Phœbus! if thy rites
"I e'er perform'd, if still I thee adore,
"Grant my sure weapon what I wish to touch."
The god consented, what he could he gave,—
The boar was struck, but struck without a wound:
Diana from the flying weapon snatch'd
The steely head, and pointless fell the wood.
More chafes the beast, like lightening fierce he burns,
Fire from his eyeballs flashes, from his chest
Clouds of hot smoke through his wide nostrils roll.
Forc'd from the close-drawn string as flies a stone,
Hurl'd at embattl'd walls, or hostile towers
With foes thick crowded: so the deadly beast
Rush'd on the heroes with unerring shock.
Eupalamus and Pelagon, who stood
The right wing guarding, on the earth he threw:
Their fellows snatch'd them from impending fate.
Not so Onesimus, of Hippocoön
The offspring, 'scap'd the death-inflicting blow;
Torn through the ham, just as for flight he turn'd;
His slacken'd nerves could bear his weight no more.
Then Nestor too, long e'er the Trojan times,
Perchance had perish'd, but beside him stood
A tree, whose branches nimbly he attain'd;
A mighty effort, aided by his spear:
Safe in his seat, he view'd the foe he fled,
Beneath him. Fiercely threatening death below,
He whets his tushes on a stumpy oak,
And bold in sharpen'd arms, ranches the thigh,
With crooked fangs, of Othrys' mighty son.
Now the twin-brothers, ere in heaven display'd
Bright constellations, both fair dazzling shone,
Mounted on steeds, whose lily'd hue surpass'd
Th' unsully'd snow; both shook their brandish'd spears,

The trembling motion sounded high in air;
Deep both had pierc'd, but 'mid the darkening trees,
Their bristly foe sought refuge, where nor steed,
Nor dart could reach him. Telamon pursues;
Ardent, and heedless of his steps, a root
Checks his quick feet, and prone the hero falls.
While Peleus aids his brother chief to rise,
The beauteous Atalanta to the string
Fits the swift dart, and from the bended bow
Speeds it; the arrow, fixt beneath his ear,
Razes the monster's skin, and drops of blood
His bristly neck ensanguine. Joys the maid
To see the blow;—but Meleager far
In joy surpass'd her. He the first beheld
The trickling blood; he to his comrades first
The wound display'd, exclaiming,—"Yon fair nymph
"The honors so deserv'dly won shall bear."—
The warriors blush with shame, and each exhorts
His fellow; shouts their souls more valiant swell;
In heaps confus'd their numerous javelins fly;
Clashing in crowds, each javelin fails to wound.
Lo now Ancæus furious, to his fate
Blind rushing, rears his double axe, and cries,—
"Behold, O youths! how much a manly arm
"Outstrikes a female's, to my prowess yield
"The palm of conquest. Let Latona's maid
"With all her power protect him, yet my force,
"Spite of Diana, shall the monster slay."—
Proud his big-boasting tongue thus speaks, then grasps
His two-edg'd weapon firmly in his hands,
And rais'd on tiptoe meditates the blow.
The watchful beast prevents him, through his groin,
To death sure passage, drives his double tusks:
Ancæus drops; his bowels gushing fall,
Roll on the earth, and soak the ground in gore.
Ixion's son, Pirithous, on the foe
Rush'd, in his nervous hand a powerful spear
Brandishing; Theseus loudly to his friend
Exclaim'd,—"O, dearer far than is myself,—
"Half of my soul, at distance wait; the brave
"At distance may engage; valor too rash
"Destroy'd Ancæus."—As he spoke he hurl'd
His massive cornel spear; its brazen head
Well pois'd, its sender's anxious wish appear'd
Fair to accomplish, when a leafy arm
Branch'd from a beech, oppos'd it in its flight.
Next Æson's son, his javelin threw, but chance
Glanc'd from its mark the weapon, and transpierc'd

An undeserving hound; the dart was drove
Through all his belly, and deep fixt in earth.
But different fortune on the arms awaits
Of Meleager, javelins two he sent;
Deep in the ground the foremost pierc'd, the next
Firm in the monster's back quivering stood fixt.
Nor stays he, whilst he raging furious whirl'd
In giddy circles round, and pour'd his foam,
Mad with the new-felt torture, close at hand
The hero plies his work, provokes his foe
To fiercer ire, and in his furious breast
Buries the glittering spear. A second shout
Loudly proclaims his thronging comrades' joy;
Each to the victor crowding, hand in hand
Congratulating grasps him; each amaz'd
Views the dire savage, as his mighty bulk
O'erspreads a space of land. Scarce think they yet
Their safety sure, him touching; each his spear
Extends, and dips it in the flowing gore.
His foot upon the head destructive fixt,
The conquering youth thus speaks:—"Nonacria fair!
"Receive the spoil my fortune well might claim:
"Fresh glory shall I gain, with thee to share
"The honors of the day."—Then gives the spoils;—
The chine with horrid bristles rising stiff,
And head, fierce threatening still with mighty tusks.
She takes the welcome gift, for much she joys
From him to take it. Envy seiz'd the rest,
And sullen murmurs through the comrades ran:
Above the rest, were Thestius' sons,—their arms
Out-stretching, clamor'd thus with a mighty noise;—
"Let not thy beauteous form thy mind deceive,
"When from thy eyes the donor of the spoil,
"Besotted with thy love, shall far be mov'd.
"Woman! restore the prize, nor hope to hold
"Our intercepted claims."—Speaking they rob
Her of the gift, him of the right to give.
Nor passive stood the warlike youth, his teeth
He gnash'd with swelling rage, as fierce he cry'd;—
"Learn, ye base robbers of another's rights,
"What difference threats and valiant actions shew.—"
Then in Plexippus' unsuspecting breast
He plung'd his impious sword: nor suffer'd long
Toxeus to doubt, who hesitating stood,
Now vengeance brooding for his brother's fate,
Now dreading for himself a like swift blow;
Again he warms the weapon, reeking still
Hot from Plexippus' bosom, in his blood.

To every temple of the favoring gods
Althæa bore donations for her son,
Victorious: When the breathless bodies came
Of both her brethren, loud the sounding blows
Of grief were heard, and all the city rung
With lamentable cries: her golden robes
Were straight to sable chang'd. But when the hand
Which struck the blow was known, her every tear
Was dry'd, and vengeance only fill'd her soul.
A log there lay when Thestius' daughter groan'd
In child-bed pangs; which on the greedy flames
The triple sisters flung; and while their thumbs
Twirl'd round the fatal thread, this was their song;—
"O newly born! to thee and to this bough
"Like date of life we give."—Then ceas'd their words,
And from her presence vanish'd: sudden snatch'd
The mother from the fire the burning brand,
And quench'd it instant in unsparing streams.
Long in most secret darkness had she hid
This fatal wood; and, thus preserv'd, her son
Had safely years mature attain'd; but now
Forth she produc'd it from its close recess.
Fragments of torches on the hearth she heap'd,
And blew the sparklings into deadly flames;
And thrice she rais'd her hands the branch to heave
On the fierce fire; and thrice her hands withdrew.
Sister and mother in one bosom fought,
To adverse acts impelling. Oft her face,
Dread of her meditated crime, bleach'd pale;
Oft to her eyes her furious rage supply'd
A fiery redness; now her countenance glow'd
With threatenings cruel; now her softening looks
To pity seem'd to melt; and when fierce ire
Had fill'd her soul, and parch'd up every tear,
Fresh tears would gush. Thus rocks a vessel, driven
By winds and adverse currents, both their force
At once obeys, and can to neither yield.
Thus waver'd Thestius' daughter, dubious thus
Affection sway'd her; now her rage is calm,
Now her calm'd rage with fourfold fury burns.
At length the sister's o'er the parent's tie
The prevalence obtains; impiously good,
With blood her own, she soothes the brethren's shades.
Now, when the fires destructive fiercely glar'd,
She cry'd:—"Here, funeral pile, my bowels burn!—"
And as the fatal wood her direful hand
Held forth, the hapless mother, at the pyre

Sepulchral, stood, exclaiming;—"Furies three!
"Avenging sisters! hither turn your eyes;
"Behold the furious sacred rites I pay:
"For retribution I commit this crime.
"By death their death must be aveng'd; his fault
"By mine be punish'd; on their funeral biers
"His must be laid; one sinning house must fall,
"In woes accumulated. Blest shall still
"Œneus enjoy his proud victorious son,
"And Thestius childless mourn? Better that both
"Should weep in concert. Dear fraternal ghosts,
"Recent from upper air, my work behold!
"Take to th' infernal realms my offering bought
"So dear! the hapless pledge my womb produc'd.

"Ah! whither am I swept? Brothers forgive
"The parent. Lo! my faltering hands refuse
"To second my intents. Well he deserves
"To perish; yet by other hands than mine.
"Unpunish'd shall he 'scape then? Victor live,
"Proud of his high success, and rule the realm
"Of Calydon, while ye are prostrate thrown
"A trivial heap of ashes, and cold shades?
"Patience no more will bear. Perish the wretch!
"Perish his father's hopes! perish the realm!
"And all the country perish! Where? O, where?
"Is then the mother's soul, the pious prayers
"A parent should prefer? Where the strong pains
"Which twice five moons I bore? O, that the flames
"First kindled, had thy infant limbs consum'd!
"Would I had not then snatch'd thee from thy fate!
"Thy gift of life is mine; now that thou dy'st
"Thy own demerits ask: take the reward
"Thy deeds deserve: yield up thy twice-given life,
"First in thy birth, then by the brand I sav'd;
"Or lay me with my brethren in their tomb.
"I wish, yet what I would my hands refuse.
"What will my soul determine? Now mine eyes
"The mangled corses of my brethren fill:
"Now filial fondness, and a mother's name
"Distract my soul. O, wretched, wretched me!
"Brothers you gain the conquest, yet you gain
"Dearly for me; but on your shades I'll wait,
"Blest in what gives you once to me again."
She said; with face averse and trembling hand,
The fateful brand amid the fires was dropt.
The brand a groan deep utter'd, or a groan
To utter seem'd: the flames half backward caught

At length their prey, which gradually consum'd.

Witless of this sad deed, and absent far,
Fierce Meleager, with the self-same fire
Burn'd inward; all his vitals felt the flame
Scorching conceal'd: th' excruciating pangs
Magnanimous he bore. Yet deep he mourn'd
By such a s othful bloodless fate to fall;
And happy call'd Ancæus in his wounds.
With deep-drawn groans he calls his aged sire,
His brother, sisters, and the nymph belov'd,
Who shar'd his nuptial couch; with final breath,
His mother too perchance. Now glows the fire,
And now the pains increase; now both are faint;
Now both together die. The soul flies forth,
And gently dissipates in empty air.

Low now lies lofty Calydon,—the youths,
And aged seniors weep; the vulgar crowd
And nobles mourn alike; the matrons rend
Their garments, beat their breasts, and tear their hair.
Stretch'd on the earth the wretched sire defiles
His hoary locks, and aged face with dust,
Cursing his lengthen'd years: the conscious hand
Which caus'd the direful end, the mother's fate
Accomplish'd; through her vitals pierc'd the steel.

Had heaven on me an hundred tongues bestow'd,
With sounding voice, and such capacious wit
As all might fill; and all the Muses' power,
Still should I fail the grieving sisters' woe
Justly to paint. Heedless of beauteous forms
They beat their bosoms livid; while the corse
Remains, they clasp and cherish in their arms
The senseless mass; the corse they kiss, and kiss
The couch on which it rests: to ashes burn'd,
Careful collected in the urn, they hug
Those ashes to their breasts; and prostrate thrown
His tomb they cover; on the graven stone
Embrace his name; and on the letters pour
Their tears in torrents. Dian' satiate now
The house of Œneus levell'd with the dust,
Rais'd them by wings in air, which sudden shot
From each their bodies. Gorgé sole, and she
The spouse of valiant Hercules, unchang'd
Were left. Long pinions for their arms were seen;
Their mouths to horny bills were turn'd; through air
Thus alter d, ample range the goddess gives.

Theseus meantime, the toil confederate done,
Homeward to Pallas' towers his journey bent;
But Acheloüs, swol'n by showery floods,
Delay'd his progress. "Fam'd Cecropia's chief,"—
He cry'd,—"here shelter, enter 'neath my roof,
"Nor through the furious torrents trust thy steps.
"Whole forests oft they root, and whirl along
"Vast rocks with thundering sound. High stalls I've seen,
"Near to the banks erected, swept away:
"Nor aught avail'd the lusty bull's strong limbs,
"Nor aught the courser's speed: the torrents oft
"Of melted snows, which from the mountains rush,
"Whelm the strong youths beneath the whirling pool.
"To rest is safer, till their wonted banks
"Again the streams confine; the lessen'd waves
"Within their channels pent."—Theseus complies,
And answers:—"Acheloüs, we approve
"Thy prudent counsel, and thy cave will use,"
The grot they enter; hollow pumice, mixt
With rugged tophus, form'd it; tender moss
The moist floor cover'd; fretwork on the roof
The purple murex and the scallop white
Alternate form'd. Now Phœbus' steeds had run
Two thirds their race, when Theseus on his couch
Reclin'd, the comrades of his toil close by;
Pirithous here, Trœzenian Lelex there,
Whose temples now some silvery hairs display'd.
With these were such as Acheloüs, joy'd
At such a noble guest, the honor deem'd
Worthy to share. The barefoot Naiäd nymphs
Heap'd on the board the banquet: food remov'd,
They brought the wine, in cups with jewels deck'd.

   The mighty hero then, the distant main
Surveying, asks:—"What land is that I see?—"
And shews the spot,—"tell me what name denotes
"That isle? and yet methinks not one it seems."
The river-god replies:—"What we behold
"A single isle is not, but five; the eye
"Is mock'd by distance. That Diana's wrath
"May less your wonder move, these once were nymphs.
"Ten bullocks had they sacrific'd, and call'd
"Each rural god to taste the sacred feast,
"And join the festal chorus, me alone,
"Forgetful, they invited not. Sore vext,
"I swell'd with rage, and as my anger rose,
"My flood increas'd; till at my greatest height,

"Woods I divorc'd from woods; from meadows tore
"The neighbouring meadows; and the Naiäds roll'd,
"Now well-remembering what my godhead claim'd,
"Down with their habitations to the main.
"My waves then, with the ocean's waters join'd,
"The land divided, and those isles you view,
"Echinades, amid the sea were form'd.

 "More distant may your vision reach;—behold
"An isle beyond them to my soul most dear;
"By sailors nam'd Perimelé. I snatch'd
"Her virgin-treasure from the much-lov'd maid.
"Hippodamas her sire in fury rav'd;
"And, from a precipice, the pregnant nymph
"Plung'd in the deep. My waves receiv'd the load;
"And whilst I bore her floating, thus I said;—
"O, trident-bearer, thou whom lot decreed
"Lord, next to heaven, o'er all the wandering waves,
"Where all the sacred rivers end their course;
"To which all rivers tend, O, Neptune, aid!
"Propitious, hear my prayer! Much have I wrong'd
"The nymph I now support: if lenient he,
"And equitable, sure Hippodamas,
"Her sire, had pity granted, and myself
"Had pardon'd. Gracious Neptune, grant thy help
"To her a parent's fury from the earth
"Wide banishes. O, I beseech thee! grant
"A place to her, paternal rage would drown:
"Or to a place transform her, where my waves
"May clasp her still. The ocean-god consents,
"And all his waters shake as nods his head.
"Still floats th' affrighted nymph; and as she swims,
"I feel her heart with trepid motion beat:
"While pressing fond her bosom, all her form
"Rigidly firm becomes, and round her chest
"Rough earth heaps high; and, whilst I wondring speak,
"A new-form'd land her floating limbs enclasps:
"Her shape transform'd, a solid isle becomes."

 Thus far the watery deity, and ceas'd.
The wondrous tale all mov'd, save one, the son
Of bold Ixion; fierce of soul, he laugh'd
To scorn their minds so credulous, the gods
Impious contemning, as he thus exclaim'd;—
"What tales, O, Acheloüs, you relate!
"Too much of potence to the gods you grant,
"To give and change our figures."—All struck dumb,
Discourage this bold speech, and Lelex first,

Mature in age, and in experience old
Beyond the rest, thus spoke:—"Celestial power,
"In range is infinite, in sway immense;
"What the gods will, completion instant finds.
"To clear your doubts, upon the Phrygian hills
"An ancient oak, and neighbouring linden stand,
"Girt by a low inclosure; I the spot
"Survey'd, when into Phrygia's realms dispatch'd
"By Pittheus, when those realms his father rul'd.
"Not far a lake extends, a space once fill'd
"With human 'habitants, whose waves now swarm
"With fenny coots, and cormorants alone.
"Here Jove in human shape, and with his sire,
"The son of Maiä, came; the last his rod
"Shorn of its wings, still bore. A thousand doors,
"Seeking repose, they knock'd at; every door
"Firm barr'd repuls'd them: one at length flew wide;
"A lowly cot, whose humble roof long reeds,
"And straw firm-matted, cover'd. Baucis there,
"A pious dame, and old Philemon match'd
"In age, had dwelt, since join'd in springtide youth;
"And there grew old together: Full content,
"Their poverty they hid not, and more light
"Their poverty on souls unmurmuring weigh'd.
"Here nor for lord, nor servant, was there need
"To seek; beneath the roof these only dwelt;
"Each order'd, each obey'd. The heaven-born guests
"The humble threshold crossing, lowly stoop'd,
"And entrance gain'd: the ancient host bade sit
"And rest their weary'd limbs: the bench was plac'd,
"Which Baucis anxious for their comfort, spread
"With home-made coverings: then with careful hand
"The scarce warm embers on the hearth upturn'd;
"And rous'd the sleeping fires of yestern's eve,
"With food of leaves and bark dry-parch'd, and fann'd
"To flame the fuel with her aged breath:
"Then threw the small-slit faggots, and the boughs
"Long-wither'd, on the top, divided small:
"And plac'd her brazen vase of scanty size,
"O'er all. Last stripp'd the coleworts' outer leaves,
"Cull'd by her husband from the water'd ground,
"Which serv'd as garden. He meantime reach'd down,
"With two-fork'd prong, where high on blacken'd beam
"It hung, a paltry portion of an hog,
"Long harden'd there; and from the back he slic'd
"A morsel thin, which soon he soften'd down
"In boiling steam. The intermediate hours
"With pleasing chat they cheat; the short delay

"To feel avoiding. On a nail high hung
"A beechen pail for bathing, by its hand
"Deep-curv'd: with tepid water this he fill'd,
"And plac'd before his guests their feet to lave.
"A couch there stood, whose feet and frame were form'd
"Of willow; tender reeds the centre fill'd,
"With coverings this they spread, coverings which saw
"The light not, but when festal days them claim'd:
"Yet coarse and old were these, and such as well
"With willow couch agreed. The gods laid down.
"The dame close-girt, with tremulous hand prepar'd
"The board; two feet were perfect, 'neath the third
"She thrust a broken sherd, and all stood firm.
"This sloping mended, all the surface clean
"With fragrant mint she rubb'd: and plac'd in heaps
"The double-teinted fruit of Pallas, maid
"Of unsoil'd purity; autumnal fruits,
"Cornels, in liquid lees of wine preserv'd;
"Endive, and radish, and the milky curd;
"With eggs turn'd lightly o'er a gentle heat:
"All serv'd in earthen dishes. After these
"A clay-carv'd jug was set, and beechen cups,
"Varnish'd all bright with yellow wax within.
"Short the delay, when from the ready fire
"The steaming dish is brought; and wine not long
"Press'd from the grape, again went round, again
"Gave place to see the third remove produc'd.
"Now comes the nut, the fig, the wrinkled date,
"The plumb, the fragrant apple, and the grape
"Pluck'd from the purple vine; all plac'd around
"In spreading baskets: snow-white honey fill'd
"The central space. The prime of all the feast,
"Was looks that hearty welcome gave, and prov'd
"No indigence nor poverty of soul.
"Meantime the empty'd bowls full oft they see
"Spontaneously replenish'd; still the wine
"Springs to the brim. Astonish'd, struck with dread,
"To view the novel scene, the timid pair
"Their hands upraise devoutly, and with prayers
"Excuses utter for their homely treat,
"At unawares requir'd. A lonely goose
"They own'd, the watchman of their puny farm;
"Him would the hosts, to their celestial guests
"A sacred offering make, but swift of wing,
"Their toiling chace with age retarded, long
"He mock'd; at length the gods themselves he seeks
"For sheltering care. The gods his death forbid,
"And speak:—Celestials are we both; a fate

"Well-earn'd, your impious neighbouring roofs shall feel.
"To you, and unto you alone is given
"Exemption from their lot. Your cottage leave
"And tread our footsteps, while of yonder mount
"We seek the loftiest summit. Each obeys;
"The gods precede them, while their tottering limbs
"A trusty staff supports; tardy from years,
"Slowly they labor up the long ascent.
"Now from the summit wanted they not more
"Than what an arrow, shot with strenuous arm,
"At once could gain; when back their view they bent:
"Their house alone they saw,—that singly stood:
"All else were buried in a wide-spread lake.
"Wondring at this, and weeping at the doom
"Their hapless neighbours suffer'd; lo! they see
"Their mouldering cot, e'en for the pair too small,
"Change to a temple; pillars rear on high,
"In place of crotchets; yellow turns the straw,
"The roof seems gilded; sculptur'd shine the gates;
"And marble pavement covers all the floor.
"Then Saturn's son, in these benignant words
"The pair address'd;—O, ancient man, most just!
"And thou, O woman! worthy of thy spouse,
"Declare your wishes.—Baucis spoke awhile
"With old Philemon; then their joint desire
"The latter to the deities declar'd.—
"To be your ministers, your sacred fane
"To keep we ask: and as our equal years
"In concord we have pass'd, let the same hour
"Remove us hence: may I her tomb not see,
"Nor be by her interr'd.—The gods comply;
"These guard the temple through succeeding life.
"Fill'd now with years, as on the temple's steps
"They stood, conversing on the wondrous change,
"Baucis beheld Philemon shoot in leaves,
"And leaves Philemon saw from Baucis sprout;
"And from their heads o'er either's face they grew.
"Still while they could with mutual words they spoke;
"At once exclaim'd,—O, dearest spouse, farewell!—
"At once the bark, their lips thus speaking, clos'd.
"Ev'n yet a Tyanæan shews two trees
"Of neighbouring growth, form'd from the alter'd pair.
"Nor dotard credulous, nor lying tongue
"The fact to me related. On the boughs
"Myself have seen the votive garlands hung;
"And whilst I offered fresher, have I said—
"Heaven guards the good with care; and those who give
"The gods due honors, honors claim themselves."

He ceas'd: the deed and author all admire,
But Theseus most; whom anxious still to hear
More wondrous actions of the mighty gods,
The stream of Calydon, as on his arm
Reclin'd, he rested, in these words address'd:—
"There are, O, valiant youth! of those once chang'd,
"Still in the new-form'd figures who remain:
"Others there are whose power more wide extends
"To many shapes to alter.—Proteus, thou
"Art one; thou 'habitant of those wide waves
"Which earth begird: now thou a youth appear'st;
"And now a lion; then a furious boar;
"A serpent next we tremble to approach;
"And then with threatening horns thou seem'st a bull.
"Oft as a stone thou ly'st; oft stand'st a tree:
"Sometimes thy countenance veil'd in fluid streams,
"Thou flow'st a river; sometimes mount'st in flames.
"Nor less of power had Erisichthon's maid,
"Spouse of Autolycus. Her impious sire
"All the divinities of heaven despis'd,
"Nor on their slighted altars offerings burn'd.
"He too, 'tis said, the Cerealean grove
"With axe prophan'd: his violating steel
"The ancient trees attacking. 'Mid the rest,
"A huge-grown oak, in yearly strength robust,
"Itself a wood, uprose: garlands hung round,
"And wreaths, and grateful tablets, proofs of vows
"For prospering favors paid. The Dryad nymphs
"Oft in its shade their festal dances held;
"Oft would they, clasping hand in hand, surround
"The mighty trunk: its girth around to mete,
"Full thrice five cubits ask'd. To every tree
"Lofty it seem'd; as every tree appear'd
"Lofty, when measur'd with the plants below.
"Yet not for that, did Erisichthon hold
"The biting steel; but bade his servants fell
"The sacred oak; lingering he saw them stand,
"His orders unobey'd; impious he snatch'd
"From one his weapon, and in rage, exclaim'd;—
"What though it be the goddess' favorite care!
"Were it the goddess' self, down should it fall,
"And bow its leafy summit to the ground.
"He said;—and pois'd his axe, and aim'd oblique.
"Deep shudderings shook the Cerealian tree,
"And groans were utter'd; all the leaves grew pale,
"And pale the acorns; while the wide-spread boughs
"Cold sweats bedew'd. When in the solid trunk

"His blow ungodly pierc'd, blood flow'd in streams
"From out the shatter'd bark: not flows more full,
"From the deep wound in the divided throat,
"The gore, when at the sacred altar's foot
"A mighty bull, an offer'd victim drops.
"Dread seizes all; and one most bold attempts
"To check his horrid wickedness, and check
"The murderous weapon: him the villain saw,
"And,—take,—he cries,—the boon thy pious soul
"Merits so well.—And from the trunk the steel
"Turns on the man, and strikes his head away:
"Then with redoubled blows the tree assails.
"Deep from the oak, these words were heard to sound:—
"A nymph am I, within this trunk enclos'd,
"Most dear to Ceres; in my dying hours,
"Prophetic I foresee the keen revenge
"Which will thy deed pursue; and this solace
"Grants comfort ev'n in death.—He, undismay'd,
"His fierce design still follows: now the tree,
"Tottering with numerous blows, by straining cords,
"He drags to earth; and half the wood below,
"Crush'd by its weight, lies prostrate. All astound,
"Of her depriv'd, and at their own sad loss,
"The sister Dryads, clad in sable robes,
"To Ceres hasten; and for vengeance call,
"On Erisichthon. To their urgent prayers
"The beauteous goddess gave assent, and shook
"Her locks; the motion shook the yellow ears,
"Which fill'd the loaded fields; and straight conceiv'd
"A torture piteous, if for pity he
"For acts like these might look:—to tear his form
"By Famine's power pestiferous. There, herself
"Approach forbidden (fate long since had doom'd
"Ceres and Famine far remov'd should dwell)
"A mountain-nymph she calls, and thus directs;—
"A region stretches on th' extremest bounds
"Of icy Scythia; dreary seems the place;
"Sterile the soil; nor trees, nor fruits are seen;
"But sluggish cold, and pale affright, and fear:
"Still-craving Famine, there her dwelling holds.
"Bid her within the inmost vitals hide
"Of this most daring, and most impious wretch.
"The proudest plenty shall not make her yield:
"For in the contest, all the power I boast
"To her shall stoop: nor let the lengthen'd way
"Appal thy mind; my car receive; receive
"My dragons; through the air their course direct
"By these long reins.—Speaking, the reins she gave.

"She, borne through ether in the granted car,
"To Scythia's realm is carried: on the ridge
"A rugged mountain offer'd, first she eas'd
"The dragons' necks; as Caucasus 'twas known.
"There she the sought-for Famine soon espy'd,
"Eagerly searching on the stony fields,
"At once with teeth and fangs, for thin-sown herbs.
"Rough matted were her locks; deep sunk her eyes;
"Pale bleach'd her face; her lips with whiten'd slime
"O'erspread; with furry crust her mouth was rough:
"Hard was her skin; and through it might be seen
"Her inwards: 'bove her hollow loins, upstood
"The arid bones: a belly's place supply'd
"A belly's form: her breasts to hang appear'd
"Held only by the chine: her fleshless shape
"Each joint in bulk increas'd: rigidly large
"The knees were swol'n, and each protruding part
"Immod'rately was big. Then as the nymph
"From far beheld her,—for a nigh approach
"She dreaded, what the goddess bade she told.
"Though brief her stay; though distant far she stood;
"Though instant there arriv'd; she felt the power
"Of Famine at the sight, and turning quick
"Her reins, she urg'd her dragons to their speed
"In retrogade direction; still on high,
"Till Thessaly they gain'd. Famine performs
"The wish of Ceres (though her anxious aim
"Is still to thwart her power) and borne on winds
"Swift through the air, the fated house she finds
"And instant enters, where the inmost walls
"The sacrilegious wretch inclose; in sleep
"Deep bury'd, for night reign'd; and with her wings
"Him clasping close, in all the man she breath'd
"Her inspiration: in his throat, his mouth,
"His chest, and in his unreplenish'd veins,
"Her hunger she infus'd. The bidden deed
"Complete, she vanish'd from those verdant fields,
"And turn'd her to the needy roofs again,
"And well-accustom'd caverns. Gentle sleep
"Fann'd Erisichthon still with soothing wings.
"Ev'n in his sleep imagin'd food he craves,
"And vainly moves his mouth; tires jaw on jaw
"With grinding; his deluded throat with stores
"Impalpable he crams; the empty air
"Greedy devouring, for more solid food.
"But soon his slumbers vanish'd, then fierce rag'd
"Insatiate hunger; ruling through his throat,
"And ever-craving stomach. Instant he

"Demands what produce, ocean, earth, and air
"Can furnish: still of hunger he complains,
"Before the full-spread tables: still he seeks
"Victuals to heap on victuals. What might serve
"A city's population, seems for him
"Too scant; whose stomach when it loads had gorg'd,
"For loads still crav'd. The ocean thus receives
"From all earth's regions every stream; all streams
"United, still requiring; greedy fire
"On every offer'd aliment thus feeds,
"Countless supplies of wood consuming;—more
"Nutrition craving, still the more it gains;
"More greedy growing from its large increase.
"So Erisichthon's jaws prophane, rich feasts
"At once devour, at once still more demand.
"All food but stimulates his gust for food
"In added heaps; and eating only seems
"To leave his maw more empty. Lessen'd now,
"In the deep abyss of his stomach huge,
"Were all the riches which his sire's bequest
"Had given: the direful torment still remain'd
"In undiminish'd strength; his belly's fire
"Implacable still rag'd. Exhausted now
"On the curst craving all his wealth was spent.
"One daughter sole remaining; of a sire
"Less impious, worthy: her the pauper sold.
"Her free-born soul, a master's sway disclaim'd.
"Her hands extending, to the neighbouring main,
"O thou!—she cry'd—who gain'd my virgin spoil
"Snatch me from bondage.—Neptune had the maid
"Previous enjoy'd: nor spurn'd her earnest prayer.
"She whom her master following close, had seen
"In her own shape but now, in manly guise
"Appears,—in garments such as fishers clothe.
"The master sees, and speaks:—O, thou! who rul'st
"The trembling reed; whose bending wire thy baits
"Conceal; so may thy wiles the water aid;
"So may the fish deceiv'd, beneath the waves,
"Thy hooks detect not, till too firmly fixt.
"Say thou but where she is, who stood but now
"Upon this beach, in humble robes array'd,
"With locks disorder'd; on this shore she stood;
"I saw her,—but no further mark her feet.—
"The aid of Neptune well the maid perceiv'd,
"And joys that of herself herself is sought,
"Thus his enquiries answering;—Whom thou art
"I know not; studious bent, the deep alone,
"And care to drag my prey, my eyes employ.

"More to remove thy doubts, so may the god
"Who rules the ocean, aid my toiling art,
"As here I swear, no man upon this shore,
"Nor female, I excepted, has appear'd.
"These words the owner credits, and the sand
"Treads with returning steps; deluded goes,
"And as he goes, her former shape returns.
"Soon as this changing power the sire perceiv'd,
"The damsel oft he sold. Now she escapes
"Beneath a mare's resemblance: now a bird,
"An heifer now, and now a deer she seem'd.
"Her greedy parent's maw with food ill-gain'd
"Supplying. When at last his forceful plague
"Had every aid consum'd, and every aid
"Fresh food afforded to his fierce disease,
"Then he commenc'd with furious fangs to tear
"For nurture his own limbs; life to support,
"By what his body and his life destroy'd.

  "But why on others' transformations dwell?
"Myself, O youths! enjoy a power, my form
"To alter; not unlimited my range.
"Now in the shape at present I assume;
"Anon I writhe beneath a serpent's form;
"Or take the figure of a lordly bull,
"And wear my strength in horns, while horns I had:
"Disfigur'd now, my forehead's side laments
"One weapon ravish'd, as you well may see." —
He spoke, and heavy sighs his words pursu'd.

THE NINTH BOOK

Combat of Acheloüs and Hercules for Dejanira. Death of Nessus. Torments and death of Hercules. His deification. Story of the change of Galanthis to a weasel. Of Dryopè to a Lotus-tree. Iölaüs restored to youth. Murmuring of the Gods. The incestuous love of Byblis. Her transformation to a fountain. Story of Iphis and Iänthe.

  The son of Ægeus begs the cause to know
Whence spring those groans, and whence that wounded front?
And thus the stream of Calydon replies; —
(His uncomb'd locks with marshy reeds entwin'd).

"A mournful task, O, warrior! you impose;—
"For who, when vanquish'd, joys to tell the fight
"Where he was worsted? yet will I relate
"In order all: vanquish'd, the shame was small;
"The honor great, for such a prize to strive:
"And such a conqueror more the mind relieves.
"Has e'er the beauteous Dejanira's name
"Reach'd to your ears? her charms the envy'd hope
"Of numerous wooers form'd; mine with the rest.
"As o'er the threshold of my wish'd-for sire
"I stepp'd, I hail'd him.—O, Parthaön's son,
"For thine accept me.—So Alcides spoke,
"And all the rest to our pretensions bow'd.
"Of Jove, his sire, he boasts; and all the fame
"His acts deserv'd; and stepdame's cruel laws
"Final completed. I (who shameful thought
"That gods should yield to mortals; then a god
"Alcides was not) thus his claim oppos'd:—
"A king of floods behold me; floods which roll
"With winding current through the land you sway;
"A son in me accept, no stranger sent
"From distant regions; of your country one,
"Part of your rule. Let it not hurt my claim,
"That Juno hates me not; that all the toil
"Of slavish orders I have ne'er perform'd.
"Alcmena was his mother, let him boast!
"Jove is a sire but feign'd, or if one true,
"Is criminally so. He claims a sire
"To prove his mother's infamy: then chuse—
"Say feign'd thy origin from Jove, or fruit
"Of intercourse adulterous, own thou art.—
"Me, speaking thus, with furious eyes he view'd,
"Nor rul'd his swelling rage, replying fierce;—
"More than my tongue I on my arm depend:
"Whilst I in fighting gain the palm, be thou
"Victor in talking.—Furious on he rush'd.
"So proudly boasting, to submit I scorn'd;
"But stript my sea-green robe, my arms oppos'd,
"And held my firm-clench'd hands before my breast;
"For stout resistance every limb prepar'd,
"To meet the fight. He in his hollow palms
"The dust collecting, sprinkled me all o'er,
"And then the yellow sand upon me threw.
"Now on my neck he seizes; now he grasps
"My slippery thighs: but only thinks to hold,
"In every part assailing. Still secure
"In bulk I stand, and he assails in vain.
"Thus stands a rock, which waves with thundering roar

"Surround: it stands unhurt in all its strength.
"A little we recede, then rush again
"To join the war: stoutly our ground we hold,
"Steady resolv'd to yield not. Foot to foot
"Fixt firm: I prone press with my ample breast,
"And hand with hand, with forehead forehead joins.
"So have I seen two mighty bulls contend,
"When each the fairest heifer of the grove
"Expects the arduous struggle to reward:
"The herds behold and tremble, witless which
"The powerful contest shall successful gain.
"Thrice while I clasp'd him close, Alcides strove
"To throw me from his breast, in vain,—the fourth
"He shook me from him, and my clasping arms
"Unloosing, instant turn'd me with his hand;
"(Truth must I speak,) and heavy on my back
"He hung. If credence may my words demand,
"Nor seek I fame through tales of false deceit,
"A mighty mountain on me seem'd to weigh:
"Scarce were my arms, with trickling sweat bedew'd,
"Loos'd from his grasp; scarce was my body freed
"From his hard gripe, when panting hard for breath,
"Ere I could strength regain, my throat he seiz'd.
"Then on the earth my knee was press'd; my mouth
"Then bit the sand. Inferior prov'd in strength,
"To arts I next betook me. Slipp'd his hands
"In form a long round serpent; while I roll'd
"In winding spires my body; while I shook
"My forked tongue with hisses dire, he laugh'd,
"And mock'd my arts; exclaiming,—snakes to kill
"I in my cradle knew; grant thou excel'st,
"O, Acheloüs! others far in size,
"What art thou mated with the Hydra's bulk?
"He fertile from his wounds, his hundred heads
"Ne'er felt diminish'd, for straightway his neck,
"With two successors, brav'd the stroke again:
"Yet him I vanquish'd with his branching heads
"From blood produc'd: from every loss more stout,
"Him prostrate I o'erthrew. What hope hast thou,
"In form fallacious, who with borrow'd arms
"Now threaten'st? whom a form precarious hides?
"He said, and fast about my throat he squeez'd
"His nervous fingers; choaking, hard I strove,
"As pincer-like he press'd me, to unloose
"From his tight grasp my neck. Conquer'd in this,
"Still a third shape, the furious bull remain'd:
"Chang'd to a bull, again I wag'd the war.
"Around my brawny neck his arms he threw

"To left, and spite of every effort try'd
"To 'scape, he dragg'd me down; the solid earth
"Deep with my horn he pierc'd, and stretch'd me prone
"On the wide sand. Unsated yet his rage,
"His fierce hand seiz'd my stubborn horn, and broke
"From my maim'd front the weapon. Naiäd nymphs
"This consecrated, fill'd with fruits, and flowers
"Of odorous fragrance, and the horn is priz'd
"By Plenty's goddess as her favorite care."

  He spoke, a nymph close-girt like Dian's train,
Her ample tresses o'er each shoulder spread,
Enter'd, supporting all of Autumn's fruit
In the rich horn, and mellowest apples came
The second course to grace. Now day appear'd:
The youths when light the loftiest summits touch'd
Of the high hills, departed; waiting not
Till the rough floods in peaceful channels flow'd;
The troubled currents smooth'd. Profound his head
Of rustic semblance, Acheloüs hides
'Reft of his horn, beneath his deepest waves.
His forehead's honor lost sore gall'd him: all
Save that was perfect. Ev'n his forehead's loss
With willow boughs and marshy reeds was hid.

  Thou too, rash Nessus, through thy furious love,
Of the same virgin, thy destruction met;
Pierc'd through thy body with the feather'd dart!
Jove's son returning to his natal soil,
Companion'd by his new-made bride, approach'd
Evenus' rapid flood. Swol'n was the stream
With wintry showers as wont, and raging whirls
Unfordable proclaim'd it; him, himself
Fearless, yet anxious for his spouse's care,
Nessus approach'd, in strength of limbs secure,
And knowledge of the fords, and thus he spoke;
"Her, O Alcides! will I safely bear
"To yonder bank; thou all thy efforts use
"In swimming." Straight the Theban hero gives
The pallid Calydonian to his care,
Shivering with dread; no less the centaur frights
Than the rough flood. The mighty warrior, prest
With his large quiver, and the lion's hide,
For on the bank opposing had he flung
His club and curved bow, exclaim'd—"the stream
"My arms will vanquish, soon as I essay."—
Nor dubious waits, but in the torrent leaps,
Not heeding where most tranquil flows the stream,

But stemming furious all its utmost rage.
Now had he reach'd the bank, now held again
The bow flung o'er, when loud his spouse's shrieks
Assail'd his ear. To Nessus, whom he saw
His trust about betraying, loud he cry'd;—
"What vain reliance on thy rapid speed
"Tempts thee to violence? O, double-shap'd!
"I speak, regard me,—to respect my rights,
"Should deference to me not move thee, think
"How whirls thy sire, and that thy rage may check
"For wishes unallow'd. Yet hope thou not
"With courser's speed to 'scape me: with my dart,
"Not feet, will I pursue thee."—His last words
With deeds he guarantees, and through and through
The flying culprit felt the javelin driv'n;
Out through his breast the forked weapon stood:
Withdrawn, from either wound gush'd forth the gore,
Mixt with the venom of Lernæa's pest.
This be preserv'd.—"Nor will I unreveng'd
"Expire,"—he murmur'd faintly to himself;
And gave his raiment, in the warm blood dipt,
A present to the nymph whose spoil he sought;
To wake again her husband's dormant love.

   Long was the intermediate time, the deeds,
Of great Alcides, and his step-dame's hate,
Fill'd all the world meanwhile. Victor return'd
From out Œchalia, when the promis'd rites,
To Jove Cæ ean, he prepar'd to pay,
Tattling report, who joys in falshood mixt
With circumstantial truth, and still the least
Swells with her lies, had in thine ears instill'd,
O Dejanira! that Alcmena's son,
With Iölé was smitten. Ardent love
Sway'd her belief, and terror-struck to hear
Of this new flame, she melted into tears;
With them her weeping grief first flow'd away:
But soon she bursted forth.—"Why weep I so?
"The harlot will but gladden in my tears!
"But ere she here arrives, it me behoves
"Each effort to employ, while time now serves,
"To hinder what he seeks; whilst yet my couch
"Another presses not. Shall I complain,
"Or rest in silence? Shall I Calydon
"Re-seek, or here remain? Shall I abscond
"His habitation, or, if nought else serves,
"Strenuous oppose him? Or if truly bent,
"O, Meleager! with a sister's pride,

"Thy wicked deeds t' outvie, a witness leave,
"The harlot's throat divided, what the rage
"Of woman may accomplish, when so wrong'd."—
In whirls her agitated mind is toss'd;
Determining last to send to him the robe,
In Nessus' blood imbu'd, and so restore
His waning love. Witless of what she sends,
Herself to Lychas' unsuspecting hands
The cause of future grief delivers. Wretch
Most pitiable! she, with warm-coaxing words,
Instructs the boy to bear her spouse the gift.
Th' unwitting warrior takes it, and straight clothes
His shoulders with Echidna's poisonous gore.
Incense he sprinkles in the primal flames
He kindles,—with the flames his prayers ascend.
As from the goblet he the vintage pours
On marble altars; hapless by the heat
The poison more was quicken'd; by the flame
Melted, it grew more potent; wide diffus'd,
Through all the limbs of Hercules it spread.
Still while he could, his fortitude, as wont
His groans suppress'd; at last his patience spent,
Fierce from the altar flinging, Œté's mount
So woody, with his plaintive shrieks he fills,
And instant from his limbs the deadly robe
Essays to tear: that, where he strips, the skin,
Stript also, follows; dreadful to describe!
Or to his limbs, his utmost struggling vain,
It clings: or bare his lacerated joints
And huge bones stand. With hissing noise his blood
Burns, as when glowing iron in a pool
Is dipp'd, so boils it with the venom fierce.
Nor hope of help remain'd, the greedy fires,
His utmost vitals waste; and purple sweat
Bedews his every limb; his scorch'd nerves crack;
And whilst his marrow, with the latent pest,
Runs fluid, high tow'rd heaven his arms he holds,
Exclaiming;—"now Saturnia, feast thy soul
"With my destruction; joy, O savage!—view
"From lofty heaven my tortures; satiate now
"Thy rancorous soul:—but if a foe may move
"Commiseration, (for thy foe I am)
"Take hence this life, grievous, through direful pains:
"Hateful to thee, and destin'd first for toils.
"Death now would be a boon; and such a boon
"A step-dame might confer. Have I for this,
"Busiris slain, who drench'd the temples deep
"With travellers' blood? For this Antæus robb'd

"Of nutriment parental? Did thy bulk,
"Of triple-form, swain of Iberia, fright?
"Or thou, three-headed Cerberus, me move?
"Wrought I for this in Elis? at the lake
"Of Stymphalis? and in Parthenian woods?
"Did not my valor seize the golden belt
"Of Thermodon's brave queen? the apples gain,
"Ill-guarded by th' unsleeping dragon's care?
"Could the fierce Centaur me resist? or could
"The mighty boar that laid Arcadia waste?
"And what avail'd the Hydra, that he grew
"From every loss, in double strength reviv'd?
"How? Saw I not the Thracian coursers gorg'd
"With human gore! whose stalls with mangled limbs
"Crowded, I overthrew, and slew their lord
"On his slain coursers? Strangled by these hands
"Nemæa's monster lies. Heaven I upbore
"Upon these shoulders. The fierce wife of Jove
"Weary'd at length with bidding, I untir'd
"Still was of acting. But at length behold
"A new-found plague, which not the bravest soul,
"Nor arms, nor darts can aught resist. Fierce fire,
"Darts through my deepest inwards; all my limbs
"Greedy devouring. Yet Eurystheus lives!
"Still are there who the deities believe?"—
He said, and o'er high Œté tortur'd rov'd
Like a mad tiger, when the hunter's dart
Stands in his body, and the wounder flies.
Oft would you see him groaning; storming oft;
Oft straining from his limbs again to fling
The vest; trees rooting up; against the hills
Fierce railing; next up to his father's skies
His arms extending. Lo! he Lychas spies,
Where trembling in a hollow rock he hides!
Then, all his fury in its utmost strength,
Raging, he cry'd;—"Thou, Lychas, thou supply'd
"This deadly gift. Thou art the author then
"Of my destruction."—Shuddering he, and pale,
In timid accents strove excuse to plead:
Speaking, and round his knees prepar'd to cling,
Alcides seiz'd him, with an engine's force
Whirl'd round and round, and hurl'd him in the waves,
Which by Eubæa roll. He, as he shot
Through air, was harden'd. As the falling showers
Concrete by freezing winds, whence snow is form'd:
As snows by rolling, their soft bodies join,
Conglomerating into solid hail:
So ancient times believ'd, the boy thus flung,

Through empty air, by strong Alcides' arm,
Bloodless through fear, and all his moisture drain'd,
Chang'd to a flinty rock. A rock e'en now
High in Eubæa's gulph exalts its head,
Which still of human form the marks retains.
Which, as though still of consciousness possess'd,
The sailors fear to tread, and Lychas call.

  Thou, Jove's renowned offspring, fell'd the trees
Which lofty Œté bore, and built a pile:
Then bade the son of Pæan bear thy bow,
Thy mighty quiver, and thy darts, to view
Once more the realm of Troy; and through his aid
The flames were plac'd below, whose greedy spires
Seiz'd on the structure. On the woody top
Thou laid'st the hide Nemæan, and thy head,
Supported with thy club, with brow serene
As though with garlands circled, at a feast
Thou laid'st, 'mid goblets fill'd with sparkling wine.

  Now the strong fires spread wide o'er every part,
Crackling, and seizing his regardless limbs,
Who them despis'd. The gods beheld with fear
The earth's avenger. Jove, who saw their care
With joyous countenance, thus the powers address'd:
"This fear, O deities! makes glad my heart;
"And lively pleasure swells in all my breast,
"That sire and sovereign o'er such grateful minds
"I hold my sway; since to my offspring too
"Your favoring care extends. No less, 'tis true,
"His deeds stupendous claim. Still I'm oblig'd.
"But from your anxious breasts banish vain fear;
"Despise those flames of Œté; he who all
"O'ercame, shall conquer even the flames you see:
"Nor shall the power of Vulcan ought consume,
"Save his maternal part: what he deriv'd
"From me, is ever-during; safe from death;
"And never vanquish'd by the force of fire.
"That we'll receive, his earthly race compleat,
"Amidst the heavenly host; and all I trust
"My actions gladly will approve. Should one
"Haply, with grief see Hercules a god,
"And grudge the high reward; ev'n he shall grant
"His great deserts demand it; and allow
"Unwilling approbation." All assent;
Not even his royal spouse's forehead wore,
A frown at ought he said; his final words
Irk'd her at length, to be so plainly mark'd.

Vulcan meantime each corruptible part
Bore off in flames, nor could Alcides' form
Remaining, now be known; nought he retain'd
Of what his mother gave; Jove's share alone.
A serpent revels thus in glittering scales,
His age and former skin thrown off at once.
So when Tirynthius from his mortal limbs
Departed, in his better part he shone,
Increas'd in stature; and majestic grace
Augustly deck'd his venerable brow.
Veil'd in a hollow cloud, and borne along
By four swift steeds, in a high car, the sire
Him plac'd in glory 'mid the radiant stars.
Atlas perceiv'd his load increas'd. Nor yet
Eurystheus 'bated in his rancorous hate,
But cruel exercis'd his savage rage,
Against the offspring of the sire abhorr'd.

  But now Alcmena, worn with constant cares,
In Argolis, to Iölé confides
Her aged plaints, to her the labors tells
Her son atchiev'd, o'er all the wide world known;
And her own griefs beside. Alcides' words
Caus'd Hyllus to his couch to take, and take
Iölé, cordial to his inmost heart:
And now with generous fruit, the nymph was large.
Alcmena, thus to her commenc'd her tale.—

  "May thee, at least, the favoring gods indulge;
"And all delay diminish, when matur'd,
"Thou to Ilithyiä shalt have need to call,
"Who o'er travailing mothers bears the rule;
"Whom Juno's influence made so hard to me.
"Of Hercules toil-bearing, now the birth,
"Approach'd, and in the tenth sign rul'd the sun.
"A mighty bulk swell'd out my womb, so huge,
"Well might you know that Jove the load had caus'd:
"Nor could I longer bear my throes (my limbs
"Cold rigors seize, while now I speak; my pains
"Part ev'n in memory now I seem to feel)
"Through seven long nights, and seven long days with pangs
"Incessant was I rack'd: my arms to heaven
"Stretching, I call'd Lucina, and the powers,
"With outcries mighty. True Lucina came,
"But came by Juno prepossest, and bent
"My life to sacrifice to Juno's rage.
"Soon as my groans she hearken'd, down she sate
"Upon the altar, plac'd without the gates:

"'Neath her right ham, her left knee pressing; join'd
"Fingers with fingers cross'd upon her breast
"My labor stay'd; and spellful words she spoke
"In whispering tone; the spellful words delay'd
"Th' approaching birth. I strain, and madly rave
"With vain upbraidings to ungrateful Jove,
"And crave for death; in such expressions 'plain
"As hardest flints might move. The Theban dames
"Around me throng; assist me with their prayers;
"And me my trying pains exhort to bear.
"Galanthis, one who tended me, of race
"Plebeïan; yellow-hair'd; and sedulous
"What order'd to perform; and much esteem'd
"For courteous deeds;—she first suspected, (what,
"I know not) somewhat, form'd by Juno's pique:
"And while she constant pass'd; now to, now fro,
"She saw the goddess on the altar sit,
"Girding her arms, with close-knit fingers o'er
"Her knees, and said;—O dame, whoe'er thou art,
"Our mistress gratulate. Alcmena now
"Argolican, is lighten'd. Now the prayers
"Of the child-bearer meet her hopes.—The dame
"Who rules the womb, straight from her station leap'd,
"And all astounded, her clench'd fingers loos'd:
"I in that moment felt my bonds undone.
"Galanthis, they report, the goddess mock'd
"Thus cheated, by her laughter. Savage, she
"Dragg'd her so laughing, by the tresses seiz'd,
"And forc'd her down to earth, as up she strove
"Erect to rise; and to forefeet her arms
"Transform'd. The same agility remains;
"Her back its colour keeps; her form alone
"Is diverse. She, 'cause then her lying mouth
"My birth assisted, by her mouth still bears:
"And round my house she harbors as before."—

  She said, and by the memory mov'd, she mourn'd
For her lost servant, whom, lamenting, thus
Her child-in-law address'd.—"If then the form
"Alter'd, of one an alien to your blood,
"O mother! thus affects you, let me tell
"The wond'rous fortune which my sister met:
"Though grief and tears will frequent choke my words.

  "Her mother, Dryopé alone could boast,
"(Me to my sire another bore) her charms
"Œthalia all confess'd; whom (rifled first
"Of virgin charms, when passively she felt

"His force, who Delphos, and who Delos rules)
"Andræmon took, and held a happy spouse.
"A lake expands with steep and shelving shores
"Encompass'd; myrtles crown the rising bank.
"Here Dryopé, of fate unconscious came,
"And what must more commiseration move,
"Came to weave chaplets for the Naïad nymphs;
"Her arms sustain'd her boy, a pleasing load,
"His first year scarce complete, as with warm milk
"She nourish'd him. The watery Lotus there,
"For promis'd fruit in Tyrian splendor bright,
"Grew flowering near. The flowers my sister cropp'd,
"And held them to delight her boy; and I,
"(For there I stood,) the same prepar'd to do;
"But from the flowers red flowing drops I saw,
"And all the boughs with tremulous shuddering shook.
"Doubtless it is, (but far too late we learn'd
"By the rough swains,) nymph Lotis, when she fled
"From Priapus obscene, her shape transform'd
"Into this tree which still retains her name.
"My sister witless of this change, in fright
"Would back retreat, and leave the nymphs ador'd,
"But roots her feet retain: these from the ground
"She strains to rend; but save her upper limbs
"Nought can she move; a tender bark grows o'er
"The lower parts, and her mid limbs invades.
"This seeing, and her locks to rend away
"Attempting: her rais'd hand with leaves was fill'd.
"Leaves cover'd all her head. Amphyssus found,
"(His grandsire had the child Amphyssus nam'd)
"His mother's breasts grow hard; nor when he suck'd
"Lacteal fluid gain'd he. I there stood,
"Of her sad fate spectator: loud I cry'd—
"But, O my sister! aid I could not bring;
"Yet what I could I urg'd; the growing trunk,
"And growing boughs, my close embraces staid:
"In the same bark I glad had been enclos'd.
"Lo! come her spouse Andræmon, and her sire
"So wretched; and for Dryopé they seek:
"A Lotus, as for Dryopé they ask,
"I shew them; to the yet warm wood salutes
"Ardent they give; and prostrate spread, the roots
"They clasp of their own tree. Now, sister dear!
"Nought save thy face but what a tree becomes.
"Thy tears, the leaves thy body form'd, bedew.
"And now, whilst able, while her mouth yet gives
"To words a passage, such like plaints as these
"She breathes;—If faith th' unhappy e'er can claim,

"I swear by all the deities, this deed
"I never merited: without a crime
"My punishment I suffer. Innocent
"My life has been. If I deceive, may drought
"Parch those new leaves; and, by the hatchet fell'd,
"May fire consume me. Yet this infant bear
"From those maternal branches; to a nurse
"Transfer him; but contrive that oft he comes
"And 'neath my boughs let him his milk imbibe;
"And 'neath my boughs sport playful. When with words
"Able to hail me, let him me salute,
"And sorrowing say;—Within that trunk lies hid
"My mother—But the lakes, O! let him dread,
"Nor dare from any tree to snatch a flower;
"But think each shrub he sees a god contains.
"Adieu! dear husband; sister dear, adieu!
"Father, farewel! if pious cares you feel,
"From the sharp axe defend my boughs, and from
"The browsing flocks. And now, as fate denies
"To lean my arms to yours,—your arms advance;
"Approach my lips, whilst you my lips may touch:
"And to them lift my infant boy. More words
"I may not;—now the tender bark my neck,
"So white, invades; my utmost summit hid.
"Move from my lids your fingers, for the bark,
"So rapid growing, will my dying eyes
"Without assistance close.—Her lips to speak
"Cease, and existence ceases: the fresh boughs
"Long in the alter'd body warm were felt."

   While Iölé the mournful fact relates;
And while Alcmena, from Eurytus' maid,
With ready fingers dry'd the tears; herself
Still weeping, lo! a novel deed assuag'd
Their grief—for Iölaüs, scarcely youth,
His cheeks with tender down just cover'd, stands
Within the porch; to early years restor'd.

   Junonian Hebé, by her husband's prayers
O'ercome, to Iölaüs gave the boon.
Who, when to vow she went, that future times
Should none such gift enjoying, e'er perceive,
Was check'd by Themis. "Now all Thebes,"—she said,
"Discordant warfare moves. Through Jove alone
"Capaneus can be conquer'd. Mutual wounds
"Shall slay the brothers. In the yawning earth
"A living prophet his own tomb shall see.
"A son avenger of his parent's death

"Upon his parent: impious for the deed,
"At once, and pious: at the action stunn'd,
"Exil'd from home, and from his senses driv'n,
"The furies' faces, and his mother's shade
"Shall haunt him; till his wife the fatal gold
"Shall ask: and till the Phegian sword shall pierce
"Their kinsman's side. Callirhoë then, the nymph
"From Acheloüs sprung, suppliant shall seek
"From Jove, her infants years mature may gain.
"Mov'd by her prayers, Jove will from thee demand,
"Son's spouse, and daughter of his wife, the boon
"And unripe men thou'lt make the youths become."

  While Themis thus, with fate-foretelling lips,
This spoke; the gods in murmuring grudgings mourn'd,
Angry why others might not grant the gift.
Aurora mourn'd her husband's aged years:
Mild Ceres 'plain'd that Jason's hairs were white:
Vulcan, for Erichthonius pray'd an age
Renew'd. E en Venus future cares employ'd,
Anxious for promise that Anchises' years
Replenishment might find: And every god
Had whom he lov'd; and dark sedition grew
From special favor; till the mighty sire
The silence broke.—"If reverence I may claim,
"Where rashly rush ye? Which of you the power,
"Fate to control, possesses? Fate it was
"Gave Iölaüs youth restor'd again:
"By Fate Callirhoë's sons ere long shall spring
"To manhood, prematurely; nor can arms
"Nor yet ambition gain this gift. With souls
"More tranquil bear this; since you see the fates
"Me also rule. Could I the fates once change,
"Old age should never bend Æacus down;
"And Rhadamanthus had perpetual spring
"Of youth enjoy'd, with Minos, now despis'd
"Through load of bitter years, nor reigns as wont."

  Jove's words the deities all mov'd; not one
Longer complain'd, when heavy press'd with years
They Æacus, and Rhadamanthus saw;
And Minos: who, when in his prime of age,
Made mightiest nations tremble at his name.
He, feeble then, at Deïoné's son
Miletus, trembled, who with youthful strength,
And Phœbus' origin proud swol'n, and known
About to rise against his rule:—yet him
He dar'd not from his household roof to drive.

But thou, Miletus, fled'st spontaneous, thou
Th' Ægean waves in thy swift ship didst pass,
And on the Asian land the walls didst found
Which bear the builder's name. Cyancë here,
Mæander's daughter, whose recurving banks
She often trode: (whose stream itself reseeks
So oft) in beauteous form, by thee was known,
And, claspt by thee, a double offspring came,
Byblis and Caunus, from the warm embrace.

  Let Byblis warn, that nymphs should ne'er indulge
Illicit warmth. Her brother Byblis lov'd;
Not as she ought; not with a sister's soul.
No fires at first the maid suspected; nought
Of sin: the thought that oft her lips to his
She wish'd to join, and clasp her arms around
His neck fraternal, long herself deceiv'd,
Beneath the semblance of a duteous love.
Love gradual bends to him her soul; she comes
Fully adorn'd to see him, anxious pants
Beauteous to seem; if one more beauteous there
She sees, invidious she that face beholds.
Still to herself unconscious was her love:
No wish she form'd beneath that burning flame,
Yet all within was fire. She call'd him lord,
Now kindred's name detesting; anxious more,
Byblis, than sister he should call her still.
Yet waking, ne'er her soul durst entertain
Lascivious wishes. When relax'd in sleep,
Then the lov'd object oft her fancy saw;
Oft seem'd her bosom to his bosom join'd:
Yet blush'd she, tranc'd in sleep. Her slumbers fly,
She lies awhile in silence, and revolves
Her dream: and thus in doubting accents speaks;
"Ah, wretch! what means this dream of silent night,
"Which yet I oft would wish? Why have I known
"This vision? Envy's eyes must own him fair,
"And but his sister am I, all my love
"He might possess; worthy of all my love.
"A sister's claim then hurts me! O! at least
"(While tempted thus I wakeful nought commit)
"Let sleep oft visit with such luscious dreams:
"No witness sees my sleeping joys; my joys,
"Though sleeping, yet are sweet. O, Venus! O,
"Thou feather'd Cupid, with thy tender dame!
"What transports I enjoy'd! what true delight
"Me thrill'd! how lay I, all my soul dissolv'd!
"How joys it me to trace in mind again

"The pleasure though so brief: for flying night
"Invidious check'd enjoyment in the bud.
"O Caunus! that an alter'd name might join
"Us closely; that thy sire a sire-in-law
"To me might be: O, Caunus, how I'd joy
"Wert thou not son, but son-in-law to mine.
"Would that the gods had all in common given,
"Save parents only. Thou in lofty birth
"I would should me excel. O beauteous youth!
"A mother whom thou'lt make I know not; I
"Ne'er can thee know but with a sister's love:
"Parents the same as thine my hapless lot.
"All that I have, me only pains the more.
"What are to me my visions? Weight have dreams?
"How much more happy are th' immortal gods!
"The gods embrace their sisters. Saturn clasps
"Ops, join'd to him by blood; Ocean enjoys
"His sister Tethys; and Olympus' king
"His Juno. Gods peculiar laws possess.
"Why seek I then celestial rites to bring
"Diverse, with human ord'nance to compare?
"Forbidden love shall from my breast be driv'n,
"Or that impossible, may death me seize
"Instant, and cold upon my couch outstretch'd,
"My brother then may kiss me as I lie.
"Yet still my wish double consent requires.
"Grant I should yield, still might the deed to him
"Seem execrable. Yet th' Æolian youth
"A sister's nuptial couch ne'er dreaded. Why,
"O, why! on this so dwell? Why thus recal
"Examples to my view? Where am I borne?
"Hence, flames obscene! hence far! a sister's love,
"And that alone my brother shall enjoy.
"But had his soul first burn'd for me, perchance
"I had indulg'd his passion. Surely then
"I may demand, who would not, ask'd, refuse.
"What couldst thou speak? Couldst thou confess thy flame?
"Love forces, and I can. If shame my lips
"Close binds; yet secret letters may disclose
"The hidden flame."—With this idea pleas'd,
These words her hesitating mind resolv'd,
Rais'd on her side, supported by her arm.—
"He shall"—she said—"now know it; all my love
"Preposterous confess'd. Alas! what depth
"Now rush I to? What fire has seiz'd my soul?"—
And then with tremulous hand the words compos'd.
Her right hand grasps the style, the left sustains
The waxen tablet smooth; and then begins.

She doubts; she writes; condemns what now she wrote;
Corrects; erases; alters; now dislikes;
And now approves. Now throws the tablet by,
Then seizes it again. Irres'lute what
She would; whate'er is done displeases, all.
Shame and audacious boldness in her face
Are mingled. Sister, once her hand had wrote,
But sister, soon as seen, her hand eras'd;
And her fair tablet bore such words as these.—
"To thee, a lover salutation sends,
"And health, which only thou to her canst give:
"Asham'd, she blushes to disclose her name.
"For should I press to gain my wish'd desire,
"Without my name, my cause I trust would find
"Successful aid. Let Byblis not be known
"Till certain hopes of bliss her mind shall cheer.
"Yet faded color, leanness, and pale face,
"With constant dripping eye, and rising sobs
"Shew my unhidden grief. Well might these prove
"To thee an index of a wounded heart.
"My constant clasping, numerous fond salutes,
"If e'er thou'st mark'd, thou well might have perceiv'd
"Not sister-like embracings. In my soul
"Though this deep wound I bear; though in my breast
"This fire consuming burns, yet strive I all,
"(Witness, ye gods! my truth) all to suppress,
"And act with wiser conduct: hapless war
"Long have I wag'd 'gainst Cupid's furious rule
"More pressure have I borne, than what a maid
"Could e'er be thought to bear. At length o'ercome,
"And forc'd to yield, thy help I must implore
"With trembling voice: thou only canst preserve,
"Thou only canst the loving nymph destroy.
"With thee the choice remains. No foe thus sues,
"But one by nearest ties to thee conjoin'd,
"Pants to be join'd more nearly; link'd to thee
"With closest bands. Let aged seniors learn
"Our laws, and seek what moral codes permit.
"What is permitted, and what is deny'd,
"Let them enquire, and closely search the laws:
"A bolder love more suits our growing years.
"As yet we know not what the laws allow;
"And judge for all things we free leave enjoy;
"Th' example following of the mighty gods.
"Nor parent stern, nor strict regard for fame,
"Nor timid thoughts should check us; absent all
"Should be each cause of fear. The dear sweet theft
"Beneath fraternal love may be conceal'd;

"With thee in secret converse I may speak,
"Embrace thee, kiss thee in the open crowd;
"How little then remains! Pity, forgive,
"The declaration of this love, ne'er told
"Had raging fire not urg'd it, nor allow
"Upon my tomb this cause of death to stand.—"

Here the fill'd tablet check'd her hand, in vain
Thus writing, at the utmost edge the lines,
But stay'd. Her crime straightway she firmly press'd,
With her carv'd gem, and moisten'd it with tears:
Her tears of utterance robb'd her. Bashful then
She call'd a page, and blandishing in fear
Exclaim'd.—"Thou faithful boy, this billet bear—"
And hesitated long ere more she said,
Ere—"to my brother, bear it."—As she gave
The tablet, from her trembling hand it fell;
The omen deep disturb'd her. Yet she sent.

A chosen hour the servant sought, went forth
And gave the secret message. Sudden rage
me youth Mæandrian petrify'd; and down
The half-read lines upon the ground he flung.
His hand scarce holding from the trembling face
Of the pale messenger. "Quick, fly!" he cry'd,
"Thou wicked pander of forbidden lust!
"Fly while thou may'st; and know, had not thy fate
"Involv'd our modest name, death hadst thou found.—"
He terrify'd escapes, and backward bears,
To his young mistress all fierce Caunus spoke.

Pale, thou, O Byblis! heardst the rough repulse;
Thy breast with frigid chills beset. But soon
Her spirits rally, and her furious love
Returns: scarce to the trembling air her tongue
Can utterance give in these indignant words;—
"Deserv'dly mourn I, who so rashly gave
"Him of my wounds the conscious tale to learn.
"Why trust so soon to words, what still might hid
"Remain, on tablets hastily compos'd?
"Why were not first the wishes of my soul
"Try'd in ambiguous hints? First, sure I ought
"Whence the wind blew have mark'd; nor loos'd my sails,
"Him flying, to pursue, and the wide main
"In all directions plough: now bellies out
"My canvas; not a single course explor'd.
"Hence am I borne against the rocks; hence 'whelm'd
"In the wide depth of ocean; nor my sails

"Know I to tack returning. Did not heaven
"Check the indulgence of my love, by marks
"Obvious to all? when from my hand down dropp'd
"The tablet, which the boy was bade to bear.
"Mark'd that my falling hopes not? More deferr'd
"Thy wishes, or the day should sure have been;
"Surely the day. For heaven itself me warn'd,
"And certain signs me gave; but those my mind
"Stupid neglected. Personal my words
"Should I have urg'd, nor trusted to the wax.
"In person should my love have been display'd.
"Then had my tears been seen; then had he view'd
"My raptur'd countenance; then had I spoke
"Far more than power of letters can convey.
"My arms around his neck I then had thrown
"Howe'er unwilling; and, had he been coy,
"In dying posture I his feet had clasp'd;
"And stretch'd before him life demanding, all
"Had I achiev'd. Perchance though, by the boy,
"My messenger commission'd, I have fail'd:
"Aptly perhaps he enter'd not; perhaps,
"And much I fear, improper hours he chose;
"Nor sought a vacant time, when nought his mind
"Disturb'd. This has, alas! my hopes destroy'd:
"For from a tiger Caunus sprung not; round
"His heart not solid steel, nor rigid flint,
"Nor adamant is girt; nor has he suck'd
"The lioness's milk. He shall be bent,
"And gain'd his heart shall be; nor will I brook
"The smallest bar to what I undertake,
"While now this spirit holds. My primal wish
"(If it were given I might revoke my deeds)
"Is, I had ne'er commenc'd: my second now
"Is, that I persevere in what's begun.
"For should I now my wishes not pursue,
"Still must he of those daring wishes think;
"And should I now desist, well might he judge
"Form'd lightly my desires: or plann'd to try
"His virtue, and involve in snares his fame:
"Or, (dreadful!) think me not by love o'ercome,
"(Who burns and rages fiercely in my breast)
"But by hot lust. For now conceal'd no more
"My guilty act can be; I've written once,
"Once have I ask'd; corrupted all my soul.
"Should further no depravity ensue,
"Guilty I must be call'd. What more remains,
"In crime is little, but in hope immense." —

She said, and such the wavering of her breast,
That, whilst the trial grieves her which she made,
Farther to try she wishes; every bound
O'erpassing: and, with luckless fate, her suit
Still meets repulsion. He, when endless seem'd
Her pressing, fled his country, and the crime;
And in a foreign region rais'd new walls.

  Then, daughter of Miletus, they report,
Forsook thee all thy senses; then in truth
Thou rent thy garments from thy breast; thy breast
Thy furious hands hard smote. Now to the world
Madly she raves; now to the world displays
Her wish'd-for love, deny'd: all hope—despair!
She too forsook her country, and the roof
So hated; and the vagrant steps pursu'd
Her flying brother trode. As Thracia's dames
O, son of Semelé! thy Thyrsus shake
When celebrating thy triennial rites,
So did the Carian matrons, Byblis see
Fly o'er the wide-spread fields, with shrieks and howls:
These left behind, o'er Caria's plains she runs,
And through the warlike Leleges, and through
The Lycian realms. Now Cragos had she left,
And Lymiré, and Xanthus' waves behind;
With the high ridge Chimæra lifts, who burns
Central with flames; his breast and front fierce arm'd
A lion—tow'rd his tail a serpent form'd.
Now all the forests past; thou Byblis, faint
With long pursuit, fall'st flat; on the hard ground
Thy locks are spread; dumb now thou ly'st; thy face
Presses the fallen leaves. Oft in their arms
So delicate, the Lelegeïan nymphs
To raise thee up attempted. Oft they strove
To give advice that might thy love control,
And offer solace to thy deafen'd ear.
Still silent Byblis lies; and with her nails
Rends the green herbage; moistens all the grass
With rivulets of tears. And here, they say,
The Naïad nymphs their bubbling art supply'd.
Ne'er drought to know: more to afford, their power
Sure could not. Straightway, as the pitchy drops
Flow from the fir's cleft bark; from solid earth
As stiff bitumen oozes; or as streams,
By cold congeal'd, thaw with the southern wind
And warming sun: Phœbean Byblis so
By her own tears exhausted, was transform'd,
A fount becoming; which still in that vale,

'Neath a dark ilex springing, keeps her name.

  Now had the rumor of this wond'rous change
Spread rapid through the hundred towns of Crete,
But Crete had lately seen a wond'rous change
In her own clime, in Iphis' alter'd form.
There in the Phestian land, near Gnossus' realm
Was Lygdus born: a man of unknown fame,
But a plebeïan of unblemish'd worth:
Nor had he, more than noble stock, estate;
Yet unimpeach'd for honesty his life.
He thus the ears of his then pregnant spouse
Address'd, when near her bearing time approach'd:—
"Two things my wishes bound; first that thy pains
"May lightly press, next that a male thou bring'st:
"More burdensome are females; strength to them
"Nature denies. Then if by fate ordain'd
"To give a female birth, which I detest,
"Unwilling I command,—O piety!
"Excuse it,—let the babe to death be given."—
He said, and tears profuse the cheeks bedew
Of him who bade, and her who heard his words.
Still Telethusa to the latest hour,
With vain petitions strives her spouse to move,
That thus he should not straighten so his hopes.
Firm to his purpose Lygdus stood. And now
Scarce could the heavy weight her womb sustain;
When in the silent space of night, in sleep
Entranc'd; or Isis stood before her bed,
Or seem'd to stand; surrounded by the pomp
To her belonging. On her forehead shone
The lunar horns, and yellow wheat them bound
In golden radiance, with a regal crown.
With her Anubis, barker came; and came
Bubastis holy; Apis various-mark'd;
He who the voice suppresses, and directs
To silence with his finger; timbrels loud;
Osiris never sought enough; and snakes
Of foreign lands full of somniferous gall.
To her the goddess thus, as rais'd from sleep
She seem'd, and manifest each object stood:—
"O vot'ry, Telethusa! fling aside
"Thy weighty cares; thy husband's mandates cheat;
"Nor waver, when Lucina helps thy pains:
"Save it whate'er it be. A goddess I,
"Assisting, still give aid when rightly claim'd:
"Nor will it e'er thee grieve to have ador'd
"An ingrate goddess."—Thus as she advis'd,

She vanish'd from the bed. The Cretan dame
Rose from the couch o'erjoy'd; and raising high
To heaven her guiltless hands, pray'd that her dream
On truth was founded. Now her pains increas'd;
And now her burthen forc'd itself to air:
A daughter came, but to the sire unknown.
The mother bade them rear it as a boy,
And all a boy believ'd it; none the truth,
The nurse excepted, knew. Glad prayers the sire
Offers, and from its grandsire is it nam'd:
(Iphis, the grandsire's appellation.) Joy'd
The mother hears the name, which either sex
May claim; and none, in that at least, deceiv'd;
The lie lay hid beneath a pious fraud.
The robes were masculine, the face was such
As beauteous boy, or beauteous girl might own.

And now three annual suns the tenth had pass'd,
Thy father, Iphis, had to thee betroth'd
Iänthé, yellow-hair'd; nymph most admir'd
'Mongst all the Phestians, for her beauteous charms:
Telestes of Dictæa was her sire.
Equal in age, and equal in fair form;
The self-same masters taught the early arts,
Suiting their years. Their unsuspecting minds
Were both by love thus touch'd, in both was fix'd
An equal wound: but far unlike their hopes.
Iänthé, for a spouse impatient looks,
With nuptial torches. Whom a man she thinks,
That spouse she hopes will be. Iphis too loves,
Despairing what she loves e'er to enjoy:
This still the more her love augments, and burns
A virgin for a virgin. Scarce from tears
Refraining;—"What,"—she cries,—"for me remains?
"What will the issue be? What cure for this
"New love, unknown to all, who prodigies
"Possess in this desire? If the high gods
"Me wish to spare, straight should they me destroy.
"Yet would they me destroy, they should have given
"A curse more natural; a more usual fate.
"Love for an heifer ne'er an heifer moves;
"Nor burns the mare for mares: rams follow ewes;
"The stag pursues his female; birds thus join:
"Nor animal creation female shews
"With love of female seiz'd. Would none were I!
"But lest all monstrous loves Crete might not shew;
"Sol's daughter chose a bull; even that was male
"With female. Yet, if candidly I speak,

"My passion wilder far than hers appears.
"She hop'd-for love pursu'd; by fraud enjoy'd;
"Beneath an heifer's form, th' adulterous spark
"Deceiving. Be from every part of earth
"Assembled here the skill: let Dædalus
"Hither, on waxen wings rebend his flight,
"What could all aid? Could all their learned art
"Change me from maid to youth? or alter thee
"Iänthé? But why resolute, thy mind
"Not fix? Why Iphis thus thyself forget,
"These stupid wishes driving hence, and thoughts
"So unavailing? Lo! what thou wast born,
"(Save thou would'st also thine own breast deceive)
"What is allow'd behold, and as a maid
"May love, love only. Hope, first snatch'd by love,
"Love feeds on still. From thee all hope is borne.
"No guardians thee debar the dear embrace;
"Nor watchful husband's care; no sire severe;
"Nor she herself denies thy pressing prayers,
"Yet art thou still forbid, though all agree;
"To reap the bliss, though gods and men unite.
"Behold, too, all my votive prayers succeed:
"The favoring gods whate'er I pray'd have given.
"My sire and hers, and even herself comply,
"But nature far more strong denies, alone
"Me irking with refusal. Lo! arrives
"The wish'd-for hour; the matrimonial light
"Approaches; when Iänthé will be mine;
"And yet far from me. In the midst of waves
"For thirst I perish. Nuptial Juno, why
"Com'st thou, or Hymen to these rites; where none
"Leads to the altar, but where both are led?"—

   Here staid her speech; nor less the other nymph
Burn'd; and O, Hymen, pray'd thy quick approach.
But what she wishes Telethusa dreads,
And searches for delays; feign'd sickness oft
Prolongs the time; oft omens dire, and dreams.
Now all her artful fictions are consum'd;
And now the long protracted period came,
For nuptial rites; and, but one day remain'd.
She from her own and daughter's head unbinds
The fillets; and with locks dishevell'd, clasps
The altar, crying;—"Isis, thou who dwell'st
"In Parætonium; Mareotis' fields;
"In Pharos; and the sev'nfold mouths of Nile.
"Help me I pray! relieve my trembling dread.
"Thee, goddess, once I saw; and with thee all

"Those images beheld; them all I know:
"Thy train, thy torches, and thy timbrels loud.
"And with a mindful soul thy words I mark'd.
"That she enjoys the light, that I myself,
"Not sinful suffer, to thy counsels, we,
"And admonitions owe. Pity us both;
"Grant us thy helping aid."—Tears follow'd words.
Straight seem'd the goddess' altars all to shake;
(And shake they did) trembled the temple's doors;
The lunar horns blaz'd bright; the timbrels rung.

  Forth goes the mother, of the omen glad,
Yet not in faith secure. Iphis pursues
His mother with a step more large than wont:
The snow-like whiteness quits his face; his strength
Increases; fiercer frowns his forehead wears:
Shorten'd his uncomb'd locks: more vigor now
Than as a nymph he felt. For thou a boy
Now art—so late a female! Bear thy gifts
Straight to the temple; and in faith rejoice.
Straight to the temple they their offerings bore,
And on them this short poem was inscrib'd.—
"Iphis a boy, the offerings pays, which maid,
"Iphis had vow'd."—The following sun illum'd
The wide world with his rays; when Venus came,
Juno, and Hymen, to the genial fires;
And the boy Iphis his Iänthé clasp'd.

THE TENTH BOOK

Marriage of Orpheus and Eurydice. Her death. Descent of Orpheus to Hell, to recover her. Her second loss. His mournful music on mount Hæmus draws the trees, birds, and beasts around him. Change of Cyparissus to a cypress-tree. Song of Orpheus. Ganymede. Hyacinth changed to a flower. The Amanthians to oxen. The Propætides to flints. Pygmalion's statue to a woman. Myrrha's incestuous love, and transformation to a tree. Venus' love for Adonis. Story of Atalanta and Hippomenes. Adonis changed to an anemoné.

THE TENTH BOOK OF THE METAMORPHOSES OF OVID

  Thence Hymen, in his saffron vesture clad,
Through the vast air departs; and seeks the land
Ciconian; by the voice of Orpheus call'd
Vainly. He came indeed, but with him brought

No wonted gratulations, no glad face,
Nor happy omen. And the torch he bore
Crackled in hissing smoke; nor gather'd flame
From whirling motion. Still more dire th' event
Prov'd, than the presage. As the new-made bride,
Attended by a train of Naïad nymphs,
Rov'd through the grass, a serpent's fangs her heel
Pierc'd, and she instant dy'd. Her, when long-mourn'd
In upper air, the Rhodopeïan bard
Ventur'd to seek in shades, and dar'd descend
Through the Tænarian cave to Stygia's realms.
'Mid shadowy crowds, and bury'd ghosts he goes,
To Proserpine, and him who rules the shades
With sway ungrateful. There he strikes the strings
Responsive to his words, and this his song.—
"Gods of this subterraneous world, where all
"Of mortal origin must come, permit
"That I the truth declare; no tedious tales
"Of falshood will I tell. Here came I not
"Your dusky Hell to view: nor to o'ercome
"The triple-throated Medusæan beast
"Snake-hair'd;—my wife alone my journey caus'd,
"Whose heel a trampled serpent venom'd stung:
"Snatch'd in her bloom of years. Much did I wish,
"My loss to bear; nor ought forbore to strive;
"But love o'ercame. Well do the upper gods
"That deity confess. In doubt I stand
"If here too he is known; but here I judge
"His power is felt: the ancient rape, if true,
"Proves love ev'n you first join'd. You I implore,
"By all those regions fill'd with dread; by this
"Chaos immense; your ample realm, all fill'd
"With silence; once again the thread renew
"Eurydicé too hasty lost. To you
"We all belong; a little while we stay,
"Then soon or late to one repose we haste:
"All hither tend; this is our final home.
"You hold o'er human kind a lengthen'd reign.
"She too, when once her years mature are fill'd,
"To you again, must by just right belong.
"I then request her only as a loan:
"But should the fates this favor me refuse,
"Certain I'll ne'er return. Two deaths enjoy."—
The bloodless shadows wept as thus he sung,
And struck the strings in concord with his words.
Nor Tantalus at flying waters caught;
Nor roll'd Ixion's wheel: the liver gnaw'd
The birds not: rested on their empty urns

The Belides: and Sisyphus, thou sat'st
Upon thy stone. Nay fame declares, then first,
Vanquish'd by song, the furies felt their cheeks
Wetted with tears. Nor could the royal spouse,
Nor he who rules deep darkness, him withstand
Thus praying; and Eurydicé is call'd.
Amid the recent dead she walk'd, and still
Halted with tardy steps from her late wound.
Her, when the bard of Thrace receiv'd, this law
Receiv'd he also: that his eyes reverse
He should not bend, till past Avernus' realms;
Else he'd the granted favor useless find.
In silence mute, through the steep path they climb
Dark, difficult, and thick with pitchy mist;
Nor far earth's surface wanted they to gain:
The lover here, in dread lest she should stray,
And anxious to behold, bent back his sight,
And instant back she sunk. As forth his arms
He stretch d, to clasp expecting, and be clasp'd:
Unhappy! nought but fleeting air he held.
Twice dying, she can nought her spouse condemn;
For how blame him because too much he lov'd?
She gives her last farewel; which scarce his ears
Receive, then sinks again to shades below.

  Orpheus, thus doubly of his spouse despoil'd,
All stunn'd appear'd: not less than he who saw
In wild affright the triple-headed dog,
Chain'd by the midmost: fear him never fled,
Till fled his former nature: sudden stone
On all his body seizing. Or than he,
Olenus, when the crime upon himself
He took, and guilty wish'd to seem; with thee
Hapless Lethæa, confident in charms.
Once breast to breast you join'd, now join as stones,
Which watery Ida bears. Beseeching vain,
And wishing once again the stream to pass,
The ferryman denies. Then on the bank
In squalid guise he sate, nor tasted food
For seven long days; his cares, and grieving soul,
And tears were all the sustenance he knew.
Cruel he call'd the gods of Erebus,
And to high Rhodopé himself betook,
And lofty Hæmus by the north-wind beat.

  Thrice had the sun the year completed, each
By watery Pisces ended. Orpheus still
Fled every female's love: or his deep woe

Made him so cold; or faithful promise giv'n.
Yet crowds there were, who wish'd the bard's embrace:
And crowds with sorrow saw their love repuls'd.
A hill there rose, and on its summit spread
A wide extended plain, with herbage green:
Shade to the place was wanting; hither came
The heaven-born poet; seated him, and touch'd
His sounding strings, and straight a shade approach'd.
Nor wanted there Chaönian trees; nor groves
Of poplars; nor the acorn's spacious leaves:
The linden soft, the beech, the virgin bay,
The brittle hazle, and spear-forming ash;
The knotless fir; ilex with fruit low-bow'd;
The genial plane; the maple various stain'd;
Stream-loving willow; and the watery lote;
Box of perpetual green; slight tamarisk;
Two-teinted myrtle; and the laurustine
With purple berries. Thou too, ivy, cam'st
Hither with flexile feet: together flock'd
Grape-bearing vines; and elms with vines entwin'd:
Wild ash, and pitch tree; and arbutus, bent
With loads of ruddy fruit; the pliant palm,
Meed of the conqueror; the pine close bound
About its boughs, but at its summit shagg'd:
Dear to the mother of celestial powers,
Since Atys Cybeleïan was transform'd,
And in the trunk a rigid tree became.

   In form pyramidal, amid the crowd,
The cypress came; now tree, but once a boy;
Dear to the god who rules the lyre's fine chords,
And rules the bowstring. Once was known a stag
Sacred to nymphs that own Carthæa's fields,
Who bore upon his head a lofty shade
From his wide-spreading horns; his horns bright shone
With gold; his collar, with bright gems bedeck'd,
Fell o'er his shoulders from his round neck hung;
A silver boss, by slender reins control'd
Mov'd o'er his brow; a brazen pair the same,
Shone o'er his temples hanging from his ears:
Devoid of fear, his nature's timid dread
Relinquish'd, oft the houses would he seek;
And oft would gently fondling stoop his neck,
Heedless who strok'd him. Cyparissus, thou
Beyond all others priz'd the sacred beast:
Thou, fairest far amongst the Cæan youths.
Thou to fresh pastures led'st the stag; to streams
Of cooling fountains: oft his horns entwin'd

With variegated garlands. Horseman-like
Now on his back thou pressest; and now here,
Now there, thou rul'st his soft jaws with the reins
Of purple tinge. 'Twas once in mid-day heat,
When burnt the bent claws of the sea-shore crab,
In Sol's fierce vapor; on the grassy earth
The weary stag repos'd his limbs, and drew
Cool breezes from the trees umbrageous shades.
Here the boy Cyparissus careless flung
His painted dart, and fix'd it in his side.
Who, when he from the cruel wound beheld
Him dying, instant bent his mind to die.
What consolation did not Phœbus speak?
Urging the loss far slighter grief deserv'd:
Yet mourn'd he still, and from the gods supreme
Begg'd this last gift, to latest times to mourn.
His blood in constant tears exhausted, now
His limbs a green hue take; his locks which late
Hung o'er his snowy forehead, rough become
In frightful bushiness; and hardening quick,
Shoot up to heaven in form a slender spire.
The mourning god, in grief exclaim'd—"By me
"Bemoan'd, thou shalt with others always grieve;
"And henceforth mourners shalt thou still attend."—
Thus did the bard a wood collect around;
And in the midst he sate of thronging beasts,
And crowding birds. The chords he amply try'd
With his impulsive thumb, and vary'd much
In sound, he found their notes concordant still;
Then to this song rais'd his melodious voice.—

  "O parent muse! from Jove derive my song:
"All yield to Jove's dominion. Oft my verse
"Before the mightiness of Jove has sung.
"I sung the giants, in a strain sublime,
"And vengeful thunders, o'er Phlegræa's plain
"Scatter'd; a tender theme now claims my lyre:
"I sing of youths by deities belov'd;
"And nymphs who with forbidden wishes burn'd,
"And met the doom their sensual lusts deserv'd.
"The king of gods made Phrygian Ganymede
"His favorite, but some other form possess'd.
"Jove must in shape be something else than Jove.
"He deems no form becomes him, save the bird
"That bears his thunder. Instant all is done;
"The Phrygian borne away: the air he beats
"With his feign'd wing. And now this youth the cup
"Of nectar hands, in Juno's spite, to Jove.

"Son of Amycla, thee had Phœbus plac'd
"Also the skies amidst, had fate allow'd
"For such position place; yet still thou hold'st
"Eternal, what fate grants: oft as the spring
"Winter repulses, and the ram succeeds
"The watery fishes, thou spring'st forth in flower
"'Mid the green sward. Beyond all else my sire
"Thee lov'd, and Delphos, plac'd in midmost earth,
"Wanted its ruling power, whilst now the god
"Eurotas lov'd, and Sparta un-intrench'd.
"Nor lyre, nor darts attention claim'd as wont;
"Of dignity unmindful, he not spurns
"To bear the nets; to curb the hounds; to climb
"With the full train the steepest mountain's ridge:
"And every toil augments his pleasure more.
"Now had the sun the midmost point near gain'd
"'Twixt flying night, and night approaching, each
"Distant in equal space; when from their limbs
"They flung their robes; with the fat olive's juice
"Their bodies shone; they enter'd in the lists
"Of the broad disk, which Phœbus first well pois'd,
"Then flung through lofty air; opposing clouds
"Flying it cleft; at length on solid earth
"It pitch'd, displaying skill with strength combin'd.
"Instant the rash Tænarian boy, impell'd
"By love of sport, sprung on to snatch the orb,
"But the hard ground repulsive in thy face,
"O, Hyacinth! it flung. Pale as the boy
"The god appear'd: he rais'd his fainting limbs,
"And in his arms now cherishes, now wipes
"The fatal wound, now stays his fleeting breath,
"With herbs apply'd; but all his arts are vain;
"Incurable the hurt. Just so, when broke,
"The violet, poppy, or the lily hang,
"Whose dark stems in a water'd garden spring;
"Flaccid they instant droop; the weighty head
"No longer upright rais'd, but bent to earth.
"So bent his dying face; his neck, bereft
"Of vigor, heavy on his shoulder laid.
"Phœbus exclaim'd;—Fall'st thou, Œbalian youth,
"Depriv'd of life in prime? and must I see
"Thy death my fault? thou art my grief, my crime;
"My hand the charge of thy destruction bears:
"I am the cause of thy untimely fate!
"But what my crime? unless with him to sport;
"Unless a fault it were too much to love.
"Would I could life for thee, or with thee quit;

"But fatal laws restrain me: yet shalt thou
"Be with me still; dwell ever on my lips;
"My hand shall sound thee on the lyre I touch;
"My songs of thee shall tell: a new-found flower
"Shall bear the letters which my griefs resound:
"And time shall come, when a most valiant chief
"Shall join him to thy flower; in the same leaf
"His name too shall be read.—As words like these
"The truth-predicting lips of Phœbus spoke,
"Behold! the blood which flow'd along the ground,
"And all the herbage ting'd, is blood no more;
"But springs a flower than Tyrian red more bright,
"A form assuming such as lilies wear:
"Like it, save purple this, that silvery white.
"Nor yet content was Phœbus; for from him
"The honor was deriv'd. Upon its leaves
"He trac'd his groans: ai, ai, on every flower
"In mournful characters is fair inscrib'd.
"Nor blush the Spartans, Hyacinth to own:
"His honors still the present age attend;
"And annual are the Hyacinthian feasts,
"In pomp surpassing aught of ancient days.

"Should you by chance of Amathus enquire,
"If williang the Propœtides it bore,
"Denying nods would equally disclaim
"Them, and the race whose foreheads once were rough
"With double horns; Cerastæ, hence their name.
"Jove's hospitable altar at their gates
"Of mournful wickedness was rear'd: who saw
"This stain'd with gore, if stranger, might conceive
"That sucking calves, or two-year's sheep there bled.
"There bled the guest! Mild Venus griev'd
"At these most impious rites, at first prepar'd
"To quit her cities, and her Cyprian fields:—
"But how,—she said,—can my beloved clime?
"How can my towns have given offence? what fault
"Abides in them? Rather the impious race,
"Shall vengeance feel in exile, or in death;
"Save death and exile medium may allow:
"How may that be, unless their shape is chang'd?—
"Then while she doubts what shape they shall assume,
"Their horns attract her eyes; struck by the hint,
"Their mighty horns she leaves them, and transforms
"To savage oxen all their lusty limbs.

"Still dar'd th obscene Propœtides deny
"Venus a goddess' power; for which, fame says

"They first, so forc'd the deity's revenge,
"Their bodies prostituted, and their charms.
"As shame them left, the blood which ting'd their cheeks
"Harden'd, and soon they rigid stone became.

  "These saw Pygmalion, and the age beheld
"With crimes o'er-run; the shameful vice abhorr'd
"Which lavish nature gave their female souls.
"Single, and spouseless liv'd he; long a mate
"Press'd not his couch. Meantime the ivory white
"With happy skill, and wond'rous art he carv'd;
"And form'd a beauteous figure; never maid
"So perfect yet was born, and his own work
"With love inspir'd him. Of a nymph her face
"Was such, you must believe the form to live,
"And move, if not by bashfulness restrain'd.
"Thus art his art conceal'd. Pygmalion stares
"In admiration; and his breast draws flames
"From the feign'd body: oft his hands his work
"Approach, if ivory or if flesh to judge;
"Nor ivory then will he confess the form.
"Kisses he gives, and thinks each kiss return'd:
"He speaks, he grasps her; where he grasps, he thinks
"His hands impression leave; and fears to see
"On the prest limbs some marks of livid blue.
"Now blandish'd words he uses; now he bears
"Those gifts so grateful to a girlish mind;
"Pearls, and smooth-polish'd gems, and smallest birds,
"With variegated flowers, and lilies fair,
"And painted figures, and the Heliads' tears,
"Dropt from the weeping tree: with garments gay
"Her limbs too he adorns, and jewels gives
"To deck her fingers; while a necklace large
"Hangs round her neck: her ears light pearls suspend;
"And a bright zone is circled round her waist.
"All well became her, yet most beauteous far
"She unattir'd appear'd. Her on a couch,
"Ting'd with the shell Sidonian, then he laid,
"And call'd her partner of his bed; and plac'd
"Her head reclin'd, as if with sense endu'd,
"On the soft pillow. Now the feast approach'd
"Of Venus, through all Cyprus' isle so fam'd,
"And snowy-chested heifers, whose bent horns
"With gold were gay, receiv'd the deadly blow;
"And incense burnt in clouds. Pygmalion stood
"Before the altar, with his offer'd gifts:
"Timid he spoke,—O ye all-potent gods!
"Give me a spouse just like my ivory nymph,—

"Give me my ivory nymph—he blush'd to say.
"Bright Venus then, as present at her feast,
"Perceiv'd the inmost wishes of his soul;
"And gave the omen of a friendly power.
"Thrice blaz'd the fire, and thrice the flame leap'd high.

  "Returning, he the darling statue seeks
"Of his fair nymph; extends him on the couch;
"Kisses, and thinks he feels her lips grow warm:
"Applies his lips again, and with his hand
"Presses her bosom: prest the ivory yields,
"Softening beneath his fingers; nor remains
"Its rigid harshness. So Hymettus' wax
"Yields to the heat, when tempering thumbs it mould
"In various forms; and fit for future use.
"Astonish'd now he joys with trembling soul,
"But fears deception; then he loves again,
"And with his hands again his wishes proves:
"'Twas flesh, the prest pulse leap'd beneath his thumb.
"Then did the Cyprian youth, in words most full
"Of gratitude and love, to Venus pray.
"Then to her living lips his lips he join'd,
"And then the damsel felt his warm salute:
"Blushing she felt it, and her timid eyes
"Op'd to the light, and with the light beheld
"Her lover. Venus bless'd the match she made;
"And when nine times the moon's full orb was seen
"Sharpen'd to horns, the damsel Paphos bore;
"Whose appellation oft the isle receives.

  "She Cinyras too bore; if childless he
"A place amongst the happiest might he claim.
"A direful song I sing! be distant far
"Ye daughters; distant far, O, parents be!
"Or if of pleasure to your minds my verse
"Aught gives, in this at least my truth suspect.
"Believe the deed not: if you must believe,
"Mark well the punishment the crime deserv'd.
"Since nature could such heinous deeds permit;
"The Thracian realms, my land, I 'gratulate;
"And joy this clime at such a distance lies,
"From that which could such monstrous acts produce.
"Let Araby be in amomum rich;
"And cinnamon, and zedoary produce;
"Incense which through the wood exudes; and flowers
"Of vary'd teints,—while Myrrha too it bears:
"Too great the price which this new tree procur'd.
"Cupid denies, O Myrrha! that his darts

"Thee wounded; vindicating from that crime
"His weapons. Thee, with Stygian torch most fierce,
"And viperous venom furies did enflame.
"Wicked to hate thy parent sure had been,
"But thus to love is worse than bitterest hate.
"The choicest nobles come from every part
"To gain thee; youths from all the East arrive,
"To struggle for thy hand. Chuse, Myrrha, chuse
"One from the crowd: one only in the world
"Whom chuse thou may'st not. She herself perceiv'd,
"And curb'd the baneful passion in her mind;
"Communing thus:—Ah! whither rove my thoughts?
"What meditate I? O, ye gods! I pray,
"O piety, O parents' sacred laws,
"Forbid this wicked act; oppose a deed
"So full of horrid guilt,—if guilt it be!
"But pious nature ne'er such love condemns.
"All animals in undistinguish'd form
"Cohabit: shame the heifer never feels
"Join'd with her sire; the steed his daughter takes
"As partner; with the female flock, who ow'd
"To him their being, couples oft the goat;
"And birds bring forth to birds who them produc'd.
"Blest those who thus enjoy; but human race
"Perversest laws invents: vexatious rules
"Forbid what nature grants. Yet am I told,
"Nations exist, where mother joins with son,
"And daughter with her sire; their pious love
"Increas'd more strongly by the double bond.
"Ah, me! unhappy, in such glorious climes
"Begotten not; I suffer but from place.
"But why on these ideas dwell? hence far
"Forbidden hopes. Well he deserves thy love,
"But as a father love him. Wert thou not
"Of mighty Cinyras the daughter, then
"Thou might'st the couch of Cinyras ascend.
"Now mine he is so much, he is not mine;
"Our very nearness is my greatest curse:
"More close, a perfect stranger had I been.
"Far hence I would depart; my country leave,
"This mischief flying; but curs'd love restrains.
"For, present, Cinyras I may behold;
"Touch, speak, my kisses to his face apply,
"If nought he'll grant beyond. How! impious maid,
"Dar'st thou hope ought beyond? perceiv'st thou not
"What laws, what names thou would'st confound? would'st thou
"The mother's rival be?—thy father's whore?
"Thy offspring's sister would'st thou then be call'd?

"Thy brother's parent? Fear'st thou not the three,
"Whose locks with sable serpents horrid curl?
"Who conscious bosoms pierce with searching eyes,
"And hurl their furious torches in the face?
"While yet thy body can resist, no more
"Cherish the heinous guilt thus in thy mind;
"Nor violate great Nature's sacred law
"With lust forbidden. Grant I should consent,
"The king would me deny: too pious he,
"Too dear to him the law. O, that in him
"Such furious passion rag'd as burns in me!—

"She ended. Cinyras, the worthy crowd
"Of suitors held in doubt; herself he ask'd,
"As name by name he counted, which as spouse
"She most would wish. Silent at first she stood,
"Then burning gaz'd on his paternal face,
"As the warm tears gush'd in her shining eyes.
"These, Cinyras effects of virgin fear
"Believing, chid her and forbade to weep.
"Drying her cheeks, he on them press'd a kiss;
"With too much pleasure she the kiss receiv'd:
"And when consulted what the spouse must be
"She would prefer, she answer'd,—one like you.—
"He witless of her meaning, prais'd her words,
"And said,—be such thy pious duty still—
"The sound of piety the virgin's eyes,
"With sense of guilt, cast conscious to the ground.

"'Twas now deep night when sleep sooth'd all the cares
"Of mortal breasts. But Myrrha wakeful laid
"Consum'd with raging fires; and rolling deep
"Her frantic wishes in her wandering mind.
"Despairing now, and now resolv'd to try;
"Now shame o'ercomes her, and anon desire:
"And undetermin'd how to act she rests.
"A mighty tree thus, wounded by the axe,
"Ere yet it feels the final blow, in doubt
"Seems where to fall; they fear on every side:
"Thus did her stagger'd mind from vary'd force
"Waver now here, now there; press'd hard by each,
"No ease for love, no rest but death appears.
"Death pleas'd. She rose, and round her throat prepar'd
"The cord to fasten; from the topmost beam
"She ty'd her girdle, and—farewel!—exclaim'd—
"Dear Cinyras! guess whence my fatal end.—
"Then drew the noose around her pallid neck.
"'Tis said, th imperfect murmuring of her words,

"Reach'd to the faithful nurse's ears, who laid
"Before the threshold of her foster-child.
"The matron rose, threw wide the door, and saw
"Prepar'd the instrument of death. At once
"She scream'd aloud, her bosom tore, deep blows
"Gave her own limbs, and from the rescu'd neck
"Tore the tight noose. Then had she time to weep,
"Then to embrace, then to inquire the cause
"Of the dread cord. But dumb the virgin sate
"And motionless, her eyes to earth were fix'd;
"Griev'd that so check'd her efforts were for death.
"More the nurse presses, bares her silver'd hairs
"And wither'd bosom; by the cradle begs,
"And the first food she tasted, to confess
"To her the cause of sorrow. Myrrha sighs,
"But turns her eyes aside as thus she begs.
"Determin'd still to know, the nurse persists
"And not content her secrecy alone
"To promise, says—yet tell me, and my aid
"Allow me to afford thee. Not yet slow,
"Though aged. Is it love? with charms and plants
"I know thy love to cure. Have envious eyes
"Thee harm'd? with magic rites their charm I'll spoil.
"Are the gods angry? with appeasing rites
"Their anger we will soothe. What ill beside
"Can be conjectur'd? Lo! thy house secure,
"And safe thy fortune; both in prosperous train.
"Yet lives thy mother, and thy father lives.—
"Her father's name when Myrrha heard she drew
"Deep from her breast a mournful sigh; nor yet
"The nurse suspected guilt was in her soul:
"But saw that love disturb'd her. In her aim
"Inflexible; again she urg'd to know
"The grief whate'er it prov'd; and lull'd her head
"Upon her aged lap, and clasp'd her form
"In her own feeble arms, as thus she spoke;—
"I see thou lovest; banish far thy fear,
"My diligence in this shall aid thee; nay
"Not e'en thy father shall the secret know.—
"Madly she bounded from the lap, and cry'd,
"While press'd the couch her face,—I beg thee go!
"And spare my grievous shame.—More pressing still—
"Or go—she said—or ask not why I mourn:
"What thou so seek'st to know is shameful guilt.—
"With horror struck, the ancient dame holds forth
"Her hands, which equal shook with fear and age;
"Then suppliant at her foster-daughter's feet
"Fell. Now she coaxes; now she threatens loud;

"If not made privy, threatens to declare
"The cord's adventure, and half-finish'd death:
"And offers a d once more her love to gain.
"She rais'd her head, and fill'd her nurse's breast
"With sudden gushing tears. And oft she strove
"All to confess; as oft her tongue was mute;
"And in her garments hid her blushing face.—
"Then,—happy mother in thy spouse!—she said;
"No more, but groan'd. Through her cold limbs and bones,
"The ancient nurse a shivering tremor felt,
"And her white hairs all o'er her head, erect
"Like bristles stood; for all the truth she saw.
"Much did she urge the direful flame to drive
"Far from her soul, if that could be. The maid
"Knows all is just she argues, yet is fix'd
"For death, unless her lover is obtain'd.
"Then she;—O live, enjoy thy—silent there,
"Enjoy thy parent—she not dar'd to say:
"Yet by a sacred oath her promise bound.

   "Now Ceres' annual feast, the pious dames
"All solemniz'd: in snowy robes enwrapt,
"They offer'd wheaten wreaths, and primal fruits.
"The rites of Venus, and the touch of man,
"For thrice three nights forbidden things they held.
"The monarch's spouse Cenchreïs, 'mid the crowd
"Forth went to celebrate the secret feast:
"And while the couch its legal partner lack'd,
"The ill-officious nurse the king espy'd
"Oppress'd with wine, and told the tale of love,
"Beneath a fictious name, and prais'd her charms.
"The virgin's years he asks.—Equal her age
"To Myrrha's—she replies.—Desir'd to bring
"The damsel, she returns:—Rejoice!—she cries,
"Rejoice! our point is gain'd.—The hapless nymph
"Felt not a general joy; presaging pangs
"Shot through her bosom; still she joy'd: her mind
"Such discord tore. Now was the silent hour;
"Boötes 'mid the Triönes had bent
"His wain with sloping pole; when Myrrha came
"To her flagitious crime. Bright Luna fled
"The skies; black clouds the lurking stars o'erspread;
"The night saw not its fires. Thou, Icarus,
"Thy face first hidst; and thou, Erigoné
"Hallow'd for thy parental love so pure.
"Thrice was she warn'd by stumbling feet, and thrice
"The owl funereal utter'd her death-note.
"Yet on she went; darkness and sable night

"Her shame diminish'd. Fast her left hand grasps
"Her nurse, the other waves t'explore the way.
"The threshold of the nuptial chamber now
"She touches; now she gently opes the door;
"Now enters. Then her trembling knees loose shook
"Beneath her bending hams; her color fled:
"Her blood flow'd back; and all her wishes sunk.
"The nearer was her crime approach'd, the more
"With horror she beheld it, and sore mourn'd
"Her daring; anxious to return unknown.
"The hoary dame, her, lingering thus, dragg'd on,
"And when presented at the lofty couch,
"Said—Cinyras receive her, she's thine own!—
"And the devoted bodies gave to join.
"The sire his proper bowels, on the bed
"Obscene, receiv'd; her virgin terrors calm'd,
"And sooth'd her trembling. Haply too, he said—
"My daughter,—from her age; and haply she—
"My sire,—lest names were wanting to their crime.
"Fill'd with her father from the bed she rose,
"Bearing in her dire womb the impious fruit;
"Carrying her crime conceiv'd. Th' ensuing night
"Her incest she repeats, nor ends she here.
"But Cinyras eager at length to know,
"After such frequent converse, who him lov'd;
"At once his daughter and his sin beheld,
"By lamps brought sudden. Grief repress'd all words;
"But from the sheath he snatch'd his glittering sword.
"Quick Myrrha fled; darkness and favoring night
"Sav'd her from death. O'er wide-spread fields she roam'd;
"Through Araby palm-bearing, and the lands
"Panchæa holds. Nine times returning light
"Had fill'd the horns of Luna, still she stray'd:
"Then weary rested in Sabæa's fields;
"While scarce she bore the burden of her womb.
"Then what to ask uncertain, 'twixt the fear
"Of death and weariness of hated life;
"In words like these she utter'd forth her prayers,—
"Ye powers, if those who guilt confess are heard,
"A punishment exemplar I deserve;
"I shrink not from it. Yet the living race
"Lest I contaminate, if left to live;
"Or lest I mix prophane with shades below,
"Drive me from either realm; from life and death
"Debar me, into some new shape transform'd.—
"The penitent some god propitious heard;
"Her final prayer at least success obtain'd:
"For as she spoke rose round her legs the earth;

"The lofty tree's foundation, crooked roots
"Shot from her spreading toes; hard wood her bones
"Became; the marrow in the midst remain'd
"As pith; as sappy juice still flow'd her blood:
"Her arms large boughs were spread; her fingers chang'd
"To slender twigs; rough bark her skin became.
"The growing tree press'd hard the gravid womb;
"Invested next her breast, and o'er her neck
"Threaten'd to spread. Impatient of delay
"She shrunk below to meet th' approaching wood,
"And hid beneath the rising bark her face.
"Human sensation with her change of shape
"She lost, yet still she weeps; and from the tree
"Warm drops yet fall, and much the tears are priz'd.
"The myrrh which oozes from the bark still holds
"Its mistress' name, well known in every age.

   "Meantime the misbegotten infant grew
"Within the trunk, and press'd to find a way
"To push to light, and leave the parent womb.
"Within the tree the gravid womb swell'd large,
"Stretch'd was the mother with the load, but mute
"Were all her woes; nor in travailing voice
"Lucina could she call. Yet hard to strain
"She seem'd; thick groans oft gave the bending bole,
"And tears flow'd copious. Mild Lucina came,
"And stood before the groaning boughs, and gave
"Assisting help, and spoke the spellful words.
"Cleft is the tree, and through the fissur'd bark
"A living burthen comes: the infant cries,
"Who on soft grass plac'd. The Naïad nymphs
"Him bathe in tears maternal: such a face
"Ev'n Envy could not blame. As painters form
"The naked Cupid's beauty, such had he;
"And that their dress no help to guess may give,
"This the light quiver take, or that resign.
"Quick passing time unheeded glides along
"Deceiving: nought than years more quickly flies.
"The child, of sister and of grandsire born,
"Late in the tree confin'd, late thence reliev'd;
"Just seen most beauteous of the infant tribe,
"Now youth, now man appears, more beauteous still:
"Now Venus charm'd, his mother's pangs aveng'd.

   "As kisses sweet the quiver-bearing boy
"Press'd on his mother's lips, he witless raz'd
"Slightly her bosom, with a dart that stood
"Protruding. Venus, wounded, angry push'd

"Her son far from her; light the wound appear'd;
"At first even her deceiving. With the blaze
"Of manly beauty caught, she now contemns
"The Cythereïan shores; nor Paphos seeks,
"Girt by profoundest seas; Cnidos, so fam'd
"For fish; nor Amathus with metals rich.
"Heaven too, she quits, to heaven she now prefers
"Adonis: him she follows, him attends;
"Whose sole employ was loitering in the shade,
"In anxious study to increase her charms.
"Bare to the knee, her robe, like Dian's train
"High-girt, o'er hills, through woods, and brambly rocks
"She roves: exhorts the dogs, and drives such game
"As threaten not with danger; fearful hares,
"High-antler'd stags, and rapid-flying deer.
"Fierce boars she shuns, and shuns the robber-wolf,
"Strong-talon'd bears, and lions slaughter-gorg'd.

    "Thou too, Adonis, admonition heardst
"These to avoid, if admonition ought
"With thee could weigh:—Be brave,—the goddess said—
"To those who fly thee; courage 'gainst the bold
"To danger drags. Dear youth, thy heart is brave;
"Indulge not to my hazard, nor provoke
"Fierce beasts by nature arm'd, nor seek for fame.
"Nor youth nor beauty, such as Venus move,
"Will move the lion, or the bristly boar:
"Their eyes and breasts untouch'd by brightest charms.
"Thunder and lightning in his bended tusks
"The fierce boar carries; rapid is the force
"The tawny lion, (hated race!) exerts:
"My cause of hatred when to thee disclos'd,
"Will raise thy wonder at the monstrous crime,
"In days of yore committed. Now hard toil
"Unwonted tires me. Lo! the poplar's shade
"So opportune invites; and the green turf
"A couch presents. Upon the ground with thee
"I'll rest:—she spoke, and as she stretch'd along,
"She press'd the grass, and press'd the lovely youth:
"Smiling, her head upon his breast reclin'd,
"'Midst intermingling kisses, thus she spoke.—

    "Perhaps thou'st heard of that renowned maid,
"Whose fleetness in the race the swiftest man's
"Surpass'd. Not fabulous the tale you heard:
"She vanquish'd all. And hard it was to say,
"If praise for swiftness, or for beauteous form,
"She most deserv'd. To her, who once enquir'd

"Of marriage, fate-predicting Phœbus said—
"A spouse would, Atalanta, be thy bane;
"Avoid an husband's couch. Yet wilt thou not
"An husband's couch avoid; but lose thyself,
"Thyself yet living.—Terror-struck to hear
"The sentence of the god, maiden she lives
"Amid the thickest woods; driving severe
"The throngs of pressing suitors from her far,
"By hard conditions.—Ne'er can I be gain'd—
"She said—till vanquish'd in the race. With me
"Your swiftness try: the conqueror in the strife,
"Shall gain me spouse, and gain a genial couch;
"But death must him who lags behind reward.
"Such be the laws of trial.—Pitiless
"The law appear'd; but (such is beauty's power)
"Crowds of rash lovers to the law agreed.
"There sat Hippomenes to view the race
"Unequal; and exclaim'd,—are there so mad,
"As seek a wife through peril so immense?—
"And the blind love of all the youths condemn'd.
"But when her face he saw, and saw her limbs
"Bar'd for the contest, (limbs like mine, or thine,
"Were thine of female mould,) amaz'd he look'd
"With uprais'd hands, and cry'd;—forgive my fault,
"Ye whom but now I blam'd; the great reward
"For which you labor, then to me unknown!—
"Thus praising, fire he feels, and hopes no youth
"More swift will run, and envious fears their speed—
"But why the fortune of this contest leave,
"Untry'd—he said,—myself? Heaven helps the bold.—
"While musing thus Hippomenes remarks
"The virgin's flying pace. Though not less swift
"Th' Aönian youth beheld her, than the dart
"Shot from the Scythian bow; her beauty more
"Ravish'd his eyes, and speed her charms increas'd.
"Th' opposing breeze, which met her rapid feet,
"Blew back the ribbons which her sandals bound;
"Her tresses floated down her ivory back;
"And loosely flow'd her garment o'er her knees,
"With painted border gay: a purple bloom
"With virgin whiteness mixt, her body shew'd;
"As when the snow-white hall a deepen'd tinge
"From purple curtains shews. While this the guest
"Intently notes, the utmost goal is pass'd:
"Victorious Atalanta with the wreath
"Is crown'd: the vanquish'd sigh, and meet the doom
"Agreed. He, by the youths' untimely fate
"Deterr'd not, forward stood, and on the nymph

"Fix'd full his eyes, and said;—Why seek you thus
"An easy conquest, vanquishing the weak?
"With me contend. So potent am I born
"You need not blush to such high rank to yield.
"Megareus was my sire, Onchestius his,
"Grandson to Neptune; thus the fourth I boast
"From Ocean's sovereign. Nor beneath my race
"Stoops aught my valor; should success me crown,
"A lofty and an everlasting fame,
"Hippomenes your conqueror, would you gain.—
"As thus he spoke, with softening eyes the maid
"Beheld him, doubtful which 'twere best to wish,
"To vanquish or be vanquish'd. While she thus
"Utter'd her thoughts—What god, an envious foe
"To beauty would destroy him: urg'd to seek
"My bed, by risking thus his own dear life?
"I cannot sure so great a prize be thought!
"His beauty melts me not; though yet I own
"Such beauty well might melt. But such a youth
"He seems, he moves me not but from his years.
"What courage in him reigns! his soul unaw'd
"By death. He springs the fourth from Ocean's king!
"Then how he loves! and prizes so my hand,
"That should hard fortune keep me from his arms,
"He'd perish. Stranger, while thou may'st, depart;
"Avoid the bloody nuptials. Marriage, I
"Too cruel make. No maid would thee refuse;
"And soon may'st thou a wiser nymph select.
"But why for him this care? from me who see
"So many die, whom he too has beheld?
"Then let him perish; since the numerous train
"Of slaughter'd lovers warns him not: he spurns
"An hated life. How! should he then be slain
"Because with me to live he wishes? Death
"Inglorious must he gain, reward of love?
"Hatred would such a conquest still attend.
"Still is not mine the fault. Do thou desist;
"Or if thy madness holds, O, that thy feet
"More swift may be! See in his youthful face
"What virgin beauties! Ah! Hippomenes,
"Would Atalanta thou had'st never seen.
"Well worthy thou of life. Were I more blest;
"Had rugged fate not me a spouse forbade,
"Thou, sole art he, by whom to Hymen's couch
"With joy I would be led.—Thus spoke the nymph,
"In fond simplicity, first touch'd by love,
"Unknowing what she felt: ardent she lov'd,
"Yet knew the passion not which rul'd her soul.

"Now loud the people, and the king demand,
"The wonted race. To me with anxious words
"Hippomenes, great Neptune's offspring pray'd—
"O Cytherea! I adjure thee, aid
"My bold attempt; from thee those flames I felt,
"Grant them thy succour.—Gales auspicious waft
"To me the tender prayers, my soul is mov'd:
"Nor long the aid so needful I delay.
"A tract there lies in Cyprus' richest lands,
"Nam'd Tamasene by those who dwell around,
"This ancient times made sacred unto me:
"And with this gift my temples were endow'd.
"'Midst of the field appears a shining tree;
"Yellow its leaves, its crackling branches gold.
"By chance there straying, from the boughs I pluck'd
"Three golden apples, bore them in my hand,
"And seen by none, except the favor'd youth,
"Approach'd Hippomenes, and taught their use.
"The trumpets gave the sign, each ready sprung—
"Shot from the barrier, and with rapid feet
"Skimm'd lightly o'er the sand. O'er the wide main
"With feet unwetted, they might seem to fly;
"Or sweep th' unbending ears of hoary grain.
"Loud shouts encouraging, and cheering words,
"On every side a stimulus afford,
"To urge the youth's exertions.—Now,—they cry,—
"Now, now, Hippomenes, the time to press!
"On, on! exert thy vigor—flag not now,—
"The race is thine.—The grateful sounds both heard,
"Megareus' son, and Schœneus' daughter; hard
"Which joy'd the most to judge. How oft her pace
"She slacken'd, when with ease she might have pass'd,
"And ceas'd unwilling on his face to gaze.
"Tir'd now, parch'd breathings from the mouth ascends
"Of Neptune's son, and far remote the goal.
"Then, as his last resource, he distant flung
"One of the tree's bright produce. In amaze
"The virgin saw it roll; and from the course
"Swerv'd, tempted to obtain the glittering fruit.
"Hippomenes o'ershoots her; all around
"Applauses ring. She soon corrects delay,
"And wasted moments, with more rapid speed,
"And leaves again the youth behind. Again,
"Delay'd to catch the second flying fruit,
"The youth is follow'd, and again o'erpass'd.
"Now near the goal they come,—O, goddess! now
"Who gave the boon assist; he said, and flung

"With youthful force obliquely o'er the plain,
"More to detain, the last bright glittering gold.
"In doubt the virgin saw it fly: I urg'd
"That she should follow; and fresh weight I gave
"The apple when obtain'd; thus by the load
"Her course impeding, and obtain'd delay.
"But lest my tale, in length surpass the race,
"The vanquish'd virgin was the victor's prize.

"Think'st thou Adonis, did I not deserve
"Most grateful thanks in smoking incense paid?
"Mindless, nor thanks, nor incense yielded he;
"And sudden anger in my bosom rag'd.
"Irk'd at the slight, I instantly provide
"That future times with less contempt behave:
"And 'gainst them both my raging bosom burns.
"Now pass'd they near a temple, long since rais'd
"By fam'd Echion, in a shady wood,
"To the great mother of the heavenly gods,
"When the long journey tempted to repose;
"And there, inspir'd by me, ill-tim'd desire
"Hippomenes excited. Near the fane
"A cave-like close recess dim-lighted stood,
"With native pumice roof'd, hallow'd of old;
"Where priests the numerous images had plac'd,
"Of ancient deities. They enter'd here,
"And with forbidden lust the place defil'd.
"The wooden images their eyes avert:
"The tower-crown'd goddess dubious stands to plunge,
"The guilty couple in the Stygian wave.
"Too light that sentence seems: straight yellow manes
"Cover their soft smooth necks; their fingers curve
"To mighty claws; their arms to fore-legs turn;
"And new-form'd tails sweep lightly o'er the sand:
"Angry their countenance glares; for speech they roar;
"They haunt the forests for their nuptial dome.
"Transform'd to lions, and by others fear'd,
"Their tam'd mouths champ the Cybeleïan reins.
"Do thou, O dearest boy! their rage avoid;
"Not theirs alone, but all the savage tribe,
"That stubborn meet with breasts the furious war;
"Not turn their backs for flight: lest bold too much,
"Thou and myself, have cause too much too mourn.—

"Thus she admonish'd; and by coupled swans
"Upborne, she cleft the air; but his brave soul
"Her cautious admonitions rash contemn'd.

"By chance his dogs the well-mark'd footprints trac'd,
"And from his lurking covert rous'd a boar;
"Whom with a stroke oblique, as from the brake
"To spring he went, the gallant youth transpierc'd.
"Instant, with crooked tusks, the gore-stain'd spear
"Wrench'd the fierce boar away, and at him rush'd,
"Trembling, and safety seeking: every fang
"Deep in his groin he plung'd, and on the sand
"Stretch'd him expiring. Cytherea, borne
"Through midmost ether in her chariot light,
"Had not at Cyprus with her swans arriv'd,
"When, known from far, she heard his dying groans;
"And thither turn'd her snowy birds. From high
"When lifeless she beheld him, in his blood
"Convulsive struggling, quick she darted down,
"She tore her garments, and she tore her hair;
"And with unpitying hands her breast she smote.
"Then, fate upbraiding first, she said;—Not all
"Shall bend to your decision; still shalt thou
"Remain, Adonis, monument of woe,
"Suffer'd by me! The image of thy death,
"Annual repeated, annual shall renew
"Remembrance of my mourning. But thy blood
"A flower shall form. Shalt thou, O Proserpine,
"A female body to a scented herb
"Transform; and I the Cinyreïan youth
"Forbidden be to change?—She said, and flung
"Nectar most odorous on the ebbing gore;
"Which instant swelling rose. So bubbles rise
"On the smooth stream when showery floods descend.
"Nor long the term, an hour's short space elaps'd,
"When the same teinted flower the blood produc'd:
"Such flowers the deep pomegranate bears, which hides
"Its purple grains beneath a flexile rind.
"But short its boast, for the same winds afford
"Its name, and shake them where they light adhere:
"Ripe for their fall in fragile beauty gay."

THE ELEVENTH BOOK

Rage of the Thracian women. Massacre of Orpheus. The women transformed to trees by Bacchus. Midas' foolish wish to change all things he touched into gold. Contest of skill between Pan and Apollo. The ears of Midas transformed to asses ears. Troy built by Apollo and Neptune. Laömedon's perfidy. Hesioné freed by Hercules, and married to Telamon. Peleus and Thetis. Birth of Achilles. Chioné ravished by Mercury, and by Apolo. Slain by Diana. Her sire Dædalion changed into an hawk. A wolf changed by Thetis to marble. Voyage of Ceÿx to Delphos. Lost in a storm. Grief of Alcyoné. Morpheus acquaints her with her husband's death. Change of both to kingfishers. Æsacus into a cormorant.

While thus the Thracian bard the forests drew,
And rocks, and furious beasts with strains divine;—
Behold the Thracian dames! their madden'd breasts
Clad with the shaggy spoil of furious beasts,
Espy'd him from an hillock's rising swell,
As to his sounding strings he shap'd the song.
When one, her tresses in the ruffling air
Wild streaming, cry'd—"Lo! him who spurns our ties!"—
And full her dart 'gainst the harmonious mouth
Of Phœbus' son she flung: entwisted round
With leaves, a bruise without a wound appear'd.
A stone another for a weapon seiz'd;
The flying stone was even in air subdu'd
By harmony and song; and at his feet
Low fell, as suppliant for its daring fault.
But now the tumult swells more furious,—bounds
It knows not! mad Erinnys reigns around.
Yet all their weapons had his music's power
Soften'd; but clamor, Berecynthian horns,
Drums, clappings, bacchanalian shouts, and howls,
Drown'd the soft lyre. Then were the stones distain'd
With silenc'd Orpheus' blood. The Bacchæ first
Drove wide the crowding birds, the snakes, the beasts,
In throngs collected by his tuneful voice;
Glory of Orpheus' stage. From thence they turn'd
Their gory hands on Orpheus, and around
Cluster'd like fowls that in the day espy
The bird of darkness. Then as in the morn
The high-rais'd amphitheatre beholds
The stag a prey to hounds; so they the bard
Attack'd, and flung their Thyrsi twin'd with leaves;
For different use first form'd. Those hurl huge clods:
These branches torn from trees; and others stones.
Lest to their fury arms were wanting, lo!
A yoke of oxen with the ploughshare broke
The ground, not distant far; with sinews there
Of nervous strength, the husbandmen upturn'd
The stubborn soil; with sweat producing fruit.
These, when the troop they saw, affrighted fled,
Quitting their instruments of toil. Their rakes,
Their ponderous harrows, and their huge long spades,

Were scatter'd left on the deserted field.
These when their furious hands had seiz'd, and tore
From the strong oxen's heads the threatening horns,
Back they return'd to end the poet's fate;
And sacrilegious, as he stretch'd his hands,
They slaughte¬'d him! Then first in vain his words
Were utter'd; nought could then his speech avail.
Then, heavenly powers! his spirit was expell'd
And breath'd in air, even through that mouth whose sound
Hard rocks had heard, and wildest beasts had own'd.
For thee, O Orpheus! mourn'd the feather'd tribe,
And crowds of savage monsters; flinty rocks
Bewail'd thee; forests, which thy tempting song
So oft had caus'd to follow, wept; the trees,
Shorn of their pride, bewail'd with falling leaves.
Each stream, 'tis said, with flowing tears increas'd
Its current. Naïad nymphs and Dryads wore
Garments of sable tinge, with streaming hair.
Wide scatter'd lie his limbs. His head and lyre
Thou, Hebrus, dost receive; and while they glide,
Wond'rous occurrence! down the floating stream,
The lyre a mournful moan sends forth; the lips,
Now lifeless, murmur plaintive; and the bank
Echoes the lamentations. Borne along
To ocean, now his native stream they leave,
And reach Methymna on the Lesbian shore.

The head, expos'd thus on the foreign sand,
And locks still dropping with the watery wave,
A snake approach'd. But Phœbus gave his aid,
And check'd the greedy bite; with open jaws
The serpent rears in stone congeal'd, as then
Widely he gap'd. The ghost from earth descends,
And views the regions he had view'd before.
Exploring through th' Elysian fields he meets
His dear Eurydicé; with longing arms
He clasps her. Here they walk, now side by side,
With equal pace; now follows he, and now
A little space precedes her: Orpheus there
Back on Eurycicé in safety looks.

But Bacchus suffer'd not the heinous deed
Unpunish'd to remain; griev'd that the bard
Who sung his praises, thus was snatch'd away,
He bound the Thracian matrons, who the crime
Had perpetrated, fast by twisted roots
To earth as trees. He stretch'd their feet and toes,
Which follow'd him so swift, and struck their points

Deep in the solid earth: A bird ensnar'd
Thus finds his leg imprison'd by the wires
Hid by the crafty fowler, and his wings
Beats, while his fluttering draws more tight the noose.
So each, as firmly fixt to earth she stood,
Affrighted strove to fly, but strove in vain:
The flexile roots detain'd them; and fast ty'd,
Spite of their struggling bounds, while they explore
For toes and nails, and while they seek for feet,
They see the wood their taper legs conceal;
Their grieving hands to beat their thighs are rais'd;
Their hands strike solid wood: their shoulders, breasts,
Are also wood become. Their outstretch'd arms
Extended boughs appear'd, and boughs they were.

  Nor sated yet was Bacchus; all their fields
He quits; attended by a worthier troop.
To Tmolus' vineyards and Pactolus' stream
He hies: the stream not yet for gold was fam'd;
Not yet so precious were its envy'd sands.
Satyrs and Bacchant' nymphs, his 'custom'd choir
Attend him, but Silenus was not found.
Him drunken had the rustic Phrygians seiz'd,
Reeling with wine, and tottering 'neath his years;
With ivy crown'd; and fetter'd to their king,
The royal Midas, brought him. Midas once
The Thracian Orpheus Bacchus' orgies taught,
With sage Eumolpus; and at once he knew
His old associate in the sacred rites;
And joyful feasted with voluptuous fare,
For twice five days, and twice five nights his guest.
Th' eleventh time Phosphor' now the lofty host
Of stars had chas'd from heaven; the jovial king
Went forth to Lydia's fields, and there restor'd
Silenus to the youth his foster-child.
He, joy'd again his nursing sire to see,
On him bestow'd his anxious sought desire,
Though useless was the gift. Greedy he crav'd
What only harm'd him,—saying—"Grant, O, power!
"Whate'er I touch may straight to gold be chang'd"—
Bacchus consents to what he wishes;—gives
The hurtful gift; but grieves to see his mind
No better wish demand. Joyful departs
The Berecynthian monarch, with ill-fate
Delighted; and, each object touching, tries
The promis'd faith. Scarcely himself believ'd,
When from a growing ilex down he tore
A sprouting bough, straight gold the bough became:

A stone from earth he lifted, pale the stone
In gold appear'd: he touch'd a turfy clod,
The clod quick harden'd with the potent touch:
He pluck'd the ripen'd hoary ears of wheat,
And golden shone the grain: he from the tree
An apple snatch'd, the fam'd Hesperian fruit
He seem'd to hold: where'er his fingers touch'd
The lofty pillars, all the pillars shone:
Nay, where his hands he in the waters lav'd,
The waters flowing from his hands seem'd such
As Danaë might deceive. Scarce can his breast
His towering projects hold; all fancy'd gold.
Th' attendant slaves before their master, joy'd
At this great fortune, heap'd the table high
With dainties; nor was bread deficient there:
But when his hands the Cerealian boon
Had touch'd, the Cerealian boon grew hard:
And when the dainty food with greedy tooth
He strove to eat, the dainty food grew bright,
In glittering plates, where'er his teeth had touch'd.
He mixt pure water with his patron's wine,
And fluid gold adown his cheeks straight flow'd.
With panic seiz'd, the new-found plague to view,
Rich, yet most wretched; from his wealthy hoard
Fain would he fly; and from his soul detests
What late he anxious pray'd. The plenteous gold
Abates his hunger nought, and parching thirst
Burns in his throat. He well deserves the curse
Caus'd by now-hated gold. Lifting his hands
And splendid arms to heaven, he cries,—"O sire
"Lenæan! pardon my offence: my fault
"Is evident; but pity me, I pray,
"And from me move this fair deceitful curse."
Bacchus, the gentlest of celestial powers,
Reliev'd him, as he thus his error own'd:
The compact first agreed dissolv'd, and void
The grant became:—"Lest still thou shouldst remain
"With gold"—he said,—"so madly wish'd, imbu'd,
"Haste to the stream by mighty Sardis' town
"Which flows; thy path along the mountain's ridge
"Explore, opposing still the gliding waves,
"Till thou the spring espy'st. Then deeply plunge
"Beneath the foaming gush thy head, where full
"It spouts its waters; and thy error cleanse,
"As clean thy limbs thou washest."—To the stream
The king as bidden hastes. The golden charm
Tinges the river; from the monarch's limbs
It passes to the stream. And now the banks

Harden in veins of gold to sight disclos'd;
And the pale sands in glittering splendor shine.

Detesting riches, now in woods he lives,
And rural dales; with Pan, who still resorts
To mountain caverns. Still his soul remains
Stupidly dull; the folly of his breast
Was doom'd to harm its owner as before.

High Tmolus rears with steep ascent his head,
O'erlooking distant ocean; wide he spreads
His bounds abrupt; confin'd by Sardis here,
By small Hypæpé there. Upon his top,
While Pan in boastful strain the tender nymphs
Pleas'd with his notes, and on his wax-join'd reeds
A paltry ditty play'd; boldly he dar'd
To place his own above Apollo's song.
The god to try th' unequal strife descends;
Tmolus the umpire. On his mountain plac'd,
The ancient judge from his attentive ears
The branches clear'd; save that his azure head
With oak was crown'd, and acorns dangling down
His hollow temples grac'd. The shepherd's god
Beholding,—"no delay, your judge,"—he said—
"Shall cause,"—and straight Pan sounds the rural reeds.
His barbarous music much the judgment pleas'd
Of Midas, who amidst the crowd approach'd.
Now venerable Tmolus on the face
Of Phœbus turn'd his eyes; and with him turn'd
Th' attentive woods. Parnassian laurel bound
His golden locks; deep dipt in Tyrian dye,
His garment swept the ground; his left hand held
The instrument with gems and ivory rich;
The other grasp'd the bow: his posture shew'd
The skilful master's art: lightly he touch'd
The chords with thumb experienc'd. Justly charm'd
With melody so sweet, Tmolus decreed
The pipe of Pan to Phœbus' lute should yield.

Much did the judgment of the sacred hill,
And much his sentence all delight, save one:
For Midas blames him, and unjust declares
The arbitration. Human shape no more
The god permits his foolish ears to wear;
But long extends them, and with hoary hairs
Fills them within; and grants them power to move,
From their foundation flexile. All beside
Was man, one part felt his revenge alone;

A slowly pacing asses ears he bears.
His head, weigh'd heavy with his load of shame,
He strove in purple turban to enfold;
Thus his disgrace to hide. But when as wont
His slave his hairs, unseemly lengthen'd, cropp'd,
He saw the change; the tale he fear'd to tell,
Of what he witness'd, though he anxious wish'd
In public to proclaim it: yet to hold
Sacred the trust surpass'd his power. He went
Forth, and digg'd up the earth; with whispering voice
There he imparted of his master's ears
What he had seen; and murmur'd to the sod:
But bury'd close the confidential words
Beneath the turf again: then, all fill'd up,
Silently he departed. From the spot
Began a thick-grown tuft of trembling reeds
To spring, which ripening with the year's full round,
Betray'd their planter. By the light south wind
When agitated, they the bury'd words
Disclos'd, betraying what the monarch's ears.
Latona's son, aveng'd, high Tmolus leaves,
And cleaving liquid air, lights in the realm
Laömedon commands: on the strait sea,
Nephelian Hellé names, an altar stands
Sacred to Panomphæan Jove, where seen
Lofty Rhætæum rises to the left,
Sigæum to the right. From thence he saw
Laömedon, as first he toil'd to build
The walls of infant Troy; with toil immense
The undertaking in progression grew,
And mighty sums he saw the work would ask.
A mortal shape he takes; a mortal shape
Clothes too the trident-bearing sire, who rules
The swelling deep. The Phrygian monarch's walls
They raise, a certain treasure for their toil
Agreed on first. The work is finished. Base,
The king disowns the compact, and his lies
Perfidious, backs with perjury.—"Boast not
"This treatment calmly borne," the ocean's god
Exclaim'd, and o'er the sordid Trojan's shores
Pour'd all his flood of billows; and transform'd
The land to sheets of water; swept away
The tiller's treasure; bury'd all the meads.
Nor sated with this ruin, he demands
The monarch's daughter should be given a prey
To an huge monster of the main; whom, chain'd
To the hard rock, Alcides' arm set free,
And claim'd the boon his due; the promis'd steeds.

Refus'd the prize his valorous deed deserv'd,
He sack'd the walls of doubly-perjur'd Troy,
Nor thence did Telamon, whose powerful arm
The hero aided, unrewarded go;
Hesioné was by Alcides given.

Peleus was famous for his goddess-spouse:
Proud not more justly of his grandsire's fame,
Than of his consort's father; numbers more
Might boast them grandsons of imperial Jove;
To him alone a goddess-bride belong'd.
For aged Proteus had to Thetis said,—
"O, goddess of the waves, a child conceive!
"Thou shalt be mother of a youth, whose deeds
"Will far the bravest of his sire's transcend:
"And mightier than his sire's shall be his name."
Hence, lest the world than Jove a mightier god
Should know, though Jove with amorous flames fierce burn'd,
He shunn'd th' embraces of the watery dame:
And bade his grandson Peleus to his hopes
Succeed, and clasp the virgin in his arms.

Hæmonia's coast a bay possesses, curv'd
Like a bent bow; whose arms enclosing stretch
Far in the sea; where if more deep the waves
An haven would be form'd: the waters spread
Just o'er the sand. Firm is the level shore;
Such as would ne'er the race retard, nor hold
The print of feet; no seaweed there was spread.
Nigh sprung a grove of myrtle, cover'd thick
With double-teinted berries: in the midst
A cave appear'd, by art or nature form'd;
But art most plain was seen. Here, Thetis! oft,
Plac'd unattir'd on thy rein'd dolphin's back,
Thou didst delight to come. There, as thou laid'st
In slumbers bound, did Peleus on thee seize.
And when his most endearing prayers were spurn'd,
Force he prepar'd; both arms around thy neck
Close clasp'd. And then to thy accustom'd arts,
Of often-varied-form, hadst thou not fled,
He might have prosper'd in his daring hope.
But now a bird thou wert; the bird he held:
Now an huge tree; Peleus the tree grasp'd firm:
A spotted tiger then thy third-chang'd shape;
Frighted at that, Æäcides his hold
Quit from her body. Then the ocean powers
He worshipp'd, pouring wine upon the waves,
And bleating victims slew, and incense burn'd:

Till from the gulf profound the prophet spoke
Of Carpathus. "O, Peleus! gain thou shalt
"The wish'd-for nuptials; only when she rests
"In the cool cavern sleeping, thou with cords
"And fetters strong her, unsuspecting, bind;
"Nor let an hundred shapes thy soul deceive;
"Still hold her fast whatever form she wears,
"Till in her pristine looks she shines again."
This Proteus said, and plung'd his head beneath
The waves, while scarce his final words were heard.

  Prone down the west was Titan speeding now;
And to th' Hesperian waves his car inclin'd,
When the fair Nereïd from the wide deep came,
And sought her 'custom'd couch. Scarce Peleus seiz'd
Her virgin limbs, when straight a thousand forms
She try'd, till fast she saw her members ty'd;
And her arms fetter'd close in every part:
Then sigh'd, and said; "thou conquerest by some god:"
And the fair form of Thetis was display'd.
The hero clasp'd her, and his wishes gain'd;
And great Achilles straight the nymph conceiv'd.

  Now blest was Peleus in his son and bride;
And blest in all which can to man belong;
Save in the crime of murder'd Phocus. Driven
From his paternal home, of brother's blood
Guilty, Trachinia's soil receiv'd him first.
Here Ceÿx, Phosphor's offspring, who retain'd
His father's splendor on his forehead, rul'd
The land; which knew not bloodshed, knew not force.
At that time gloomy, sad, himself unlike,
He mourn'd a brother's loss. To him, fatigu'd
With trave , and with care worn out, the son
Of Æacus arriv'd; and in the town
Enter'd with followers few: the flocks and herds
That journey'd with him, just without the walls,
In a dark vale were left. When the first grant
T'approach the monarch was obtain'd, he rais'd
The olive in his suppliant hand; then told
His name, and lineage, but his crime conceal'd.
His cause of flight dissembling, next he beg'd,
For him and his, some pastures and a town.
Then thus Trachinia's king with friendly brow:
"To all, the very meanest of mankind,
"Are our possessions free; nor do I rule
"A realm inhospitable: add to these
"Inducements strong, thine own illustrious name,

"And grandsire Jove. In praying lose not time.
"Whate'er thou wouldst, thou shalt receive; and all,
"Such as it is, with me most freely share;
"Would it were better." Speaking thus, he wept:
His cause of grief to Peleus and his friends,
Anxious enquiring, then the monarch told.

  "Perchance this bird, which by fierce rapine lives,
"Dread of the feather'd tribe, you think still wings
"Possess'd. Once man, he bore a noble soul;
"Though stern, and rough in war, and fond of blood.
"His name Dædalion: from the sire produc'd
"Who calls Aurora forth, and last of stars
"Relinquishes the sky. Peace my delight;
"Peace to preserve was still my care: my joys
"I shar'd in Hymen's bonds. Fierce wars alone,
"My brother pleas'd. His valor then o'erthrew
"Monarchs and nations, who, in alter'd form,
"Drives now Thisbæan pigeons through the air.
"His daughter Chioné, in beauty rich,
"For marriage ripe, now fourteen years had seen;
"And numerous suitors with her charms were fir'd.
"It chanc'd that Phœbus once, and Maiä's son,
"Returning from his favorite Delphos this,
"That from Cyllené's top, together saw
"The nymph,—together felt the amorous flame.
"Apollo his warm hopes till night defers;
"But Hermes brooks delay not: with his rod,
"Compelling sleep, he strokes the virgin's face;
"Beneath the potent touch she sinks, and yields
"Without resistance to his amorous force.
"Night spread o'er heaven the stars, when Phœbus took
"A matron's form, and seiz'd fore-tasted joys.
"When its full time the womb matur'd had seen,
"Autolycus was born; the crafty seed
"Of the wing'd-footed god; acute of thought
"To every shade of theft; from his sire's art
"Degenerate nought; white he was wont to make
"Appear as black; and black from white produce.
"Philammon, famous with the lyre and song,
"Was born to Phœbus (twins the nymph brought forth).
"But where the benefit that two she bears?
"Where that the favorite of two gods she boasts?
"What that a valiant sire she claims? and claims
"As ancestor the mighty thundering god?
"Is it that glory such as this still harms?
"Certain it hurtful prov'd to her, who dar'd
"Herself prefer to Dian', and despise

"The goddess' beauty; fierce in ire she cry'd,—
"At least I'll try to make my actions please.—
"Nor stay'd; the bow she bent, and from the cord
"Impell'd the dart; through her deserving tongue
"The reed was sent. Mute straight that tongue became;
"Nor sound, nor what she try'd to utter, heard:
"Striving to speak, life flow'd with flowing blood.
"What woe (O hapless piety!) oppress'd
"My heart! What solace to her tender sire
"I spoke; my solace just the same he heard,
"As rocks hear murmuring waves. But still he moan'd
"For his lost child; but when the flames he saw
"Ascending, four times 'mid the funeral fires
"He strove to plunge; four times from thence repuls'd,
"His rapid limbs address'd for flight, and rush'd
"Like a young bullock, when the hornet's sting
"Deep in his neck he bears, in pathless ways.
"Ev'n now more swift than man he seem'd to run:
"His feet seem'd wings to wear, for all behind
"He left far distant. Through desire of death,
"Rapid he gain'd Parnassus' loftiest ridge.
"Apollo, pitying, when Dædalion flung
"From the high rock his body, to a bird
"Transform'd him, and on sudden pinions bore
"Him floating: bended hooks he gave his claws,
"And gave a crooked beak; valor as wont;
"And strength more great than such a body shews.
"Now as an hawk, to every bird a foe,
"He wages war on all; and griev'd himself,
"He constant cause for others grief affords."

  While these miraculous deeds bright Phosphor's sob
Tells of his brother, Peleus' herdsman comes,
Phocian Anetor, flying, and, with speed
Breathless, "O Peleus! Peleus!" he exclaims,
"Of horrid slaughter messenger I come!"
Him Peleus bids, whate'er he brings, to speak;
Trachinia's monarch even with friendly dread
Trembles the news to hear. When thus the man:
"The weary cattle to the curving shore
"I'd driv'n, when Sol from loftiest heaven might view
"His journey half perform'd, while half remain'd.
"Part of the oxen on the yellow sand,
"On their knees bending view'd the spacious plain
"Of wide-spread waters; part with loitering pace
"Stray'd here, and thither; others swam and rear'd
"Their lofty necks above the waves. There stood
"Close to the sea a temple, where nor gold,

"Nor polish'd marble shone; but rear'd with trees
"Thick-pil'd, it gloom'd within an ancient grove.
"This, Nereus and the Nereïd nymphs possess.
"A fisherman, as on the shore he dry'd
"His nets, inform'd us these the temple own'd.
"A marsh joins near the fane, with willows thick
"Beset, which waves o'erflowing first has form'd.
"A wolf from thence, a beast of monstrous bulk,
"Thundering with mighty clash, with terror struck
"The neighbouring spots: then from the marshy woods
"Sprung out; his jaws terrific, smear'd with foam
"And clotted gore; his eyes with red flames glar'd.
"Mad though he rag'd with ire and famine both,
"Famine less strong appear'd; for his dire maw
"And craving hunger, he not car'd to fill
"With the slain oxen; wounding all the herd:
"All hostile overthrowing. Some of us,
"Ranch'd by his deadly tooth, to death were sent
"Defence attempting. The shore and marsh
"With bellowings echoing, and the ocean's edge
"Redden with blood. But ruinous, delay!
"For hesitation leisure is not now.
"While ought remains, let all together join;
"Arm! arm! and on him hurl united spears."
The herdsman ceas'd, Peleus the loss not mov'd;
But conscious of his fault, infers the plague
Sent by the childless Nereïd to avenge
Her slaughter'd Phocus' loss. Yet Ceÿx bids
His warriors arm, and take their forceful darts;
With them prepar'd to issue: but his spouse
Alcyöné, rous'd by the tumult, sprung
Forth from her chamber; unadorn'd her locks,
Which scatter'd hung around her. Ceÿx' neck
Clasping, she begg'd with moving words and tears,
Aid he would send, but go not; thus preserve
Two lives in one. Then Peleus to the queen;
"Banish your laudable and duteous fears.
"For what the king intended, thanks are due.
"Arms 'gainst this novel plague I will not take:
"Prayers must the goddess of the deep appease."

   A lofty tower there stood, whose summit bore
A beacon; grateful object to the sight
Of weary mariners. Thither they mount,
And see with sighs the herd strew'd o'er the beach;
The monster ravaging with gory jaw,
And his long shaggy hairs in blood bedy'd.
Thence Peleus, stretching to the wide sea shore

His arms, to Psamathé cerulean pray'd,
To finish there her rage, and grant relief.
Unmov'd she heard Æäcides implore:
But Thetis, suppliant, from the goddess gain'd
The favor for her spouse. Uncheck'd, the wolf
The furious slaughter quits not, fierce the more
From the sweet taste of blood, till to a stone
Transform'd, as on a bull's torn neck he hung.
His form remains; and, save his color, all;
The color only shews him wolf no more:
And shews no terror he shall now inspire.

  Still in this realm the angry fates deny'd
Peleus to stay; exil'd, he wander'd on,
And reach'd Magnesia: from Acastus there
Thessalian, expiation he receiv'd.

  Ceÿx meantime, with anxious doubts disturb'd;
First with the prodigy, his brother's change,
Then those which follow'd; to the Clarian god
Prepar'd to go, the oracles to seek,
Which sweetly solace men's uneasy minds.
Delphos was inaccessible; the road
Phorbas prophane, with all his Phlegians barr'd.
Yet first Alcyöné, most faithful spouse!
He tells thee of his purpose. Instant seiz'd
A death-like coldness on her inmost heart:
A boxen paleness o'er her features spread;
And down her cheeks the tears in torrents roll'd.
Thrice she attempted words, but thrice her tears
Her words prevented; then her pious plaints,
Broken by interrupted sobs, she spoke.
"My dearest lord! what hapless fault of mine
"Thy soul has alter'd? Where that love for me
"Thou wont'st to shew? Canst thou now unconcern'd
"Depart, and leave Alcyöné behind?
"Glads thee this tedious journey? Am I lov'd
"Most dearly farthest absent? Yet by land
"Was all thy journey, then I should but grieve,
"Not tremble: sighs would then of fears take place.
"The sea, the dread appearance of the main,
"Me terrifies. But lately I beheld
"Torn planks bestrew the shore: and oft I've read
"On empty tombs, the names of dead inscrib'd.
"Let not fallacious confidence thy mind
"Mislead, that Æölus I call my sire;
"Who binds the furious winds in caves, and smoothes
"At will the ocean. No! when issu'd once,

"They sweep the main, no power of his can rule:
"And uncontroll'd they ravage all the land:
"Nor checks them aught on ocean. Clouds of heaven,
"They clash; and ruddy lightnings hurl along
"In fierce encounter. More their force I know,
"(For well I knew, and oft have mark'd their power,
"While yet an infant at my sire's abode,)
"The more I deem them such as should be fear'd.
"Yet dearest spouse, if thy firm-fixt resolve
"No prayers can change, and obstinate thou stand'st
"For sailing, let me also with thee go:
"Together then the buffeting we'll bear.
"Then shall I fear but what I suffer; then
"Whate'er we suffer we'll together feel:
"Together sailing o'er the boundless main."

  Her words and tears the star-born husband mov'd;
For less of love he felt not. Yet his scheme
To voyage o'er the deep he could not change;
Nor yet consent Alcyöné should share
His peril: and with soothing soft replies,
He try'd to calm her timid breast. Nor yet
Himself approv'd the arguments he try'd,
His consort to persuade consent to yield
To his departure. This at length he adds
As solace, which alone her bosom mov'd.
"All absence tedious seems; but by the fires
"My father bears, I swear, if fates permit,
"Returning, thou shalt see me, ere the moon
"Shall twice have fill'd her orb." Hope in her breast
Thus rais'd by promise of a quick return,
Instant the vessel, from the dock drawn forth,
He bids them launch in ocean, and complete
In all her stores and tackling. This beheld
Alcyöné; and, presaging again
Woes of the future, trembled, and a flood
Of tears again gush'd forth; again she clasp'd
His neck; at length, as, wretched wife, she cry'd,—
"Farewell" she, swooning, lifeless sunk to earth.

  The rowers now, while Ceÿx sought delays,
To their strong breasts the double-ranking oars
Drew back, and cleft with equal stroke the surge.
Her humid eyes she rais'd, and first beheld
Her husband standing on the crooked poop,
Waving his hand as signal; she his sign
Return'd. When farther from the land they shot,
Her straining eyes no more indulg'd to know

His features; still, while yet they could, her eyes
Pursu'd the flying vessel. This at length
Increasing distance her forbade to see;
Still she perceiv'd the floating sails, which spread
From the mast's loftiest summit. Sails at length
Were also lost in distance: then she sought
Anxious her widow'd chamber; and her limbs
Threw on the couch. The bed, the vacant space,
Renew'd her tears, reminding of her loss.

  Now far from port they'd sail'd, when the strong ropes
The breeze began to strain; the rowers turn
Their oars, and lash them to the vessel's side;
Hoist to the mast's extremest height their yards;
And loose their sails to catch the coming breeze.
Scarce half, not more than half, the sea's extent
The vessel now had plough'd; and either land
Was distant far; when, as dim night approach'd,
The sea seem'd foaming white with rising waves;
And the strong East more furious 'gan to blow.
Long had the master cry'd,—"Lower down your yards,
"And close furl every sail!"—he bids; the storm
Adverse, impedes the sound; the roaring waves
Drown every voice in noise. Yet some, untold,
Haste to secure the oars; part bind the sails;
Part fortify the sides: this water laves,
Ejecting seas on seas; that lowers the yards.
While thus they toil unguided, rough the storm
Increases; from each quarter furious winds
Wage warfare, and with mounting billows join.
Trembles the ruler of the bark, and owns
His state; he knows not what he should command,
Nor what forbid; so swift the sudden storm;
So much more strong the tempest than his skill.
Men clamorous shout; cords rattle; mighty waves
Roar, on waves rushing; thunders roll through air;
In billows mounts the ocean, and appears
To meet the sky, and o'er the hanging clouds
Sprinkles its foam. Now from the lowest depths,
As yellow sands they turn, the billows shine;
Now blacker seem they than the Stygian waves;
Now flatter'd, all with spumy froth is spread.
The ship Trachinian too, each rapid change
In agitation heaves; now rais'd sublime
The deeper'd vale she views as from a ridge
So lofty: down to Acheron's low depths,
Now in the hollow of the wave she falls,
And views th' o'erhanging heaven from hell's deep gulf.

Oft bursting on her side with loud report
The billows sound; nor with less fury beat
Than the balista, or huge battering ram,
Driv'n on the tottering fort: or lions fierce,
Whose strength and rage increasing with their speed,
Rush on the armour'd breast and outstretch'd spear.
So rush'd the waves with wind-propelling power
High o'er the decks; and 'bove the rigging rose.

  Now shook the wedges; open rents appear'd,
The pitchy covering gone, and wide-display'd,
A passage opens to the deadly flood.
Then from the breaking clouds fell torrent showers;
All heaven seem'd sweeping down to swell the main;
And the swol'n main, ascending to invade
Celestial regions, soak'd with floods each sail:
And ocean's briny waters mix'd with rain.
No light the firmament possess'd, and night
Frown'd blacker through the tempest. Lightning oft
Reft the thick gloom, and gave a brilliant blaze;
And while the lightnings flame the waters burn.

  Now o'er the vessel's cover'd deck the waves
High tower; and as a soldier, braver far
Than all his fellows, urg'd by thirst of fame,
(The well-defended walls to scale oft try'd,)
At length his hope obtains, and singly keeps
His post, by foes on every side assail'd:
So when the furious billows raging beat
The lofty side, the tenth impetuous rears
Above the rest, and forceful rushes on;
The battery ceasing not on the spent bark,
Till o'er the wall, as of a captur'd town,
Downward it rushes. Part without invade,
And part are lodg'd within. In terror all
In trembling panic stand: not more the crowd
Which fill a city's walls, when foes without
Mine their foundations; while an entrance gain'd
Within, part rage already. Art no more
Can aid; all courage droops; as many deaths
Seem rapid rushing as the billows break.
This wails in tears his fate; that stupid stands;
This calls those blest whom funeral rites await:
One to his deity rich offerings vows,
And vainly stretching forth to heaven his arms,
The heaven he sees not, begs for aid: his friends,
Brethren and parents, fill of this the mind;
Of that his children, or whate'er he leaves.

Alcyöné, alone in Ceÿx' soul
Found place; and but Alcyöné, his lips
Nought utter'd. Her alone he wish'd to see;
Yet joy'd she far was absent. Much he long'd
To view once more his dear paternal shores;
And turn his last looks tow'rd his regal dome:
But where to turn he knows not; in a whirl
So boils the sea; and all the heaven is hid
In shade, by more than pitchy clouds produc'd:
Night doubly darken'd. Now the whirlwind's force
Shivers the mast, and tears the helm away:
And like a victor, proud to view his spoils,
Mounts an high wave, and scornfully beholds
The lower billows; thundering down it sweeps,
Impell'd by force that Athos might o'erturn,
Or Pindus, from their roots; and plunge in sea.
Down in the lowest depths, the weight and blow
Bury'd the vessel; with her most the crew
Sunk in the raging gulf: some met their fate,
Ne'er to return to air: some floated still;
To splinter'd fragments of the bark they clung.
Ceÿx himself, grasp'd only in that hand
A shatter'd plank, which once a sceptre held;
And Æölus and Phosphor' call'd in vain:
But chiefly from his lips was, as he swam,
Alcyöné resounded; that lov'd name
Remember'd constant, and repeated most.
He prays the billows may his body bear
To meet her eyes; and prays her friendly hands
His burial may perform. While thus he swims,
Alcyöné he names, whene'er the waves
To gasp for breath permit him; and beneath
The billows, tries Alcyöné to sound.
Lo! a black towering arch of waters broke
Midst of the surges; in the boiling foam
Involv'd, o'erwhelm'd he sunk. That mournful night
Was Phosphor' dark, impalpable to view:
And since stern fate to heaven his post fast bound,
He veil'd in densest clouds his grieving face.

  Meantime Alcyöné her height of woe
Unknown, counts each sad night, and now with haste
The garments he should wear prepares; and now
Those to adorn herself when him she meets;
Cherishing emptiest hopes of his return.
Devoutest offerings to the heavenly powers
She bore; but incense far before the rest

On Juno's altar burn'd; and oft she pray'd
For him who was not. For his safety pray'd;
For his return; and that his love might still
Without a rival hers remain: the last
Of all her ardent prayers indulgence found.
But longer bore the goddess not to hear
Such vain petitions for the dead; these hands
Polluted, from her altars to remove,
To Iris thus she spoke:—"O, faithful maid!
"Most trusty messenger, with speed repair
"To Somnus' drowsy hall; him bid to send
"A vision form'd in lifeless Ceÿx' shape
"To tell Alcÿöné her woes' extent."
She ended: in her various-teinted robe
Attir'd, and spreading o'er the spacious heaven
Her sweeping arch, Iris the dwelling sought
The goddess order'd. Hid beneath a steep
Near the Cimmerians, in a deep dug cave,
Form'd in a hollow mountain, stands the hall
And secret dwelling of inactive sleep;
Where Phœbus rising, or in mid-day height,
Or setting-radiance, ne'er can dart his beams.
Clouds with dim darkness mingled, from the ground
Exhale, and twilight makes a doubtful day.
The watchful bird, with crested head, ne'er calls
Aurora with his song; no wakeful dog,
Nor goose more wakeful, e'er the silence breaks;
No savage beasts, no pastur'd flocks, no boughs
Shook by the breeze; no brawl of human voice
There sounds: but death-like silence reigns around.
Yet from the rock's foundation, gently flows
A stream of Lethe's water, whose dull waves
In gentle murmuring o'er the pebbles purl,
Tempting to slumber. At the cavern door
The fruitful poppy, and ten thousand plants,
From which moist night the drowsy juices drains,
Then scatters o'er the shady earth, grew thick.
Round all the house no gate was seen, which, turn'd
On the dry hinge should creak; no centry strict
The threshold to protect. But in the midst
The lofty bed of ebon form'd, was plac'd.
Black were the feathers; all the coverings black,
And stretch'd at length the god was seen; his limbs
With lassitude relax'd. Around him throng'd
In every part, vain dreams, in various forms,
In number more than what the harvest bears
Of bearded grains; the woods of verdant leaves;
Or shore of yellow sands. Here came the nymph;

Th' opposing dreams push'd sideways with her hands,
And through the sacred mansion from her robe
Scatter'd refulgent light. With pain the god,
His eyelids weigh'd with slothful torpor, rais'd;
But at each effort down they sunk again:
And on his breast his nodding chin still smote.
At length he rous'd him from his drowsy state;
And, on his elbow resting, ask'd the nymph,
For well he knew her, why she thither came.
Then she—"O Somnus! peaceful rest of all!
"Somnus! most placid of immortal powers;
"Calm of the soul; whom care for ever flies;
"Who soothest bosoms, with diurnal toil
"Fatigu'd; and renovat'st for toil again;
"Dispatch a vision to Trachinia's town,
"(By great Alcides founded,) in the form
"Its hapless monarch bore: let it display
"The lively image of her husband's wreck,
"To sad Alcyöné. This Juno bids."—
Iris, her message thus deliver'd, turn'd:
For more the soporific mist, which rose
Around, she bore not; soon as sleep she felt
Stealing upon her limbs, abrupt she fled,
Mounting the bow by which she glided down.

    The drowsy sire, from 'midst a thousand sons,
Calls Morpheus forth, an artful god, who well
All shapes can feign. None copies else so close
The bidden gait, the features, and the mode
Of converse; vesture too the same he wears,
And language such as most they wont to speak.
Mankind alone he imitates. To seem
Fierce beasts, and birds, and long-extended snakes
Another claims: this Icelos the gods
Have nam'd; by mortals as Photebor known.
A third is Phantasus of different skill;
His change is happiest when he earth becomes,
Or rocks, or waves, or trees, or substance aught
That animation lacks. These shew their forms
By night to mighty heroes and to kings;
The rest before th' ignobler crowd perform.
All these the ancient Somnus pass'd, and chose
Morpheus alone from all his brethren crowd,
The deed Thaumantian Iris bade, to do;
Then, weigh'd with slumber, dropp'd again his head,
And shrunk once more within the sable couch.

    He flies through darkness on unrustling wings,

And short the space, ere in Trachinia's town
He lights; and from his shoulders lays aside
His pinions; when he Ceÿx' form assumes.
In Ceÿx' ghastly shape pallid he stood,
Despoil'd of garments, at the widow'd bed
Of the sad queen: soak'd was his beard, and streams
Seem'd from his heavy dripping locks to flow.
Then leaning o'er the couch, while gushing tears
O'erspread his cheeks, he thus his wife bespoke;—
"Know'st thou thy Ceÿx, wretched, wretched wife?
"Or are my features chang'd by death? Again
"View me, and here behold thy husband's shade,
"Instead of husband: all thy pious prayers
"For me, Alcyöné, were vain. I'm lost!
"No more false hopes encourage, me to see.
"The showery southwind, on th' Ægean main,
"Seiz'd on our vessel, and with mighty blast
"Shiver'd it wide in fragments; and the waves
"Rush'd in my throat as loud thy name I call'd;
"But call'd in vain. No doubtful author brings
"To thee these tidings; no vague rumor this,
"In person I relate it. Shipwreck'd I,
"My fate to thee detail. Rise, and assist!
"Pour forth thy tears; in sable garments clothe;
"Nor send my ghost to wander undeplor'd,
"In shady Tartarus." Thus Morpheus spoke;
And in such accents, that the queen, deceiv'd,
Believ'd her husband spoke. Adown his cheeks
Seem'd real tears to flow; and even his hand
With Ceÿx' motion mov'd. Deeply she groan'd,
Ev'n in her sleep, and rais'd her longing arms
To clasp his body; empty air she clasp'd:
Exclaiming;—"stay; O whither dost thou fly?
"Together let us hence!"—Rous'd with the noise,
And spectre of her spouse; sleep fled her eyes,
And round she cast her gaze for that to seek
Which she but now beheld. Wak'd by her voice,
Her slaves approach'd with lights; but when in vain
She search'd for what she lack'd, her face she struck;
Rent from her breasts her garments; beat her breasts
Themselves: nor stay'd her twisted hair to loose,
But tore the bands away; then to her nurse
Anxious the subject of her grief to learn—
"Alcyöné,"—she cries—"is now no more!
"She with her Ceÿx in one moment fell.
"Hence with your soothing words; shipwreck'd he dy'd.
"I saw; I knew him; as he fled me, stretch'd
"My arms to hold the fugitive.—Ah! no!

"The shadow fled, 'twas but his ghost; but shade
"My husband mere resembling ne'er was form'd.
"Yet had he not his wonted looks, nor shone
"In former brightness his beloved face.
"I saw him, hapless stand with pallid cheek,
"Naked, with tresses dropping still. Lo! here
"Wretched he stood, just on the spot I point:"—
Then anxious try'd his footmarks there to trace.—
"This did my mind foreboding fear; I pray'd
"When me thou fled'st, the winds thou would'st not trust:
"But since to sure destruction forth thou went'st,
"Would that by me companion'd thou had'st gone.
"With thee my bliss had been;—with thee to go.
"Unwasted then one moment of the space
"For life allow'd; not ev'n in death disjoin'd.
"But now I perish, and upon the waves,
"Though absent, float; the main me overwhelms,
"Though from the main far distant. Mental storms
"To me more cruel were than ocean's waves,
"Should I but longer seek to spin out life,
"And combat such deep grief? I will not strive
"Nor wretched thee desert; but now, though late,
"Now will I join thee; and the funeral verse
"Shall us unite; not in the self-same urn,
"Yet in the self-same tomb; bones join'd with bones,
"Allow'd not, yet shall name with name be seen."—
The rest by grief was chok'd, and sounding blows
Each sentence interrupted; while deep groans
Burst from her raving bosom. Morning shone,
And forth she issu'd to the shore, and sought
In grief the spot, where last his face she view'd
Departing. "Here,"—she said,—"as slow he went,
"As slow he loos'd his cables; on this beach
"The parting kiss he gave." While her mind's eye
Retraces every circumstance, she looks,
And something sees far floating on the waves,
Not much unlike a man: dubious at first
What it may be, she views it: nearer now
The billows drive it; and though distant still,
Plain to the eye a body was descry'd.
Whose body, witless, still a shipwreck'd wretch
With boding omen mov'd her; and in tears
She wail'd him as a stranger in these plaints.—
"Unhappy wretch! whoe'er thou art; and she
"Thy wife, if wife thou had'st"—but now the surge
More near the body bore. The more she views
Nearer the corps; the more her senses fly.
And now close driven to shore it floats, and now

Well she discern'd it was, it was—her spouse!
"'Tis he!"—she loudly shriek'd, and tore her face,
Her hair, her garments. Then her trembling arms
To Ceÿx stretching; "Dearest husband!"—cry'd.
"Art thou restor'd thus to my wretched breast?"

High-rais'd by art, adjoining to the beach
A mole was form'd, which broke the primal strength
Of ocean's fury, and the fierce waves tir'd.
Hither she sprung, and, wond'rous that she could!
She flew; the light air winnowing with her wings
New-sprung; a mournful bird she skimm'd along
The water's surface. As she flies, her beak
Slender and small, a creaking noise sends forth,
Of mournful sound, and full of sad complaint.
Soon as the silent bloodless corse she reach'd,
Around his dear-lov'd limbs her wings she clasp'd,
And gave cold kisses with her horny bill.
If Ceÿx felt them, or his head was rais'd
To meet her by the waves, th' unlearned doubt.
But sure he felt them. Both at length, the gods
Commisserating, chang'd to feather'd birds.
The same their love remains, and subject still
To the same fates; and in the plumag'd pair
The nuptial bond is sacred; join'd in one
Parents they soon become; and Halcyon sits
Sev'n peaceful days 'mid winter's keenest rule
Upon her floating nest. Safe then the main:
For Æölus with watchful care the winds
Guards, and prevents their egress; and the seas
Smooths for the offspring, with a grandsire's care.

These, as they skimm'd the surface of the main,
An ancient sire beheld, and prais'd their love:
Constant in death: his neighbour or himself
Also repeats;—the bird which there you see,
Brushing the ocean with his slender legs,
(And shews a corm'rant with his spacious maw)
A monarch's offspring was; would you descend
Through the long series, 'till to him you reach;
Ilus; Assaracus; and Ganymede,
Borne up to heaven by Jove, supply'd the stock
From whence he sprung; Laömedon the old;
And Priam doom'd to end his days with Troy.
Hector his brother; but in spring of youth
He felt this strange adventure, he perchance
As Hector's might have left a towering name:
Though from old Dymas' daughter Hector sprung.

Fair Alixirrhoë, so fame reports,
Daughter of two-horn'd Granicus, brought forth,
By stealth, Æsacus 'neath thick Ida's shade.
Wall'd cities he detested; and remote
From glittering palaces, secluded hills
Inhabited, and unambitious plains;
And scarce at Troy's assemblies e'er was seen.
Yet had he not a clownish heart, nor breast
To love impregnable. By chance he saw
Cebrenus' daughter, fair Hesperië—oft
By him through every shady wood pursu'd—
As on her father's banks her tresses, spread
Adown her back, in Phœbus' rays she dry'd.
The nymph, discover'd, fled. So rapid flies
Th' affrighted stag to 'scape the tawny Wolf;
Or duck, stream-loving, from the hawk, when caught,
Far from her wonted lakes. The Trojan youth
Quick follows, swift through hope; she swift through fear.
Lo! in the herbage hid, her flying foot
With crooked fang a serpent bit, and pour'd
O'er all her limbs the poison: with her flight
Her life was stopp'd. Frantic, he clasps her form
Now lifeless, and exclaims—"how grieve I now,
"That e'er I thee pursu'd; not this I fear'd!
"How mean my conquest, bought at such a price!
"Both, hapless nymph! in thy destruction join'd:
"I gave the cause, the serpent but the wound.
"I guiltier far than he, unless my death
"Shall thine avenge."—He said, and in the main,
From an high rock, by hoarsely-roaring waves
Deep-worn beneath, prepar'd to plunge. Receiv'd
By pitying Tethys softly in his fall,
She clothes him, as he swims the main, with wings;
And death, so much desir'd, denies him still.
The lover, furious at th' unwelcome gift
Of life upon him forc'd, and his pent soul,
Bent on escaping from its hated seat
Confin'd, soon as the new-shot plumes he felt
Spring from his shoulders, up he flew, and plunged
Again his body in the depths below:
His feathers broke his fall. Æsacus rav'd,
And deeply div'd; with headlong fury still,
And endless perseverance death he sought.
Love keeps him meagre still; from joint to joint
His legs still longer grow; his outstretch'd neck
Is long; and distant far his head is plac'd.
He loves the ocean, and the name he bears,
From constant diving, seems correctly giv'n.

Rape of Helen. Expedition of the Greeks against Troy. House of Fame. The Trojan war. Combat of Achilles and Cygnus. The latter slain and transformed to a swan. Story of Cæneus. Fight of the Lapithæ and Centaurs. Change of Cæneus to a bird. Contest of Hercules with Periclymenos. Death of Achilles. Dispute for his arms.

THE TWELFTH BOOK OF THE METAMORPHOSES OF OVID

Priam the sire, much mourn'd, to him unknown
That still his son, on pinions borne, surviv'd:
While Hector and his brethren round the tomb,
A name alone possessing, empty rites
Perform'd. Save Paris, from the solemn scene
None absent were; he with the ravish'd wife
Brought to his shores a long protracted war.
Quick was he follow'd by confederate ships
Ten hundred, and the whole Pelasgian race.
Nor had their vengeance borne so long delay,
But adverse raging tempests made the main
Impassable; and on Bœotia's shores,
In Aulis' port th' impatient vessels bound.

Here, while the Greeks the rites of Jove prepare,
Their country's custom, as the altar blaz'd,
They saw an azure serpent writhe around
A plane, which near the altar rear'd its boughs.
Its lofty summit held a nest; within
Eight callow birds were lodg'd; on these he seiz'd,
And seiz'd the mother, who, with trembling wings,
Hover'd around her loss, all burying deep
Within his greedy maw. All stare with dread.
But Thestor's son, prophetic truths who still
Beheld, exclaim'd—"Rejoice! O Greeks, rejoice!
"Conquest is ours, and lofty Troy must fall.
"But great our toil, and tedious our delay."
Then shew'd the birds a nine years' war foretold.
The snake, entwining 'mid the virid boughs,
Hard stone becomes, but keeps his serpent's form.

But still th' Aönian waves in violent swell
Were lash'd by Neptune, nor their vessels bore;
And many deem'd that Troy he wish'd to spare,

Whose walls his labor rais'd. Not so the son
Of Thestor thought: neither he knew hot so,
Nor what he knew conceal'd:—a victim dire
The virgin-goddess claim'd; a virgin's blood!
When o'er affection public weal prevail'd,
The king o'ercame the father; and before
The altar Iphigenia stood, prepar'd
Her spotless blood to shed, as tears gush'd forth
Even from the sacrificial 'tendants. Then
"Was Dian' mov'd, and threw before their sight
A cloud opaque, and (so tradition tells)
The maid Thycenian to an hind was chang'd,
Amid the priests, the pious crowd and all
Who deprecating heard her doom. This done,
Dian' by such a sacrifice appeas'd
As Dian' best became; and sooth'd her ire,
The angry aspect of the seas was smooth'd;
And all the thousand vessels felt the breeze
Abaft, and bore the long impatient crowd
To Phrygia's shores. A spot there lies, whose seat
Midst of created space, 'twixt earth, and sea,
And heavenly regions, on the confines rests
Of the three-sever'd world; whence are beheld
All objects and all actions though remote,
And every sound by tending ears is heard.
Here Fame resides; and in the loftiest towers
Her dwelling chuses; and some thousand ways,
And thousand portals to the dwelling makes:
No portal clos'd with gates. By day, by night,
Open they stand; of sounding brass all form'd;
All echoing sound; all back the voice rebound:
And all reit'rate every word they hear.
No rest within, no silence there is found,
Yet clamor is not, but a murmur low;
Such as the billows wont to make when heard
From far, or such as distant thunder sends,
When Jove the dark clouds rends and drives aloof.
Crowds fill the halls: the trifling vulgar come
And issue forth. Ten thousand rumors vague
With truth commingled to and fro are heard.
Words in confusion fly. Amid the throng
These preach their words to vacant air, and those
To others tales narrate; the measure still
Of every fiction in narration grows;
And every author adds to what he hears.
Here lives credulity; and here abides
Rash error; transports vain; astonied fear;
Sedition sudden; and, uncertain whence,

Dark whisperings. Fame herself sits high aloft,
And views what deeds in heaven, and earth, and sea
Are done, and searches all creation round.
The news she spreads, that now the Grecian barks
Approach with valiant force; nor did the foe
Unlook'd-for threat the realm. All Troy impedes
Their landing, and the shores defends. Thou first,
Protesilaüs! by great Hector's spear
Unluckily wast slain. The war begun,
Their valiant souls, ere yet they Hector knew,
Dear cost the Greeks. Nor small the blood which flow'd
From Phrygia's sons, by Grecia's valor spill'd.

  Now blush'd Sigæum's shores with spouting blood,
Where Cygnus, Neptune's offspring, gave to death
Whole crowds. Achilles in his chariot stood,
And with his forceful Pelian spear o'erthrew
Thick ranks of Trojans; and as through the fights
Cygnus or Hector to engage he sought,
Cygnus he met: delay'd was Hector's fate
To the tenth year. Then to his white-neck'd steeds,
Press'd by the yoke, with cheering shouts he spoke;
And full against the foe his chariot drove.
His quivering lance well-pois'd he shook, and call'd,
"Whoe'er thou art, O youth! this comfort learn
"In death, that by Achilles' arm thou dy'st."
Thus far Pelides; and his massive spear
Close follow'd on his words. With truth it fled;
Yet did the steely point, unerring hurl'd,
Fall harmless: with a deaden'd point his breast
Was struck. Then he;—"O goddess-born! (for fame
"Thy race to me has long before made known)
"Why wonder'st thou that I unwounded stand?"
(For wondering stood Pelides.) "Not this helm,
"Which thou behold'st, gay with the courser's mane.
"Nor the curv'd buckler by my arm sustain'd,
"For aid are worn. For comely grace alone
"They deck me. Thus is Mars himself adorn'd.
"Thrown every guard far from my limbs, my limbs
"Unwounded would remain. Sure I may boast!
"Sprung not from Nereus' daughter, but from him
"Who rules o'er Nereus; o'er his daughter rules;
"And all th' extent of ocean." Cygnus spoke:
And at Pelides launch'd his spear to pierce
His orbed shield; its brazen front it pierc'd,
And nine bull-hides beneath; stay'd at the tenth,
The warrior shook it forth; with strenuous arm
The quivering weapon hostile back return'd:

Cygnus again unwounded felt the blow.
Nor felt his naked bosom, to the force
Of the third weapon vauntingly expos'd,
Aught harm'd. Less fiercely in the Circus wide
Rages the bull not, when the scarlet vests
To urge his fury fixt, with furious horn
To gore attempting, finds elusion still,
The unhurt limbs invading. Seeks he now
If fall'n the metal from his weapon's point:
Fast to the wood the metal still appears;
And cries he;—"Weak is then my hand? and spent
"On one, is all the strength I once could boast?
"For surely strength that arm could boast, which erst
"Lyrnessus' wall o'erthrew, and when with gore
"In Tenedos, and Thebes made stream; or when
"Caÿcus purple flow'd, stain'd with their blood
"Who on its banks had dwelt; and when twice prov'd
"By Telephus, the virtue of my spear.
"This nervous arm has here too shewn its force
"In hills of slain by me up-heap'd; these shores
"Attest it." Speaking so, his spear he sent
Against Menœtes 'mid the Lycian crowd,
As doubting faintly deeds perform'd before:
And pierc'd at once his corslet and his breast.
From the hot smoking wound as forth he drew
The dart,—as with his dying head was struck
The solid ground, he spoke:—"This is the hand,
"And this the spear which conquest knew before:
"This will I 'gainst him use. May it, when sent,
"The same success attend."—Ere ceas'd his words
Cygnus again with aim he sought, nor swerv'd
His ashen weapon whence he aim'd, but rung,
Unshrunk from, on the shoulder: thence repell'd,
As from a wall or rugged rock it fell:
Yet where the blow was felt, did Cygnus seem
With blood distain'd. Achilles' joy was vain,
For wound was not. Menœtes' blood was there.
Then furious from his lofty car he sprung,
And close at hand his braving foe assail'd
With glittering falchion; by the falchion broke,
The helm and shield he saw, but the keen edge
His stubborn body blunted. More the son
Of Peleus bore not, but the warrior's face
With furious buffets from his shield, unclaspt
First from his arm, he smote, and with his hilt
Heavy his temples; and with headstrong rage
Bore on him: nor to his astounded soul
Respite allow'd. Dread through his bosom spread;

Before his eyes swam darkness: when amidst
The plain, a stone his retrogressive feet
Oppos'd. Pelides, with his mightiest strength,
Struck Cygnus against it, and to earth
Hard forc'd him, thrown supine. Pent with his shield,
And nervous knees upon his bosom prest
Tight, he the lacing of the helmet drew,
Which 'neath his chin was ty'd; close press'd his throat,
His breathing passage and his life at once
Destroy'd he. When his conquer'd foe to spoil
Of all his arms he went, the arms he found
Vacant. The ocean-god had to a bird
Of snowy plumage chang'd his offspring's form:
A bird which still the name of Cygnus bears.

  Here stay'd the toil, here did the battle gain
Of numerous days a respite, either power
Resting on arms unhostile. Then, while guards,
Watchful, the Trojan walls protective kept;
And sentries equal wakeful o'er the trench
Form'd by the Argives watch'd, a feast was held,
Where Cygnus' victor, stout Achilles, gave
An heifer ribbon-bound to Athen's maid.
The sever'd flesh was on the altar plac'd,
Whose smoking fragrance, grateful to the gods,
High to th' ethereal regions mounted. Part,
Their due, th' official sacrificers took;
To swell the feast the rest was given. Outstretch'd
On couches, laid the noble guests, and fill'd
With the drest meat their hunger; and with wine
At once their thirst and all their cares assuag'd.
No lyre them sooth'd; no sound of vocal song;
Nor long extended boxen pipe with holes
Multiferous pierc'd: but all night long, discourse
Protracted; valiant deeds alone the theme.
Alike the valiant acts their foes perform'd,
And those their own they speak. Much they enjoy
To tell by turns what hazards they o'ercame;
And what they oft successless try'd. What else
Could e'er Achilles' speech employ? What else
By great Achilles could with joy be heard?
Chief in the converse, was the conquest late
O'er Cygnus gain'd, the topic. Strange to all
Seem'd it; the youth, from every weapon safe
By wound unconquerable, and with skin
Blunting the keenest steel. Wonder the Greeks,
And wonders ev'n Pelides: when in words
Like these, old Nestor hail'd them. "Cygnus, proof

"'Gainst stee ,—unpierceable by furious blows
"Your age alone has known. These eyes have seen
"Perrhæbian Cæneus bear ten thousand strokes
"Unhurt. He, fam'd for warlike actions, dwelt
"On Othrys, and more strange those warlike deeds,
"Since female was he born." The wondering crowd,
Mov'd with the novel prodigy, beseech
(Their spokesman was Achilles) that the tale
Nestor would give them. "Eloquent old man!
"Of all our age most prudent, tell, for all
"The same desire prevails o'er, who was he,
"This Cæneus? why was chang'd his sex? what wars
"Of fierce encounter made him known to thee?
"And if by any conquer'd, tell the name."

    Then thus the senior: "Though decrepid age
"Weighs heavy on me, and the deeds beheld
"In prime of youth, in numbers 'scape my mind;
"Yet than these facts, 'mid all of peace and war,
"Nought on my bosom made a deeper print.
"Yet may extended age of all beheld
"Part of the numerous acts and objects seen
"Relate,—I twice one hundred years have pass'd;
"Now in the third I breathe. Cænis, a nymph
"Sprung from Elateus, fam'd was all around
"For brightest beauty; fairest of the maids
"Who Thessaly adorn; theme of vain hopes
"To crowds of wooers through the neighbouring towns;
"And ev'n through thine, Achilles; for the land
"Thou claim'st produc'd her. Nay, her nuptial couch,
"Peleus perchance had sought, save that the rites
"Already with thy mother were compleat,
"Or were in promise ready. Nuptial couch
"She never press'd, for on the lonely shore
"Strolling, so fame declares, the vigorous clasp
"Of Ocean's god she felt. The charms possest
"Of his new object, Neptune said—whate'er
"Thou wishest, chuse, secure of no repulse.—
"This too does fame report, that Cænis cry'd—
"Wrongs such as mine no trivial gift deserve,
"That ne'er such shame again I suffer, grant
"I woman be no longer; that will all
"Favors comprize.—Her closing words betray'd
"A graver sound; manly appear'd her voice:
"And masculine it was. Deep ocean's god
"Acceded to her wish, and granted, more,
"That wounds should never harm her, nor by steel
"Should she e'er fall. Joy'd at the gift, the god

"Atracia's hero leaves—employs his age
"In studies warlike; and among the fields,
"Where fertilizing Peneus wanders, roams.

"Now bold Ixion's son had gain'd the hand
"Of Hippodamia; and the fierce-soul'd crowd
"Cloud-born, had bidden to attend the boards,
"In order rang'd within a cavern's mouth,
"By trees thick-shaded. All the princes round
"Of Thessaly attended: I, myself
"Amongst them went. Loud rung the regal feast
"With the mixt concourse; all most joyful sung
"O Hymen! Iö Hymen! and each hall
"Blaz'd bright with fires. The virgin then approach'd
"Pre-excellent in fairness, with a band
"Of matrons and unwedded nymphs begirt.
"Most blest, we all exclaim'd, in such a spouse
"Must be Pirithoüs—but such boding hopes
"Well nigh deceiv'd us. For when drunken lust
"O'er thee, Eurytus! govern'd, of the blood
"Of savage Centaurs, far most savage, fir'd
"Whether by wine, or by the virgin's charms
"Thou saw'st, thy breast. Instant, the board o'erturn'd,
"Routed the guests convivial, and the bride
"Caught by her locks, was forceful dragg'd away.
"Eurytus Hippodamia seiz'd; the rest
"Grasp'd such as pleas'd them, or whoe'er they met.
"It show'd the image of a captur'd town.

"With female shrieks the place resounded; swift
"We start, and Theseus foremost thus exclaims:—
"What frenzy, O Eurytus! thee impels
"Pirithoüs thus to wrong me still in life!
"Ign'rant that two thou wound'st in one?—Nor vain
"The chief magnanimous his threat'nings spoke:
"Th' aggressors back repell'd; and, while they rag'd,
"The ravish'd bride recover'd. Nought he said,
"Nor could such acts defence by words allow;
"But with rude inconsiderate hands he press'd
"Full on her champion's face; his valiant breast
"Assaulting. Near by chance a cup there stood,
"Of mould antique, and rough with rising forms:
"Mighty it was, but Theseus, mightier still,
"Seiz'd it, and full against his hostile face
"It dash'd; he vomits forth, with clots of gore,
"His brains, and wine; these issuing from the wound;
"That from his mouth; and on the soaking sand
"Supine he sprawls. With rage the two-form'd race

"Burn for their brother's slaughter; all with voice
"United, eager call—to arms! to arms!
"Wine gave them courage, and the primal fight
"Was goblets, fragile casks, and hollow jars,
"Dash'd on: once instruments to feasts alone
"Pertaining; now for slaughter us'd and blood.

"First Amycus, of Ophion son, not fear'd
"To rob the sacred chambers of their spoils;
"And from its cord suspensive, tore away,
"As from the roof it hung, a glittering lamp;
"And hurl'd it, lofty-pois'd, full in the front
"Of Lapithæan Celadon. So falls
"On the white neck the victim bull presents,
"The sacrificial axe, and all his bones
"Were shatter'd left; one all confounded wound.
"His eyes sprang forth; his palate bones displac'd,
"His nose driv'n back within his palate falls.
"Him Belates Pellæan with a foot
"Torn from a maple table, on the ground
"Stretch'd prone; his chin forc'd downward on his breast;
"And sputtering teeth, with blackest gore commixt,
"Sent by a second blow to Stygia's shades.

"As next he stood, and with tremendous brow
"The flaming altar view'd, Gryneus exclaim'd—
"Why use we this not? and the ponderous load
"With all its fires he seiz'd, and 'mid the crowd
"Of Lapithæans flung: two low it press'd;
"Broteas and bold Orion. From her sphere
"Orion's mother Mycalé, by charms
"The moon to drag to earth has oft been known.

"Loud cry'd Exodius:—Were but weapons found
"That death impunity would boast not. Horns
"An ancient stag once brandish'd, on a pine
"Hung lofty, serv'd for arms; the forky branch
"Hurl'd in his face deep dug out either eye.
"Part to the horns adhere; part flowing down
"His beard, thence hang in ropes of clotted gore.
"Lo! Rhætus snatches from the altar's height
"A burning torch of size immense, and through
"Charaxus' dexter temple, with bright hair
"Shaded, he drives it. Like the arid corn
"Caught by the rapid flame, the tresses burn;
"And the scorch'd blood the wound sent forth, a sound
"Of horrid crackling gave. Oft whizzes steel
"So, drawn forth glowing from the fire, with tongs

"Bent, and in cooling waters frequent plung'd;
"And crackling sounds, immers'd in tepid waves.
"The wounded hero from his tresses shook
"The greedy flames, and in his arms upheav'd,
"Tom from the earth, a mighty threshold stone,
"A waggon's burthen; but the ponderous load
"Forbade his strength to hurl it on the foe:
"And on Cometes, who beside him stood,
"Dropp'd the huge bulk. Nor Rhætus then his joy
"Disguis'd, exclaiming:—Such may be the aid
"That all your friends receive!—Then with his brand
"Half burnt, his blows redoubling, burst the skull
"With the strong force; and on the pulpy brain
"By frequent strokes the bones beat down. From thence
"Victor, Evagrus, Corythus, he met
"And Dryas. Corythus o'erthrown, whose cheeks
"The first down shaded; loud Evagrus cry'd:—
"What glory thine, thus a weak boy to slay?—
"No more to utter Rhætus gave, but fierce
"Plung'd the red-flaming weapon in his mouth,
"Thus speaking; and deep forc'd it down his throat.
"Thee also, furious Dryas! with the brand,
"Whirl'd round and round his head, he next assails.
"But thee the same sad fortune not befel:
"Him, proud triumphing from increas'd success
"In blood, thou piercest with an harden'd stake,
"Where the neck meets the shoulder. Rhætus groan'd:
"And from the hard bone scarce the wood could draw;
"As drench'd in blood his own, by flight he scap'd.
"With him fled Lycabas; and Orneus fled;
"Thaumas; Pisenor; Medon, who was struck
"'Neath the right shoulder; Mermeros, who late
"In rapid race all else surpass'd, but now
"Mov'd halting with his wound; Abas, of boars
"The spoiler; Pholus, and Melaneus too;
"With Astylos the seer, who from the war
"Dissuaded, but in vain, his brethren crowd.
"Nay more, to Nessus, fearing wounds, he cry'd—
"Fly not!—thou'lt for Alcides' bow be sav'd.

  "Euronymus, nor Lycidas, their fate,
"Areos, nor Imbreos fled; whom face to face
"Confronting, Dryas' hand smote down. Thou too,
"Crenæus! felt thy death in front, though turn'd
"For flight thy feet; for looking back thou caught'st
"Betwixt thine eyes the massy steel; where joins
"The nose's basement to the forehead bones.

"With endless draughts of stupefactive wine
"Aphidas lay, 'mid all the raging noise
"Unrous'd; and grasping in his languid hand
"A ready-mingled bowl: stretch'd was he seen,
"On a rough bear-skin, brought from Ossa's hill.
"Him from afar, as Phorbas saw, no arms
"Dreading, he fix'd his fingers in the thongs,
"And said—with Stygian waters mixt, thy wine
"Now drink;—and instant round his javelin twin'd
"The youth: for as supinely stietch'd he lay
"The ash-form'd javelin through his throat was driv'n.
"No sense of death he felt; his dark brown gore
"Flow'd in full stream upon the couch, and flow'd
"In his grasp'd goblet. I, Petræus saw,
"An acorn-loaded oak from earth to rend
"Endeavoring; which while compass'd with both arms
"He strains, now this way, now the other, shook
"Appear'd the tottering tree. Pirithous' dart
"Driv'n through the ribs, Petræus' straining breast
"Nail'd to the rigid wood. Pirithous' arm
"Lycus o'erthrew; and 'neath Pirithous' force
"Fell Chromis,—so they tell. But less of fame
"The conqueror gain'd from these, than from the death
"Of Helops, and of Dictys. Helops felt
"The dart through both his temples; swift it whizz'd
"His right ear enter'd, shewing at his left.
"But Dictys, from a dangerous mountain's brow
"As flying, trembling from Ixion's son
"Close following, he descended, headlong down
"He tumbled; with his ponderous fall he broke
"A mighty ash; within his riven side
"The stumps his bowels tore. Aphareus fierce,
"Came on for vengeance; and a massive rock,
"Torn from the hill, upheav'd to throw—to throw
"Attempted Theseus with an oaken club
"Prevented, and his mighty elbow broke:
"Nor now his leisure suits, nor cares he now
"A foe disabled to dispatch to hell:
"But on Biamor's lofty back he springs,
"Unwont to bear, except himself, before:
"Press'd with his knees his ribs, and grasping firm,
"With his left hand his locks, he bruis'd his face,
"His frowning forehead, and his harden'd skull,
"With the rough club. With the same club he lays
"Nidymnus prostrate; and Lycotas, skill'd
"To fling the javelin; Hippasus, whose beard
"Immense, his breast o'ershaded; Ripheus sprung
"From lofty woods; and Tereus wont to drag

"Home furious bears still living, on the hills
"Thessalian, caught. Nor longer in the fight
"Raging with such success, Demoleon bore
"Theseus to see, but from a crowded wood,
"With giant efforts strove a pine to rend,
"Of ancient growth, up by the roots, but foil'd
"He flung the broken fragment 'mid the foe.
"Warn'd by Minerva, from the flying wood
"Theseus withdrew; so would he we believe.
"Yet harmless fell the tree not; from the breast
"And shoulder of great Crantor, was the neck
"Sever'd. The faithful follower of thy sire
"Was he, Achilles. Him, Amyntor, king
"Of all Dolopia, in the warlike strife
"O'ercome, as pledge of peace and faithful words
"Gave to Æäcides. Him mangled so
"With cruel wound, Peleus far distant saw;
"And thus exclaim'd,—O, Crantor! dearest youth!
"Thy funeral obsequies behold.—He said,
"And hurl'd his ashen spear with vigorous arm,
"And with a spirit not less vigorous, forth,
"Full on Demoleon: tearing through the fence
"Of his strong chest, it quiver'd in the bones.
"The pointless wood his hand dragg'd out; the wood
"With difficulty dragg'd he: in his lungs
"Deep was the steel retain'd. To his fierce soul
"Fresh vigor gave the smart. Hurt as he was
"He rear'd against the foe, and with his hoofs
"Trampled thy sire. He, with his helm and shield,
"Wards off the sounding blows; his shoulders guards;
"Holds his protended steel, and his foe's chest
"Full 'twixt the shoulders; one strong blow transpierc'd.
"Yet had he slain by distant darts before
"Both Hylis and Phlegræus; and in fight
"More close, had Clanis and Hipponous fall'n.
"To these must Dorilas be added, he
"A wolf skin round his forehead wore; and, bent,
"A double wound presenting, o'er his brows
"He bore the weapons of a savage bull;
"With streaming gore deep blushing. Loud I cry'd,
"While courage gave me strength—see how my steel
"Thy horns surpasses—and my dart I flung.
"My dart to 'scape unable, o'er his brow
"To ward the blow, his hand he held; his hand
"Was to his forehead nail'd. Loud shouts were heard,
"And Peleus at him, wounded thus, rush'd on,
"(He nearer stood) and with a furious blow
"Mid belly plac'd, dispatch'd him. High he sprung

"On earth his entrails dragging;—as they dragg'd
"Madly he trampled;—what he trampled tore:
"These round his legs entwining, down he falls;
"And with an empty'd body sinks to death.

  "Nor could thy beauty, Cyllarus, avail
"Aught in the contest! if to forms like thine
"Beauty we grant. His beard to sprout began,
"His beard of golden hue; golden the locks
"That down his neck, and o'er his shoulders flow'd.
"Cheerful his face; his shoulders, neck, and arms,
"Approach'd the models which the artists praise.
"Thus all that man resembled. Nor fell short
"The horse's portion: beauteous for a beast.
"A neck and head supply'd, a steed were form'd,
"Of Castor worthy: so was for the seat
"Fitted his back; so full outstood his chest:
"His coat all blacker than the darkest pitch;
"Save his white legs, and ample flowing tail.
"Crowds of his race him lov'd; but one alone,
"Hylonomé, could charm him; fairest nymph
"Of all the two-form'd race that roam'd the groves.
"She sole enraptur'd Cyllarus, with words
"Of blandishment; beloved, and her love
"For him confessing. Grace in all her limbs
"And dress, for him was studied; smooth her hair
"For him was comb'd; with rosemary now bound;
"Now with the violet; with fresh roses now;
"And oft the snow-white lily wore she; twice
"Daily she bath'd her features in the stream,
"That from Pagasis' woody summit falls;
"Twice daily in the current lav'd her limbs.
"Nor cloth'd she e'er her shoulders, or her side,
"Save with the chosen spoils of beasts which best
"Her form became. Most equal was their love:
"As one they o'er the mountains stray'd; as one
"The caves they sought; and both together then
"The Lapithæan roof had enter'd; both
"Now wag'd the furious war. By whom unknown,
"From the left side a javelin came, and pierc'd
"Thee deep, O Cyllarus! 'neath where thy chest
"Joins to thy neck. Drawn from the small-form'd wound,
"The weapon.—with the mangled heart, the limbs
"Grew rigid all. Hylonomé supports
"His dying body, and her aiding hand
"Presses against the wound; leans face to face,
"And tries his fleeting life awhile to stay.
"When fled she saw it, with laments which noise

"Drown'd ere my ears they reach'd, full on the dart
"Which through him stuck she fell; and clasp'd in death
"Her dear-lov'd husband's form. Before my eyes
"Still stands Phæöcomes, whom, closely-join'd,
"Six lions' hides protected; man and horse
"Equal the covering shar'd. Phonoleus' son
"Fierce on the skull he smote, with stump immense,
"Huge as four oxen might with labor move.
"Crush'd was the rounding broadness of the head;
"And the soft brain gush'd forth at both his ears;
"His mouth, his hollow nostrils, and his eyes.
"So through the straining oaken twigs appears,
"Coagulated milk: so liquid flows
"Through the fine sieve, by supercumbent weights
"Prest down, the thick curd at the small-form'd holes.
"Deep in his lowest flank the foe I pierc'd,
"As from our fallen friend the arms to strip
"Prepar'd, he stoop'd. Thy father saw the deed.
"Chthonius too fell beneath my sword, and fell
"Teleboas. Chthonius bore a forky bough;
"A javelin arm'd the other; with its steel
"He pierc'd me. Lo! the mark the wound has left:—
"Still the old scar appears. Then was the time
"They should have sent me to the siege of Troy:
"Then had I power great Hector's arm to stay;
"To check, if not to conquer. Hector then
"Was born not, or a boy. Now age me robs
"Of all my force. Why should I say how fell
"Two-form'd Pyretus, by the strength o'erthrown
"Of Periphantes? Why of Amphyx tell,
"Who in Oëclus' hostile front deep sunk,
"(Oëclus centaur-born) a pointless spear?
"Macareus, Erigdupus, (near the hill
"Of Pelethronus born, against his chest
"Full-bearing,) prostrate laid. Nor should I pass,
"How I the spear beheld, by Nessus' hands
"Launch'd forth, and bury'd in Cymelus' groin.
"Nor think you Mopsus, Amphyx' son, excell'd
"Alone to teach the future. By the dart
"Of Mopsus, fell Odites double-form'd.
"To speak in vain he strove, for tongue to chin,
"And chin to throat were by the javelin nail'd.

  "Cæneus ere this had five to death dispatch'd
"Bromius, Antimachus with hatchet arm'd;
"Pyracmon, Stiphelus, and Helimus.
"What wounds them slew I know not; well their names,
"And numbers I remember. Latreus big

"In body and in limbs, sprung forth adorn'd
"In the gay arms Halesus once had own'd;
"Halesus of Thessalia by him slain:
"'Twixt strong virility and age his years,
"Still strong virility his arm could boast;
"Gray hairs his temples sprinkled. Lofty seen
"In helm and shield, and Macedonian spear,
"Proudly between the adverse ranks he rode;
"And clash'd his arms, and circling scower'd along.
"These boasting words to the resounding air
"Brave issuing—Cænis, shall I bear thee so?
"Still will I think thee Cænis;—female still
"By me thou'lt be consider'd. 'Bates it nought
"Thy valor, when thy origin thy soul
"Reflects on? When thy mind allows to own
"What deed the grant obtained? What price was paid
"To gain the false resemblance of a man?
"What thou was born, remember: mark as well
"Who has embrac'd thee. Go, the distaff take,
"And carding basket. With thy fingers twirl
"The flax, and martial contests leave to men.
"The spear which Cæneus hurl'd, deep in his side
"Bare as he cours'd, expos'd the blow to meet,
"Pierc'd him when boasting thus, just where the man
"Join'd the four-footed form. With smart he rag'd,
"And to the Phyllian warrior's face his spear
"Presented. Back the spear rebounded: so
"Bound the hard hailstones from the roof; so leap
"The paltry pebbles on the hollow drum.
"Now hand to hand he rushes to engage,
"And in his harden'd sides attempts to plunge
"His weapon deep. Pervious his weapon finds
"No spot. Then cry'd he,—still thou shalt not 'scape:
"Though blunted is my point my edge shall slay;—
"And aim'd a blow oblique, to ope his side,
"While round his flank was grasp'd his forceful arm.
"Sounded the stroke as marble struck would sound;
"The shiver'd steel rebounding from his neck.
"His limbs unwounded, to the wondering foe
"Thus long expos'd, loud Cæneus call'd;—Now try
"Our arms thy limbs to pierce!—Up to the hilt
"His deadly weapon 'twixt his shoulders plung'd;
"Then thrust and dug with blows unseeing 'mid
"His entrails deep; thus forming wounds on wounds.

 "Now all the furious crowd of double forms
"Rush raging round him; all their weapons hurl;
"And all assail with blows this single foe.

"Blunted their weapons fall, and Cæneus stands
"Unpierc'd, unbleeding, from ten thousand strokes:
"Astonish'd at the miracle they gaze;
"But Monychus exclaims;—What blasting shame
"A race o'erthrown by one; that one a man,
"But dubious. Grant him man, our coward deeds
"Prove us but what he has been. What avail
"Our giant limbs? What boots our double strength;
"Strength of created forms the mightiest two,
"In us conjoin'd? A goddess-mother we
"Assur'dly should not boast; nor boast for sire
"Ixion, whose great daring soul him mov'd
"To clasp the lofty Juno in his arms.
"Now vanquish'd by a foe half-male. Him whelm
"With trees, with rocks: whole mountains heap'd on high,
"Whole falling forests, let that stubborn soul
"Crush out. The woods upon his throat shall press,
"And weight for wounds shall serve.—The centaur spoke,
"Seizing a tree which lay by chance uptorn
"By raging Auster; on his valiant foe
"The bulk he hurl'd. All in like efforts join'd:
"And quickly Othrys of his woods was stript:
"Nor Pelion shade retain'd. Cæneus opprest
"Beneath the pile immense—the woody load,—
"Hot pants, and with his forceful shoulders bears,
"To heave th' unwieldy weight: but soon the heap
"Reaches his face, and then o'ertops his head:
"Nor breath is left his spirit can inhale.
"Now faint he sinks, and struggles now in vain
"To lift his head to air, and from him heave
"The heap'd-up forests: then the pile but shakes,
"As shakes the lofty Ida you behold,
"When by an earthquake stirr'd. Doubtful his end.
"His body, by the sylvan load down prest,
"Some thought that shadowy Tartarus receiv'd.
"But Mopsus this deny'd, who spy'd a bird
"From 'mid the pile ascend, and mount the skies
"On yellow pinions. I the bird beheld,
"Then first, then last. As wide on buoyant wing
"Our force surveying, Mopsus saw him fly,
"And rustling round with mighty noise, his eyes
"And soul close mark'd him, and he loud exclaim'd,—
"Hail, Cæneus! of the Lapithæan race
"The glory! once of men the first, and now
"Bird of thy kind unique!—The seer's belief
"Made credible the fact. Grief spurr'd our rage.
"Nor bore we calmly that a single youth
"By hosts of foes should fall. Nor ceas'd our swords

"In gore to rage 'till most to death were given:
"The rest by favoring darkness say'd in flight."

  While thus the Pylian sage, the wars narrates
Wag'd by the Lapithæan race, and foe
Centaurs half-human; his splenetic ire
Tlepolemus could hide not, when he found
Alcides' deeds past o'er; but angry spoke.—
"Old sire, astonish'd, I perceive the praise
"The deeds of Hercules demand, has 'scap'd
"Your mind. My father has been wont to tell
"Whom, he of cloud-begotten race o'erthrew:
"Oft have I heard him." Nestor sad reply'd;
"Why force me thus my miseries to recal
"To recollection; freshening up the woes
"Long years have blunted; and confess the hate
"I bear thy sire for injuries receiv'd.
"He, (O, ye gods!) has deeds atchiev'd which far
"All faith surpass; and has the wide world fill'd
"With his high fame. Would I could this deny!
"For praise we e'er Deïphobus? or praise
"Give we Polydamas, or Hector's self?
"Who can a foe applaud? This sire of thine
"Messenia's walls laid prostrate, and destroy'd
"Elis and Pylos, unoffending towns;
"Rushing with fire and sword in our abode.
"To pass the rest who 'neath his fury fell,—
"Twice six of Neleus' sons were we beheld;
"Twice six save me beneath Alcides' arm,
"There dy'd. With ease were conquer'd all but one;
"Strange was of Periclymenos the death;
"Whom Neptune, founder of our line, had given,
"What form he will'd to take; that form thrown off.
"His own again resume. When vainly chang'd
"To multifarious shapes; he to the bird
"Most dear to heaven's high sovereign, whose curv'd claws
"The thunders bear, himself transform'd; the strength
"That bird possesses, using, with bow'd wings,
"His crooked beak and talons pounc'd his face.
"'Gainst him Tyrinthius his unerring bow
"Bent, and as high amid the clouds he tower'd,
"And poising hung, pierc'd where his side and wing
"Just met: nor deep the hurt; the sinew torn
"Still him disabled, and deny'd the power
"To move his wing, or strength to urge his flight.
"To earth he fell; his pinions unendow'd
"With power to gather air: and the light dart
"Fixt superficial in the wing, his fall

"Deep in his body pierc'd; out his left side,
"Close by his throat the pointed mischief stood.

  "Now, valiant leader of the Rhodian fleet,
"Judge what from me the great Alcides' deeds
"Of blazonry can claim? Yet the revenge
"I give my brethren, is on his brave acts
"Silent to rest: to thee still firm ally'd
"In friendship." Thus his eloquent discourse
The son of Neleus ended, and the gift
Of Bacchus, oft repeated, circled round
To the old senior's words; then from the board
They rose, and night's remainder gave to sleep.

  But now the deity, whose trident rules
The ocean waters, with a father's grief
Mourns for his offspring to a bird transform'd.
Savage 'gainst fierce Achilles, he pursues
His well-remember'd ire with hostile rage.
And now the war near twice ten years had seen,
When long-hair'd Phœbus, thus the god address'd;
"O power! to me most dear, of all the sons
"My brother boasts! whose hands with mine uprear'd
"In vain the walls of Troy! griev'st thou not now
"Those towers beholding as they ruin'd fall?
"Griev'st thou not now such thousands to behold
"Slain, those high towers attempting to defend?
"Griev'st thou not (more I need not speak) to think
"Of Hector's body round his own Troy dragg'd,
"When still the fierce Achilles, ev'n than war
"More ruthless, of our works destroyer, lives?
"Would it to me were given—my trident's power,
"Well know I, he should prove; but since deny'd
"To rush, and hand to hand this foe engage,
"Slay him with unsuspected secret dart."
The Delian god consented, and at once
His uncle's vengeance and his own indulg'd.
Veil'd in a cloud amid the Ilian host
He darts, and 'mid a slaughter'd crowd beholds
Where Paris, on plebeïan foes his shafts
Unerring hurls: to him confess'd, the god
Exclaims;—"Why wast'st thou in ignoble blood
"Thy weapons? If thy friends employ thy care,
"Turn on Pelides every dart, revenge
"Thy murder'd brothers."—Phœbus spoke, and shew'd
Where with his steel Achilles ranks on ranks
Of Troy o'erthrew. On him the bow he turns;
To him he guides the sure, the deadly dart.

Now may old Priam joy for Hector slain;
For thou, Achilles, victor o'er such hosts,
Fall'st by the coward's hand, who stole from Greece
The ravish'd wife. O! if foredoom'd thy lot
By woman-warrior to be slain, to fall
By Amazonian weapon had'st thou chos'n.
Now burns Æacides, the Phrygians' dread;
The pride, the guardian of the Grecian name;
The chief in war unconquer'd: and the god
Who arm'd him once, consumes him. Ashes now;
Nought of the great Pelides can be found,
Save what with ease a little urn contains.
But still his glory lives, and fills all earth:
Such bounds alone the hero suit; his fame
Equals himself, nor sinks he to the shades.

His shield itself, as conscious whose the shield,
Fomented wars; and quarrels for his arms
Arose. Tydides fear'd to urge his claim;
Ajax, Oïleus' son; Atrides' each,
Him youngest, and the monarch who surpass'd
In age and warlike skill; and all the crowd.
Laërtes' son, and Telamon's alone
Try'd the bold glorious contest. From himself
All blame invidious Agamemnon mov'd:
The Grecian chiefs amid the camp he plac'd,
And bade the host around the cause decide.

THE THIRTEENTH BOOK

Contest of Ajax and Ulysses for the arms of Achilles. Success of Ulysses and death of Ajax. Sack of Troy. Sacrifice of Polyxena to the ghost of Achilles. Lamentation of Hecuba. She tears out the eyes of Polymnestor, and is changed into a bitch. Birds arise from the funeral pile of Memnon, and kill each other. Escape of Æneas from Troy, and voyage to Delos. The daughters of Anius transformed to doves. Voyage to Crete and Italy. Story of Acis and Galatea. Love of Glaucus for Scylla.

THE THIRTEENTH OF THE METAMORPHOSES OF OVID

The princes sate; the common troops in crowds
Circled them round; when Ajax in the midst,
Lord of the seven-fold shield, arose, with rage
Uncurb'd. Sigæum's shores he fiercely view'd;
And ship-clad beach, while with extended arms,

"O, Jupiter!" he cry'd, "before this fleet
"Must then our cause be try'd? With me contends
"Ulysses? He who yielded all a prey
"To Hector's fires; whom I alone repell'd?
"Fires which I from that fleet drove far? More safe
"'Tis sure with artful language to contend,
"Than battle hand to hand. Hard 'tis for me
"To speak; for him 'tis no less hard to fight.
"And much as I in keen-urg'd blows excel,
"And arduous contest, such in words is he.
"My deeds, O Grecians! to rehearse what need?
"Have you not seen them? Let Ulysses tell
"His actions, feats without a witness done;
"Night only privy. Mighty is the prize,
"I own; but Ajax' glory suffers much,
"Striving with such a rival. Granted, great
"Its value; where the boast to have obtain'd
"What this Ulysses hop'd for? He ev'n now
"Enjoys th' advantage of the contest. Foil'd,
"His pride will be to boast with me he strove.
"But I, if doubtful is my valor deem'd,
"Have claims most potent in my noble race:
"Sprung from great Telamon, who Troy's proud town,
"'Neath brave Alcides captur'd; and explor'd
"The shores of Colchis in th' Hæmonian bark.
"His sire was Æäcus, who equal law
"Dispenses 'mid the silent shades; where toils
"Æölian Sisyphus beneath his stone.
"Well mighty Jove knows Æäcus, and owns
"Him son. Thus Ajax ranks but third from Jove.
"Nor yet, O, Greeks! should this descent my cause
"Assist, save that Achilles claim'd the same.
"Of brothers born, a kinsman's right I ask.
"Why should one sprung of Sisyphæan blood,
"Like his progenitor in theft and fraud,
"Ingraft an alien name upon the stock
"Of Æäcus? Am I the arms refus'd
"That first I join'd the warriors? join'd your host
"Betray'd not by informers? Worthier he,
"That last his arms he took? with madness feign'd
"Shunning the warfare; till more crafty came
"Naupliades, though luckless for himself;—
"Who shew'd his coward soul's devices plain;
"And hither dragg'd him to the hated wars?
"Now let him arms most glorious take, who arms
"To wear refus'd. Let me unhonor'd go,
"Robb'd of my kindred right, who first arriv'd
"To face the perils. Would, ye gods! that true,

"Or thought so, his insanity had been.
"Then, counsellor of cruel deeds, he ne'er
"Had join'd our camp before the Phrygian walls.
"Then thou, O Pæän's son! had Lemnos ne'er
"Known—to our shame abandon'd on the shore.
"Thou now, so fame reports, in woody caves
"Shelter'd, ev'n rocks mov'st with thy rending groans;
"Pray'st that Laërtes' son his justest meeds
"May gain. Ye gods! ye gods! grant ye his prayers
"A favoring ear! Now he, by oath combin'd
"With us in war;—O, heavens! a leader too!
"Heir to employ Alcides' faithful darts,
"Sinks both by famine and disease opprest:
"By birds sustain'd, and cloth'd by birds, he spends
"Upon his feather'd prey, the darts design'd
"To end the fate of Troy. Yet still he lives:
"For here he never with Ulysses came.
"Content had hapless Palamedes been
"Deserted so. Life might he have enjoy'd
"Perchance; and blameless sure to death had sunk.
"He whom this wretch, too mindful of the time
"His counterfeited madness was expos'd,
"Feign'd had betray'd the Greeks; and prov'd the crime
"By forg'd assistance: shewing forth the gold
"First bury'd by himself. Thus he destroys
"The strength of Greece, by exile or by death.
"Thus fights Ulysses; thus must he be fear'd
"Who, though old faithful Nestor he surpass'd
"In eloquence, not all would e'er avail,
"To prove deserting Nestor was no shame:
"Who press'd with age, and with a wounded horse
"Delay'd, Ulysses' aid besought: behind
"His coward comrade left him. Well, this deed
"Tydides can declare, by me not feign'd,
"Who oft him reprimanded by his name,
"And curs'd the flying of his trembling friend.
"Gods with just eyes all mortal actions view.
"Lo! he who aid would give not, aid requires!
"Who Nestor left, deserted was himself:
"Himself prescrib'd the treatment which he found.
"Loud call'd he to his friends. I come, I see,
"Pale trembling, where he lies, with dread to view
"Impending death. My mighty shield I fling;
"Beneath it shade him, and his coward breast
"(My smallest claim to glory) I protect.
"If still persisting, thou the strife wilt urge,
"Thither again return. Recal the foe;
"Thy wound; thy wonted terror; and lie hid

"Beneath my shield. 'Neath that with me contend.
"Lo! him I snatch'd from death, whose wounds refus'd
"Ev'n power to stand; retarded not by wounds,
"In agile flight sped on. Now Hector comes,
"Whom in the fight the deities attend.
"Where'er he swept, not thou Ulysses sole
"Wast struck with dread; the bravest of our host
"Shrunk, such the terror which then fill'd the field.
"When hand to hand engag'd, him prone I laid,
"Proud of his slaughter, on th' ensanguin'd plain,
"With a huge stone. I singly him oppos'd,
"All single challeng'd; all the Greeks to me
"Pray'd for the lot: nor vain your prayers were found.
"Enquire ye, what the fortune of the fight?
"I stood, by him unconquer'd, when all Troy
"Rush'd on the fleet of Greece, with fire, with sword,
"And aiding Jove: Where was Ulysses then?
"The eloquent Ulysses? I alone,
"A thousand ships, the hopes of your return,
"Defended with my breast: this crowd of ships
"Deserves those arms. Nay, if with truth to speak
"You grant, those arms more glory gain from me
"Than I from them; our honor is conjoin'd.
"Ajax the arms demand, not Ajax arms.
"Let Ithacus compare his Rhæsus slain;
"And slain unwarlike Dolon; and trepann'd
"Helenus, Priam's son; and Pallas' form.
"In open day nought done, and nought perform'd,
"Save Diomed' assisted. Grant for once,
"Such paltry service could the armour claim;
"Divide the prize, and lo! the largest share
"Tydides must demand. But why this prize
"Seeks Ithacus? who all his deeds performs
"In private; traversing unarm'd; the foe,
"While unsuspecting, conquering by deceit.
"This helmet's radiance from the glittering gold
"Darting, would shew his plots, and open lay
"The latent spy. But his Dulichian head,
"Cas'd in Achilles' casque, the weight would 'whelm,
"And for his languid arms, the Pelian spear
"Too weighty would be found. That shield engrav'd,
"With all earth's various scenes, but ill would grace
"His arm, for stealthy deeds alone design'd.
"Presumptuous fool! to seek a prize, which gain'd
"Would only mar thy power. By erring votes
"Of Grecians giv'n to thee, cause would it be
"The foe would strip thee; not thy prowess fear.
"And flight, in which, O trembler! erst alone

"Thou all surpass'd, slow would'st thou then pursue;
"Such ponderous armor dragging. Those, thy shield
"Which bears so rare the brunt of battle, shines
"Yet whole: a new successor mine demands,
"Which gash'd by weapons, shews a thousand rents.
"To end, what need of words? let actions shew
"Each one's deserts. Amid the foe be thrown
"The valiant warrior's arms. Thence bid us bring
"The prize;—who brings it, let him wear the spoil."

  So spake the Telamonian warrior; round
A murmur follow'd from the circling crowd.
Till up the chief of Ithaca arose;
His eyes (awhile cast down) rais'd from the earth;
The chiefs with anxious look'd-for sounds address'd:
Nor grace was wanting to persuasive words.
"O Grecians! had your prayers and mine been heard,
"Owner of what such cause of strife affords
"Were now not dubious: thou, Pelides, still
"These arms possessing, we possessing thee.
"But since unpitying fate, to you, to me,
"Denies him"—(here as weeping, o'er his eyes
His hand he draws)—"who with so just a right
"Can great Achilles now succeed, as he
"Who great Achilles brought the Greeks to join?
"Let it not aid his cause, that fool he seems,
"Or stupid is indeed; nor aught let harm
"The ingenuity I claim, to mine:
"Which, O, ye Argives! still has aided you.
"Let not my eloquence, if such I boast,
"And words, whose 'vantage often you have prov'd,
"Now for their author, move invidious thoughts:
"Nor what each claims his proper gift, refuse.
"Scarce can we call our ancestry, our race,
"Or deeds by them perform'd, merits our own:
"Yet since of grandsire Jove this Ajax boasts,
"I too, can boast him author of my line:
"Nor more degrees remov'd. My sire was nam'd
"Laërtes; his Arcesius; and from Jove
"Arcesius came direct: nor in this line,
"E'er any exil'd or condemn'd appear'd.
"Cyllenius too, his noble lineage adds
"Through my maternal stock. Each parent boasts
"A god-descended race. Yet claim I not
"The arms contested, merely that I spring
"Maternally more noble; nor them claim
"That from a brother's blood my sire is free:
"By merits solely you the cause adjudge.

"These only none to Ajax, that his sire,
"And Peleus brethren were, e'er grant. The prize
"Desert, and not propinquity of blood,
"Should gain. If kindred, then the hero's heir
"Demands it: Peleus still survives, his sire;
"And Pyrrhus is his son. Where Ajax' right?
"To Phthia, or to Scyros be it borne.
"Nor less is Teucer cousin than himself;
"Yet does he ask, or does he hope the arms?
"But since the obvious contest is by deeds
"Perform'd, though mine outnumber far what words
"Can easy compass; yet will I relate
"In order some:—

      "The Nereïd mother knew
"His future fate; her offspring's dress disguis'd;
"And all, ev'n Ajax, the fallacious robes
"Deceiv'd. With female wares I mingled arms,
"Which stir the martial soul. Nor had the youth
"Disrob'd him of his virgin dress, when grasp'd
"As in his hand the shield and lance he held,
"I cry'd'—O, goddess-born! reserv'd for thee
"Is Ilium's fate. The mighty Trojan walls
"Why to o'erthrow demur'st thou?—Him I seiz'd.
"Sent the brave youth, brave actions to atchieve:
"And all his actions as my own I claim.
"My spear then conquer'd Telephus in fight;
"And after heal'd the suppliant vanquish'd foe.
"Thebes low by me was laid. I, you must own,
"Lesbos, and Tenedos, and Scyros took;
"Chrysa, and Cylla, bright Apollo's towns.
"My arm Lyrnessus' walls shook, and laid low.
"But other deeds I well may pass: since I
"Gave to the host what dreadful Hector slew;
"By me renowned Hector fell. Those arms
"I claim, who gave those arms, which to the Greeks
"Achilles found. Living, those arms I gave;
"Him dead, those arms I gave, again demand.

  "The wrongs of one through every Grecian breast
"Spread wide; a thousand ships th' Eubœan port
"Of Aulis fill'd. The long-expected gales
"Or came not, or blew adverse to the fleet.
"The rigid oracle Atrides bade
"His guiltless daughter sacrifice to calm
"Ruthless Diana. Stern the sire deny'd,
"And rag'd against the gods: the sovereign all
"Lost in the father. I with soothing words

"The parent's bosom mollify'd, and turn'd
"To thoughts of public good. Still, I confess,
"(And such confession will the king excuse;)
"An arduous cause I pleaded, where my judge
"Was by affection warp'd. The people's weal,
"His brother, and the lofty rank he held
"Mov'd him at length; and glory with his blood
"He bought. Then to the mother was I sent,
"Where reasoning had no force, but subtle craft.
"There had you sent the son of Telamon,
"Still had jour sails the needful breezes lack'd.
"Sent was I also to the Ilian towers,
"A daring envoy. Troy's fam'd court I saw;
"Troy's court I enter'd, then with heroes fill'd.
"There undismay'd, I pleaded all that Greece
"Bade for their common cause; Paris accus'd;
"Helen demanded, and the stolen spoil;
"And Priam and Antenor both convinc'd.
"But Paris, Paris' brethren, and the crowd
"Who aided in the rape, their impious hands
"Could scarce withhold. (Thou, Menelaüs, know'st,
"Who then with me the dawning of the war
"Didst prove in danger.) Long the tale, to speak
"Of all my deeds have done, the public cause
"To aid; since first the lengthen'd war began:
"By counsel or by valor. Wag'd the first
"Rough skirmish, long our foes within their walls
"Protected lay; no scope for open war:
"But in the tenth year now we fight again.
"In all that period what hast thou, who know'st
"But fighting, done? Where was thy service then?
"I, if my deeds thou seek'st, the foe betray'd
"By subtilty; girt us with trenches round;
"Inspirited our soldiers; made them bear,
"With mind unmurmuring, all the tedious war;
"Taught where to find the means to gain supplies
"Of food and arms; wherever need me call'd,
"There always was I sent. Lo! when the king,
"From Jove's deceptive dream, gave word to quit
"Th' unfinish'd war, he might the deed defend
"Through him who bade. But Ajax disapproves
"The flight; insists Troy shall in ruins lie,
"Asserts our power may do it! No! our troops
"Embarking, he not stay'd. Why seiz'd he not
"His arms? Why somewhat to the wavering crowd
"Said not, to fix? no weighty task to him
"Who ne'er harangues, except on mighty themes.
"Why? but that Ajax fled himself! I saw,

"But blush'd to see thee, when thy back thou turn'dst
"Hasting, thy coward sails to hoist; I spoke
"Instant—O fellow soldiers! whither now?
"What voice insane now urges you to leave
"Already-captur'd Troy? What will you bear
"Homeward, a lengthen'd ten years' shame besides?—
"With words like these back from the flying fleet
"I brought them; eloquence had sorrow's aid.

  "Atrides call'd the council, all with dread
"Trembling were dumb; nor there dar'd Ajax gape:
"But there Thersites durst with galling words
"The king provoke; vengeance he met from me.
"I rose, our panic-stricken friends, once more
"Rous'd 'gainst the foe: I, by my words recall'd
"Departed valor. Hence, whoever boasts
"Since then of valiant deeds, those deeds are mine,
"Who back recall'd him, as he turn'd for flight.
"Last, tell me which of all the Greeks applauds,
"Or as a comrade seeks thee. All his acts
"With me Tydides shares, allows me praise:
"Ulysses still his confidential friend.
"Sure from such thousands of the Argive ranks
"By Diomed' selected, I may boast.
"Nor lot me bade to go, when void of fear,
"Through double danger of the foe and night,
"I went; and Phrygian Dolon slew, who dar'd
"On our adventure come; but slew him not
"Till made to utter all; the wiles betray
"Perfidious Troy intended. All I learnt;
"Nor ought for further search remain'd. Now I,
"The camp with fame sufficient might have gain'd;
"But not content, for Rhesus' tents I push;
"Him, and his guard surrounding, in his camp
"I slay. Victorious so, possess'd of all
"My hopes design'd, the car I mount, and proud
"A glad triumpher ride. Now me deny
"The arms of him, whose steeds the spy had hop'd
"Meed of his bold excursion. Ajax say
"More worthy. Why Sarpedon's Lycian troop
"Vanquish'd, should I with boastful tongue relate?
"I vanquish'd Ceranos, Iphitus' son;
"Alastor, Chromius, and Alcander stout;
"Halius, Noëmon, Prytanis, with crowds
"Slaughter'd beside. Thoön to hell I sent,
"Chersidamas, and Charops; and to fates
"Unpitying, Ennomus dispatch'd: with these
"Beneath yon' walls whole heaps of meaner rank

"This hand has slain. And, fellow soldiers, lo!
"My wounds are honorable all in place:
"Believe not empty words, yourselves behold."—
Then stript his robe, exclaiming—"Here the breast
"Still for your good employ'd. No drop of blood
"Has Ajax shed since first our host he join'd:
"In all these years, his body still remains
"Unwounced. Yet on this why should I dwell,
"If he must boast, that for the Argive fleet
"He fought alone 'gainst Jupiter and Troy?
"He fought, I grant it; no malignant spite
"Shall move detraction from his valiant deeds.
"But let him not the common rites of more
"Monopolize; let him to each allow
"The honor which they claim. Patroclus, fear'd
"In great Pelides' semblance, backward drove
"All Troy and Troy's protector from the ships,
"Then burning. Next his vanity would boast
"He only in the field of Mars durst strive
"With Hector; of the king, the chiefs, and me
"Forgetful; in the list the ninth alone,
"Solely by lot preferr'd. Yet, warrior brave,
"What was the issue of this daring fight?
"Hector unwounded left you. Mournful theme!
"With what deep sorrow I the time recal,
"When, bulwark of the Greeks, Achilles fell!
"Nor tears, vain lamentations, nor pale fear
"Me check d; the prostrate body from the ground
"I rais'd. Upon those shoulders—yes, I swear,
"These very shoulders, I Pelides bore,
"With all his arms. The arms I now require.
"Strength I must have to bear with such a load:
"As sure your votes will meet a grateful mind.
"Was it because the bright celestial gift
"Might clothe the limbs of one without a soul,
"Stupidly dull, that all her anxious care
"The green-hair'd mother on her son employ'd;
"Arms wrought with art so great? Knows he the least
"The shield's engravings? Ocean, or the land:
"The lofty sky; the planets; Pleiäds bright;
"Hyäds; the bear, ne'er plung'd beneath the main;
"Orion's glittering sword, or various towns?
"Arms he demands he cannot understand.
"But how asserts he I the toils of war
"Evaded; joining late the fighting host,
"Nor sees he scandalizes too the fame
"Of great Pelides? If indeed a crime
"Dissembling must be call'd,—dissembled both.

"If faulty all delay, the first I came.
"A tender wife me kept; a tender tie,
"A mother, kept Achilles. Our life's spring
"To them was given, the rest reserv'd for you.
"Nor should I fear, even were this crime, I share
"With such a man, of all defence deny'd.
"Yet his disguise Ulysses' cunning found:
"Ajax ne'er found Ulysses. Needs surprize
"To hear th' abusing of his booby tongue,
"When with like guilt he stigmatizes you?
"Shames most that I this Palamedes brought,
"Falsely accus'd your sentence to receive,
"Or that you doom'd him so accus'd to die?
"But Nauplius' son not ev'n defence could urge,
"So plain his crime appear'd; nor did you trust
"The accusation heard: obvious you saw
"The bribe for which you doom'd him. Nor of blame
"Deserve I ought, that Philoctetes stays
"In Vulcan's Lemnos. You the deed excuse:
"All to the deed assented. Yet my voice,
"Persuasive, will I not deny, I us'd;
"That spar'd from travel, and from war's fatigue,
"In rest he might his cruel pains assuage:
"He lik'd my words, and lives. My counsel here
"Not merely faithful (though our faith the whole
"Our promise can insure) but happy prov'd.
"His presence since the seers prophetic ask
"T' achieve the fall of Troy, dispatch not me;
"Ajax will better go, will better soothe
"With eloquence of tongue, a man who burns
"With raging choler, and with smarting pains:
"Or with some stratagem him thence allure.
"But Simoïs' stream shall sooner backward flow;
"Ida unwooded stand: Achaïa aid
"The Trojan power, than Ajax' stupid soul
"Shall help the Greeks, when first my anxious mind
"Striving to aid you, has been found to fail.
"O, stubborn Philoctetes! though enrag'd
"Against thy comrades, 'gainst the king, and me;
"Though thou may'st curse me, and my head devote
"Through endless days; though in thy grief thou ask'st
"To meet me, and to glut thee with my blood,
"Still will I try thee, and if fortune smiles,
"So will I gain thy arrows, as I gain'd
"The Trojan prophet, whom I captive made;
"As I the oracles of heaven laid ope;
"And all the fate of Troy: as from its room
"Close-hidden, I the form of Pallas brought,

"The charm of Troy, through ranks of hostile foes.
"Mates Ajax here with me? Fate had deny'd
"Of Troy the capture till that prize obtain'd.
"Where then the mighty Ajax? Where the boasts
"Of this brave hero? Why this risk evade?
"Why dar'd Ulysses through the watchful guards
"Steal 'mid the darkling night? and find his way,
"Not merely past the Trojan walls, but high
"Through raging swords their loftiest turrets scale;
"Bear off the goddess from her sacred fane,
"And with the prize again repass the foe?
"This deed not done, Ajax had bore in vain
"On his huge arm the sevenfold oxen hide.
"From that night's deeds I Ilium's conquest share.
"Then Troy I conquer'd, when the fact was done,
"Which made Troy vincible. Cease thou to mark
"With looks and mutterings Diomed' my friend;
"His share in all was glorious. Nor wast thou
"Single, when with thy buckler thou didst guard
"The general fleet; crowds aided, I was one.
"He, but re knows too well that less esteem
"Valor demands than wisdom; that the prize,
"A mere unconquer'd arm not justly claims,
"Had also sought: thy milder namesake too;
"Or fierce Eurypilus; or Thoas, son
"Of bold Andræmon. Equal right to hope,
"Idomeneus, Meriones, might boast,
"Each Cretan born; and who the sovereign king
"His brother claims; but all their valorous breasts
"(Nor does their martial prowess stoop to thine)
"Yield to my wisdom. In the fight thy arm
"Is mighty; prudence boast I, which that arm
"Directs. To thee a force immense is given,
"Without a brain; foresight is given to me.
"Well, thou canst wage the war; the time that war
"To wage, Atrides oft with me resolves.
"Thou aidest with thy body, I with mind:
"And as the guider of the ship transcends
"Him who but plies the oar: as soars above
"The soldier, he who leads him, so must I
"Thee far surpass; for far the mental powers
"In me surpass the merits of my arm:
"In mind my vigor lies. Ye nobles, speak;
"Give to your watchful guardian this reward,
"For the long annual care with anxious mind
"He gave you. This reward at length bestow,
"To his deserts but due: his labor done.
"Th' obstructing destinies by me remov'd,

"High Troy by me is captur'd; since by me
"The means high Troy to overthrow are given.
"Now beg I by our hopes conjoin'd; the walls
"Of Troy already tottering; by the gods
"Gain'd from the foe so lately; by what more
"Through wisdom may be done, if aught remains;
"Or aught of boldness, which through peril sought,
"Wanting, you still may deem to fill Troy's fate.
"If mindful of my merits you would rest,
"The arms award to this, if not to me:"
And pointed to Minerva's fateful form.

Mov'd were the band of nobles. Plainly shewn
What eloquence could do:—persuasion gain'd
The valiant warrior's arms. Then he who stood
'Gainst steel, and fire, and the whole force of Jove,
So oft, his own vexation now o'ercame:
Grief conquer'd his unconquerable soul.
He seiz'd his sword,—"And surely this"—he cry'd—
"Still is my own! or claims Ulysses this?
"Against myself this steel must now be us'd:
"This stain'd so oft with Phrygian blood, be stain'd
"With his who owns it; lest another hand
"Than Ajax' own should Ajax overcome."—
No more; but where his breast unguarded lay,
Pervious at length to wounds, his deadly blade
He plung'd, nor could his hand the blade withdraw;
The gushing blood expell'd it. Straight there sprung
Through the green turf, form'd by the blood-soak'd earth,
A purple flower, like that which sprung before
From Hyäcinthus' wound. Amid the leaves
Of each the self-same letters are inscrib'd;
The boy's complainings, and the hero's name.

Victorious Ithacus his sails unfurls,
To seek the land Hypsipylé once rul'd,
And Thoäs fam'd. An isle of old disgrac'd
By slaughter of its males, to bring the darts,
The weapons of Tyrinthius. These obtain'd
To Greece, and with their owner brought, at length
The furious war was finish'd. Priam falls
With Troy; and Priam's more unhappy spouse,
To crown her losses, loses human shape;
With new-heard barkings shaking foreign climes.
Where the long Hellespont's contracted bounds
Are seen, Troy blaz'd: nor yet the fires were quench'd.
The scanty drops of blood Jove's altar soak'd,
Which flow'd from aged Priam. By her locks

Dragg'd on, Apollo's priestess vainly stretch'd
To lofty heaven her arms. The victor Greeks
Tear off the Trojan mothers as they clasp
Their country's imag'd gods; and as they cling
To flaming temples—an invidious prey.
Astyänax is from those turrets flung,
Whence erst he wont to view his sire, whose arm
Him guarding, and his ancestorial realm
In fight, his mother shew'd. And Boreas now
Departure urg'd. Swol'n by a favoring breeze
The rattling canvas warn'd the sailor crew.
"O, Troy! farewel!"—The Trojan matrons cry—
"Hence are we borne."—They kiss their natal soil;
And leave the smoking ruins of their domes.
Last—mournful object! Hecuba, descry'd
Amid her children's graves, the bark ascends.
Ulysses' hand her dragg'd, as close she grasp'd
Their tombs, and kiss'd their bones which still remain'd.
Yet snatch'd she hastily, and bore away
Of Hector's ashes some, and in her breast
Hugg'd them: and on the top of Hector's tomb
Left her grey hairs; her hairs, and flowing tears.
Oblation fruitless to his last remains.

   Oppos'd to Phrygia, where Troy once was seen,
A country stands, where live Bistonia's race:
Where Polymnestor, wealthy monarch, rul'd,
To whom, O. Polydore! thy cautious sire
Thee sent; from Iliüm's battles far remov'd,
For safe protection. Wisdom sway'd the king;
Save that he sent him store of treasure too,
Reward of wickedness; and tempting much
His greedy soul. Soon as Troy's fortune sank,
Impious the Thracian monarch plung'd his sword
In his young charge's throat: as if his crime
And body from his sight at once 'twere given
To move, he flung him in the dashing main.

   Now on the Thracian coast, Atrides moor'd
His fleet, till placid were the waves again,
And favoring more, the winds. Achilles here,
Out from the earth, by sudden rupture rent,
Appear'd in 'semblance of his living form:
Threatening his brow appear'd, as when so fierce
He Agamemnon with rebellious sword
Sought to assail.—"Depart ye then, O, Greeks!"
He cry'd—"of me unmindful? Is the fame
"Of all my valiant acts with me interr'd?

"Treat me not thus. That honors due my tomb
"May want not, let Polyxena be given
"In sacrifice to soothe Achilles' ghost."
He said; his fellows with the ruthless shade
Complying, from the mother's bosom tore
Her whom she sole had left to cherish. Brave
Than female more, the hapless maid was led
To the dire tomb in sacrificial pomp.
She, of her state still mindful, when before
The cruel altar brought; when all prepar'd
The savage-urg'd oblation of herself
She saw; and Neoptolemus beheld
There stand, the steel there grasping; on his face
Her eyes firm-fixing, spoke.—"My noble blood
"This instant spill. Delay not—plunge thy blade
"Or in my throat, or bosom;"—and her throat
And bosom, as she spoke she bar'd—"for ne'er
"Polyxena, a slavish life had borne.
"Yet grateful is this victim to no god!
"My only wish, that from my mother dear
"May be my death conceal'd: my mother clogs
"My final passage; damps the joys of death.
"Yet should she wail my death not, but my life.
"But distant stand ye all, that to the shades
"Inviolate I sink; if what I ask
"Be just, let every hand of man avoid
"A virgin's touch. Whoe'er your steel prepares
"To move propitiatory with my blood,
"A victim quite untainted best must please.
"And should the final accents that I speak,
"(King Priam's daughter, not a captive sues)
"My corse unransom'd to my mother give.
"Let her not buy the sad sepulchral rites
"With gold, but tears. Yet time has been, with gold
"I might have been redeem'd."—The princess ceas'd,
And save her own no cheek unwet was seen.
And ev'n the priest reluctant, and in tears,
Op'd by a sudden plunge the offer'd breast.
She, to earth sinking, 'neath her tottering limbs,
Wore to the last a face unmov'd; ev'n then
Her final care was in her fall to veil
Limbs that a veil demanded, as she sank;
And decent pride of modesty preserve.

The Trojan dames receive her, and recount
The woes of Priam's house, the streams of blood
That single stock has spent. Thee too, O, maid!
They weep; and thee, a royal spouse so late,

And royal parent stil'd; pride of the realm
Of glorious Asia; now a mournful lot
Amid the spoil; whom Ithacus would scorn
To own, great Hector hadst thou not brought forth:
The name of Hector scarce a master finds,
To claim h s mother. She, the lifeless trunk
Embracing, which had held a soul so brave,
Tears pour'd; tears often had she pour'd before,
For country, husband, children—now for her
Those tears gush'd in the wound; lips press'd to lips;
And beat that breast which oft with grievous blows
Was punish'd. Sweeping 'mid the clotted blood
Her silver'c tresses; all these plaints, and more
She utter'd, as she still her bosom rent.

  "My child thy mother's last afflicting grief
"(For who is spar'd me?) low, my child, thou ly'st;
"And in thy wound, I all my wounds behold.
"Yes, lest a single remnant of my race
"Unslaughter'd should expire, thou too must bleed.
"A female, thee, safe from the sword I thought:
"A female, thee the sword has stretch'd in death.
"The same Achilles, ruiner of Troy,
"Bereaver of my offspring, all destroy'd,—
"Yes, all thy brethren, he, now murders thee!
"Yet when by Paris' and Apollo's darts
"He fell,—now, surely,—said I,—now no more
"Pelides need be dreaded! Yet ev'n now,
"Dreadful to me he proves. Inurned, rage
"His ashes 'gainst our hapless race; we feel
"Ev'n in his grave the anger of this foe.
"I fruitful only for Pelides prov'd.
"Low lies croud Iliüm, and the public woe,
"The heavy ruin ends: if ended yet:
"For Troy to me still stands; my sufferings still
"Roll endless on. I, late in power so high,
"Great in my children, in my husband great,
"Am now dragg'd forth in poverty; exil'd
"From all my children's tombs; a gift to please
"Penelopé; who, while my daily task
"She gives to Ithaca's proud dames, will taunt,
"And cry;—of Hector, the fam'd mother see!
"Lo! Priar's spouse!—And thou who sole wast spar'd
"To soothe maternal pangs, so many lost,
"Now bleed'st, atonement to an hostile shade:
"And funeral victims has my womb produc'd
"T' appease a foe. Why holds this stubborn heart?
"Why still delay I? What to me avails

"This loath'd, this long-protracted life? Why spin,
"O, cruel deities! the lengthen'd thread
"Of an old wretch, save that she yet may see
"More deaths? Who e'er could Priam happy deem,
"Iliüm o'erthrown? Yet happy was his death,
"Thy sacrifice, my daughter! not to see;
"At once of life and realm bereft. Yet sure
"O, royal maid! funereal rites await
"Thy last remains; thy corse will be inhum'd
"In ancestorial sepulchres. Ah, no!
"Such fortune smiles not on our house; the tears
"A mother can bestow, are all thy gifts;
"Sprinkled with foreign dust. All have I lost.
"Of the whole stock I could as parent boast,
"To tempt me now still longer to sustain
"This life, my Polydore alone is left;
"Once least of all my manly sons, erst given
"To Thracia's monarch's care, upon these shores.
"But why delay to cleanse that ghastly wound
"With water, and that face, with spouting blood
"Besmear'd."—She ceas'd, and bent her tottering steps,
With torn and scatter'd locks down to the shore.
And as the hapless wretch—"O, Trojans!"—cry'd,
"An urn supply to draw the liquid waves;"—
The corse of Polydore, flung on the beach
She saw, pierc'd deep with wounds of Thracian steel.
Loud shriek'd the Trojan matrons; she by grief
Dumb-stricken stood. Affliction keen suppress'd
Her rising moans, and ready-springing tears:
Stupid, and like a rigid stone she stood.
Now on the earth her eyes are fixt; and now
To heaven her furious countenance she lifts:
Now dwells she on his face, now on the wounds
Her son receiv'd, and on the wounds the most:
And now her bosom with collected rage
Furiously burning, all on vengeance fierce
Her soul is bent, as still in power a queen.
As storms a lioness robb'd of her cub,
The track pursuing of her flying foe,
Whom yet she sees not: rage and grief were mixt
Just so in Hecuba; of her old years
Regardless, mindful of her ire alone.
She Polymnestor seeks, of the dire deed
The perpetrator, and his ear demands—
That more of gold, intended for her boy,
Her wish was to disclose. The Thracian king
Heard credulous; lur'd by his wonted love
Of gain, with her withdrew, and wily thus;

With coaxing words;—"quick, Hecuba!"—exclaim'd,
"Give for thy son the treasure. By the gods!
"I swear, all shall be his; what more thou giv'st,
"And what thou gav'st before."—Him, speaking so,
And falsely swearing, savagely she view'd,
And her fierce bosom swell'd with double rage.
Then instant on him, by the captive dames
Fast held, she flies; in his perfidious face
Digs deep; her fingers (rage all strength supply'd)
Tear from their orbs his eyes; bury'd her hands,
Streaming with blood, where once the eyes had been;
Widening the wounds, for eyes no more remain'd.

   Fir'd at their monarch's fate the Thracian crowd
With stones and darts t'attack the queen began.
The queen with harsher voice, as they pursue,
Bites at th' assailing stones, and, trying words,
Barkings her jaws produce. The place remains
Nam'd from the change. She, of her ancient woes
Long mindful, grieving still, Sithonia's fields
With howlings fill'd. Her fate with pity mov'd
Her fellow Trojans; and the hostile Greeks;
Nay, all the gods above; and all deny,
(Ev'n she, the sister-wife of mighty Jove)
That Hecuba so harsh a lot deserv'd.

   Nor leisure now Aurora had to mourn
(Though strong their cause she favor'd) the sad fall,
And mournful fate of Hecuba, and Troy.
A nearer case, a more domestic woe,
The loss of Memnon, wrung the goddess' breast:
Whom on the Phrygian plains the mother saw
Beneath the weapon of Achilles sink.
She saw—that color which the blushing morn
Displays, grew pale, and heaven with clouds was hid.
Still could the parent not support the sight,
Plac'd on the funeral pyre his limbs, but straight
With locks dishevell'd, not disdain'd to sue
Prostrate before the knees of mighty Jove.
These words her tears assisting.—"Meanest I,
"Of those the golden heaven supports; to me
"The fewest temples through earth's space are rais'd:
"Yet still a goddess sues. Not to demand
"Temples, nor festal days, nor altars warm'd
"With blazing fires; yet if you but behold
"What I, a female, for you all atchieve,
"Bounding night's confines with new-springing light,
"Such boons you might consider but my due.

"But these are not my care. Aurora's mind
"Not now e'en honors merited demands.
"I come, my Memnon lost, who bravely fought,
"But vainly, in his uncle Priam's cause:
"And in his prime of youth (so will'd your fates)
"Fell by the stout Achilles. Lord supreme!
"Of all the deities, grant, I beseech
"To him some honor, solace of his death;
"Allay the smarting of a mother's wounds."

Jove nodded, round the lofty funeral pile
Of Memnon, rose th' aspiring flames; black clouds
Of smoke the day obscur'd. So streams exhale
The rising mists which Phœbus' rays conceal.
Mount the black ashes, and conglob'd in one
They thicken in a body, and a shape
That body takes, and heat and light receives
From the bright flames. Its lightness gave it wings:
Much like a bird at first, and soon indeed
A bird, its pinions sounded. And a crowd
Of sister birds, their pinions sounded too;
Their origin the same. Thrice they surround
The pile, and thrice with noisy clang the air
Resounds; the fourth time all the troop divide:
Then two and two, they furious wage the war
On either side; fierce with their crooked claws
And beaks, they pounce their adversary's breast,
And tire his wings. Each kindred body falls
An offering to the ashes of the dead,
And prove their offspring from a valiant man.
These birds of sudden origin receive
Their name, Memnonides, from him whose limbs
Produc'd them. Oft as Sol through all his signs
Has run, the battle they renew again,
To perish at their parent-warrior's tomb.
Thus, while all others Dymas' daughter weep
In howling shape, Aurora still on griefs
Her own sad brooding, her maternal tears
Sprinkles in dew o'er all th' extent of earth.

Yet fate doom'd not with Iliüm's towers the fall
Of Iliüm's hopes. The Cythereän prince
Bore off his gods; and on his shoulders bore
A no less sacred, venerable load,
His sire. Of all his riches these preferr'd.
The pious hero, with his youthful son
Ascanius, from Antandros, o'er the main
Borne in the flying fleet, leaves far the shore

Of savage Thrace, still moisten'd with the blood
Of Polydore, and enters Phœbus' port;
Aided by currents, and by gentle gales,
With all his social crew. Anius receives
The exile, in his temple,—in his dome;
Where o'er the land he monarch rul'd; and where,
As Phœbus' priest, he tended due his rites:
The city, and the votive temples shew'd,
And shew'd two trees, once by Latona grasp'd
In bearing throes. The incense in the flames
Distributed, wine o'er the incense thrown,
The entrails of the offer'd bulls consum'd
As wont; the regal roof approach they all;
And high on tapestry reclin'd, partake
Of Ceres' gift, and Bacchus' flowing boon.
Then good Anchises, thus—"O chosen priest
"Of Phœbus! was I then deceiv'd? methought,
"As far as memory aids me to recal,
"When first mine eyes these lofty walls beheld,
"That twice two daughters, and a son were thine."
Old Anius shook his head, begirt around
With snowy fillets, as in grief, he said:—
"No, mighty hero! not deceiv'd art thou,
"Me hast thou seen of five the parent; now
"Thou well-nigh childless see'st me: (such to man
"The varying change of sublunary things)
"For, ah! what can an absent son bestow
"To aid me, who, in Andros' isle now dwells,
"Where for his sire the realm and state he holds?
"Delius on him prophetic art bestow'd;
"And Bacchus, to my female offspring, gave
"A boon beyond all credit, and their hopes.
"For all whate'er, which felt my daughters' touch
"To corn, and wine, and olives, was transformed:
"A mighty treasure in themselves they held.
"But Agamemnon, Troy's destroyer learn'd
"This gift (think not but that your overthrow
"In some respect we shar'd,) by ruthless force,
"Tore them unwilling from their parent's arms;
"And stern commanded that the heavenly gift
"Should feed the Grecian fleet. Each as she can
"Escapes. Eubœä two attain, and two
"Fraternal Andros seek. The troops pursue
"And threaten warfare, if withheld the maids.
"Fraternal love was vanquish'd in his breast
"By fear, (that thou this terror mayst excuse,
"Reflect, Æneäs was not there, nor there
"Was Hector, Andros to defend, whose arms

"To the tenth year made Iliüm stand.) And now
"Chains were prepar'd their captive arms to bind.
"While yet unchain'd, those arms to heaven they rais'd,
"O father Bacchus!—crying—grant thy aid.—
"And aid the author of the gift bestow'd:
"If them to lose by an unheard-of mode
"Be aid bestowing. Then could I not know,
"Nor now relate the order of the change
"Which lost their shapes; the summit of my grief
"I know; with plumage were they cloth'd; transform'd
"To snowy doves, thy spouse's favor'd bird."

  With these, and tales like these, the feast was clos'd:
The board remov'd, all sought repose. With day
Arising, all Apollo's shrine attend;
Who bids that they their ancient mother seek,
And kindred shores. The king attends them, gives
His presents as they go. Anchises holds
A sceptre, while a quiver and a robe
Ascanius boasts; Æneäs holds a cup,
Erst from Bœötia's shores to Anius sent,
By Theban Therses. Therses sent the gift;
Sicilian Alcon form'd it, and engrav'd
A copious tale around. A town was there,
And seven wide gates appear'd: for name were these,
What town it was displaying. All without
Its walls were funeral trains, and tombs beheld;
And fires; and piles; and matrons, whose bare breasts,
And locks dishevell'd, shew'd their mournful woe.
Weeping the nymphs appear'd, and seem'd to wail
Their arid streams; the leafless trees were hard;
The goats were browsing on the naked rocks:
And, lo! amid the Theban town was seen
Orion's daughters: this her naked throat
Offering, with more than female courage; that
On the sharp weapon's point forth leaning, dy'd,
To save the people: round the town are borne
Their pompous funerals, they in splendor burn.
Then, lest the race should perish, spring two youths
From out their virgin ashes; which by fame
Are call'd Coronæ, and the pomp attend,
When their maternal ashes are interr'd.

  Thus far the images on ancient brass
Were grav'n; the bordering summit of the cup
In gold acanthus rough appear'd. Nor gave
The Trojans gifts less worthy than they took.
To hold his incense, they a vase present

The royal priest; a goblet, and a crown,
Shining with gold, and bright with sparkling gems.

   Thence, mindful that the Trojan race first sprung
From Teucer's blood, tow'rd Crete their course they bend:
But long Jove s native clime they could not bear.
The hundred-city'd isle now left behind,
Ausonia's port they hope to gain. Rough swell
The wintry storms, and toss them on the main;
And in the port of faithless Strophades
Receiv'd, the wing'd Aëllo scares them far.
Now had they sail'd beyond Dulichium's bay;
Samos; and Ithaca, Neritus' soil;
The realms Ulysses, so perfidious, sway'd:
And saw Ambracia, for the strife of gods
Renown'd, and stone to which the judge was chang'd;
Now as Apollo's Actium far more fam'd:
And saw Dodona's land with vocal groves;
And deep Chaonia's bay, where vain-urg'd flames
Molossus' sons, on new-sprung pinions 'scap'd.
Phæäcia's neighbouring country, planted thick
With grateful apples, now they reach; from thence
Epirus and Buthrotus, by the seer
Of Iliüm govern'd, image true of Troy.
Thence of the future certain, full of faith,
In all that Helenus of fate them told,
Sicilia's isle they enter, which extends
Midst of the waves its promontories three.
Pachymos, tow'rd the showery south is plac'd;
And Zephyr soft on Lilybæum blows:
But 'gainst the Arctic bear that shuns the sea,
And Boreas' rugged storms, Pelorus looks.
By this the Trojans steer; urg'd by their oars,
And favoring tide, by night on Zanclé's beach
The fleet is moor'd. Here Scylla on the right;
Charybdis, restless, on the left alarms.
This sucks the destin'd ships beneath the waves,
And whirls them up again: fierce dogs surround
The other's sable belly, while she bears
A virgin's face; and, if what poets tell
Be feign'd not all, she had a virgin been.

   Her many wooers sought; these all repuls'd,
She join'd the ocean nymphs; by ocean's nymphs
Much favor'd was the maid; and told the loves
Of all the baffled youths. Her, while she gave
Her locks to comb, thus Galatea fair,
Bespoke, but first suppress'd a rising sigh.

"'Tis true, O maid! a gentle race thee seeks,
"Whom safely, as thou dost, thou may'st deny:
"But I, whose sire is Nereus; who was born
"Of blue-hair'd Doris; who am potent too
"In crowds of sisters, refuge only found
"From the fierce Cyclops' love, in my own waves."
Tears chok'd her utterance here; which when the maid
Had wip'd with marble fingers, and had sooth'd
The goddess.—"Dearest Galatea! speak;
"Nor from thy friend this cause of grief conceal:
"Faithful am I to thee." The goddess yields,
And to Cratæis' daughter, thus replies.

   "From Faunus and the nymph Symethis sprung
"Acis, his sire's delight, his mother's pride;
"But far to me more dear. For me the youth,
"And me alone, lov'd warmly; twice eight years
"Had o'er him pass'd; when on his tender cheek
"A doubtful down appear'd. Him I desir'd,
"As ceaseless as the Cyclops sought for me.
"Nor should you ask, if in my bosom dwelt
"For him most hate, or most for Acis love,
"Could I inform you: equal both in force.
"O, gentle Venus! with what mighty power
"Thou sway'st; lo! he, the merciless, the dread
"Of his own woods; whom hapless guest ne'er saw
"With safety; spurner of the power of Jove,
"And all the host of heaven, what love is, feels!
"Seiz'd with desire of me he flames, forgets
"His flocks, and caverns. All thy anxious care
"Thy beauty, Polyphemus! to improve,
"And all thy anxious care is now to please.
"And now with rakes thou comb'st thy rugged hair;
"Now with a scythe thou mow'st thy bushy beard:
"Thy features to behold in the clear brook,
"And calm their fire employs thee. All his love
"Of slaughter; all his fierceness; all his thirst
"Cruel of blood, him leaves; and on the coast,
"Ships safely moor, and safe again depart.
"Meantime at Etna Telemus arriv'd,
"Of Eurymus the son, whom never bird
"Deceiv'd; he to dread Polyphemus came,
"And spoke:—Thee, of the single light thou bear'st
"Mid front, Ulysses will deprive.—Loud laugh'd
"The monster, saying;—Stupidest of seers,
"How much thou err'st!—already is it gone.—
"So spurns the truth the prophet told in vain.
"Then moving on along the shore, he sinks

"The sand with heavy steps, or tir'd returns
"To his dark caves. Far stretching in the main
"A wedge-like promontory rears its ridge
"Aloft; on either side the surging waves
"Foam on it. To its loftiest height ascends
"The Cyclops fierce; his station in the midst
"Assumes; his woolly flocks his steps pursue
"Unshepherded. He when the pine immense,
"Which serv'd him for a staff, though fit to serve
"For sailyard, low beneath his feet had thrown;
"And grasp'd the pipe, an hundred 'pacted reeds
"Compos'd; the pastoral whistling all around
"The hills confess'd, and all the waters nigh.
"I, hid beneath a rock, my head reclin'd
"On my dear Acis' bosom, heard these words—,
"And still the words are noted in my breast.—

   "O, Galatea! brighter than the leaves
"Of snow-white lilies; fresher than the meads;
"More lofty far than towering alder trees;
"Than chrystal clearer; than the wanton kid
"More gay; than shells, by ocean's constant waves
"Smooth polish'd, smoother; dearer than the shade
"In summer's heat; than winter's sun more dear;
"More than the apple bright; and fairer far
"Than lofty planetrees; clearer than the frost;
"More beauteous than the ripen'd grape; more soft
"Than the swan's plumage; or the new-prest milk:
"And, but thou fly'st, more than the garden fine
"With water'd streamlets. Yet the same art thou,
"Wild Galatea, than the untam'd steer
"More fierce; more stubborn than the ancient oak;
"Than water more deceitful; slippery more
"Than bending willows, or the greenest vines;
"More stubborn than these rocks; than seas more rough;
"Than the prais'd peacock prouder; sharper far
"Than fire; and piercing more than thistles keen.
"More savage than a nursing bear; more deaf
"Than raging billows; than the trodden snake
"More pitiless: and, what I more than all
"Would wish thou wast not, fleeter than the deer,
"Chas'd by shrill hunters; fleeter than wing'd air,
"Or winds. If well thou knew'st me, much thou'dst grieve
"That e'er thou fled'st; thou'dst blame thy dull delay,
"And sue and labor to retain my love.
"Caverns I have, scoop'd in the living rock
"Beneath the mountain's side, where never sun
"In mid-day heat, nor winter's cold can come.

"My apples bend the branches; grapes are mine
"On the long vine-trees clustering; some like gold;
"Some of a purple teint; and these and those
"Will I preserve for thee. Thy own fair hands
"Shall gather strawberries soft, beneath the shade;
"Autumnal cornels; and the purple plumb,
"Dark with its juice, and that still nobler kind
"Like new-made wax in hue. Nor shalt thou lack
"The chesnut; nor the red arbutus' fruit:
"Be but my spouse. All trees shall thee supply.
"Mine are these flocks, and thousands more besides
"Which roam the vallies; thousands like the woods;
"And thousands shelter in the shady caves:
"Nor could I, should'st thou ask, their numbers tell.
"Poor he who counts his store. Believe not me
"When these I praise; before thine eyes behold
"How scarce their legs the swelling udder bear.
"Mine are the tender lambs, in the warm fold
"Secure; and mine are kids of equal age
"In folds apart. The whitest milk have I;
"But still for drink shall serve, and thicken'd, part
"Shall harden into cheese. Nor wilt thou find
"But cheap delights, and common vulgar gifts:
"For deer, and hares, and goats, thou shalt possess;
"Pigeons in pairs, and nests from mountains gain'd.
"Upon the hills, a shaggy bear's twin cubs
"I found; so like, no difference could be seen,
"With thee to play I found them: these, I said,
"These will I force my mistress to obey.
"O Galatea! raise thy lovely head
"Above the azure deep; come! only come;
"Nor scorn my gifts. Right well myself I know:
"I view'd me lately in the liquid stream;
"And much my image satisfy'd my view.
"Behold, how vast my bulk! Jove, in his heaven,
"(For of some Jove ye oft are wont to tell
"Who rules there) towers not in a mightier size.
"Thick bushy locks o'er my stern forehead hang,
"And like a forest down my shoulders spread.
"Nor deem my body, with hard bristles rough,
"Unseemly; most unsightly is the tree,
"Without a leaf; unsightly is the steed,
"Save on his neck the flowing mane is spread:
"Plumes clothe the feather'd race; and their own wool
"Becomes the sheep; so beards become mankind,
"And bushy bristles, o'er their limbs bespread.
"True in my forehead but one light is plac'd;
"But huge that light, and like a mighty shield

"In size. Yet does not Sol from heaven's high round
"All view? and Sol possesses lights no more.
"Remember too, my father o'er your realm
"Rules sovereign; I in him a sire-in-law
"Would give thee. Only pity me, I pray,
"And hear my suppliant vows. To thee alone
"I bend: and while I scorn your mighty Jove,
"His heaven, and piercing thunder, thee, O nymph!
"I fear: then fiercest lightnings dreading more
"Thy anger. Far more patient should I rest
"With this contempt, all didst thou thus contemn.
"But how, the Cyclops first repuls'd, dar'st thou
"This Acis love? this Acis dare prefer
"To my embraces? Yet may he himself
"Delight; nay let him Galatea please,
"If so it must be, though what most I'd spurn:
"Let but the scope be given, soon should he prove
"My strength is equal to my mighty bulk.
"Living his entrails would I tear, and spread
"His mang ed members o'er the fields, and o'er
"Thy waters: let him mingle with thee so.
"For oh! I burn; more fierce my injur'd love
"Now rages: in ray breast I seem to bear
"All Etna and its fires. But all my pains
"Can nought, O Galatea! thee affect.—

    "Thus with vain 'plainings (for the whole I saw)
"He rises, raging like a furious bull
"Robb'd of his heifer; paces restless round,
"And bourds along the forests and the coasts.
"When me and Acis, heedless of such fate,
"And unsuspecting, he beheld, and roar'd:—
"I see ye! but the period of your love
"Will I accomplish.—Loud his threats were heard,
"As all the Cyclops' power of voice could raise.
"All Etna trembled at the sound. In fright
"I plung'd for safety in the neighbouring waves;
"While fair Symethis' son for flight prepar'd;
"And—help me, Galatea!—he exclaim'd—
"Help me, O help! and ye, my parents, aid;
"And, perishing, receive me in your realm.—
"Close at his heels the Cyclops comes, and hurls
"A mighty fragment from a mountain rent;
"A corner only of the mighty rock
"Him reach'd: that corner Acis all o'erwhelm'd.
"But I, what fate alone would grant, perform'd,
"That Acis still his ancestorial race
"Should join: his purple gore flow'd from the rock;

"And soon the redness pal'd; it seem'd a stream
"Disturb'd by drenching showers; and soon this stream
"Was clear'd to limpid purity. The rock
"Gap'd wide, and living reeds sprung up erect,
"On either brink. Loud roars the pressing flood
"In the rock's hollow womb, and (wond'rous sight!)
"A youth, his new-form'd horns with reeds begirt,
"Sudden appear'd, 'mid waist above the waves;
"Who but in stature larger, and his skin
"Of azure teint, might Acis well be deem'd.
"Acis indeed it was, Acis transform'd
"To a clear stream which still his name retains."

  Here Galatea ceas'd, the listening choir
Dividing, all depart. The Nereïd train
Swim o'er the placid waves. Scylla returns;
Fearful to venture 'mid the boundless main,
And vestless roams along the soaking sand;
Or weary'd; finding some sequester'd pool,
Cools in the shelter'd waters her fair limbs.
Lo! Glaucus, lately of the mighty deep
An 'habitant receiv'd, his shape transform'd
Upon Bœötia's shores, cleaves through the waves;
And feels desire as he the nymph beholds.
All he can urge to stay her flight he tries;
Yet still she flies him, swifter from her fear.
She gains a mountain's summit, which the shore
O'erhung. High to the main the lofty ridge
An undivided sbrubless top presents,
Down shelving to the sea. In safety here
She stood; and, dubious monster he, or god,
Admir'd his color, and the locks which spread
Adown his shoulders, and his back below:
And that a wreathing fish's form should end
His figure from his groin. He saw her gaze;
And on a neighbouring rock his elbow lean'd,
As thus he spoke.—"No monstrous thing am I,
"Fair virgin! nor a savage of the sea;
"A watery god I am; nor on the main
"Has Proteus; Triton; or Palæmon, son
"Of Athamas, more power. Yet time has been
"When I was mortal, yet even then attach'd
"To the deep water, on the ocean I,
"Still joy'd to labor. Now the following shoal
"Of fishes in my net I dragg'd; and now,
"Plac'd on a rock, I with my flexile rod
"Guided the line. Bordering a verdant mead
"A bank there lies, the waves its circuit bound

"In part; in part the virid grass surrounds;
"A mead which ne'er the horned herd had cropp'd:
"Where ne'er the placid flock, nor hairy goats
"Had brows'd; nor bees industrious cull'd the flowers
"For sweets: no genial chaplets there were pluck'd
"To grace the head; nor had the mower's arm
"E'er spoil'd the crop. The first of mortals, I
"On the turf rested. As my nets I dry'd;
"And as my captur'd scaly prey to count,
"Upon the grass I spread,—whatever the net
"Escape prevented, and the hook had snar'd
"Through their own folly. (Like a fiction sounds
"The fact, but what avails to me to feign?)
"Soon as the grass they touch, my captiv'd prey
"Begin to move, and on their sides to turn;
"And ply their fins on earth as in the main.
"Then, while with wonder struck I pause, all fly
"The shore in heaps, and their new master quit,
"Their native waves regaining. I, surpriz'd,
"Long doubtful stand to guess the wond'rous cause.
"Whether some god, or but the grasses' juice
"Accomplish'd this. What herb—at last, I said—
"Can power like this possess?—and with my hand
"Pluck'd up, and with my teeth the herbage chew'd.
"Scarce had my throat th' untasted juice first try'd,
"When all my entrails sudden tremblings shook,
"And with a love of something yet unknown
"My breast was mov'd; nor could I longer keep
"My place.—O earth! where I shall ne'er return—
"Farewel! I cry'd,—and plung'd below the waves.
"Worthy the ocean deities me deem'd
"To join their social troop, and anxious pray'd
"To Tethys, and old Ocean, Tethys' spouse,
"To purge whate'er of mortal I retain'd.
"By them lustrated, and the potent song
"Nine times repeated, earthly taints to cleanse,
"They bade me 'neath an hundred gushing streams
"To place my bosom. No delay I seek;
"The floods from numerous fountains pour'd, the main
"O'erwhelm'd my head. Thus far what deeds were done
"My memory helps me to relate; thus far
"Alone can I remember; all the rest
"Dark to my memory seems. My sense restor'd,
"I found my body chang'd in every part;
"Nor was my mind the same. Then first I saw
"This beard of dingy green, and these long locks
"Which through the seas I sweep; these shoulders huge;
"Those azure arms and thighs in fish-like form

"Furnish'd with fins. But what avails this shape?
"What that by all the deities marine
"I dear am held? a deity myself?
"If all these honors cannot touch thy breast."
These words he spoke, and more to speak prepar'd,
When Scylla left the god. Repuls'd, he griev'd
And sought Titanian Circé's monstrous court.

THE FOURTEENTH BOOK

Scylla transformed to a monster by Circé through jealousy; and ultimately to a rock. Continuation of Æneas' voyage. Dido. Cercopians changed to apes. Descent of Æneas to hell. The Cumæan Sybil. Adventures of Achæmenides with Polyphemus: and of Macareus amongst the Lestrigonians. Enchantments of Circé. Story of the transformation of Picus to a woodpecker; and of the nymph Canens to air. The Latian wars. Misfortunes of Diomede. Agmon and others changed to herons. Appulus to a wild olive. The Trojan ships changed to sea-nymphs. The city Ardea to a bird. Deification of Æneas. Latin kings. Vertumnus and Pomona. Story of Iphis and Anaxareté. Wars with the Sabines. Apotheösis of Romulus; and of his wife Hersilia.

THE FOURTEENTH BOOK OF THE METAMORPHOSES OF OVID

  Now had Eubœan Glaucus, who could cleave
The surging sea, left Etna, o'er the breasts
Of giants thrown, and left the Cyclops' fields,
Unconscious of the plough's or harrow's use;
And unindebted to the oxen yok'd.
Zanclé he left, and its opposing shore
Where Rhegium's turrets tower; and the strait sea
For shipwreck fam'd, which by incroaching shores
Press'd narrow, forms the separating bound
Betwixt Ausonia's and Sicilia's land.
Thence glides he swift along the Tyrrhene coast,
By powerful arms impell'd, and gains the dome,
And herbag'd hills of Circé Phœbus sprung:
(The dome with forms of wildest beasts full cramm'd)
Whom, soon as greeting salutations pass'd,
He thus address'd:—"O powerful goddess! grant
"Thy pity to a god; and thou alone,
"If worth that aid thou deem'st me, canst afford
"Aid to my love. For, O Titanian maid!
"To none the power of plants is better known
"Than me, who by the power of plants was chang'd.
"But lest the object of my lore, to thee
"Unknown, be hid; I Scylla late beheld

"Upon th' Italian shore: Messenia's walls
"Opposing. Shame me hinders to relate
"What promises, what prayers, what coaxing words
"I us'd: my words all heard with proud contempt.
"Do thou with magic lips thy charms repeat,
"If power in charms abides: or if in herbs
"More force is found, then use the well-try'd strength
"Of herbs of power. I wish thee not to soothe
"My heart; wish thee not these wounds to cure;
"Still may they last, let her such flames but feel."

  Then Circé spoke, (and she a mind possess'd
Most apt to flame with love, or in her frame
The stimulus was plac'd; or Venus, irk'd
At what her sire discover'd, caus'd the heat.)
"O, better far the willing nymph pursue
"Who would in wishes meet thee; wh'o is seiz'd
"With equal love: well worthy of the maid
"Thou wast; nay shouldst have been the first besought;
"And if but hope thou wilt afford, believe
"My words, thou shalt spontaneously be lov'd.
"Fear not, but on thy beauteous form depend;
"Lo! I, a goddess! of the splendid sun
"A daughter, who with powerful spells so much
"And herbs can do, to be thy consort sue.
"Spurn her who spurns thee; her who thee desires
"Desiring meet; and both at once avenge."
But to her tempting speeches Glaucus thus
Reply'd—"The trees shall sooner in the waves
"Spring up, and sea-weed on the mountain's top,
"Than I, while Scylla lives, my love transfer."
The goddess swol'n with anger, since his form
To harm 'twas given her not, and love deny'd,
Turn'd on her happier rival all her rage.
Irk'd at her slighted passion, straight she grinds
Herbs infamous, to gain their horrid juice;
And mixes all with Hecatéan spells.
Then clothes her in a sable robe, and forth
Through crowds of fawning savage beasts she goes,
From her gay palace. Rhegium's coast she seeks
O'erlooking Zanclé's rocks; and on the waves
With fury boiling, steps; o'er them she walks
As on a solid shore, and skims along
The ridgy billows with unwetted feet.

  A little pool, bent in a gentle curve,
With peaceful surface oft did Scylla tempt;
And often thither she herself betook

To 'scape from ocean's, and from Phœbus' heat,
When high in noon-tide fierceness short the shade
Was from the head describ'd. Before she came
The goddess poison'd all the pool; she pour'd
Her potent juice, of monster-breeding power,
Prest from pernicious roots, within the waves;
And mutter'd thrice nine times with magic lips,
In sounds scarce audible, her well-known spells.
Here Scylla came, and waded to the waist;
And straight, with barking monsters she espies
Her womb deform'd: at first, of her own limbs
Not dreaming they are part, she from them flies;
And chides them thence, and fears their savage mouths.
But what she flies she with her drags; she looks
To find her thighs, and find her legs, and feet;
But for those limbs Cerberean jaws are found.
Furious the dogs still howl; on their fierce backs
Her shorten'd groin, and swelling belly rest.

   The amorous Glaucus griev'd, and spurn'd the love
Of Circé, who so rancorously had us'd
The power of plants. Her station Scylla kept;
And soon as scope for vengeance she perceiv'd,
In hate to Circé, of his comrade crew
Depriv'd Ulysses. Next the Trojan fleet
Had she o'erwhelm'd; but ere they pass'd, transform'd
To stone, she tower'd aloft a flinty rock,
And still do mariners that rock avoid.

   The Phrygian ships that danger 'scap'd, and 'scap'd
Charybdis fell, by oars propell'd; but now
Ausonia's shore well nigh attain'd, were driv'n
By adverse tempests to the Libyan coast.
Æneäs then the queen Sidonian took
Most welcome to her bosom, and her dome;
Nor bore her Phrygian spouse's sudden flight,
With calm indifference: on a lofty pile
Rear'd for pretended sacred rites, she stood,
And on the sword's point fell; herself deceiv'd,
She all around outwitted. Flying far
The new-rais'd city of the sandy plains
To Eryx' country was he borne; where liv'd
Acestes faithful: here he sacrific'd,
And gave due honors to his father's tomb.
Then loos'd his ships for sea, well nigh in flames
By Juno's Iris: all th' Æoliän realm;
The islands blazing with sulphuric fire;
And rocks of Acheloüs' siren nymphs,

He left. The vessel now, of him who rul'd
The helm, bereft, along Ænaria's shore;
And Prochytas; and Pithecusa, plac'd
Upon a sterile hill, its name deriv'd
From those who dwelt there, coasted. Erst the sire
Of gods, detesting perjuries and fraud,
Which that deceitful race so much employ'd,
Chang'd to an animal deform'd their shapes;
Where still a likeness and unlikeness seems
To man. Their every limb contracted small;
Their turn'd-up noses flatten'd from the brow;
And ancient furrows plough'd adown their cheeks.
Then sent them, all their bodies cover'd o'er
With yellow hairs, this district to possess.
Yet sent them not till of the power of speech
Depriv'd; and tongue for direst falsehoods us'd:
But left their chattering jaws the power to 'plain.
These past, and left Parthenopé's high towers
To right; and musical Misenus' tomb,
And Cuma's shores to left; spots cover'd thick
With marshy reeds, he enters in the cave
Where dwelt the ancient Sybil; and in treats
That through Avernus' darkness he may pass,
His father's shade to seek. Then she, her eyes,
Long firmly fixt on earth, uprais'd; and next,
Fill'd with the god, in furious raving spoke.

    "Much cost thou ask, O man of mighty deeds!
"Whose valor by the sword is amply prov'd,
"And piety through flames. Yet, Trojan chief,
"Fear not; thou shalt what thou desir'st attain:
"By me conducted, thou th' Elysian field,
"The lowest portion of the tri-form realm,
"And thy beloved parent's shade shalt see:
"No path to genuine virtue e'er is clos'd."
She spoke, and pointed to th' Avernian grove,
Sacred to Proserpine; and shew'd a bough
With gold refulgent; this she bade him tear
From off its trunk. Æneäs her obeys,
And sees the treasures of hell's awful king;
His ancestors', and great Anchises' shades:
Is taught the laws and customs of the dead;
And what deep perils he in future wars
Must face. As then the backward path he trode
With weary'd step; the labor he beguil'd
By grateful speech with his Cumæan guide.
And, while through darkling twilight he pursu'd
His fearful way, he thus:—"Or, goddess, thou,

"Or of the gods high-favor'd, unto me
"Still shalt thou as a deity appear.
"My life I own thy gift, who hast me given
"To view the realms of death: who hast me brought,
"The realms of death beheld, to life again.
"For these high favors, when to air restor'd
"Statues to thee I'll raise, and incense burn."
Backward the prophetess, to him her eyes
Directs, and heaves a sigh; as thus she speaks:
"No goddess I; deem not my mortal frame
"The sacred incense' honors can deserve:
"Err not through ignorance. Eternal youth
"Had I possess'd, if on Apollo's love
"My virgin purity had been bestow'd.
"This while he hop'd, and while he strove to tempt
"With gifts,—O, chuse—he said,—Cumæan maid!
"Whate'er thou would'st—whate'er thou would'st is thine.
"I, pointing to an heap of gather'd dust,
"With thoughtless mind, besought so many years
"I might exist, as grains of sand were there:
"Mindless to ask for years of constant youth.
"The years he granted, and had granted too
"Eternal youth, had I his passion quench'd.
"A virgin I remain; Apollo's gift
"Despis'd: but now the age of joy is fled;
"Decrepitude with trembling steps has come,
"Which long I must endure. Seven ages now
"I have existed; ere the number'd grains
"Are equall'd, thrice an hundred harvests I,
"And thrice an hundred vintages must see.
"The time will come, my body, shrunk with age,
"And wither'd limbs, shall to small substance waste;
"Nor shall it seem that e'er an amorous god
"With me was smitten. Phœbus then himself
"Or me will know not, or deny that e'er
"He sought my love. Till quite complete my change,
"To all invisible, by words alone
"I shall be known. Fate still my voice will leave."

   On the steep journey thus the Sybil spoke:
And from the Stygian shades Æneäs rose,
At Cuma's town; there sacrific'd as wont,
And to the shores proceeded, which as yet
His nurse's name not bore. Here rested too,
After long toil, Macareus, the constant friend
Of wise Ulysses: Achæmenides,
Erst left amid Etnæan rocks, he knows:
Astonish'd there, his former friend to find,

In life unhop'd, he cry'd; "What chance? What god
"O Achæmerides! has thee preserv'd?
"How does a Greek a foreign vessel bear?
"And to what shores is now this vessel bound?"

Then Achæmenides, not ragged now,
In robes with thorns united, but all free,
Thus answer'd his enquiries. "May I view
"Once more that Polyphemus, and those jaws
"With human gore o'erflowing; if I deem
"This ship to me than Ithaca less dear;
"And less Æneäs than my sire esteem.
"For how too grateful can I be to him,
"Though all to him I give? Can I e'er be
"Unthankful or forgetful? That I speak,
"And breathe, and view the heavens and glorious sun
"He gave: that in the Cyclops' jaws my life
"Was clos'd not; that when now the vital spark
"Me quits, I may be properly intomb'd,
"Not in the monster's entrails. Heavens! what thoughts
"Possess'd my mind, (unless by pallid dread
"Of sense and thought bereft) when, left behind,
"I saw you push to sea. Loud had I call'd,
"But fear'd my cries would guide to me the foe.
"Ulysses' clamor near your ship destroy'd.
"I saw the monster, when a mighty rock,
"Torn from a mountain's summit, in the waves
"He flung: I saw him when with giant arm
"Huge stones he hurl'd, with such impetuous force,
"As though an engine sent them. Fear'd I long,
"Lest or the stones or waves the bark would sink;
"Forgetful then that not on board was I.
"But when you 'scap'd from cruel death, by flight,
"Then did he madly rave indeed; and roam'd
"All Etna o'er; and grop'd amid the woods;
"Depriv'd of sight he stumbles on the rocks;
"And stretching to the sea his horrid arms,
"Blacken'd with gore, he execrates the Greeks;
"And thus exclaims;—O! would some lucky chance
"Restore Ulysses to me, or restore
"One of his comrades, who might glut my rage;
"Whose entrails I might gorge; whose living limbs
"My hand might rend; whose blood might sluice my throat;
"And mangled members tremble in my teeth.
"O! then how light, and next to none the curse
"Of sight bereft.—Raging, he this and more
"Fierce utter d. I, with pallid dread o'ercome,
"Beheld his face still flowing down with blood;

"The orb of light depriv'd; his ruthless hands;
"His giant members; and his shaggy beard,
"Clotted with human gore. Death to my eyes
"Was obvious, yet was death my smallest dread.
"Now seiz'd I thought me; thought him now prepar'd
"T'inclose my mangled bowels in his own:
"And to my mind recurr'd the time I saw
"Two of my comrades' bodies furious dash'd
"Repeated on the earth: he, o'er them stretcht
"Prone, like a shaggy lion, in his maw
"Their flesh, their entrails, their yet-quivering limbs,
"Their marrow, and cranch'd bones, greedy ingulf'd.
"Horror me seiz'd. Bloodless and sad I stood,
"To see him champ, and from his mouth disgorge
"The bloody banquet; morsels mixt with wine
"Forth vomiting: and such a fate appear'd
"For wretched me prepar'd. Some tedious days
"Skulk'd I, and shudder'd at the smallest sound:
"Fearful of death, yet praying much to die;
"Repelling hunger by green herbs, and leaves,
"With acorns mixt; a solitary wretch,
"Poor, and to sufferings and to death decreed.
"Long was the time, ere I, not distant far,
"A ship beheld; I by my gestures shew'd
"My wish for flight, and hasten'd to the shore.
"Their hearts were mov'd, and thus a Trojan bark
"Receiv'd a Greek.—And now, my friend most dear,
"Tell thy adventures, and the chief's, and crew's,
"Who with thee launch'd upon th' extended main."

  He tells how Æölus his kingdom holds
On the deep Tuscan main, who curbs the winds
In cavern'd prisons; which, a noble boon!
Close pent within an ox's stubborn hide,
Dulichium's chief, from Æölus receiv'd.
How for nine days with prosperous breeze they sail'd;
And saw the long-sought land. How on the tenth,
Aurora rising bright, his comrades, urg'd
By envy, and by thirst of glittering spoil,
Gold deeming there inclos'd, the winds unloos'd.
How, driven by them, the ship was backward sped
Through the same waves she had so lately plough'd;
And reach'd the port of Æölus again.
"Thence,"—he continued—"to the ancient town
"Of Lestrygonian Lamus we arrive,
"Where rules Antiphates; to him dispatch'd
"I go, by two attended. I with one
"Scarce find in flight our safety: with his gore

"The hapless third, the Lestrigonians' jaws
"Besmears: our flying footsteps they pursue,
"While fierce Antiphates speeds on the crowd.
"Around they press, and unremitting hurl
"Huge rocks. and trunks of trees; our men o'erwhelm,
"And sink o_r fleet; one ship alone escapes,
"Which great Ulysses and myself contains.
"Most of our band thus lost, and angry much,
"Lamenting more, we floated to these isles,
"Which hence, though distant far, you may descry.
"Those isles, by me too near beheld, do thou
"At distance only view! O, goddess-born!
"Most righteous of all Troy, (for now no more,
"Æneäs, must thou enemy be stil'd
"To us, war ended) fly, I warn thee, fly
"The shore of Circé. We, our vessel moor'd
"Fast to that beach, not mindless of the deeds
"Antiphates perform'd, nor Cyclops, wretch
"Inhuman, row to tempt this unknown land
"Refuse. The choice by lot is fix'd. The lot
"Me sends, and with me sends Polites true;
"Eurylochus: and poor Elphenor, fond
"Too much of wine; with twice nine comrades mote,
"To seek the dome Circéan. Thither come;
"We at the entrance stand: a thousand wolves,
"And bears. and lionesses, with wolves mixt,
"Meet us, and terror in our bosoms strike.
"But ground for terror none: of all the crew
"None try our limbs to wound, but friendly wave
"Their arching tails, and fawningly attend
"Our steps; till by the menial train receiv'd,
"Through marbled halls to where their mistress sate,
"Our troop is led. She, in a bright recess,
"Upon a lofty throne of state, was plac'd,
"Cloth'd in a splendid robe; a golden veil
"Around her head, and o'er her shoulders thrown.
"Nereïds, and nymphs around (whose fingers quick
"The wool ne'er drew, nor form'd the following thread)
"Were plants arranging, and selecting flowers,
"And various teinted herbs, confus'dly mixt
"In baskets. She compleats the work they do;
"And well she knows the latent power each leaf
"Possesses. well their force combin'd she knows:
"And all the nice-weigh'd herbs inspects with care.
"When us she spy'd, and salutations pass'd
"Mutual; her forehead brighten'd, and she gave
"Our every wish. Nor waited more, but bade
"The beverage of the roasted grain be mix'd;

"And added honey, all the strength of wine,
"And curdy milk, and juices, which beneath
"Such powerful sweetness undetected lay.
"The cup from her accursed hand, I take,
"And, soon as thirsty I, with parch'd mouth drink,
"And the dire goddess with her wand had strok'd
"My head (I blush while I the rest relate)
"Roughen'd with bristles, I begin to grow;
"Nor now can speak; hoarse grunting comes for words;
"And all my face bends downwards to the ground;
"Callous I feel my mouth become, in form
"A crooked snout; and feel my brawny neck
"Swell o'er my chest; and what but now the cup
"Had grasp'd, that part does marks of feet imprint;
"With all my fellows treated thus, so great
"The medicine's potency, close was I shut
"Within a sty: there I, Eurylochus
"Alone unalter'd to a hog, beheld!
"He only had the offer'd cup refus'd.
"Which had he not avoided, he as one
"The bristly herd had join'd; nor had our chief,
"The great Ulysses, by his tale inform'd
"To Circé come, avenger of our woe.
"To him Cyllenius, messenger of peace
"A milk-white flower presented; by the gods
"Call'd Moly: from a sable root it-springs.
"Safe in the gift, and in th' advice of heaven,
"He enters Circé's dome; and her repels,
"Coaxing to taste th' invidious cup; his head
"To stroke attempting with her potent wand;
"And awes her trembling with his unsheath'd steel.
"Then, faith exchang'd, hands join'd, he to her bed
"Receiv'd, he makes the dowry of himself
"That all his comrades' bodies be restor'd.

  "Now are we sprinkled with innocuous juice
"Of better herbs; with the inverted wand
"Our heads are touch'd; the charms, already spoke,
"Strong charms of import opposite destroy.
"The more she sings her incantations, we
"Rise more from earth erect; the bristles fall;
"And the wide fissure leaves our cloven feet;
"Our shoulders form again; and arms beneath
"Are shap'd. Him, weeping too, weeping we clasp,
"And round our leader's neck embracing hang.
"No words at first to utter have we power,
"But such as testify our grateful joy.

"A year's delay there kept us. There, mine eyes
"In that long period much beheld; mine ears
"Much heard. This with the rest, in private told
"To me, by one of four most-favor'd nymphs
"Who aided in her spells: while Circé toy'd
"In private with our leader, she me shew'd
"A youthful statue carv'd in whitest stone,
"Bearing a feather'd pecker upon his head;
"Plac'd in a sacred shrine, with numerous wreaths
"Encircled. Unto my enquiring words,
"And wish to know who this could be, and why
"There worshipp'd in the shrine, and why that bird
"He bore,—then, Macareus,—she said—receive
"Thy wish; and also learn what mighty power
"My mistress boasts; attentive hear my words.

"Saturnian Picus in Ausonia's climes
"Was king, delighted still was he to train
"Steeds for the fight. The beauty you behold
"As man was his. So strong the 'semblance strikes,
"His real form in the feign'd stone appears.
"His mind his beauty equall'd. Nor as yet,
"The games quinquennial Grecian Elis gives,
"Four times could he have seen. He, by his face
"The Dryad nymphs who on the Latian hills
"Were born, attracted. Naiäds, river-nymphs,
"Him sought, whom Albula, and Anio bear;
"Almo's short course; the rapid stream of Nar;
"And Numicus; and Farfar's lovely shades;
"With all that Scythian Dian's woody realm
"Traverse; and all who haunt the sedgy lakes.
"But he, all these despis'd, lov'd one fair nymph,
"Whom erst Venilia, fame reports, brought forth
"To Janus on Palatiura's mount. When reach'd
"The nuptial age, preferr'd before the rest,
"Laurentian Picus gain'd the lovely maid.
"Wond'rous was she for beauty, wond'rous more
"Her art in song, and hence was Canens nam'd.
"Wont was her voice forests and rocks to move;
"Soothe savage beasts; arrest the course of streams;
"And stay the flying birds. While warbling thus
"With voice mature her song, Picus went forth
"To pierce amid Laurentium's fields the boars,
"Their native dwelling; on a fiery steed
"He rode; two quivering spears his left hand bore;
"His purple vestment golden clasps confin'd.
"In the same woods Apollo's daughter came,
"And from the fertile hills as herbs she cull'd,

"She left the fields, from her Circæan nam'd.
"When, veil'd by twigs herself, the youth she saw,
"Amaz'd she stood. Down from her bosom dropp'd
"The gather'd plants, and quickly through her frame
"The fire was felt to shoot. Soon as her mind
"Collected strength to curb the furious flame,
"She would have told him instant what she wish'd,
"But his impetuous steed, and circling crowd
"Of followers, kept her far.—Yet shalt thou not,
"If I but know my power, me fly; not should
"The winds thee bear away; else is the force
"Of plants all vanished, and my spells deceive.
"She said; and form'd an incorporeal shape
"Like to a boar; and bade it glance across
"The monarch's sight; and seem itself to hide
"In the dense thicket, where the trees grew thick:
"A spot impervious to the courser's foot.
"'Tis done; unwitting Picus eager seeks
"His shadowy prey; leaps from his smoking steed;
"And, vain-hop'd spoil pursuing, wanders deep
"In the thick woods. She baneful words repeats,
"And cursing charms collects. With new-fram'd verse
"Invokes strange deities: verse which erst while
"Has dull'd the splendid circle of the moon;
"And hid with rain-charg'd clouds her father's face.
"This verse repeated, instant heaven grew dark,
"And mists from earth arose: his comrades roam
"Through the dark paths; the king without a guard
"Is left. This spot, and time so suiting gain'd,
"Thus Circé cry'd—O fairest thou of forms!
"By those bright eyes which me enslav'd, by all
"Thy beauteous charms which make a goddess sue,
"Indulge my flame; accept th' all-seeing sun,
"My sire, for thine; nor, rigidly austere,
"Titanian Circé spurn.—She ceas'd; he stern
"Repuls'd the goddess, and her praying suit;
"Exclaiming,—be thou whom thou may'st, yet thine
"I am not; captive me another holds;
"And fervently, I pray, to lengthen'd years
"She still may hold me. Never will I wrong
"The nuptial bond with stranger's lawless love,
"While Janus' daughter, my lov'd Canens lives.—
"Sol's daughter then (re-iterated prayers
"In vain oft try'd) exclaim'd:—Nor shalt thou boast
"Impunity; nor e'er returning see
"Thy Canens; but learn well what may be done
"By slighted, loving woman: Circé loves,
"Is woman, and is slighted.—To the west

"She turn'd her twice, and turn'd her twice to east;
"Thrice with her wand she struck the youth, and thrice
"Her charm-fraught song repeated. Swift he fled,
"And wondering that more swift he ran than wont,
"Plumes on his limbs beheld. Constrain'd to add
"A new-form'd 'habitant to Latium's groves,
"Angry he wounds the spreading boughs, and digs
"The stubborn oak-tree with his rigid beak.
"A purple tinge his feathers take, the hue
"His garment shew'd; the gold, a buckle once,
"Which clasp'd his robe, to feathers too is chang'd;
"The shining gold circles his neck around:
"Nor aught remains of Picus save the name.

   "Meantime his comrades vainly Picus call,
"Through all the groves; but Picus no where find.
"Circé they meet, for now the air was clear'd,
"The clouds dispers'd, or by the winds or sun;
"Charge her with crimes committed, and demand
"Their king; force threaten, and prepare to lift
"Their savage spears. The goddess sprinkles round
"Her noxious poisons and envenom'd juice;
"Invokes old night, and the nocturnal gods,
"Chaos, and Erebus; and Hecat's help,
"With magic howlings, prays. Woods (wond'rous sight!)
"Leap from their seats; earth groans; the neighbouring trees
"Grow pale; the grass with sprinkled blood is wet;
"Stones hoarsely seem to roar, and dogs to howl;
"Earth with black serpents swarms; unmatter'd forms
"Of bodies long defunct, flit through the air.
"Tremble the crowd, struck with th' appalling scene:
"Appall'd, and trembling, on their heads she strikes
"Th' envenom'd rod. From the rod's potent touch,
"For men a various crowd of furious beasts
"Appear'd: his form no single youth retain'd.

   "Descending Phœbus had Hesperia's shores
"Now touch'd; and Canens with her heart and looks
"Sought for her spouse in vain: her servants all,
"And all the people roam through every wood,
"Bearing bright torches. Not content the nymph
"To weep, to tear her tresses, and to beat
"Her bosom, though not one of these was spar'd,
"She sally'd forth herself; and frantic stray'd
"Through Latium's plains. Six times the night beheld,
"And six returning suns, her, wandering o'er
"The mountain tops, or through the vallies deep,
"As chance directed: foodless, sleepless, still.

"Tiber at length beheld her; with her toil,
"And woe, worn out, upon his chilling banks
"Her limbs extending. There her very griefs,
"Pour'd with her tears, still musically sound.
"Mourning, her words in a soft dying tone
"Are heard, as when of old th' expiring swan
"Sung his own elegy. Wasted at length
"Her finest marrow, fast she pin'd away;
"And vanish'd quite to unsubstantial air.
"Yet still tradition marks the spot, the muse
"Of ancient days, still Canens call'd the place,
"In honor of the nymph, and justly too.

 "Many the tales like these I heard; and much
"Like this I saw in that long tedious year.
"Sluggish and indolent for lack of toil,
"Thence are we bid to plough the deep again;
"Again to hoist the sail. But Circé told
"So much of doubtful ways, of voyage vast,
"And all the perils of the raging deep
"We must encounter; that my soul I own
"Trembled. I gain'd this shore, and here remain'd."

 Here Macareus finish'd; to Æneäs' nurse
Inurn'd in marble, this short verse was given:
"Cajeta here, sav'd from the flames of Greece,
"Her foster-son, for piety renown'd,
"With fires more fitting burn'd." Loos'd are the ropes
That bound them to the grassy beach, and far
They leave the dwelling of the guileful power;
And seek the groves, beneath whose cloudy shade
The yellow-sanded Tiber in the main
Fierce rushes. Here Æneäs gains the realm,
And daughter of Latinus, Faunus' son:
But not without a war. Battles ensue
With the fierce people. For his promis'd bride
Turnus loud rages. All the Tuscans join
With Latium, and with doubtful warfare long
Is sought the conquest. Either side augment
With foreign aid their strength. Rutilians crowds
Defend, and crowds the Trojan trenches guard.

 Not bootless, suppliant to Evander's roof
Æneäs went; though Venulus in vain,
To exil'd Diomed's great town was sent.
A mighty city Diomed' had rear'd
Beneath Apulian Daunus, and possess'd
His lands by marriage dower. But when made known

By Venulus, the message Turnus sent,
Beseeching aid, th' Etolian hero aid
Der y'd. For neither was his wish to send
His father's troops to fight, nor of his own
Had he, which might the strenuous warfare wage.—
"Lest this but feign'd you think," he said, "though grief
"The sad relation will once more renew,
"Yet will I now th'afflicting tale repeat.

  "When lofty Ilium was consum'd,—the towers
"Of Pergamus a prey to Grecian flames,
"The Locrian Ajax, for the ravish'd maid,
"Drew vengeance on us all; which he alone
"Deserv'd from angry Pallas. Scatter'd wide,
"And swept by tempests through the foaming deep,
"The Grecians, thunders, rains, and darkness bore,
"All heaven's and ocean's rage; and all to crown,
"On the Capharean rocks the fleet was dash'd.
"But not to tire you with each mournful scene
"In order; Greece might then the tears have drawn
"Ev'n from old Priam. Yet Minerva's care
"Sratch'd me in safety from the surge. Again
"From Argos, my paternal land, I'm driven;
"Bright Venus bearing still in mind the wound
"Of former days. Upon th'expanded deep
"Such toils I bore excessive; on the land
"So in stern combat strove, that oft those seem'd
"To me most blest, who in the common wreck,
"Caphareus sunk beneath the boisterous waves;
"A fate I anxious wish'd I'd with them shar'd.
"Now all my comrades, of the toilsome main,
"And constant warfare weary; respite crav'd
"From their long wanderings. Not was Agmon so,
"Fierce still his bosom burn'd; and now he rag'd
"From his misfortunes fiercer, as he cry'd—
"What, fellows! can remain which now to bear
"Your patience should refuse? What, though she would,
"Possesses Cytherea to inflict?
"When worse is to be dreaded, is the time
"For prayers: but when our state the worst has seen
"Fear should be spurn'd at; in our depth of woe
"Secure. Let she herself hear all my words;
"And let her hate, as hate she does, each man
"Who follows Diomed'! Yet will we all
"Her hatred mock, and stand against her power
"So mighty, with a no less mighty breast.—
"With words like these Etolian Agmon goads
"Th' already raging goddess, and revives

"Her ancient hate. Few with his boldness pleas'd;
"Far most my friends his daring speech condemn.
"Aiming at words respondent, straight his voice
"And throat are narrow'd; into plumes his hair
"Is alter'd; plumes o'er his new neck are spread;
"And o'er his chest, and back; his arms receive
"Long pinions, bending into light-form'd wings;
"Most of his feet is cleft in claws; his mouth
"Hardens to horn, and in a sharp beak ends.
"Lycus, Rhetenor, Nycteus, Abas, stare
With wonder, and while wondering there they stand
"The same appearance take; and far the most
"Of all my troop on wings up fly: and round
"The ship the air resounds with clapping wings.
"If what new shape those birds so sudden form'd
"Distinguish'd, you would know: swans not to be,
"Nought could the snowy swan resemble more.
"Son now to Daunus, my diminish'd host
"Scarce guards this kingdom, and those barren fields."

  Thus far Diomedes; and Venulus
Th' Apulian kingdom left, Calabria's gulf
Pass'd, and Messapia's plains, where he beheld
Caverns with woods deep shaded, with light rills
Cool water'd: here the goatish Pan now dwelt;
Once tenanted by wood-nymphs. From the spot
Them, Appulus, a shepherd drove to flight;
Alarm'd at first by sudden dread, but soon,
Resum'd their courage, his pursuit despis'd,
They to the measur'd notes their agile feet
Mov'd in the dance. The clown insults them more,
Mimics their motions in his boorish steps,
To coarse abusing adding speech obscene:
Nor ceas'd his tongue 'till bury'd in a tree.
Well may his manner from the fruit be known;
For the wild olive marks his tongue's reproach,
In berries most austere: to them transferr'd
The rough ungrateful sharpness of his words.

  Return'd the legates, and the message told,
Th' Etolians' aid deny'd; without their help
Wage the Rutilians now the ready war:
And streams of blood from either army flow.
Lo! Turnus comes, and greedy torches brings
To fire the cover'd ships; the flames they fear
Whom tempests spar'd. And now the fire consum'd
The pitch, the wax, with all that flame could feed;
Then, mounting up the lofty mast, assail'd

The canvas; and the rowers' benches smok'd.
This saw the sacred mother of the gods,
And mindful that from Ida's lofty top
The pines were hew'd, with clash of tinkling brass,
And sounds of hollow box, fill'd all the air.
Then borne through ether by her lions tam'd,
She said; "Those flames with sacrilegious hand
"Thou hurl'st in vain: I will them snatch away.
"Ne'er will I calmly view the greedy fire
"Aught of the forests, which are mine consume."
Loud thunders rattled as the goddess spoke;
And showery floods with hard rebounding hail,
The thunder follow'd. In the troubled air
The blustering brethren rag'd, and swell'd the main:
The billows furious clash'd. The mother us'd
One blast's exerted force; the cables burst,
Which bound the Phrygian vessels to the shore;
Them swiftly swept along, and in the deep
Low plung'd them. Straight the rigid wood grows soft
The timber turns to flesh; the crooked prows
To heads are chang'd: the oars to floating legs,
And toes; while what were ribs, as ribs remain;
The keels, ceep in the vessels sunk, become
The spinal bones; in soft long tresses flows
The cordage; into arms the sailyards change:
The hue of all cerulean as before.
And now the Naiäds of the ocean sport
With girlish play, amid those very waves
Ere while so dreaded: sprung from rugged hills
They love the gentle main; nor aught their birth
Their bosoms irks. Yet mindful still what risks
Themselves encounter'd on the raging main,
Oft with assisting hand the high-tost bark
They aid; save Greeks the hapless bark contains.
Mindful of Iliüm's fall, they still detest
The Argives; and with joyful looks behold
The shatter'd fragments of Ulysses' ship:
With joy behold the bark Alcinous gave
Harden to rock, stone growing from the wood.

  'Twas hop'd, the fleet transform'd to nymphs marine,
The fierce Rutilians, struck with awe, might cease
The war; but stubborn either side persists.
Each have their gods, and each have godlike souls.
Nor seek they now, so much the kingdom dower,
Latinus' sceptre, or Lavinia! thee,
As conquest: waging war through shame to cease.
Venus at last beholds, brave Turnus slain,

Her son's victorious arms; and Ardea falls,
A mighty town when Turnus yet was safe:
It cruel flames destroy'd; and every roof
The smoking embers hid; up from the heap
Of ruins, sprung a bird unknown before,
And beat the ashes with its sounding wings:
Its voice, its leanness, pallid hue, and all,
Suit well a captur'd city; and the name
Retaining still, with beating wings it wails.

   Now had Æneäs' virtues, all the gods,
Ev'n Juno, forc'd to cease their ancient hate.
The young Iülus' growing empire fixt
On firm foundations, ripe was then for heaven
The Cytheréan prince. Venus besought
That favor of the gods; round her sire's neck
Her arms she clasp'd—"O, father!"—she exclaim'd—
"Indulgent still, be more than ever kind:
"Grant that a deity, though e'er so low,
"Æneäs may become! who through my blood
"Claims thee as grandsire; something let him gain.
"Let it suffice, that he has once beheld
"The dreary realm; and once already past
"The Stygian stream."—The deities consent:
Nor does the heavenly queen, her forehead stern
Retain, consenting with a cheerful mien.
Then spoke the sire. "Both, daughter, merit well
"The boon celestial: what thou ask'st receive,
"Since thou desir'st it, and since he deserves."
He ceas'd. O'erjoy'd, she grateful thanks returns;
And by yok'd turtles borne through yielding air,
She seeks Laurentum's shore, where gently creep
Numicius' waters 'midst a reedy shade
Into the neighbouring main. She bids him cleanse
All of Æneäs that to death was given;
And bear him silent floating to the sea.
The horned god, what Venus bade perform'd:
All that Æneäs had of mortal mould
He purg'd away, and wash'd him with his waves.
His better part remain'd. Odours divine,
O'er his lustrated limbs, the mother pour'd;
And with ambrosia and sweet nectar touch'd
His lips, and perfect is the new-made god:
Whom Indiges, the Roman people call,
Worship with altars, and in temples place.

   Alba, and Latium then beneath the rule
Of young Iülus, call'd Ascanius, came.

Him Sylvius follow'd. Then Latinus held
The ancient sceptre, with his grandsire's name.
Alba to fam'd Latinus was the next.
Then Epitus; Capetus; Capys reign'd:
Capys before Capetus. After these
The realm was sway'd by Tiberinus; sunk
Beneath the billows of the Tuscan stream,
The waters took his name. His sons were two,
Fierce Remulus, and Acrota; the first
Pre-eminent in years, the thunder mock'd;
And by the thunder dy'd. Of meeker mind
His brother, to brave Aventinus left
The throne; who bury'd 'neath the self-same hill
Where once he reign'd, gave to the hill a name;
And Procas now the Latian people rul'd.

  Beneath this monarch fair Pomona liv'd,
Than whom amongst the Hamadryad train
None tended closer to her garden's care;
None o'er the trees' young fruit more anxious watch'd;
And thence her name. In rivers, she, and woods,
Delighted not, for fields were all her joy;
And branches bending with delicious loads.
Nor grasps her hand a javelin, but a hook,
With which she now luxurious boughs restrains,
And prunes the stragglers, when too wide they spread:
Now she divides the rind, and in the cleft
Inserts a scion, and supporting juice
Affords th' adopted stranger. Ne'er she bears
That drought they feel, but oft with flowing streams
Waters the crooked fibres of their roots:
This all her love, this all her care, for man
She heeded not. Yet of the lawless force
Of rustics fearful, she her orchard round
Well fenc'd, and every part from access barr'd,
And fled from all mankind. What was there left
Untry'd, by satyrs, by the wanton fawns,
Or pine-crown'd Pan; Sylvanus, ever youth;
Or him whose sickle frights nocturnal thieves
To gain her? These Vertumnus all excell'd
In passion; but not happier he than they.
How oft a basket of ripe grain he bore,
Clad like a hardy reaper, and in form
A real reaper seem'd! Oft with new hay
His temples bound, who turns the fresh cut grass
He might be thought. Oft in his horny hand
He bears a goad; then might you swear, that now
The weary oxen he had just unyok'd.

Arm'd with a pruning hook, he one appears
Who lops the vines. When he the ladder lifts,
Apples about to pluck he seems. His sword
Shews him a soldier; and his trembling reed
An angler. Thus a thousand shapes he tries,
T' enjoy the pleasure of her beauteous sight.
Now leaning on a staff, his temples clad
In painted bonnet, he an ancient dame,
With silver locks thin scatter'd o'er her head,
Would seem; and in the well-trimm'd orchard walks;
Admires the fruit—"But, O! how far beyond
"Are these;"—he said, and kiss'd the lips he prais'd:
No ancient dame such kisses e'er bestow'd.
Then rested on the swelling turf, and view'd
The branches bending with th' autumnal load.

  An elm there stood right opposite, full spread
With swelling grapes, which, with its social vine,
He prais'd;—"Yet should that trunk there single stand"—
Said he,—"without its vine, nought but the leaves
"Desirable would seem. As well the vine
"Which rests now safe upon its wedded elm,
"If not so join'd, were prostrate on the ground.
"Yet does the tree's example move not thee.
"Thou fly'st from marriage; fly'st from nuptial joys;
"Would they could charm thy soul. Not Helen e'er
"Such crowds of wooers sought; not her who mov'd
"The Lapithæan war; nor the bright queen
"Of Ithacus, still 'gainst the coward brave,
"As would pursue thee. Now, though all thou fly'st,
"Thy suitors scorning, thousands seek thy hand,
"Both demi-gods and gods, whoever dwell
"Of deities on Alba's lofty hills.
"Yet wisely would'st thou act, and happy wed,
"Attend my aged counsel (thee I love
"More than all these, and more than thou'dst believe)
"Reject such vulgar offers, and select
"Vertumnus for the consort of thy bed:
"And for his worth accept of me as pledge.
"For to himself not better is he known
"Than me. No truant through the earth he roves;
"These spots he dwells in, and in these alone,
"Nor loves he, like thy wooer's greatest share,
"Instant whate'er he sees. Thou his first flame
"Shalt be, and be his last. He will devote
"His every year to thee, and thee alone.
"Add too his youth, and nature's bounteous gifts
"Which decorate him; and that changed with ease,

"He every form can take, and those the best
"That thou may'st like, for all thou may'st command.
"Are not your pleasures both the same? the fruits
"Thou gatherest first, are they not given to him?
"Who takes thy offerings with a grateful hand.
"But now he seeks not fruits pluck'd from thy trees,
"Nor herbs thy garden feeds with mellow juice,
"Nor aught, save thee. Have pity on his flame:
"Think 'tis himself that sues; think that he prays
"Through me. O fear the vengeance of the gods!
"Affronted Venus' unrelenting rage;
"And fear Rhamnusia's still vindictive mind.
"That these you more may dread, I will relate
"(For age has much to me made known) a fact
"Notorious through all Cyprus which may urge
"Your soul more quickly to relent and love.

"Iphis of humble origin beheld
"The noble Anaxareté—the blood
"Of ancient Teucer: he beheld, and felt
"Love burn through all his frame; he struggled long
"By reason to o'ercome the flame, in vain.
"He came a humble suppliant to her gate.
"To her old nurse, he now his hapless love
"Confess'd, and pray'd her by her nurseling's hopes,
"She would not be severe. Now he assails
"All her attendants with his flattering speech,
"And anxious begs of each to intercede.
"Oft, grav'n on tablets, were his amorous words
"Borne to her. Oft against her door he hung
"Garlands, wet dropping with the dew of tears.
"Plac'd on the threshold hard his tender side,
"Venting reproaches on the cruel bar.
"But she more deaf than surges which arise
"With setting stars; and harder than the steel
"Numician fires have temper'd; or the rock
"Still living in its bed, spurn'd him, and laugh'd:
"And cruel, added lofty words to deeds
"Unmerciful, and robb'd him ev'n of hope.
"Impatient Iphis, now no longer bore
"The pangs of endless grief, but at her gate
"Thus utter'd his last 'plaints—Thou hast o'ercome
"O Anaxareté! for never more
"Will I molest thy quiet. Now prepare
"Glad triumphs; Pæan call; and bind thy brows
"With laurel bright, for thou victorious art,
"And joyfully I die. O heart of steel!
"Enjoy thy bliss. Now will I force thy praise

"In something;—somehow find a way to please,
"And thee constrain to grant I have desert.
"Yet still remember, that my love for thee
"Leaves me not but with life! at once I lose
"A double light. But fame shall not announce
"To thee my death, for I myself will come.
"Lest thou should'st doubt, thou shalt thyself behold
"My death, and on my lifeless body glut
"Thy cruel eyes. But, O ye gods above!
"If mortal deeds ye view, remember me:
"No more my tongue can dare to ask, than this,
"That distant ages may my fortune know;
"Grant fame to him, whom ye of life deprive.—
"He spoke, and to the porch so oft adorn'd
"With flowing chaplets, rais'd his humid eyes,
"And stretch'd his pallid arms; then to the post,
"The cord with noose well-fitted, fastening, cry'd:—
"Nymph, pitiless and cruel! pleas'd the best
"With garlands such as these!—Then in the cord,
"His head inserted; tow'rd the maid still turn'd,
"As, hapless load! with strangled throat he hung.
"Struck by his dangling feet, the portals seem'd
"A sound to give, which mighty seem'd to mourn;
"And open thrown, the horrid deed display'd:
"Loudly the servants shriek, and vainly bear
"His breathless body to his mother's dome.
"(Defunct his sire) She clasp'd him to her breast,
"Embrac'd his clay-cold limbs; and all she said
"That wretched parents say; and all she did
"That hapless mothers do: then through the town
"The melancholy funeral pomp she led,
"The lurid members following, on a bier
"For burning. In the road the dwelling stood
"Through which the sad procession took its way,
"And sound of lamentation struck the ears
"Of Anaxareté, whom now the power
"Of vengeance follow'd. Mov'd, she now exclaim'd—
"I will this melancholy prospect view.—
"And to the open casement mounted high.
"Scarce had she Iphis on the bier beheld,
"When harden'd grew her eyes; a pallid hue
"O'erspread her body as the warm blood fled.
"Her feet to move for flight she try'd, her feet
"Stuck fast; her face she try'd to turn away;
"She could not turn it; and by small degrees
"The stony hardness of her breast was spread
"O'er all her limbs. Believe not that I feign,
"For Salamis the figure of the nymph

"Still keeps; and there a temple is high rear'd
"Where Venus, the beholder, they adore.
"Mindful of this, O dearest nymph! lay by
"That cold disdain, and join thee to a spouse.
"So may no vernal frosts thy budding fruits
"Destroy, nor sweeping storms despoil thy flowers."
When this the god, to various shapes in vain
Transform'd, had utter'd; he assum'd again
The youth, and flung the garb of age aside:
And so appear'd, as seems the radiant sun,
Freed from opposing clouds, and darting bright
His glory round. Force he prepar'd, but force
He needed not. The nymph his beauty mov'd,
And straight her bosom felt a mutual flame.

Th' Ausonan realm Amulius' force unjust
Commanded next; and ancient Numitor
By his young grandsons the lost realm regain'd.
The city's walls on Pales' feast were laid.
Now Tatius and the Sabine sires wage war
Against it; and the fortress' gate unclos'd,
Tarpeïa, well-deserving of her fate,
Breathes out her soul beneath a pile of shields.
Thence Cures' sons, each sound of voice repress'd,
Silent as wolves, steal on them drown'd in sleep,
And gain the gates, which Ilia's son had clos'd
With massive bars. But Juno one threw ope,
Nor creak'd the portal on its turning hinge.
Venus alone the fastening of the gate
Withdrawn, perceiv'd, and had it clos'd again,
Save that the acts a deity performs,
No deity can e'er undo. A spot
Near Janus' temple, cool with flowing streams,
Ausonia's Naiäds own'd; and aid from these
She sought. Nor could the nymphs deny a boon
So just; and instant all their rills and floods
Burst forth. But still to Janus' open gate
The way was passable, nor could the waves
Oppose their way. They to the fruitful springs
Apply blue sulphur, and the hollow caves
Fire with bitumen; to the lowest depth
They forceful penetrate, both this, and that.
And streams that late might vie with Alpine cold,
To flames themselves, not now in heat would yield.
The porches of the deity two-fac'd
Smok'd with the fiery sprinkling; and the gate,
Op'd to the hardy Sabine troops in vain,
Was by the new-sprung fountain guarded, 'till

The sons of Mars had girt them in their arms.
Soon Romulus attack'd them, and Rome's soil
Was strew'd with Sabine bodies and her own:
And impious weapons mingled blood of sires
With blood of sons-in-law; yet so it pleas'd,
War settled into peace, nor rag'd the steel
To ultimate destruction; in the realm
Tatius as equal sovereign was receiv'd.

  Tatius deceas'd, thou, Romulus, dispens'd,
To the joint nations, equitable laws.
When Mars, his helmet thrown aside, the sire
Of gods and men, in words like these, address'd.—
"O parent! (since the Roman realm has gain'd
"A strong and wide foundation, nor should look
"To one protector only) lo! the time
"To grant the favor, promis'd me so long,
"To thy deserving grandson. Snatch'd from earth
"Let him in heaven he plac'd. Time was, long since,
"In a full council of the gods thou said'st,
"Well I remember, well my mindful breast
"The tender words remark'd; a son of mine
"By thee should in the azure sky be plac'd:
"Now be the fulness of thy words complete."
Th' Omnipotent consented; with black clouds
Darken'd the air; and frighten'd all the town
With flaming thunders. When the martial god
Perceiv'd this fiat of the promis'd change,
Propp'd on his spear he fearless mounts the steeds,
Press'd by the bloody yoke; loud sounds the lash,
And prone the air he cleaves, lights on the top
Of shady Palatine. There Ilia's son
Delivering regal laws to Romans round,
He saw, and swept him thence: his mortal limbs
Waste in the empty air, as balls of lead
Hurl'd from a sling, melt in the midmost sky:
More fair his face appears, and worthy more
Of the high shrines: such now appears the form
Of great Quirinus, clad in purple robe.

  His spouse him wept as lost, when heaven's high queen
Bade Iris on her sweeping bow descend,
And thus her orders to Hersilia speak:—
"O matron! glory of the Latian land;
"Pride of the Sabine race; most worthy spouse
"Of such an hero once; spouse worthy now
"Of god Quirinus, cease thy tears: if wish
"To see thy husband warms thee, led by me,

"To yonder grove upon Quirinus' hill
"Which flourishes, and overshades the fane
"Of Rome's great monarch, haste."—Iris obeys;
Upon her painted bow to earth slides down,
And hails Hersilia in the bidden words.
Her eyes scarce lifting, she with blushing face
Replies—"O goddess! whom thou art, to me
"Unknown; that thou a goddess art is plain.
"Lead me, O lead! shew me my spouse's face:
"Which if fate grant I may once more behold,
"Heaven I'll allow I've seen." Nor waits she more,
But with Thaumantian Iris, to the hill
Of Romulus proceeds. There, shot from heaven,
A star tow'rd earth descended; from its rays
Bright flam'd Hersilia's hair, and with the star
Mounted aloft. Rome's founder's well-known arms
Receive her. Now her former name is chang'd,
As chang'd her body: known as Ora, now,
A goddess, with her great Quirinus join'd.

THE FIFTEENTH BOOK

Numa's journey to Crotona. The Pythagorean philosophy of transmigration of the soul, and relation of various transformations. Death of Numa, and grief of Egeria. Story of Hippolytus. Change of Egeria to a fountain. Cippus. Visit of Esculapius to Rome, in the form of a snake. Assassination and apotheösis of Julius Cæsar. Praise of Augustus. Prophetic conclusion.

THE FIFTEENTH BOOK OF THE METAMORPHOSES OF OVID

  Meantime they seek who may the mighty load
Sustain; who may succeed so great a king.
Fame, harbinger of truth, the realm decreed
To noble Numa. Not content to know
The laws and customs of the Sabine race,
His mind capacious grasp'd a larger field.
He sought for nature's laws. Fir'd by this wish,
His country left, he journey'd to the town
Of him, who erst was great Alcides' host:
And as he sought to learn what founder first
These Grecian walls rear'd on Italia's shore,
Thus an old 'habitant, well vers'd in tales
Of yore, reply'd.—"Jove's son, rich in the herds
"Iberia bred, his prosperous journey bent
"By ocean unto fair Lacinia's shores:

"Enter'd himself the hospitable roof
"Of mighty Croto, while his cattle' stray'd
"Amid the tender grass; and his long toil
"Reliev'd by rest. Departing, thus he spoke—
"Here in thy grandson's age a town shall rise.—
"And true the promis'd words; for Myscelos,
"Argive Alemon's son, dear to the gods,
"Beyond all mortals of that time, now liv'd.
"The club-arm'd god, as press'd with heavy sleep,
"He lay, hung o'er him, and directed thus.—
"Haste leave thy native land;—where distant flows
"The rocky stream of Æsaris, go seek.—
"And threaten'd much if disobedient found:
"Then disappear'd the god and sleep at once.
"Alemon's son arose; with silent care
"Revolv'd the new-seen vision in his soul,
"And undetermin'd waver'd long his mind.
"The god commands,—the laws forbid to go:
"Death is the punishment to him decreed
"Who would his country quit. Now glorious Sol
"Had in the ocean hid his glittering face,
"And densest night shew'd her star-studded head;
"Again the god was seen to come; again
"Admonish, and with threats more stern demand
"Obedience. Terror-struck he now prepar'd
"His property and household gods to move
"To this new seat. Quick through the city flies
"The rumor; as a slighter of the laws
"Is he denounc'd. The trial ends at once;
"Th' acknowledg'd crime without a witness prov'd.
"The wretched culprit lifts his eyes and hands
"To heaven, exclaiming;—Thou whose toils twice six
"Have given thee claim to glory, lend thy aid;
"Thou art the cause that I offence have given.—
"Sentence in old, by stones of white and black
"Was shewn: by these th' accus'd was clear'd, by those
"Condemn'd. Thus is the heavy doom now pass'd,
"And in the fatal urn each flings a stone
"Of sable hue. Inverted then to count
"The pebbles, lo! their color all is chang'd
"From black to white; and thus, the doom revers'd,
"Alemon's son by Hercules is freed.
"Thanks to Alcmena's son, his kinsman, given,
"He o'er th' Ionian sea with favoring winds
"Sail'd, and Tarentum, Sparta's city, pass'd,
"And Sybaris, Neæthus Salentine,
"The gulph of Thurium, and Japygia's fields,
"With Temeses; which shores at distance seen

"By him, were scarcely pass'd, when he beheld
"The mouth of Æsaris, the destin'd flood:
"And thence not far a lofty heap of earth,
"Where Croto's hallow'd bones were safe inhum'd.
"There he as bidden rais'd the walls, which took
"From the high sepulchre their lasting name.
"Plain then the city's origin appears
"By fame, thus built upon Italia's shores."

Here dwelt a sage whom Samos claim'd by birth,
But Samos and its masters he had fled;
A willing exile from tyrannic rule.
Though from celestial regions far remov'd
His mind to heaven could soar; with mental eyes
He things explor'd which to the human ken
Nature deny'd. When all with watchful care
Was learnt in secret, to the listening crowd
He public spoke. Told to their wondering ears
The primal origin of this great world;
The cause of things; what nature is; what god;
Whence snow; and whence tremendous thunder springs,—
From Jove, or from the rattling of rent clouds;
What shakes earth's pillars; by what law the stars
Wander; and what besides lies hid from man.
And first that animals should heap the board
For food, he strict forbade; and first in words
Thus eloquent, but unbeliev'd he spoke.

"Cease, mortals, cease your bodies to pollute
"With food unhallow'd: plentiful is grain;
"The apples bend the branches with their load;
"The vines bear swelling heaps of clustering grapes;
"Bland herbs you have; and such as heat require
"To mollify for use. Nor do you lack
"The milky fluid, or the honey sweet,
"Fragrant of thyme. The lavish earth supplies
"Mild aliments, her riches and affords
"Dainties, with nought of slaughter or of blood.
"Their hunger beasts alone with flesh allay,
"And beasts not all; the generous steed, the flock,
"The herd, on grass subsist. But lions grim,
"Armenian tigers, bears, and wolves, delight
"In bloody feasts. How impious to behold
"Bowels in bowels bury'd! greedy limbs
"Fatten on limbs digested, and prolong'd
"One's animation by another's death.
"In vain the earth, benignant mother, gives
"Her copious stores, if nought can thee delight,

"Save with a savage tooth this living food
"To chew, and Cyclopéan feasts renew.
"Can'st thou not cloy the appetite's keen rage,
"Deprav'd desire! unless another die?
"That early age, to which we give the name
"Of golden, happy was in mellow fruits,
"And plants, by earth produc'd; nor e'er did gore
"The mouth defile. In safety through the air
"Fowls way'd their feathers: fearless through the fields
"Wander'd the hare: nor, on the barb'd hook hung
"By his credulity, was snar'd the fish.
"Fraud was not, none suspicious of deceit;
"And all was fill'd with harmony and peace.
"But soon some wretch (whatever wretch was he)
"Such food disliking, in his greedy maw
"Bury'd what animation once possess'd.
"He led the way to wickedness. And first
"The weapon smok'd with blood of ravenous beasts:
"And there it should have stay'd. Just is the plea
"To take their lives that follow us for prey;
"But not devour them when destroy'd. From thence
"Wide spread the horrid practice, and the sow,
"Doom'd the first victim, is decreed to die,
"For digging up with crooked snout the seed;
"And blasting all the prospect of the year.
"The goat had gnaw'd the vine;—the culprit bled
"On Bacchus' altars to appease his ire.
"These two their fate deserv'd. But how, O sheep!
"Ye harmless flocks, have ye this merited,
"Form'd to receive protection from mankind?
"Who in your swelling dugs bland liquors bear,
"Who give your fleecy coverings, garments soft
"For us to form; and more in life than death
"Assist our wants. What has the ox deserved?
"A simple harmless beast, and born for toil,
"Of guile and fraud devoid? Forgetful man!
"And undeserving of the harvest's boon,
"Who could, the crooked joke just from his neck
"Remov'd, his faithful tiller sacrifice;
"Smite with the axe that neck with labor worn,
"With which so oft he had the soil renew'd;
"Which had so many crops on him bestow'd.
"Nor is this all, the savage deed perform'd,
"They implicate the heavenly gods themselves,
"Pretend th' almighty deities delight
"To see the slaughter of laborious steers.
"Spotless must be the victim; in his form
"Perfection: (fatal thus too much to please!)

"With golc and fillets gay, the beast is led
"Before the altar, hears the unknown prayers,
"And sees the meal, the product of his toil,
"Betwixt his horns full in his forehead flung:
"Then struck, he stains the weapon with his blood,
"The weapon in reflecting waves beneath
"Haply beheld before. Next they inspect
"His torn-out living entrails, and from thence
"Learn what the bosoms of the gods intend.
"Whence, man, such passion for forbidden food?
"How dar'st thou, mortal man! in flesh indulge?
"O! I conjure you, do it not; my words
"Deep in your minds revolve, when to your mouth
"The mangled members of the ox you raise,
"Know, and reflect, your laborer you devour.

"And now the god inspires my tongue, my tongue
"Shall follow what th' inspiring god directs,
"My truths I will disclose, display all heaven,
"And oracles of mind divine reveal.
"I sing of mighty things, by none before
"Investigated; what has long lain hid.
"It glads me through the lofty heavens to go;
"To sail amid the clouds, the sluggish earth
"Left far below; and on the shoulders mount
"Of mighty Atlas; thence from far look down,
"On wandering souls of reasoning aid depriv'd,
"Shivering and trembling at the thoughts of death.
"I thus exhort, and scenes of fate unfold.

"O race! whom terror of cold death affrights,
"Why fear ye Styx? why darkness? why vain names,
"The dreams of poets? why in fancy'd worlds
"Severe atonements? Whether slow disease,
"Or on the pile the body flames consume,
"Think not that any suffering it can feel.
"The soul from death is free, and one seat left,
"Another habitation finds and lives.
"Well I remember I was Pantheus' son,
"Euphorbus, in the fatal war of Troy,
"Whose breast the young Atrides' massive spear
"Transpierc'd in fight. I lately knew the shield
"My left arm bore, in Juno's temple hung,
"In Abantean Argos. All is chang'd,
"But nothing dies. The spirit roams about
"From that to this, from this to that again;
"And enters vacant bodies at its will.
"Now from a beast's to human frame it goes,

"Now from the man it passes to a beast;
"And never perishes. As yielding wax
"Is with new figures printed, nor remains
"Long in one form, nor holds its pristine shape;
"And yet is still the same: so do I teach,
"The soul the same, though vary'd are its seats.
"Hence, lest thy belly's keen desire o'ercome
"All piety, (and prophet-like I speak)
"Forbear by impious slaughter to disturb
"The souls of kindred friends; and let not blood
"With blood be fed. Now on the boundless sea
"Since I am borne, and to the breeze have loos'd
"My swelling sail, this more:—Nought that the world
"Contains, is in appearance still the same
"All moving alters; changeable is form'd
"Each image. And with constant motion flows
"Ev'n time itself, just like a passing stream;
"For nor the river, nor the flying hour
"Can be detain'd. As wave by wave impell'd,
"The foremost prest by that behind; itself
"Urging its predecessor; so time flies,
"And so is follow'd, ever seeming new.
"For what has been, is lost; what is, no more
"Shall be, and every moment is renew'd.
"You see the night emerge to glorious day,
"And the bright sun in shady darkness sink.
"Nor shews the sky one hue when nature all
"Worn out, in midnight quiet rests; and when
"Bright Lucifer dismounts his snowy steed:
"Varying again when fair Aurora comes
"Of light fore-runner, and the world, to Sol
"About to yield, dyes deep. The orbed god,
"When from earth's margin rising, in the morn
"Blushing appears, and blushing seems at eve
"Descending to the main, but at heaven's height
"Shines in white splendor; there th' ethereal air
"Is purest, earth's contagion distant far.
"Nor can nocturnal Phœbe always shew
"Her form the same, nor equal: less to-day,
"If waxing, than to-morrow she'll appear;
"If waning, greater. Note you not the year
"In four succeeding seasons passing on?
"A lively image of our mortal life.
"Tender and milky, like young infancy
"Is the new spring: then gaily shine the plants,
"Tumid with juice, but helpless; and delight
"With hope the planter: blooming all appears,
"And smiles in varied flowers the feeding earth;

"But delicate and pow'rless are the leaves.
"Robuster now the year, to spring succeeds
"The summer, and a sturdy youth becomes:
"No age is stronger, none more fertile yields
"Its stores, and none with heat more fervid glows.
"Next autumn follows, all the fire of youth
"Allay'd, mature in mildness, just between
"Old age and youth a medium temper holds;
"Some silvery tresses o'er his temples strew'd.
"Then aged winter, frightful object! comes
"With tottering step, and bald appears his head;
"Or snowy white the few remaining hairs.
"Our bodies too themselves submit to change
"Without remission. Nor what we have been,
"Nor what we are, to-morrow shall we be.
"The day has been when we were but as seed,
"And in his mother's womb the future man
"Dwelt. Nature with her aiding power appear'd,
"Bade that the embryo bury'd deep within
"The pregnant mother, should not rack her more:
"And from its dwelling to the free drawn air
"Produc'd it. To the day the infant brought,
"Lies sinewless; then quadruped he crawls
"In beast-like guise; then trembling, by degrees
"He stands erect, but with a leg unfirm,
"His knees assisting with some strong support.
"Now is he strong and swift, and youth's brisk stage
"Quick passes; then, the flower of years o'ergone,
"He slides down gradual to descending age:
"This undermines, demolishes the strength
"Of former years. And ancient Milo weeps,
"When he beholds those aged feeble arms
"Hang dangling by his side, once like the limbs
"Of Hercules; so muscular, so large.
"And Helen weeps when in her glass she views
"Her aged wrinkles, wondering to herself
"Why she was ravish'd twice. Consuming time!
"And envious age! all substance ye destroy;
"All things your teeth decay; and you consume
"By gradual progress, but by certain death.
"These also, which the elements we call,
"Their varying changes know: lo! I explain
"Their regular vicissitudes,—attend.

  "Four elements th' eternal world contains;
"Two, earth and water, which their ponderous weight
"Sinks low; and two, the air and purer fire,
"Void of dense gravity, soar up on high,

"Free, unconfin'd. Though distant far in space,
"Yet from these four are all things form'd, and all
"To them resolve again. The earth dissolv'd
"Melts into liquid dew; more subtile grown
"It passes to the breezes and the air;
"And air again, when in its thinest form,
"Depriv'd of weight, springs to the fires on high.
"Thence retrogade they come, inverting all
"This order: fire is thicken'd to dense air;
"Air into water; water to hard earth;
"Nor aught retains its form. Nature, of things
"Renewer, figures from old figures makes.
"Nought that the world contains (doubt not my truth)
"E'er perishes, but changes; and receives
"An alter'd shape. What to be born we call,
"Is to begin in different guise to seem
"Than what we were; and what we call to die,
"Is but to cease to wear our wonted form.
"Though haply some part hither may be mov'd,
"Some thither, still the aggregate's the same.
"Nor can I think that aught can long endure
"Unalter'd. Soon the primal ages came
"From gold to iron. Quite transform'd is oft
"The state of places. I have seen what once
"Was earth most solid, chang'd to fluid waves.
"Land have I seen from ocean form'd; and shells
"Marine, lie scatter'd distant from all shore:
"Old anchors bury'd in the mountain tops.
"The rush of waters hollow vallies forms
"Where once were plains; and level lie the hills
"Beneath the deluge: dry the marshy ground
"With barren sand becomes; and what was parch'd
"Is soak'd, a marshy fen. Here nature opes
"New fountains; there she closes up the old.
"Rivers have bursted forth, when earthquakes shook
"The globe; some chok'd have disappear'd below.
"Thus Lycus, swallow'd by the yawning earth,
"Bursts far from thence again, another stream:
"The mighty Erasinus, now absorb'd,
"Now flows, to Argive fields again restor'd.
"And Myssus, they relate, who both his stream
"And banks disliking, as Caïcus now
"'Twixt others flows. With Amenane who rolls
"O'er sands Sicilian, flowing oft, and oft
"With clos'd-up fountains dry. Anigros, once
"Sweet to the thirsty, now his waters pours
"Untouch'd by lips, since (save we must deny
"To poets faith) the double-body'd race

"There bath'd the wounds Alcides' arrows gave.
"And is not Hypanis, the flood that springs
"From Scythia's hills, once sweet, with bitter salts
"Now tainted? By the waves begirt were once
"Antissa, Pharos, and Phœnician Tyre;
"And not a spot an island now remains.
"The ancient clowns, Leucadia to the land
"Saw join'd; now surges beat around its base;
"And Zanclé, they relate, was once conjoin'd
"To Italy, 'till ocean burst his bounds,
"And rent the land, and girt it with his waves.
"For Helicé or Buris should you seek,
"Achaïan towns, o'erwhelm'd beneath the waves
"You'll find them: boatmen oft are wont to shew
"The tottering cities, and their walls immers'd.
"Near Pitthean Trœzen is a lofty hill
"By trees unshaded; now indeed an hill
"But once a level plain. Wond'rous to tell
"The wind's resistless force, in caverns deep
"Inclos'd, for exit somewhere as it strain'd,
"And struggled long in vain, a freer range
"Of air to sweep; when all the prison round
"Was found no fissure pervious to the blast,
"It swell'd the high-rais'd ground: just so the breath
"Puffs out the bladder, or the horn'd goat's skin.
"The tumor still remains, and now appears,
"Grown hard by lapse of time, a lofty hill.
"Though numbers to my mind occur, or seen
"Or heard, but few beside I will relate.
"Do not streams too receive and lose new powers?
"Thy fountain, horned Ammon, at mid-day
"Is icy cold, but hot at morn and eve.
"The waters of Athamanis, are said,
"Sprinkled on wood, when Luna's lessening orb
"Shines in the heavens, to warm it into flame.
"A river have the Cicones, which turns
"To marble what it touches: whoso drinks
"Instant his inwards harden into stone.
"Cathis and Sybaris, which border near
"Our pastures, make the hair resemble gold.
"More wond'rous still, waters there are, with power
"The mind to change as well as change the limbs.
"Who has not heard of Salmacis obscene?
"And Ethiopa's lake, which whoso drinks
"Or furious raves, or sinks in sleep profound?
"Whoe'er his thirst at the Clitorian fount
"Quenches, he loathes all wine: abstemious, joys
"To drink pure water: whether power the waves

"Possess to thwart the heating vinous juice,
"Or, as the natives tell, with herbs and charms
"When the mad Prætides Melampus cur'd,
"He in the stream the mental medicine flung;
"And hate of wine the fountain still retains.
"Lyncestius' river flows with different power;
"Of this who swallows but the smallest draught
"Staggers, as charg'd with plenteous cups of wine.
"A dangerous place Arcadia holds (of yore
"Call'd Pheneos) for its waters' two-fold force:
"Dreaded by night: for drank by night they harm,
"But guiltless of all mischief drank by day.
"Thus lakes and rivers now these powers possess;
"Now those. Time was Ortygia on the waves
"Floated, now firm she rests. Argo, first ship
"Dreaded the isles Cyanean scatter'd round
"And clashing oft amid the roaring waves;
"Which rest unmov'd now, and the winds despise.
"Nor Etna whose sulphureous furnace flames
"Will always burn; time was it burn'd not yet:
"For let earth be an animated mass,
"Which lives, and breathing holes in various parts
"Exhaling flame, possesses, she may change,
"Each time she moves, those passages of air;
"These caverns close, and others open throw.
"Or whether wind, confin'd in those deep caves,
"Hurls rocks on rocks, and what the seeds of fire
"Contain; and flames from the concussion burst;
"The winds appeas'd, cold will the caves be left.
"Or if the flame be by bitumen caught,
"Or by pale sulphur, fiercely will it burn
"To the last particle; but when the earth
"Fuel and oily nutriment no more
"The flame shall give; a tedious length of years
"Its force exhausting, and its nutriment
"By nature's tooth consum'd, the famish'd flames
"Will this desert, deserted by their food.
"Fame says, the men who in Pallené live,
"A northern clime, when nine times in the lake
"Tritonian plung'd, in plumage light are clad.
"This scarce can I believe. They also tell
"That Scythia's females, sprinkling on their limbs
"Rank poisons, such like transformation gain.
"Yet when well-try'd experience us instructs,
"Faith may be given. Do we not bodies see
"Decaying slow with moisture and with heat,
"To animalcules chang'd? Nay, go, inter
"A chosen slaughter'd steer, (well known the fact,

"And much in use;) lo! from the putrid paunch
"Swarms of the flower-collecting bee will rise,
"Which rove the meadows as their parent rov'd:
"And urge their toil and labor still in hope.
"The warlike courser, prostrate on the ground,
"Becomes the source whence angry hornets rise.
"Cut from the sea-shore crab his crooked claws,
"And place the rest in earth, a scorpion thence,
"Will come, and threaten with his hooked tail.
"The meadow worms too, which with silky threads
"(Well noted is the fact,) are wont to weave
"The foliage, change the figures which they wear,
"Like the gay butterfly of funeral fame.
"The life-producing seeds of grass-green frogs
"Mud holds; and forms them first devoid of feet,
"Then gives them legs for swimming well contriv'd;
"And, apt that they for lengthen'd leaps may suit,
"Behind these far surpass the first in length.
"The cub the bear brings forth, at its first birth
"Is but a lump of barely living flesh:
"Licking, the mother forms the limbs, and gives
"As much of shape as she herself enjoys.
"See we the young not of the honey'd bee,
"Clos'd in the wax hexagonally shap'd,
"First form'd a body limbless, gaining late
"Their feet and wings? And who could e'er suppose,
"Except the fact he knew, that Juno's bird
"Which bears the starry tail; that Venus' doves;
"The thunder-bearer of almighty Jove;
"And all the race of birds, their being owe
"To a small egg's still smaller central part?
"There are, who think the human marrow chang'd,
"A snake becomes, when putrid turns the spine
"In a close sepulchre. These, each and all,
"Their origin from other things derive.
"One bird there is, which from herself alone
"Springs, and regenerates without foreign aid:
"Assyrians call her Phœnix. Not on grain,
"Nor herbs she lives, but on strong frankincense,
"And rich amomums' juice: when she has pass'd
"Five ages of her life, with her broad bill
"And talons, she upon the ilex' boughs,
"Or on the summit of the trembling palm,
"A nest constructs: on this she cassia strews,
"Spikes of sweet-smelling nard, the dark brown myrrh,
"And cinnamon well bruis'd: then lays herself
"Above, and on the odorous pile expires.
"Then, they report, an infant Phœnix springs

"From the parental corse, to which is given
"Five ages too, to live. When years afford
"Due strength to lift, and bear the ponderous load,
"She lightens of the weighty nest the boughs;
"With pious duty her own cradle takes,
"And parent's sepulchre; then, having gain'd
"Hyperion's city through the yielding air,
"Before the sacred portal lays it down.
"If of stupendous wonder aught ye find
"In this, hyænas must your wonder move;
"Alternate changing, females now they bear;
"And annual alter unto males again:
"That reptile too, which feeds on wind and air;
"And what it touches, straight its hue assumes.
"India by cluster-bearing Bacchus gain'd,
"Lynxes upon the conquering god bestow'd:
"And, (so they tell) whate'er their bladders void,
"Concretes to gems, and hardens in the air.
"Thus too, the coral hardens to a stone;
"A plant so flexible beneath the waves.
"Day would desert us; Phœbus' panting steeds
"Would in the mighty deep be plung'd, ere I
"Could finish, should I every substance tell
"Chang'd to new form. This we perceive, that time
"All turns. These nations mighty strength attain:
"Those sink in power. Thus Troy in wealth and strength
"Was mighty; and for ten long years could shed
"Her blood in torrents. Low she lies, and shews
"Her ancient ruins, and her numerous tombs
"For all her riches. Sparta once was great;
"And fam'd Mycené once in power was strong;
"With Athens; and the town Amphion rais'd.
"Now a mean spot is Sparta; low now lies
"Lofty Mycené; what of Thebes remains,
"The town of Œdipus, except his tale?
"What of Pandion's Athens, but the name?
"And now begins the fame of Dardan Rome
"To rise; the waves of Tiber from the hills
"Of Appenine descending, bathe her walls:
"Plac'd on a huge foundation shall she fix
"Her empire's base. By increase shall she change;
"And shall hereafter of the mighty world
"Be head. This prophets, they assert, have said,
"And fate-predicting oracles. Myself
"Remember Helenus, old Priam's son,
"Address'd Æneas, when the Trojan towers
"Were tottering, weeping,—and of future fate
"Doubtful, in words like these—O goddess born!

"If the prognostics of my soul I read
"Rightly, Troy ne'er, while thou art safe, will fall.
"Flames and the sword shall ope to thee a path
"Thou shalt depart, and with thyself convey
"An Iliüm, till a foreign land thou find'st;
"A land more friendly both to thee and Troy.
"Now, to the Phrygians' offspring due, I see
"A city rais'd; such former ages ne'er
"Beheld; such is not; such will never be.
"Thousands of worthies in a length of years,
"Its power shall spread; but lord of all the globe
"Shall he, descended of Iülus, reign;
"Who, when by earth awhile enjoy'd, shall gain—
"A seat celestial; and the heavens shall be
"The bound of his career.—Well does my mind
"Retain, that Helenus in such like words
"Address'd the chief who bore his country's gods.
"Joy'd I behold my kindred walls increase;
"And Grecia's conquest happy prove for Troy.
"But lest too wide I wander, and my steeds
"Forget the goal; know, heaven, and all beneath;
"Earth, and all earth's contents their shapes must change.
"Let us then, members of the world (not form'd
"Of body only, but with winged souls
"Which to the bodies of wild beasts may pass,
"Or dwell within the breasts of grazing herds)
"Permit those forms which may the souls contain
"Of parents, brethren, or of those once join'd
"To us by other bonds, certain of men,
"To rest secure and safe from savage wounds;
"Nor load our bowels at Thyestes' board.
"Soon, by ill custom warp'd, does he prepare
"To bathe his impious hands in human gore,
"Who severs with his knife the lowing throat
"Of the young calf, and turns a deafen'd ear
"To all its cries: or who the kid can slay,
"Moaning in plaintive tone like children's cries:
"Or who the fowl he fed before, can eat.
"What more is wanting, that may now complete
"The measure of iniquity? From thence
"Where the next step? Then let thine oxen plough,
"And let their death be due alone to age.
"Let from dread Boreas' piercing cold the sheep
"Defend thee with her wool. Let the full goat
"Present her udder to thy hand to press.
"Throw far thy nets, thy nooses, and thy snares,
"And all thy treacherous skill; nor with lim'd twig
"Deceive the bird; nor with strong toils the deer;

"Nor hide the barbed hook with treacherous bait.
"If animals annoy ye, them destroy:
"But slay them only. From the taste of flesh
"Free be your mouths, while food more fit ye eat."

  His breast with these, and such like doctrines fill'd,
Numa, 'tis said, back to his country came;
And held, unsought for, the supreme command
O'er Latium's realm. Blest with the nymph his spouse,
And by the muses guided, all the rites
Of sacrifice he taught: the people train'd,
Fond of fierce war, to arts of gentle peace.
When late he finish'd reign at once, and life,
The Latian females, nobles, commons, all
In streaming tears, bewail'd their Numa dead.
His consort Rome deserted, and lay hid
In the deep forests of Aricia's vale;
And with her wailings and her mournful sighs,
The rites impeded in Diana's fane.
How oft the nymphs who dwelt in lakes and groves,
Kind admonitions gave her not to mourn,
And sooth'd her with consolatory words!
How oft the son of Theseus weeping, said;
"Cease thus to grieve, nor think your fate alone
"Is hard. Look round awhile on others' woes;
"More mild your own you'll bear. Would that not mine
"Were such as might assuage your woe; but mine,
"When heard, to calm your grief may something yield.

  "Haply report has sounded in your ears
"Of one Hippolytus the fate, destroy'd
"Through his most impious step-dame's treacherous fraud,
"And sire's credulity. With much surprize
"You'll hear,—nay scarcely will you trust my words,
"But he am I! Pasiphaë's daughter me
"Accus'd, that I with vain endeavour try'd
"To violate my parent's nuptial couch:
"Me feigning guilty of the crime she wish'd;
"On me th' offence retorting, or through fear
"I might accuse, or rage at her repulse.
"My sire, me guiltless from the city drove,
"And curs'd me going with most hostile prayers.
"To Pitthean Træzen I my exil'd flight
"Directed: and now drove along the shore
"Of Corinth's sea; when ocean sudden heav'd;
"A mighty heap of waters bent appear'd,
"Like an huge hill, and increase seem'd to gain;
"Then roaring loud was at its summit cleft.

"Thence, from the bursting waves a horned bull
"Rush'd forth, breast-high uprearing in the air;
"Spouting the waves through his capacious mouth
"And nostrils. Terror seiz'd my comrades' breasts:
"Fill'd with the thoughts of exile, mine alone
"Unmov'd remain'd. While my impatient steeds,
"Turn'd to the main their heads; with ears erect
"Affrighted stood; then by the beast appall'd,
"Rush'd rapid with the car o'er lofty rocks.
"With a vain hand I strive to gird the curb,
"Besmear'd with foaming whiteness; bending back
"With all my might I pull the pliant reins.
"Nor had my horses' furious madness mock'd
"My strength, save that the fast-revolving wheel
"A tree opposing struck, and shatter'd: wide
"The fragments flew. I from the car was thrown,
"Entangled in the harness: plain to view
"Were seen my living bowels dragg'd along;
"My sinews twisted round the stump; my limbs
"Part swept away, and part entangled left:
"Loud crash'd my fractur'd bones; my weary'd soul
"At length exhal'd; my body nought retain'd
"That could be known, one all-continued wound.
"Can you, O nymph! or dare you, now compare
"Your woe with mine? Since then I have beheld
"The realm of darkness, and my mangled limbs
"Bath'd in the waves of Phlegethon. Nor life
"Had been restor'd, but through the forceful help,
"Of medicine that Apollo's offspring gave.
"From him Pæonian aid when I had gain'd
"By plants of power, though much in Pluto's spite,
"Cynthia me cover'd with her densest clouds:
"And lest my sight their hatred should increase,
"That safe I might remain, and without risk
"Be seen, she gave to my appearance age,
"Nor left me features to be known again:
"And long deliberated, whether Crete
"Or Delos, for my dwelling she would chuse.
"But, Crete and Delos both abandon'd, here
"She plac'd me, and my name she bade renounce
"Which still reminded me of my wild steeds;
"Saying—O thou, Hippolytus who wast!
"Be Virbius now! Thenceforth within these groves
"I dwell,—a minor deity, I tend
"My heavenly mistress, and increase her train."

  But foreign griefs possess'd not power to chase
Egeria's woe; who at a mountain's foot

Thrown prostrate, melted in a flood of tears;
'Till Phœbus' sister by her sorrow mov'd,
Transform'd her body to a cooling fount;
And her limbs melted to still-during streams.

  The miracle the wondering nymphs beheld;
Nor stood the son of Amazonia's queen
With less surprize than on the bosom seiz'd
Of the Tyrrhenian ploughman, when he view'd
The fate-foretelling clod, amidst the fields.
At first spontaneous and untouch'd it mov'd;
Then took a human figure; shook off earth,
And op'd its new-form'd prophesying mouth:
Tages the natives call'd him, who first taught
Th' Etruscan race the future to explain:
Or Romulus, when he his spear beheld
Stuck on Palatium's hill, and sudden sprout:
By a new root, not by its steely point,
Fixt fast: no more a weapon, but a tree,
With pliant branches, which afford a shade
Unlook'd for to the wondering people round:
Or Cippus, when he in the flowing stream
Beheld his new-form'd horns (for them he saw)
But thought th' appearance false; and what he view'd,
Oft rais'd his fingers to his head to touch:
No more his eyes distrusting, then he stood,
(As victor from a conquer'd foe he came,)
And raising up to heaven his hands and eyes,
"Ye gods!" he said, "whatever this portends,
"If happy, to my country, to the state,
"Be it;—if ominous of ill, to me."
And then with odorous fires the gods ador'd,
On grassy altars of the green sward form'd;
And from the goblets pour'd the wine; and search'd,
The panting entrails of the slaughter'd sheep,
For what was meant. Th' Etruscan seer beheld
That mighty revolutions they foretold;
But yet obscurely: till his piercing eye
He from the entrails turn'd to Cippus' horns.
Then cry'd;—"Save thee, O king! for lo! the place
"For thee, O Cippus! and thy horns, the towers
"Of Latium will obey. Thou only haste;
"Delay not, but within the open gates
"Enter; so fate commands. In them receiv'd
"King wilt thou be; in safety wilt enjoy
"An ever-during kingdom." Back he drew
His feet, and from the city's walls he turn'd
Sternly his looks; exclaiming; "far, ye gods!

"O, far avert these omens! Better I
"An exile roam for life, than monarch rule
"The Capitol." Then he assembled straight
The reverend senate, and the people round:
But first with peaceful laurel veil'd his horns:
Then on a mound, there by the soldiers rais'd,
He stood; and pray'd in ancient mode to heaven.
"Lo! here," he cry'd, "is one, whom save ye drive
"Far from your city, will your monarch be;
"By marks, but not by name I him describe:
"Two horns his forehead bears. He is the man,
"Once in the town receiv'd, the augur tells,
"With servile laws will rule ye. Nay, he might
"Your open gates have enter'd, but myself
"Oppos'd him; though more near to me is none.
"Expel him, Romans! from your city far;
"Or, if he merit them, with massive chains
"Load him: or rid yourself at once of fear
"By the proud tyrant's death." Such murmurs sound
'Mid lofty pines, when Eurus whistles fierce;
Such is the roaring of the ocean waves
Rolling far distant, as the crowd sent forth:
Till from amidst the all-confounding noise
One spoke more loud, and—"which is he?" exclaim'd.
Then all the brows they search'd, the horns to find.
Cippus again address'd them. "What you seek
"Behold!" and from his head the garland tore,
Spite of their efforts, and his forehead shew'd,
With double horns distinguish'd. All their eyes
Depress'd, and sighs from every bosom burst:
Unwillingly (incredible!) they view
That head so bright with merit. Then, no more
Bearing that honors due he should not gain,
They bind his temples with a festal crown.
Thee, Cippus! since within the walls forbid
To enter, now the senators present
A grateful gift; a tract of land so large
As with a plough, by two yok'd oxen drawn,
Thou canst from morn till close of day surround.
The horns, the type of this stupendous fact,
Long shall remain on brazen pillars grav'd.

  Ye muses, patrons of the poet's song,
Explain (for all complete your knowledge, age
Most distant ne'er deceives you) why the isle
In Tiber's bosom, by his billows wash'd,
The rites of Esculapius introduc'd
Into the town of Romulus! A plague

Of direst form infected Latium's air,
And the pale bloodless bodies wasted thin
Squalid in poison. When the numerous deaths
Prov'd every effort of mankind was vain,
And vain the art of medicine, they beseech
Celestial aid, and unto Delphos go,
Apollo's oracle, 'mid place of earth;
Pray him to help their miserable state
With health-affording words; and end at once
The dreadful pest which scourg'd their mighty town.
The fane, the laurel, and the quiver, slung
Upon his shoulder, shook; and this reply
The tripod from its secret depth return'd;
Thrilling their fear-struck bosoms: "What you seek,
"O Romans! here, you should have nearer sought:
"And nearer now ev'n seek it. Phœbus' aid
"Your woe can lessen not; but Phœbus' son
"Can help ye: therefore with good omens go,
"And call my offspring to afford relief."
Soon as the prudent senators receiv'd
The god's commands, with diligence they seek
What city's walls Apollo's son contain;
Depute a band, whom favoring breezes waft
To Epidaurus' shores. Soon as their keels
Touch'd on the strand, they to th' assembled crowd
Of Grecian elders haste; and earnest beg
To grant their deity, to check the rage
Of death amongst the hapless Latian race,
By his mere presence. So unerring fate
Had said. Divided is the council's voice:
Some would the aid besought, be granted; some,
And many, these oppose; refuse to send
To foreign lands their patron, and their god.
While dubious they deliberated, eve
Chas'd the remains of light, and the earth's shade
Threw darkness round; when, lo! the helping god
Appear'd in sleep before the Roman's bed
To stand, in form like what his temples grace.
His left hand bore a rugged staff; his right
Strok'd down the hairs of his expanded beard;
As thus with words of import mild he spoke;
"Fear not, for I will come; my temple leave.
"View but this snake which with his circling folds
"My staff entwines; remark him, that again
"You well may know him; chang'd to such a form
"Will I be; but more huge I will appear;
"Mighty in bulk as heavenly beings ought."
The vision ceas'd, and vanish'd with the words:

And with the god fled sleep; and cheerful light
Follow'd the flight of Somnus. Now the morn
Had chas'd the starry fires; the Grecian chiefs,
Still dubious, in the splendid temple meet
Of the intreated deity, and pray
That some celestial sign he should display,
To prove which country for his seat he chose.
Scarce had they ended, when the shining god
Fore-running hisses sent; and as a snake
With lofty crest appear'd: at his approach
His statue, altars, portals, gilded roofs,
And marble pavement shook. He rear'd his chest
Sublime amid the temple; and around
Darted his eyes, which shone with living fire.
Trembled the fear-struck crowd. The sacred priest,
His hair encircled with a snowy band,
Straight knew him; and, "the God! the God!" exclaim'd:
"All present, him with hearts and tongues adore!
"O glorious deity! may thou, thus seen,
"Propitious be; thy worshippers protect,
"Who keep thy rites." All present to the god
Adoring bend, and all his words repeat;
And Rome's embassadors with fervor join
In mind and voice. To these the god consents,
And his crest moving, certain signs affords:
Thrice hissing, thrice he shakes his forked tongue,
Then down the shining steps he glides, his head
Retorted; as he thence departs he views
His ancient altars, and a last salute,
His wonted seat, his long-own'd temple, gives.
Thence rolls he huge along the ground bestrew'd
With scatter'd flowers, in curving folds entwin'd;
And through the city's centre takes his way,
To where the bending mole the port defends.
Here rested he; and to dismiss appear'd
His followers, and the kind attending crowd,
With gracious looks; then in th' Ausonian ship
He plac'd his length. A deity's huge weight
The ship confess'd; the keel beneath the load
Bent. Glad Æneäs' offspring felt, and loos'd
(A bull first sacrific'd upon the shore,)
The cables which their crowded galley bound.
Light airs impell'd the vessel. High aloft
The god appear'd; upon the curving poop
Rested his neck, and view'd the azure waves.
By zephyrs wafted o'er th' Iönian sea,
They reach'd Italia when the sixth time rose
Aurora. Pass'd Scylacea, and the fane

Of Juno, on Lacinia's noted shore;
Japygia left, and shunn'd Amphissia's rocks
With larboard oars; and, coasting on the right,
Ceraunia, and Romechium pass'd, and pass'd
Narycia and Caulonia; they, (the risks
Of sea, and of Pelorus' narrow straits
Surmounted) pass th' Æolian monarch's isles;
Metallic Themesis; Leucasia's land;
And warm and rosy Pæstus. Thence they coast
Along Capræa; and Minerva's cape;
And pass Surrentum, rich in generous wine,
The town of Hercules; Parthenopé,
Built for soft ease; with Stabia; and from thence
Pass the Cumæan Sybil's sacred dome.
Hence by Linternum, with the mastich rich;
And boiling fountains are they borne; and past
Vulturnus sucking sand within the gulf;
And Sinuessa, fill'd with milk-white doves:
Marshy Minturnæ; with Cajeta, rais'd
By him she nurs'd; Antiphates' abode;
Trachas, by fens encompass'd; Circé's land;
And Antium's solid shore. Here when the crew
Had with toe flying vessel reach'd, (for now
Rough was the main) the god his folds untwines,
Glides on in frequent coils, and spires immense;
Entering a temple of his sire that stood
Close by the yellow beach. The ocean calm'd,
The Epidaurian god his father's fane
Now leaves; a deity to him close join'd
Thus hospitable found: the sandy shore
Ploughs in a furrow with his rattling scales:
Then, in the steersman confident, he rests
On the high poop his head, till they approach
Lavinium's city, and her sacred seat,
And Tiber's mouth. The people rush in heaps,
And crowds of matrons and of fathers rush,
Confus'dly hither; even the vestal maids
Who guard the sacred fire: and all salute
The god with joyful clamor. Then where'er
The rapid vessel cleaves th' opposing stream,
The incense crackles on the banks, and rais'd
Are lines of altars, thick on either shore;
The smoke perfumes the air; the victims bleed
In heaps, and warm the sacrificial knife.
The Roman city now, the world's great head,
They enter'd, up erect the serpent rose;
From the mast's loftiest summit tower'd his neck,
And round he look'd to chuse a fit abode.

The waves circumfluent in two equal streams
Divide; the isle has thence its name, the arms
On either side are stretch'd, land in the midst.
Hither the Æsculapian snake himself
Betook, departing from the Latian ship;
Resum'd his form celestial, and their griefs
Dispersing, came health-bearer to the land.

 A foreign power he in our temples stands,
But Cæsar, in his native town a god
Is worshipp'd. In the forum, and the field
Fam'd equal: yet not his well-finish'd wars,
His triumphs, nor the deeds in peace perform'd
So justly chang'd him to an heavenly shape,
A blazing star, as did the son he left.
For no atchievement Cæsar e'er perform'd
Can with the boast to be Augustus' sire
Compare. Far greater this than to subdue
The sea-girt Britons:—his victorious fleets
To seven-mouth'd Nile to lead;—to bring the realms
Cinyphian Juba rul'd, 'neath Rome's control,
Rebel Numidia; and, puff'd high in pride
With Mithridates' glory, Pontus' land;
Rich triumphs to have gain'd, and triumphs more
To merit, as a man so great produce;
To whose presiding care, O bounteous gods!
Mankind ye gave, and them completely blest.
And lest he seem from mortal seed to spring
His sire must mount to heaven, in form a god.
This the bright mother of Æneäs saw,
And for the priest beheld a mournful fate
Prepar'd, and moving saw the arms conspir'd.
She trembled, and to every god she met
Address'd her: "Lo! what deep and potent plots
"Against me they prepare. See, with what art
"His life is sought, who sole to me is left
"Of my Iülus. Why must I alone
"Be harrass'd still with never-ceasing cares?
"Whom now Tydides' Calydonian spear
"Wounds; now the walls of ill-protected Troy
"Lie prostrate. Who my darling son behold
"Driv'n to long wanderings; on the ocean toss'd;
"Entering the silent mansions of the dead;
"Waging fierce war with Turnus; or, if truth
"I speak, with Juno rather. Yet why now
"Record I former sufferings in my sons?
"Terror prevents all memory of the past;
"See, where at me their impious swords they point!

"O, I conjure you! stay them; and prevent
"The horrid deed; lest, spilt the high-priest's blood,
"The fires of Vesta be for ever dark."
With words like these did troubled Venus move
Each power of heaven, in vain; yet all were touch'd,
And, though the stern decrees of rigid fate
To break unable, tokens plain they gave,
That some immense calamity was nigh.
They tell, that clashing arms 'mid the black clouds,
And dreadful horns and trumpets in the heavens
Sounded, to warn us of the impious deed.
Full of solicitude the earth beheld
The pale wan image of sad Phœbus' face.
Torches were often seen 'mid heaven to glare;
And from the clouds oft gory drops were shed.
Blue Lucifer a dusky hue o'ercast;
And Luna's car was sprinkled o'er with blood.
Th' infernal owl in numerous places shriek'd,
A direful omen! In a thousand fanes
The ivory statues wept; the sacred groves
Re-echo'd all with songs and threatening sounds.
No victim seem'd appeasing; tumults vast
Approaching shew'd the entrails; and appear'd
The liver always with a wounded head.
Around the domes, and temples of the gods
Loud howl'd the midnight dogs; the silent shades
Flitted along; and tremblings shook the town.
Yet could not these forebodings of the heavens
Crush the conspiracy, or ward his fate;
And in the temple were the weapons drawn:
For, but the senate-house, no spot could please
The vile assassins for the bloody deed.
Then Cytherea smote her lovely breast
In anguish; and beneath an heavenly cloud
Sought to conceal him: such a cloud as once
From furious Menelaüs Paris sav'd;
And snatch'd Æneäs from Tydides' sword.
Then thus her sire: "O daughter! hast thou power
"Th' immutable decrees of fate to change?
"To thee 'tis granted to inspect the dome
"Of the three sisters; there thou wilt behold
"Th' eternal tablets of events engrav'd
"On steel and brass, a work of mighty toil.
"Safe, they nor fear the clashing of the sky,
"Nor rage of thunder, nor of ruin aught.
"There wilt thou written find thy offspring's fate
"On ever-during adamant. Myself
"Have read it, and record it in my mind;

"And lest thou should'st be to the future blind,
"I will relate it. He for whom thou toil'st,
"O Cytherea! has his time fulfill'd;
"The sum of years which to the earth he ow'd.
"That he a deity in heaven may rise,
"And be in temples worshipp'd is thy care,
"And his successor's; who his name will take,
"And on his shoulders bear the wide world's rule;
"On him impos'd. He, of his murder'd sire
"Valiant avenger, shall in all his wars
"Our favoring influence feel. Mutina's walls,
"By him besieg'd, in conquest shall confess
"His power, and sue for peace. Pharsalia, him
"Shall feel; and, drench'd in Macedonian blood
"Again, Philippi. On Sicilia's seas
"His mighty name shall conquer. Egypt's queen,
"Falsely relying on the nuptial bond
"With Rome's triumvir, falls: all vain her threats,
"That Tiber should subservient bend to Nile.
"Why should I speak to thee of barbarous hordes,
"Nations which dwell at either seas' extreme?
"Whatever habitable earth contains
"Will to his empire bend. Ocean will own
"His sway. Peace on th'extended earth bestow'd,
"To civil studies will his breast be turn'd;
"And laws most equitable will he frame.
"By his example curb licentious souls;
"And, stretching forward to a future age
"His anxious care, which their sons' sons may feel,
"His offspring, nurtur'd in a pious womb,
"At once his name and station will assume.
"Nor shall he touch th' ethereal seats, nor join
"His kindred stars till full like him in years.
"Meantime his soul, snatch'd from the mangled corse,
"Form to a brilliant star, a god divine:
"That Julius from his lofty seat may still
"Our forum, and our Capitol behold."
Scarcely the sire had ceas'd, when Venus, bright,
But unperceiv'd by all, stood in the midst
Of Rome's assembled senate; from the breast
Of her lov'd Cæsar took the recent soul,
Nor let it waste in air. Up to the stars
She bore it. Rapid as she swept along,
She saw it shine with light, she saw it burn;
Then from her bosom spring above the moon:
Lofty it flies, it shines a glittering star,
Dragging a flaming tail's stupendous length.
Viewing the glorious actions of his son,

Candid he grants them mightier than his own,
And thus surpast rejoices. Let him frown,
If to his parent's deeds we his prefer;
Yet fame quite free will such commands despise,
Give him unwish'd-for precedence; and here,
And here alone he'll disobedience find.
So Atreus yielded to the mighty fame
Of Agamemnon; Theseus so surpass'd
Ægeus; and Achilles Peleus so.
Nay more, examples nearer to themselves
If I should use, Saturn submits to Jove.
Jove rules th' ethereal sky, the triform world;
And all the earth beneath Augustus lies:
Each is the sire and ruler of his realm.

  O, I implore, ye gods! who did attend
Æneäs,—who made fire and sword retreat!
Ye native deities of Latium's soil!
Quirinus, founder of the walls of Rome!
Mars, of Quirinus never-conquer'd, sire!
Vesta, held sacred midst the Cæsars' gods!
Domestic Phœbus, with chaste Vesta plac'd!
And Jove, who guards the high Tarpeiän walls!
With all whom pious poets may invoke;
Slow may that day arrive, and older far
Than what our age may see, when to the clouds
His glorious head shall mount, quitting this globe
He rules so well, and our beseeching prayers
Bending with condescending ear to grant.

  Now is my work complete, which not Jove's ire,
Nor flame, nor steel, nor gnawing tooth of age,
Shall e'er destroy. Come when it will, that day
Which nothing, save my mortal frame, can touch.
Which ends the being of a dubious life,
My better part unperishing shall mount
Above the loftiest stars. Eternal still
Shall be my name. Where'er Rome's power extends
O'er conquer'd earth, my verses shall be read;
And, if the presages by poets given
Be true, to endless years my fame shall live.

www.ingramcontent.com/pod-product-compliance
Lightning Source LLC
Chambersburg PA
CBHW030818090426
42737CB00009B/780